Psychology Builds a Healthy World

Psychology Builds a Healthy World

OPPORTUNITIES FOR RESEARCH AND PRACTICE

Edited by

Ronald H. Rozensky

Norine G. Johnson

Carol D. Goodheart

W. Rodney Hammond

American Psychological Association
Washington, DC

Published by
American Psychological Association
750 First Street, NE
Washington, DC 20002
www.apa.org

To order
APA Order Department
P.O. Box 92984
Washington, DC 20090-2984
Tel: (800) 374-2721
Direct: (202) 336-5510
Fax: (202) 336-5502
TDD/TTY: (202) 336-6123
Online: www.apa.org/books/
E-mail: order@apa.org

In the U.K., Europe, Africa, and the Middle East, copies may be ordered from
American Psychological Association
3 Henrietta Street
Covent Garden, London
WC2E 8LU England

Typeset in Goudy by World Composition Services, Inc., Sterling, VA

Printer: Data Reproductions, Auburn Hills, MI
Cover Designer: Naylor Design, Washington, DC
Technical/Production Editor: Kristen S. Boye

The opinions and statements published are the responsibility of the authors, and such opinions and statements do not necessarily represent the policies of the American Psychological Association. The views expressed in this book do not necessarily represent the official policies or opinions of the Centers for Disease Control and Prevention (CDC) or the U.S. Department of Health and Human Services.

Library of Congress Cataloging-in-Publication Data

Psychology builds a healthy world : opportunities for research and practice / edited by Ronald H. Rozensky . . . [et al.]. — 1st ed.
    p. cm.
   Includes bibliographical references and indexes.
   ISBN 1-59147-047-1 (alk. paper)
   1. Clinical health psychology. I. Rozensky, Ronald H.

  R726.7.P79165   2003
  616.89—dc22   2003014261

British Library Cataloguing-in-Publication Data
A CIP record is available from the British Library.

Printed in the United States of America
First Edition

CONTENTS

CONTRIBUTORS

Judith L. Alpert, PhD, Department of Applied Psychology, New York University, New York

Ileana Arias, PhD, Etiology and Surveillance Branch, Division of Violence Prevention, National Center for Injury Prevention and Control, Centers for Disease Control and Prevention, Atlanta, GA

Thomas E. Boyce, PhD, Psychology Department, University of Nevada, Reno

Yolanda Bruce Brooks, PsyD, The Dallas Cowboys Football Club; private practice, Dallas, TX

Victor De La Cancela, PhD, ABPP, Department of Psychiatry, Columbia University College of Physicians and Surgery, New York; Salud Management Associates, New York

Dorothy W. Cantor, PsyD, past president of the American Psychological Association; private practice, Westfield, NJ

Cary L. Cooper, PhD, The University of Manchester Institute of Science and Technology, Manchester, England

Will Courtenay, PhD, McLean Hospital, Harvard Medical School, Men's Health Consulting, Berkeley, CA

Shoshana L. Dachs, MA, Department of Applied Psychology, New York University, New York

Joanne H. Gavin, PhD, Marist College, Poughkeepsie, NY

Carol D. Goodheart, EdD, private practice, Princeton, NJ

W. Rodney Hammond, PhD, Division of Violence Prevention, National Center for Injury Prevention and Control, Centers for Disease Control and Prevention, Atlanta, GA

Lynn Jenkins, MA, Analysis and Field Evaluations Branch, National Institute for Occupational Safety and Health, Centers for Disease Control and Prevention, Morgantown, WV

Norine G. Johnson, PhD, past president of the American Psychological Association; private practice; Department of Neurology, Boston University Medical School; ABCS Psychology Resources, Boston, MA

Suzanne Bennett Johnson, PhD, Florida State University, Tallahassee

Russell T. Jones, PhD, Department of Psychology, Virginia Polytechnic Institute and State University, Blacksburg

John R. Lutzker, PhD, Prevention Development and Evaluation Branch, Division of Violence Prevention, National Center for Injury Prevention and Control, Centers for Disease Control and Prevention, Atlanta, GA

Susan H. McDaniel, PhD, University of Rochester School of Medicine and Dentistry, Rochester, NY

Susan Pick, PhD, Instituto Mexicano de Investigación de Familia y Población (IMIFAP-Educación salud y vida); Faculty of Psychology, National University of Mexico, Mexico City

Chaya Piotrkowski, PhD, Fordham University, New York

Mary Pipher, PhD, private practice, Lincoln, NE

William S. Pollack, PhD, Centers for Men and Young Men at McLean Hospital, Belmont, MA; Department of Psychiatry, Harvard Medical School, Boston, MA

James Campbell Quick, PhD, Center for Research on Organizational and Managerial Excellence, University of Texas at Arlington

Jonathan D. Quick, MD, MPH, World Health Organization, Geneva, Switzerland

Rena L. Repetti, PhD, Department of Psychology, University of California, Los Angeles

Michael C. Roberts, PhD, Clinical Child Psychology, University of Kansas, Lawrence

Ronald H. Rozensky, PhD, ABPP, Department of Clinical and Health Psychology, University of Florida, Gainesville

Samuel F. Sears, PhD, Department of Clinical and Health Psychology, University of Florida, Gainesville

David A. Sleet, PhD, Division of Unintentional Injury, National Center for Injury Prevention and Control, Centers for Disease Control and Prevention, Atlanta, GA

Annette L. Stanton, PhD, Department of Psychology, University of California, Los Angeles

Nina Thomas, PhD, International Trauma Consultant; New York University postdoctoral program in psychotherapy and psychoanalysis, New York

Lenore E. A. Walker, EdD, Center for Psychology Studies, Nova Southeastern University, Fort Lauderdale, FL

Billy Whitt, Department of Psychology, Virginia Polytechnic Institute and State University, Blacksburg

David A. Wolfe, PhD, Department of Psychology, University of Western Ontario, London, Canada

Tom Wolff, PhD, private practice, Amherst, MA

FOREWORD: PSYCHOLOGY IN A GLOBALIZED WORLD

MARY PIPHER

> There is a timeless wisdom that survives failed human economies
> and wars.
>   It's a nameless wisdom stressed by all people. It is understanding how
> to live a decent life, how to behave properly toward other people and
> the land.
>   —Barry Lopez

It is a great honor to write the foreword for *Psychology Builds a Healthy World*. I was asked to prepare this foreword because I have written a book entitled *The Middle of Everywhere: The World's Refugees Come to Our Town* (2002).[1] This book, as well as my keynote at the American Psychological Association convention in August of 2001, explores the effects of globalization on the mental health of us all. It examines the role psychology can play in our new century and recommends changes in our theory and practice, changes that are necessary to prepare us for our world.

I live in Lincoln, a town of about 200,000 in southeastern Nebraska. Not long ago this area was all short grass prairie inhabited by the Ponca and Omaha tribes. In the late 1800s, settlers from German, Czech, and other European backgrounds homesteaded in the area. For 100 years, Nebraska was mainly a White, Christian, conservative place. Then in the 1980s the Vietnamese and Cambodians came to our town. The Mexicans who had been migrants began to stay through the winter. Exiles from the political unrest in Latin America came to Lincoln.

In the 1990s Lincoln became an official resettlement community. Because of our low unemployment figures and cheap housing, refugees from all over the world were sent to Lincoln. These newcomers had no choice: They disembarked at JFK or San Francisco International Airport, and they

---

[1] Pipher, M. (2002). *The middle of everywhere: The world's refugees come to our town.* New York: Harcourt.

were handed plane tickets to Lincoln. Most refugees did not even know where Nebraska was. Some thought they were in Alaska and asked about grizzly bears and glaciers.

We now have 52 languages in our public schools. Lincoln is filled with people from the former Soviet Union, Iraq, Ethiopia, Iran, Afghanistan, Bosnia, Croatia, Ukraine, Somalia, Sudan, and now Sierra Leone.

I have always been interested in how others live. As a girl in Beaver City, I played the globe game. Sitting outside in the thick, yellow weeds, or at the kitchen table while my father made bean soup, I would shut my eyes, put my finger on the globe, and spin it. Then I would open my eyes and imagine what it was like in whatever spot my finger was touching. What were the streets like, the sounds, the colors, the smells? What were the people doing there right now?

I felt isolated in my small town of White Protestants surrounded by cow pastures and wheat fields. I had no contact with people who were different from me. Native Americans had a rich legacy in Nebraska, but I knew nothing of them, not even the names of the tribes who lived in my area. I had never seen a Black person or a Latino. Until I read *The Diary of Anne Frank*, I had never heard of Jewish people.

Adults talked mostly about crops, pie, and rainfall. I couldn't wait to grow up and move someplace exotic and faraway and, living where I did, every place appeared faraway and exotic. As a young adult, I escaped for a while. I lived in San Francisco, Mexico, London, and Madrid. But much to my surprise, I missed the wheat fields, the thunderstorms, and the meadow-larks. I returned to Nebraska in my mid-20s, married, raised a family, worked as a psychologist, and ate a lot of pie. I have been happy in Nebraska, but until recently I thought I had to choose between loving this rural place and experiencing all the beautiful diversity of the world.

Now the world has moved to my town. I can study the question I have always found the most fascinating: How does culture affect personality? I have been able to talk with families from all over the world about their family situations, their past traumas, their reactions to America, and their dreams. Then I can sleep in my own bed.

My husband and I sponsored a family of six Kurdish sisters and their mother. This family had escaped Saddam Hussein and walked into Iran where they were placed in a refugee camp. Then they rode horses into Pakistan where they lived in a hut in Quetta for 10 years. Finally, the family threatened to starve themselves to death if they were not allowed to leave their hut. Workers from the United Nations moved them to Islamabad and eventually to Nebraska.

We also sponsored a family of Kakuma refugees. This family was from the Dinka tribe and consisted of three brothers and one sister who had lost their parents in the civil war in Sudan. They had walked across three countries and survived crocodiles, lions, and starvation before they reached a camp in Kenya where they lived for 9 years. The Kakuma family arrived from equatorial Africa on a 20-below-zero day. The first thing that happened was they fell down the escalator at our airport. We bought them gloves, hats, a calendar, and a clock.

Both the Kurdish and Kakuma families came from traditional cultures. Thomas Friedman talked of the world being divided into slow cultures and fast cultures. Kurdish culture and Dinka culture are slow cultures. They are also more holistic and less compartmentalized than our culture. Both our families came from places where community and family responsibility came before individual needs. Working with these families I have developed a much more nuanced and complex view of how families function. I no longer see many aspects of our lives as "givens."

The work I have done with refugees has been the most satisfying work of my life. Intellectually I have grown enormously, and emotionally I have been deeply touched. My understanding of what it means to be human has broadened and deepened. I have learned what humans will do to each other and for each other.

Garrison Keillor described how the refugees' stories, if known, would break our heart.

Refugees learn about America in two ways, first through what I call cultural brokers, teachers, and others who have their best interest in mind and who try to teach them what they need to know about our culture. Second, refugees learn about our culture by watching television and through advertising. Many, such as the Kakuma refugees, are naive and have no antidotes to consumer culture. They eat what is advertised on television; they order Discover cards and buy things on time; and they are swindled by telemarketers. Soon they are in financial trouble. They have few external resources and many mental health needs.

I was involved with a project called Thrive that trained mentors from different cultures to be cultural brokers on mental health issues. The project began with 10 classes about mental health, which included everything from when Americans toilet train their children, to what is the difference between a psychiatrist and a psychologist, to how to deal with a suicidal person. Mentors shared their new knowledge with their ethnic communities, and they educated us professionals on how other cultures deal with emotional pain. The mentors then worked with people from their own countries, easing them into our system or helping them in more traditional ways. We therapists supervised their work.

The value of the project was not what we taught the Bosnian, Vietnamese, Kurdish, Russian, and Caribbean mentors, but what they taught us. They told us about the psychological problems that people from their countries experienced, and they listened to our advice about cases from their cultures. Often, they politely told us why our advice would not apply.

The mentors defined their roles broadly. They were action-oriented and did not wear watches. If their clients were stressed by hungry children, rather than discussing stress management theory, the mentors drove them to the grocery store. A traditional supervisor might say that these mentors did not have good boundaries. But I came to see it differently. The mentors were not compartmentalized the way we Americans are. They did not make distinctions between clients and friends, and professional and nonprofessional relationships. By their behavior they said, we are all humans in need of each other's nurturance.

Early on, I noticed that the Thrive mentors who were least like mental health professionals were the most popular with their own people. The ones who acted the most like us were not in great demand. The busiest mentors were holistic. For example, once when I chided a Sudanese caseworker for taking calls at night, he said to me, "You don't understand. All the Sudanese people are my family. I will help them all day and all night. It is not a job to me. It is my life."

Our Bosnian mentor knew a woman who had lost 22 male family members in Srebrenica. This woman said to Vanya, "My pain has killed my soul." Vanya listened to the woman's stories, then she invited her to the circus, which she told me later "was a big hit."

Vanya had another client who had suffered greatly during the war. All she wanted was a child, and she feared she could not get pregnant. Vanya took her to a women's clinic where the doctor reassured the woman she could have another child. Then Vanya invited the woman and her husband to her home. The two families stayed up all night drinking plum brandy and singing.

Vanya was my most creative mentor. She was warmhearted, helpful, and good-natured. She had common sense and intelligence. When she heard I was writing a book on refugees, she said, "Tell families to get a kitten. We were very lonely and sad until we got our little kitty. Now we have reason to laugh. My daughter jumps out of the bed every morning to check on her kitty. It is the best thing."

At first, the goal of Thrive had been to train mentors to use our system and to encourage their countrymen to use it. As the group proceeded, I grew to respect the mentors' ways of helping. I found myself asking, "Why was I assuming that our system was better?"

Refugees have much to teach us. They have suffered more than most of us and also have recovered more than most of us. They are resilient in the ways we all need to be. Refugees do not fit our theoretical models. With all their stress and sadness they should be the most miserable of people.

They experience the most difficult environments humans can endure, yet all over America they bring vitality into slums, enchant school teachers with their eagerness to learn, and impress employers with their willingness to work. Refugees give us new ways of looking at humans, more positive ways that assume that humans have more resiliency than our earlier theories suggested.

Nithal is a young girl from the Nuba Mountains in Sudan, new to this country and helping her mother with many younger siblings, even as she studies to make As at high school in her fourth language. She wants to be a doctor and help her people. Her father was Yousif Kowa, leader of the Nuba people and leading their fight for survival in the Nuba Mountains in Sudan. Nithal has prepared a speech to raise money for supplies for him and the Nuba left behind in the mountains. This speech tells of children cut in half by bombs and of children praying for peace as they bleed to death. Her people receive no international relief aid. Many are literally naked as their clothes have long ago eroded. One quarter million of the Nuba people have died since Nithal's father sent her and the family to America to be safe.

Nithal has suffered an enormous amount of stress, loss, dislocation, and disruption in her life, yet she is flourishing in Nebraska. When Nithal's father died, her mother returned for his funerals in Kenya and Sudan. Nithal stayed here, watching her siblings, going to school, and looking for a part-time job. I stopped by to see her and asked how she was doing. She said of her father's death, "He was gone so much these last few years, it's easy to think of him as on a journey. I like to think that this trip is a safe one and that we will be together when it is over."

All cultures have systems of healing. Universal methods of healing include food, music, love, touch, truth telling, and forgiveness. Laughter is a part of many healing systems. There is really no period in history when humans did not laugh. Many cultures have healing ceremonies, purification, and forgiveness rituals. Talking to friends, enjoying children, watching the stars, creating art, and helping others are ways of healing that have been used for thousands of years. People recover with "tincture of time."

In the Middle East, troubled people often visit the saints' houses. Usually these are peaceful retreats with kind people to assist the travelers. The guests visit with food to share. They pray, cry, talk to others, and rest. Most return home feeling much better.

Buddhism has an ancient and sophisticated set of practices for calming and healing. Breathing properly, meditating, and focusing on the impermanence of all things are healing activities. In fact, some of our most successful psychotherapy incorporates aspects of Buddhism.

Traditional healers and customs work because they are believed to work. They are about faith. Almost all mental health cures are about placebo effects. Placebo effects are not negligible. They are about hope and faith. Praying works whether or not people believe in God. Prayer is a more active, trusting process than worrying. It is calming and hopeful. Talking to God is generally more satisfying to people than talking to Freud. Also with prayer, there is no need for diagnosis, treatment, or comprehensive health insurance.

Refugees seem to understand the value of positive emotions and joyful events. An old Iraqi saying goes something like, "Three things are calming: grass, water, and the face of a beautiful woman." Latinos have all night fiestas. The Vietnamese are masters of potlucks.

Refugees often help other people. Social activism provides meaning and assuages survivor guilt. Documenting the abuses of an authoritarian regime or working for human rights is what saves many victims of a repressive government. Bringing family over from the old country is profoundly healing.

As I worked with refugees, I found myself acting less and less like a traditional therapist. This was partly because of the practical difficulties. Refugees just do not show up in private practice therapy offices with their checks and insurance cards the second Tuesday of every month at 5:00 p.m. Also, I worked with many people who did not use verbal skills and self-disclosure to solve problems. My traditional ways of working seemed bizarre to them. Depending on the need, I was a cultural broker, college advisor, mom, driving instructor, collaborator, case manager, advocate, or cook. I did coaching, cheerleading, consulting on the ways of Americans, life planning, values clarification, mediation, money and time management, and strength building. Sometimes I was a driver, a personal shopper, a math mentor, a friend, or a dance partner. Sometimes I was a magician or a faith healer. As I said, I learned to be flexible, to do what the situation required.

What we call professional boundaries can also be called being compartmentalized. Most other cultures do not divide their worlds into neat little boxes. As I spent time with newcomers, I became less compartmentalized. I talked as much about parties, international phone cards, and visas as I did about feelings and relationships. I showed families pictures of my kids. I gave little gifts and received them. I worried less about time and slowed down.

To work with refugees, we must expand our ideas of therapy. We will need new ways of looking at humans—more positive ways that assume humans have strong psychological immune systems. We need to value research on how the positive emotions of joy, contentment, and awe strengthen the psychological immune system.

A psychoeducative approach works well with refugees. They are suspicious of psychology but respectful of education. Psychoeducational approaches are less rule-bound and less prone to pathologizing. They carry no stigma, no shame, and no hierarchy. Psychoeducation happens all the time. Teaching healthy attitudes is not just the job of experts. Everyone can help everyone. Whereas therapy can make people feel weird, damaged, and alone, psychoeducation, especially in groups, makes people feel more normal and connected.

In America if families are not careful they end up stressed, rushed, unhealthy, addicted, and broke. We therapists can teach the importance of intentionally regarding media, money, and relationships. We can teach newcomers that time is their greatest wealth and that they must spend it carefully. And that to be strong in America, parents must protect their family from what is harmful and connect them to what is good and beautiful.

Therapists should be flexible and teach flexibility. We can teach the skill "cultural switching," which is behaving one way at home and another way outside the family. This is an especially important skill during transitions and when dealing with age and gender issues. We can emphasize that whatever adaptations and compromises people make are temporary and can be renegotiated as they learn more about America.

As cultural therapists, we can help people cope with the pain of cultural collisions around work, family, and community issues. We can learn about healing from each other and select from all cultures that which might work for us. In an ideal world we would all be able to pray, to dance and feast, to watch sunsets and moons rise, and to talk to each other about our pain. We would use both laughter and tears as well as that great antidote to despair, being useful.

We would create healing ceremonies. We would find symbols that gave meaning to our grief. We would teach each other to endure, that greatest of human strengths. Where there is endurance there is hope. Langston Hughes lamented that when dreams abandon us, life becomes like a barren field frozen with snow.

Our broadest goal is to reintroduce refugees to the human community of love. Many have been dehumanized by their experiences. Our caring can rehumanize them. Good touch can ameliorate memories of bad touch. Warmth and respect can rebuild a person who has been systematically humiliated and degraded by torturers.

What works best is a real person connecting to a real person. The first casualty of trauma is trust. People lose their protective shields of invulnerability and have no illusions that they are safe. This puts them in a difficult bind. They cannot heal without relationships, but relationships seem dangerous. Therapy can offer relationships that are nurturing, consistent, and continuous.

Therapy reawakens hope, that greatest of all elixirs. It is important to say, "You have lost a lot but you have not lost everything." Therapists have been "purveyors of hope." We can all be in that great society of encouragers.

Mark Twain described calmness as a language that the deaf can hear and the blind can read. Our best work is asking what is your experience and then listening closely. In the end our work is about finding dignity adequate to the sorrow. Isak Dinesen implied that sorrows could be borne if put in a story. Nietzsche implied a similarity between truth and a mobile army of metaphors.

Therapy is a meaning-building activity. We engage in the alchemy of healing by turning pain and sorrow into empathy and wisdom. We help our clients construct new stories that offer them new possibilities. To say that people can grow and learn from any experience is not to justify their experience or even to say that people could not have learned from easier lives, but it is to say that healthy people learn and grow from everything, even trauma. After trauma people often see the world in a new way—in a more layered, complex, and empathic way.

Globalization is creating one small, very interconnected world. I was influenced by Michael Featherstone's belief that we are living in each other's backyards. Kenneth Prewitt, director of the 2000 census, noted that America is on the way to becoming a microcosm of the entire world. One in five school children in our country is foreign born. My town with all its beautiful diversity is just like your town. Our job as psychologists is to help people learn to live peacefully together in this new world and new century. We can ease people into each other's cultures and teach our citizens to say, welcome. We can provide a healthier environment for all people by using psychological research on healthy communities, families, and work—which is the subject of this book.

PREFACE

It is hard to be a good citizen of the world in any great sense; but if we render no interest or increase to mankind out of that talent that God gave us, we can at least preserve the principle unimpaired. One would like to be making large dividends to society out of that deposit capital in us, but he does well for the most part if he proves a secure investment only without adding to the stock.

—Henry David Thoreau (*Journal*, March 26, 1842)

Psychology is a learned profession, and all psychologists who serve as educators, scientists, practitioners, or advocates for human welfare not only are good citizens of the world but also are truly dedicated to improving the quality of life of all the citizens of our planet.

In 2001, the American Psychological Association amended its mission statement to include the term *health*, stating that psychology's focus is "to advance as a science and a profession, and as a means of promoting *health* and human welfare." The addition of this one word, health, to the mission statement formally recognized the fact that "psychology has long been in the forefront of the scientific inquiry into the understanding of health" (Resnick & Rozensky, 1996, p. 1) and that, as health care providers, psychologists have been members of the health care team for decades (Matarazzo, 1994). As can be seen from this book, health has a broad definition that ranges from traditional medical and behavioral health activities to the prevention of illness, injury, and trauma to the building of healthy schools, workplaces, and communities. Furthermore, we strongly believe that this text highlights the roles and contributions that psychologists have contributed to the general health and well-being of all people.

The U.S. Surgeon General has noted that both behavioral and psychosocial variables are directly related to morbidity and mortality in the U.S. population (U.S. Department of Health and Human Services [USDHHS], 1990). In fact, each entry on the list of "The Leading Health Indicators" from *Healthy People 2010* (USDHHS, 2000) involves changes in health-oriented behavior, and thus, by definition, involves the work of psychology. These "health indicators" were chosen by the USDHHS to reflect the major health concerns in the United States at the beginning of the 21st century and were selected on the basis of their ability to motivate action, the availability of data to measure progress, and their importance as major public health issues; they include physical activity, overweight and obesity, tobacco use, substance abuse, responsible sexual behavior, mental health, injury and violence, environmental quality, immunization, and access to health care (USDHHS, 2000). Clearly, each of these is directly related to increases in health-oriented behavior or the avoidance of or decrease in health-threatening activity. A major goal of the Healthy People 2010 program is to increase both the quality and years of healthy living. Furthermore, "the underlying premise of Healthy People 2010 is that the health of the individual is almost inseparable from the health of the larger community and that the health of every community in every State and territory determines the overall health status of the Nation," and "community health is profoundly affected by the collective beliefs, attitudes, and behaviors of everyone who lives in the community" (USDHHS, 2000, p. 1). By this definition then, we cannot have a healthy world without healthy communities, and healthy communities are composed of healthy people and the healthy organizations in which they function, be those organizations the family, neighborhoods, schools, or workplaces. Schneiderman and Speers (2001), in reviewing the scientific and clinical interface of psychology and public health, noted that "the control of most causes of morbidity and mortality involves the use of behavioral-social sciences interventions. Application of these interventions occurs at many levels and requires the application of different skills both within and across levels. Thus, for many individual-based (i.e., intrapersonal, interpersonal) interventions to succeed, they may have to take place in a sociocultural environment that also involves concomitant population-based (i.e., organizational, societal) interventions" (p. 22). Thus, psychology builds a healthy world by enhancing the positive interplay of the individual and his or her personal, local, and global environment.

ORGANIZATION OF THIS BOOK

This book is the product of the American Psychological Association (APA) 2001 Presidential Initiative, "Psychology Builds a Healthy World," held as part of the 109th Annual Convention of the APA. More than 50 psychologists, specialists in a wide array of health promotion, illness prevention, public health, and health care, served as expert speakers to a well-attended, 3-day program. The major purpose of this book is to provide the reader with a survey of many of the topics and speakers who added to the vibrant nature of the conference. Space does not allow all topics and all speakers to be included in the text, but those included highlight the range of psychology's contribution to building a healthy world. Theoretical, clinical, and research discussions are included along with presentations of actual programming ideas across the venues of the family, the workplace, and the community as the targets for healthy living. The individual in need of traditional health care is discussed along with opportunities to promote healthy lifestyles across venues. The introduction to this volume is written by Norine G. Johnson, who served as president of the APA in 2001 and whose "healthy world" initiative is described in that chapter. Part I of the book looks at building healthy families. Chapter 1, the overview to the part, considers healthy connections within the home to prevent violence in society. Chapter 2 reviews the biopsychosocial model of health and applications to specific illnesses and building healthy families and healthy home environments. Injury and violence prevention in the home are topics of chapter 3, whereas the final chapter in this part looks at the interplay between gender and stress and their impact on general health.

Part II of the book looks at building healthy communities and begins with chapter 5, an overview of healthy sexuality in the community setting as a first step to assuring healthy communities. The next chapter focuses on community-based health psychology programming and program development and then details responses to community trauma focusing on child sexual abuse prevention. It ends with a focus on building healthy communities. The final chapter in this part reviews the literature and programs pertaining to injury control in the community, violence prevention, fire and burn safety, and the traumatic aftermath of violence in the community.

Part III of the book begins with chapter 8, an overview of cooperation and collaboration in the healthy workplace, and then goes on, in the next chapter, to look at issues of balancing the family and workplace, violence prevention at work, and managing stress at work. The last chapter in this part looks at occupational health, workplace safety, and preparing for a healthy retirement.

The final part, or "afterword," of this book then reviews the contributions that psychology has made to building a healthy world. It offers suggestions for future research, education and training, applied services, and public policy that assure that psychologists continue to take an active role in all endeavors that likewise assure a high quality of life and health for ourselves, our families, our coworkers, and our global neighborhood.

> Health is a state of complete physical, mental and social well-being, and not merely the absence of disease or infirmity.
> —Constitution of the World Health Organization

REFERENCES

Matarazzo, J. D. (1994). Health and behavior: The coming together of science and practice in psychology and medicine after a century of benign neglect. *Journal of Clinical Psychology in Medical Settings, 2*, 21–38.

Resnick, R. J., & Rozensky, R. H. (1996). Introduction. In R. J. Resnick & R. H. Rozensky (Eds.), *Health psychology through the life span: Practice and research opportunities* (pp. 1–6). Washington, DC: American Psychological Association.

Schneiderman, N., & Speers, M. A. (2001). Behavioral science, social science, and public health in the 21st century. In N. Schneiderman, M. A. Speers, J. M. Silva, H. Tomes, & J. H. Gentry (Eds.), *Integrating behavioral sciences with public health* (pp. 3–28). Washington, DC: American Psychological Association.

U.S. Department of Health and Human Services. (1990). *Healthy people 2000: National health promotion and disease prevention objectives* (DHHS Publication No. 91-50212). Washington, DC: U.S. Government Printing Office.

U.S. Department of Health and Human Services. (2000, November). *Healthy people 2010: Understanding and improving health* (2nd ed.). Washington, DC: U.S. Government Printing Office.

ACKNOWLEDGMENTS

The editors wish to thank the following individuals who helped make this volume possible: Drs. Dorothy W. Cantor, Susan H. McDaniel, Rick Price, Marilyn Puder-York, and Michael C. Roberts as well as Elizabeth Kaplinski and Judith Strassburger. To all those who participated in the 2001 American Psychological Association Presidential Miniconvention, "Psychology Builds a Healthy World," this book celebrates your dedication to improving the lives of all people.

Psychology Builds a
Healthy World

INTRODUCTION:

PSYCHOLOGY AND HEALTH— TAKING THE INITIATIVE TO BRING IT TOGETHER

NORINE G. JOHNSON

We must remove the line between health and mental health in our research, in our practices, in our educational programs, and in our public policies. Parity in health services and insurance coverage are but one step in the battle to remove this deceptive line between health and mental health. As will be the focus of this book, health is an interaction among many elements including the environment, culture, and the individual. And within each there are physical and psychological elements that contribute to health and others that contribute to illness, disability, and death. Therefore, why continue this false dialogue and carry on our conversations as if one could separate the mind from the body and as if we could ignore the influence of culture, class, and gender on the health of our minds and bodies? There are powerful forces in our society, including our historic roles and current funding sources, that continue to perpetuate an obviously deceptive mode of questioning and treating. Just as physicians for over two thousand and five hundred years continued bloodletting as a cure for most illnesses (Starr, 2002), so does health science continue an arbitrary division between the health or illness of mind and the body.

As psychology expands its role in all aspects of heath, Thomas Jefferson's query on head and heart resonates and leaders in our field warn of the danger of un-integrated approaches, whether occurring individually or systemically: "a failure in the internal dialogue between thinking and feeling, thought and emotion, head and heart can lead to unhealthy and adverse consequences" (Quick, Gavin, Cooper, & Quick, chap. 8, this volume). And from medical statistics we see graphic evidence of the fallacy of dividing physical and mental health care, as the WHO Collaborative Project found 24% of patients in primary care presented with psychological problems (Global Forum for Health Research, 2002). And yet a patient's psychological problems are unrecognized or untreated by most primary care physicians. In the United States, one of the most developed countries in the world, we find the health systems continue as if the mind and body were two separate entities with little or no relevance for each other's well-being or illness.

This book is one product of the 2001 Presidential Initiative "Psychology Builds a Healthy World" and illustrates the work of leaders in psychology and health. The Healthy World Initiative exceeded all expectancies for innovation, involvement of the best and brightest from our discipline, and breadth and depth of issues covered, thanks to the cochairs of the initiative, Carol D. Goodheart, EdD, W. Rodney Hammond, PhD, and Ronald H. Rozensky, PhD. Drs. Goodheart, Hammond, and Rozensky brought a diversity of expertise and perspectives on psychology and health, modeling for the field a respectful, collaborative, biopsychosocial approach to health. The convention presenters and writers for this book were selected for their contributions to the field, their forward look into the labyrinth of connections between the mind and body, and their understanding of the importance of social/cultural context and of the role of behavior in health promotion and disease prevention.

The 2001 Healthy World Initiative's three goals were to promote systematic physical, mental, social, and spiritual health; to promote research and practice that integrates physical and mental health; and to promote psychology as a core discipline in the provision of health care. The Healthy World mission is to inform psychologists of psychological cutting edge research and practice in health; to inform the public of psychology's contributions to health; and to expand health-based partnerships with the public, policymakers, and other professionals. And as Pat DeLeon, the American Psychological Association's (APA) 108th President, wrote in his "Presidential Reflections" (2002),

> psychologists have a special responsibility to affirmatively address society's pressing needs and collectively provide proactive vision and affirmative leadership. Almost all of the problems addressed daily by the

national media possess a major behavioral science (e.g., psychological) component, wherever one addresses the U.S. health care system. . . . In this light, Norine G. Johnson's presidential initiative is most timely. The interrelatedness of psychologists as providers of health services and their role in the construction of a socially healthy society. (p. 425)

This introduction will select but a few of the thousands of examples of biopsychosocial behavioral aspects of health and is dedicated to all the psychology researchers and practitioners who—study by study, patient by patient—have added so much to our knowledge of psychology and health. For those of you not specifically trained in health, health psychology, or working in the health arena, I encourage you to scan the literature over the past year. I guarantee you will be amazed, perhaps even astonished, at the breadth and depth of psychological research that explores a galaxy of questions related to the universe of health.

APA'S MISSION STATEMENT

In 2001, during my APA presidential year, the association amended its mission statement to include as a primary mission of the APA "to advance psychology as a science and a profession, and as a means of promoting *health* and human welfare." This bylaw change was approved by one of the largest pluralities ever. Over 95% of the members voted to include health as one of psychology's primary missions. In the last section of this chapter, I will talk about some of the present initiatives and future implications of this important bylaw change for psychology as a field and for psychologists.

DEFINITIONS OF HEALTH

The "Psychology Builds a Healthy World" initiative uses the biopsychosocial model of health, which incorporates the World Health Organization's (1948) definition of health as a state of complete physical, mental, and social well-being and not merely the absence of disease or infirmity. The biopsychosocial model (Engel, 1977) proposed an integration of mind and body to provide a more comprehensive approach to health and illness. The Institute of Medicine (2000) added further emphasis to the importance of psychological research and intervention in health policy and funding when it asserted that a key to helping people enjoy longer, healthier lives is understanding how to promote behavior change and to create healthier environments. The contributors to this volume provide a plethora of research and interventions that support the thesis that all illnesses have a biopsychosocial basis and that the interventions to restore health or reduce the effects of an illness benefit from a partnership between health and mental health.

STRENGTH-BASED APPROACHES

My address as president of the Society for the Psychological Study of Women raised the issue of the importance of the psychological study of strengths and how concepts of strengths were changing (Johnson, 1995). I proposed that women were changing their concepts of what it meant to be strong from a traditional valuing of endurance to a concept of strength as embracing enacting. In 1993 the National Conference on Education and Training in Feminist Practice endorsed as a core tenet of feminist therapy, focusing on strengths rather than deficits, and resulted in the edited book, *Shaping the Future of Feminist Psychology: Education, Research, and Practice* (Worell & Johnson, 1997).

The twin themes of valuing diversity and valuing strengths were endorsed by the APA Presidential Task Force on Adolescent Girls in 1994 by then APA President Dorothy Cantor, and they became the spine for the task force's two books, *Beyond Appearance: A New Look at Adolescent Girls* (Johnson, Roberts, & Worell, 1999) and *The Inside Story on Teen Girls* (Zager & Rubenstein, 2002). By changing the focus of the lens to strengths, the task force was endorsing a health-based model for viewing adolescent girls. A well-designed national study, looking at adolescent health and interested in issues of vulnerability and resilience, used a similar focus on strengths. Resnick and colleagues (1997) chose to investigate children who, although at high risk for health-compromising behaviors, instead successfully navigated adolescence and avoided health-compromising behaviors.

Mary Pipher (see the foreword, this volume) used the immigrant experience in Nebraska as a stepping-stone to ask psychologists to include healing and resiliency in our models: "What models could we develop from our experience with refugees that would allow us to expand our knowledge of the human race? What are the universal components of healing? What are the cross-cultural aspects of resiliency?"

Across settings—individual, family, or community—and across health conditions, psychology research and interventions are increasingly looking at strength-building strategies and outcomes. The approach advocated in positive psychology focuses on positive human traits that may serve as a defense against psychopathology: "We must bring the building of strength to the forefront in the treatment and prevention of mental illness" (Seligman, 2002, p. 3). I would add that we must bring the building of strength to the forefront in the treatment and prevention of illness, for the promotion of wellness and health.

Psychology research is documenting the effects of cognition upon health outcomes (Salovey, Rothman, Detweiler, & Steward, 2000; Taylor, Kemeny, Reed, Bower, & Gruenewald, 2000). Negative self-appraisal or negative assessment of one's potential for recovery from a health event was found to correlate with health outcomes (Taylor, Klein, et al., 2000). For example, this research suggests that practitioners with clients who are heart disease survivors need to incorporate therapeutic approaches for increasing the client's ability to visualize improved health and improved self-empowerment in dealing with the medical regime.

The questions for psychology are: How do we do this? How do we help individuals engage in healthy thinking and health promoting behavior? Boyce (Cantor, Boyce, & Repetti, chap. 10, this volume) encourages psychologists to study the natural consequences of at-risk behavior and then design wellness programs that compete with the natural consequences. Another example of following these principles is Strader, Collins, and Roe's (2000) Creating Lasting Family Connections program designed to work with youths at high risk from substance abuse. They concluded that "building from strengths, rather than attacking problems, has proved to be critical to our successful program development" (p. viii).

Teaching positive coping skills at the individual, family, and community level has demonstrated efficacy and effectiveness in decreasing health-risk behaviors in social and behavioral contexts such as sexual abuse, HIV/AIDS, and youth substance abuse. Susan Pick's (chap. 5, this volume) work at the Mexican Institute for the Study of Family and Population (IMIFAP) is an outstanding example of utilizing psychological research to design and evaluate culturally appropriate interventions within the community.

While in Mexico City I had the opportunity to learn in some detail about Pick's work in IMIFAP, which focuses on teaching skills and competencies to women and promotes sexual and reproductive health within their native communities. Pick's address at the 2001 American Psychological Association convention and her chapter in this book give a few examples of these extensive programs and the evaluation research that documents their effectiveness in reducing violence and increasing healthy sexual behavior through the use of strength- and competency-based interventions.

FAMILY, COMMUNITY, AND WORK CONTRIBUTIONS TO HEALTH

The biopsychosocial approach to health is not limited to individuals. Although currently the vast amount of medical research dollars are spent on individual trials, psychology research is increasingly focused on systemic and cultural efforts on health. The Healthy World Initiative focused on three major systems—family, community, and work—to provide a unifying forum for these newer perspectives of health and psychology. Using systemic approaches to the biopsychosocial approach to health unites psychologists working in these seemingly diverse settings. Family psychologists, community psychologists, and occupational health psychologists are making major contributions to the understanding and treatment of health issues across the spectrum from wellness and prevention to death and dying.

Family dynamics impact the course of disease and the effectiveness of medical treatment. The integration of family psychologists into primary care has produced research and practice that spotlights the importance of family members in all phases of the treatment of illnesses: assessment, decision making, and treatment (McDaniel, Johnson, & Sears, chap. 2, this volume). By integrating primary care and mental health, opportunities are presented for emphasizing wellness and the prevention of mental illness.

William S. Pollack (chap. 1, this volume) has a body of work (Pollack, 1999, 2000) that focuses on the psychological underpinnings that sap the health of our boys and lead to paths of violence. He provides the hope of health through the protective bonding of families. His writings emphasize the importance of a boy's connection to his family and the importance of community relationships for boys. He writes passionately about the violence that threatens the foundations of our country and calls for society to support families "of all stripes and colors" so they can provide the cement to sustain health for individual members as well as the community as a whole. He provides psychological guidance for families to create safety for their children. While focusing on boys, he provides evidence for how the code of masculinity that requires men and boys to tough it out alone, reject connections, and be emotionally detached relates to the health menace of violence that has been expressed in school shootings throughout our nation.

The community health psychology perspective presented by Victor De La Cancela and colleagues (chap. 6, this volume) places the focus of intervention in the community, with an emphasis on the health and well-being of underserved communities. For an example of effective community approaches we can look at research-based psychological approaches used with teens at high risk for addictive behavior.

Alcohol, tobacco, and marijuana are the top three substances abused by youth. Statistics on heavy drinking in youth indicate that almost one third of 12th graders self-report heavy recent alcohol use. Starting in the 1980s, there was a shift from school-based programs that did not involve parents, to community-based programs dealing with youth issues of addictions. Approaches such as the Creating Lasting Family Connections program (Strader, Collins, & Roe, 2000), which was designed to prevent substance abuse in high-risk youth, focus on the importance of connections in promoting health in teens. The CLFC program uses positive approaches to develop and maintain relationships and uses these relationships to provide models and information about maintaining drug-free, healthy lifestyles.

Psychologists are leading the way to designing healthy workplaces. The United States is frequently seen as the center of a global economic village. We have an obligation as a country to set the bar for healthy workplaces around the world. Psychologists are contributing to changes in business practices that promote health in the workplace just as psychological knowledge has influenced the theory and practice in areas such as business leadership skills and profitability.

Rosch's (2001) assertion that job stress is a health epidemic is the jumping-off place for James Campbell Quick's argument that psychology research and interventions are vital for the health of modern workplaces (Quick et al., chap. 9, this volume). Also, because the causes of disabilities in the workplace are shifting from injury-based investigations to stress-based inquiries, psychological principles appropriately applied can result in a reduction in workplace injury with a resultant financial savings for the company (Cantor, Boyce, & Repetti, chap. 10, this volume).

An example of the potentially positive influence of psychological inferences and interventions in the workplace is seen in approaches to downsizing. Phenomena such as organizational downsizing (Brockner, Siegel, Daley, Tyler, & Martin, 1997) have psychological sequelae. Fifty people committed suicide, untold hundreds of family members were affected and entire communities disrupted by the bankruptcy and demise of Eastern Airlines. In contrast, psychologists today, according to Quick and colleagues (chap. 8, this volume), are working with organizations and using interventions based on research that suggests when downsizing is done with fairness, justice, and heart it can lead to significantly more positive outcomes.

The workplace has a psychological effect on all aspects of our lives and on the lives of our family members. Parental job stressors result in family social interactions that are less sensitive and supportive, more negative and conflicted, leading to an impact on children's biological responses to stress, emotional regulation, and social competence (Cantor, Boyce, & Repetti, chap. 10, this volume). As women have increasingly entered the workforce there have been innumerable studies documenting the negative consequences of work upon parent–child interaction. Clearly, stress at work, previous experiences, and upbringing can have negative consequences on family life. Isn't it time we as a society use psychological principles to develop public policies that support healthy conditions and support for both mothers and fathers who work?

Work consumes much of the time and energy of most Americans, and yet there has been limited research or interventions specifically geared to how to voluntarily leave the workforce or how to prepare for a predetermined retirement. Given the numbers of people entering retirement age, combined with a possibly uncertain economic picture, psychology has an important role to play in this life stage. Research and interventions using the biopsychosocial model of healthy behavior, combined with knowledge of the psychology of work are needed to develop processes by which people may utilize healthy psychological strategies to enter retirement. Cantor (Cantor, Boyce, & Repetti, chap. 10, this volume), while commenting that many look upon retirement as a form of death, recommends instead that retirement be looked upon as a developmental stage with possibilities for growth. She suggests cognitive, behavioral, and emotional interventions whereby the individual actively engages in a review and planning process geared to promote better emotional and physical health.

RANGE OF HEALTH ISSUES WITH MAJOR BEHAVIORAL PSYCHOSOCIAL RESEARCH AND INTERVENTION COMPONENTS

When I was around 10 years old, I gathered frog eggs and set up a crude laboratory to watch their development to adulthood. We lived in the country and having spent several summers looking at the eggs close to the pond's edge and listening to the nighttime croaks of the adult frogs—and probably wondering about sex but unwilling to ask—I turned our little-used garage into a world that preoccupied my days.

As the project expanded and the eggs turned to tadpoles which then metamorphosed into small frogs, the garage filled with various-sized containers of pond water and vegetation. Getting more and more complex and more and more revealing and more and more interesting, each phase was different than I had expected.

The evolution of psychology in the health field is similar to this early experiment. We are moving out of the earlier stages of development into more complex questions, models, and structures. Our interventions are getting more complex and focused. And just as not all my frog eggs made it to adulthood and hence back to the pond, not all our early ideas and findings are surviving.

Psychology health science and psychology health practice are beyond their early embryonic stages. Similar to early adolescence they are ready to seek independence and identity. How far we've come. How exciting the journey. How awesome the continuing exploration ahead. I am struck over and over again by the foresight of the pioneers in psychology and health and the intellect, dedication, and creativity of its current scientists, practitioners, educators, and policymakers.

As we look at the span of health issues that include psychological components, the current research blankets the entire spectrum from wellness, prevention, acute and chronic illness, reoccurrence of an illness, to death and dying. And we add depth to our widening perspective through the research and practices that include the impact of poverty, ethnicity and race, sexual orientation, and gender upon the health of individuals and nations. This section will use examples from wellness and prevention, chronic illness, and behavioral, social, and cultural influences to illustrate the importance of a biopsychosocial model of health that infuses psychology research and practice in all facets of our nation's health research, health care, and health policies.

WELLNESS AND PREVENTION

The behavioral sciences have a well-known body of outcome research related to wellness and prevention for individuals, families, and communities. Strength-based approaches and positive psychology focus research and interventions on looking at individuals, families, and communities that are healthy and what sustains health. Ryff and Singer (2002) raise the crucial questions that positive psychology brings to the discussion on health: "What does it mean to be psychologically well? And, what factors promote such well-being?" (p. 541).

Psychologists already have contributed much to the dialogue. We have developed techniques for teaching the major components of health-sustaining behaviors: exercise, nutrition, weight control, stress management, relaxation training, smoking cessation, alcohol and drug treatment, and violence prevention. The Institute for the Future (2000) looked at the top 10 determinants of illness and death and the top 10 underlying causes for these, to reach the conclusion that a biomedical model of health and disease was insufficient and that a more comprehensive biopsychosocial model was needed (p. 167). The ranking of the top 10 illnesses was (in order from most to less prevalent) cardiovascular disease, cancer, cerebrovascular disease, chronic obstructive pulmonary disease, unintentional injury, pneumonia and influenza, diabetes, HIV/AIDS, suicide, and homicide. And the top ten underlying causes were, from most to least prevalent, tobacco, poor diet, lack of exercise, alcohol, infectious agents, pollutants and toxins, firearms, sexual behavior, motor vehicles, and illicit drug use.

Therefore, to prevent illness and sustain wellness it is necessary for individuals, families, and communities to engage in healthy behaviors and interactions. Communities working together have tackled health issues as diverse as lifestyle issues (e.g., smoking cessation, alcohol and drug abuse);

crime related health traumas (e.g., violence against women, child sexual abuse); and environmental hazards (e.g., clean water, identifying cancer hot spots). Victor De La Cancela identifies the healthy communities' movement as emerging from the World Health Organization. There the prescriptions for a healthy community—peace, shelter, education, food, income, a stable ecosystem, sustainable resources, social justice, and equity—were proposed (Ottawa Charter for Health Promotion, 1986).

Medical insurance considers annual checkups and screening as part of prevention where prevention means detecting a health problem while still medically manageable and hopefully therefore, to prevent extensive medical intrusiveness and possible death. The value of screening—mammograms, colorectal, heart—is currently part of our national debate and yet the psychological impact of screening has not been integrated into medical practice. Psychologists in private practice are well aware of the anxiety for women as they approach their annual mammogram and then wait for the results. Or parents who hear a pediatrician say, "Your child is borderline for diabetes." In mid-2002, the American Heart Association released new guidelines that proposed evaluating everyone starting at age 20, in an attempt to catch even earlier those at risk of having a heart attack or stroke. A 30-year-old major league baseball player died in his sleep of heart disease, raising again the anxiety of men in this age bracket with family histories of coronary deaths.

Participation in screening by those designated at high risk is also a psychological event and we have much to contribute to understanding the resistance to screening, to increasing compliance, and to helping support individuals and families afterwards. Physician and family support are key variables for predicting whether or not the high-risk patient actually follows through on the screening. For example, practitioners working with Huntington's disease families know full well how devastating the illness is and how complicated is the process by which a family member, not yet affected, struggles with the decision whether or not to test. In my experience even the "good news" of finding that one might be the only survivor in one's family, can have a major negative disruptive impact on a life that had been organized around the high probability of early death. For example, a client in her late 40s decided to have the Huntington's disease screening she had declined to have throughout her life. She became acutely depressed upon finding out she did not have the disease. As she explained in treatment, her life decisions—not to marry, not to have children—had been made on her belief that she was a carrier and would die. She did not want her spouse or children to experience what she had as her parents died and she did not want to risk having children with the disease. She had built her life on the assumption she would die of Huntington's. What was expected by the screeners to be good news instead filled her with despair that her life choices left her empty and alone.

CHRONIC ILLNESS

Four chronic diseases will be used as examples of psychology's impact on the understanding and treatment of the chronic illnesses that are ranked as the major causes of human death and disability. Cardiovascular disease, cancer, diabetes, and HIV/AIDS are among the major chronic diseases affecting adults and children in the United States today (Institute for the Future, 2000). And mental illness negatively affects the course and outcome of comorbid chronic conditions such as cancer, heart disease, diabetes, and HIV/AIDS. For example, depressed patients are at increased risk for complications and death from chronic diseases and their recovery from surgery is slower.

Each of these four illnesses can be used to illustrate the importance of removing the barriers between health and mental health and recognizing and incorporating treatment and prevention of the psychological factors that affect and are affected by these diseases. Good mental health contributes to well-being, increases productivity, and improves social cohesiveness.

Cardiovascular Disease

The entire course of heart disease has been studied extensively by psychologists: causes, risk indicators, compliance with treatment, rehabilitation, prevention of second occurrences, and death. In January 2001, the APA Monitor on Psychology started a series on health issues for the "Psychology Builds a Healthy World" presidential initiative. The first issue focused on cardiac psychology research and practice (Clay, 2001) and featured the cutting-edge cardiac research of several prominent psychologists, Blumenthal, Krantz, Frasure-Smith, Matthews, Williams, and their colleagues. Their research has delineated several psychological factors as contributing significantly to heart disease: hostility, anger, stress, depression, social isolation, and lifestyle behavioral habits. A few examples are that depressed patients with heart conditions are more likely to die; hostility in adults and young people is related to coronary artery calcification (Miller, Smith, Turner, Guyarro, & Hallet, 1996); and emotional factors impact on myocardial ischemia through a reduced blood supply to the heart. Behavioral contributions found to increase the risk of heart disease include smoking and eating habits.

The intervention research demonstrates that various psychological treatments are effective in reducing rates of reoccurrence of types of cardiac distress. In a well-designed research program (Blumental et al., 1997), cardiac patients with ischemia were assigned to one of three groups. Over a 3-year period the group that was taught stress management techniques had significantly less additional heart problems than either the exercise program or control group.

The importance of psychological interventions in responding to and complying with treatments for cardiac illness is dramatically seen in the Sears and Conti discussion (chap. 2, this volume) on the patients with implantable cardioverter defibrillator (ICD). ICDs save lives but may cause anxiety and depression: that is, 13% to 38% of patients with ICD experience significant emotional symptoms. Januzzi, Stern, Pasternak, and DeSanctis (2000) found that anxiety and depression resulted in decreased compliance in using the ICD. Appropriate psychological intervention increases both positive mental health and compliance with appropriate treatment with the ICD. So again, the mind affects the body, the body affects the mind, and it is imperative to recognize the unity and treat both.

One of the special delights of being APA President was the opportunity to talk with members about their experiences as psychologists: what they are doing, what they see in the future, and what excites them. During a governance meeting I was talking with a student and asked him how his internship was coming. His internship was at a major teaching hospital where he served as a member of the heart transplant team. Organ transplantation is a growing medical field and psychologists are increasingly becoming integral members of transplant teams. As a member of the team, the psychologist's input as to the suitability of a patient for heart transplant is highly valued. He spoke at length about his preparation to assume this responsibility, his inner voyage to accept the responsibility, and the role of his psychology supervisor. Finally, he spoke of his struggle with knowing that, given the scarcity of acceptable hearts, his skilled psychological recommendations were as life- or death-producing as the surgeon's skilled hands. That week one of the patients on his team was up for review, and a heart was available. The team was mixed and awaited his recommendation.

Cancer

The incidence of cancer is rising in most countries. In the United States, some estimates place the incidence of breast cancer in women at 1 in 8. Whether or not stress causes cancer, the research findings consistently indicate that cancer causes stress. This stress, if not addressed, results in significant emotional distress with a preponderance of symptoms of depression and chronic anxiety, and can have a negative effect on subsequent life functioning (Anderson, 2002). Given the vastness of the epidemic of cancer and the range of types of cancer, with each having its own body of research, this section only focuses on a small body of the intervention research for women with breast cancer as an example of the role psychological research is playing in the total treatment of this disease.

There is a plethora of interventions in the cancer research being evaluated for a range of effects, from maintaining wellness, prevention of the disease, to lack of recurrence, to the psychological factors that increase feelings of well-being, to lifestyle and behavioral changes—such as exercise, diet, smoking, and condom use (the last is important because cervix cancer is hypothesized to be putting women at risk for breast cancer). In two separate reviews of breast cancer and psychobehavioral approaches, Anderson (1992, 2002) found that interventions such as relaxation, individual cognitive therapy, and educationally based support groups resulted in a decrease in reported emotional distress. However, her review also found little evidence for educational or supportive services reducing mortality. This is in marked contrast to the enthusiasm of the research in the early 80s and early 90s that found psychological interventions increased the life span of women with metastatic breast cancer (Anderson, 2002).

There are a variety of theories as to why in the new studies psychological intervention does not appear to extend life. Anderson concludes that the practice of excluding patients with other physical and mental health conditions from the breast cancer research may be adversely affecting the ability to explore intervention effects. One psychology cancer researcher, George Miller of Washington University (DeAngelis, 2001), speculated that the increased support given cancer patients today and the effects of medical improvements in increasing survival might be why psychological interventions appear less likely to improve survival rates.

What strikes one in reading Anderson's review is the high rate of mortality when the studies include women with late stage breast cancer: after 10 years, two studies found 59% and 66% respectively of the women died; after 5 years, two other studies found that 48% and 80% respectively of the women died; one study after 2 years found 60% of the women died; and another study found 85% of the women died. One cannot help but wonder if we are not looking at the wrong end of the disease to evaluate the effectiveness of psychological interventions. Utilizing a strength-based or positive psychological approach one would investigate women who remain free of Stage III, IV, and V cancer, looking for health and wellness indicators.

Psychologists Haber (1993) and Woznick and Goodheart (2001) translated the research in cancer into interventions for use by independent practitioners and families. Haber's work alerted psychologists to the importance of understanding the medical aspects of concern as well as the appropriate psychological approaches. Woznick and Goodheart wrote a brilliantly knowledgeable and compassionate guide for parents of children with cancer. Both translated psychology research and interventions in health into quality mental health interventions.

Diabetes

In the 1980s I made a trip to the Marshall Islands to visit one of my daughters, who was in the Peace Corps there, located on a remote atoll. As I readied to board a small, 16-seat plane, to fly the final leg from Majuro, the capital of the Marshalls, to her atoll, I was asked to wait while they carried an elderly woman amputee to her seat. She was returning to her home after having surgery to remove her legs due to advanced diabetes. As I heard story after story of children and adults affected by the disease, I was stunned to learn that diabetes is in epidemic proportions in the Marshalls, a U.S. protectorate. It affects the young and the old and results in part from excessive reliance on coconuts as a primary food and from a sedentary lifestyle. This experience began my voyage toward recognizing the crucial importance of integrating culture and health care to best service our world's diverse populations.

The treatment of diabetes requires constant medical attention, regular exercise, and controlled eating. As the incidence of diabetes, especially Type 1, explodes in the United States, some blame lifestyle issues in children and adolescents. Suzanne Bennett Johnson (McDaniel, Johnson, & Sears, chap. 2, this volume) reports that childhood diabetes (Type 1) affects over 100,000 children and their families, with increasing numbers being diagnosed each year. Childhood diabetes has become the number one chronic illness for children (LaPorte, Matsushima, & Chang, 1995). The treatment of diabetes is not just a medical issue: it affects the family and requires psychological interventions based on an understanding of developmental stages, knowledge of the course of the disease and its medical treatment, and sensitivity to the emotional and life issues that may sabotage the treatment (McDaniel, Johnson, & Sears, chap. 2, this volume). Again, we see the need to erase the line between health and mental health, to integrate psychological knowledge into the treatment, and to use a biopsychosocial model of intervention.

HIV/AIDS

The HIV/AIDS epidemic is like a modern black plague. In some countries it is affecting one in two families and leaving millions of children orphans. Worldwide, since the first cases were diagnosed almost 58 million people have been infected with HIV/AIDS with almost 22 million deaths.

In the United States one estimate places as many as 900,000 people infected with HIV and it is the leading cause of death for African American men (U.S. Department of Health and Human Services, 2000).

Although we think of HIV/AIDS as a behaviorally transmitted disease, and in most cases it is, the recent explosion in diagnosed HIV/AIDS in China apparently is the result of how blood products were collected, sold, and distributed. In the case of China it appears to be the behavior of unscrupulous businesses with government consent that set the stage in rural villages for massive infections. When I hear the stories of villagers who have lost their families and are dying themselves, I cannot even begin to comprehend the greed that would cause some people to prey upon others, that would use their poverty to exploit them for the money made from their blood.

Attacking the disease globally requires developed countries to assist developing countries through the sharing of resources: financial aid, medication, trained personnel, and knowledge. Psychology has an important role to play in the battle against this devastating disease. Nationally and internationally, health workers have used psychologically based interventions that focus on teaching the importance of safe and consensual sexual behavior. Susan Pick's research and interventions with IMIFAP (chap. 5, this volume) are a model of HIV/AIDS prevention on the community level with indigenous people. In Africa psychological understanding of the role of cultural beliefs and gender dynamics will be crucial to changing the sexual behavioral patterns that are wiping out the adults in entire families, leaving, some estimate, millions of children orphaned.

In addition to these biopsychosocial programs, the APA has an opportunity to express its opinion on issues of world health, such as the HIV/AIDS epidemic. APA recently became a National Government Organization (NGO) at the United Nations. As an NGO we have an opportunity to participate in policy debates. Psychology has a voice at the table that is formulating policy and recommending resource allocations for the global response to HIV/AIDS. This is another example of how psychology research, interventions, and public policy formulation are having and can have significant impact on the health of people and nations.

The psychology community has been actively involved in all facets of U.S. health efforts to understand and stem the devastation caused by the virus and the disease. Let me use just one example from the extensive psychological research looking at the individual issues of people at risk for HIV/AIDS or who have the disease. A review of research (Taylor, Kemeny, Reed, Bower, & Gruenewald, 2000) of individual personality variables and coping style concluded that men with HIV with positive thinking and optimism had significantly better health indicants than men who were pessimistic, bereaved, or experienced other negative emotions.

Unlike the black plague that was carried by rodents and required a change in hygiene and community water systems, the current plague is transmitted by humans and requires changes in human behavior and belief systems. Again psychology's role as a partner with public health is clear and crucial.

BEHAVIORAL AND SOCIAL CAUSES OF DEATH AND ILLNESSES

Behavioral, emotional, and social causes are seen as major contributors to the world's health problems (Institute for the Future, 2000). As immunization increased worldwide, there was a significant shift in the causes of illness, disability, and death. It is predicted that by 2020 noncommunicable diseases will account for 70% of the deaths in the developing world (Global Forum for Health Research, 2002). The biopsychosocial model allows us to move from the false simplicity of mind–body to better understand the role of race, ethnicity, immigration, social economic status, and gender on the health of individuals, families, and communities.

The behavioral and emotional causes most associated with illness and death are addiction (alcohol, tobacco, and illicit drug use), stress, injury, and violence. Crucial social and cultural influences are poverty, class, race, ethnicity, immigration, and gender. This section will share a few examples of some of the psychological research and interventions that address the questions regarding the influence of behavioral, emotional, and social causes of illness and are covered in much greater detail throughout this book.

Alcohol, Tobacco, and Illicit Drug Use

As an example of the extent of the impact of one behavior—tobacco use—let me share briefly some of the statistics on the primary cause of poor health and death. In 1990, tobacco was estimated to account for 3 million deaths worldwide. By 1998, tobacco-attributable deaths rose to 4 million and are projected to reach 8.4 million in 2020, and 20 million annual deaths in 2030. Psychological research regarding smoking is vast. In just one issue of the journal *Health Psychology* (July 2002) there were four articles that included research on smoking. They range in the health spectrum from prevention, such as stopping teens before they smoke; stopping or relapse (Perkins et al., 2002); exploring the influence of peers on young adults' substance use (Andrews, Tildesley, Hops, & Fuzhong, 2002); gender effects in stopping smoking (Westmaas, Wild, & Ferrence, 2002); to an interesting study on light smokers, called "chippers" (Presson, Chassin, & Sherman, 2002).

The numbers tell it all. Over 40% of Americans surveyed reported alcoholism in their family and 45% reported illicit drug use either by a family member, close friends, or themselves (Institute for the Future, 2000). These statistics and others almost as startling caused the Institute for the Future (2000) to place alcohol and drug abuse among the most pervasive of the U.S. health and social problems. I opened my APA presidential column (Johnson, 2001) on addictions as a major health hazard with these thoughts:

> The United States has a history of ambivalence to alcohol and drugs. The macho cowboy ambling up to the bar and the stumbling Bowery drunk are past pictorial depictions of the glory and tragedy of drink. Legends of Carrie Nation's hatchet-swinging starving widows and children compete with beliefs that the Prohibition Act, which limited the sale of alcohol, began the era of organized crime. Television images of 1970s college students in drugged states dancing merrily are set awry by today's headlines of college students falling off buildings because of alcohol and/or drugged states.

The ambivalence of the United States toward alcohol and drug use, as I said in the column, is expressed in limited funding for prevention and treatment in contrast to the ever expanding funds for law enforcement. Again psychology and psychologists have been leaders in the research on addictions and innovators in the development of techniques for intervention. The National Institute on Drug Abuse (NIDA) launched in 1999 a multisite research program that is looking at three protocols using pharmacological and cognitive treatments. The NIDA studies' goal is to use the results to transfer to the community effective, research-based interventions for drug abuse treatments.

Stress

Frequently there is assumed to be a link between stress and illness. Twenge's (2000) meta-analysis found Americans shifting toward higher anxiety during the years between 1952 and 1993. What must it be now since 9-11 and the economic changes of 2002? Might not we expect an increase not just in mental health problems but also in physical symptoms among those most susceptible to stress-related illnesses? Twenge's (2000) research made the connection between her findings of increased anxiety and increases in certain physical illnesses, "with asthma, irritable bowel syndrome . . . on the increase" (p. 1018). Stress is a complicated phenomenon, operating at the individual and system level, and in interaction among entities. Communities can experience stress from traumatic events like the terrorists attacks on September 11, 2001, as well as the individual stress reactions to the event and its constant repetitive televising. An individual's stress can affect the health of a system, such as a family or school, and of course a system's stress, such as a business going into bankruptcy as was discussed earlier, can affect the health of individuals, families, and whole communities.

At the individual level, psychological researchers are looking at how stress affects the immune system, raising such questions as the following: What body events affect brain activity? What brain activity affects the body? How does the immunization system serve as a link between the brain and the body (Taylor, 2002)? Psychoneuro-immunology (PNI) studies the relationships among and between stress, the immune system, health, and disease.

As I have in other sections, let me use one small area in a disease—arthritis—to illustrate how psychology has contributed to an understanding of how stress affects the pain experienced by arthritis sufferers. Studies linking interpersonal stress and disease activity in arthritis (Zautra, Burleson, Matt, Roth, & Burows, 1994) illuminate how psychology looks at the connectedness of stress and health. Arthritis is a painful disease affecting many elderly people, and even children and young adults. The pain connected with arthritis can have a major impact on quality of life. Daily stressors in the lives of rheumatoid arthritis patients were found to be significantly related to increased joint pain. Even minor stressors appeared to result in increased inflammation in the joints (Affleck et al., 1997).

Stress also interacts with other social behavioral phenomena such as ethnicity, race, immigration status, socioeconomic status, and gender to produce a cascade of interactive factors that contribute to illness, injury, and death. It would be beyond the scope of this chapter to even attempt a summary or even to use an example to illustrate decades of work in the effect of stress on mental health. What is relatively new and ever expanding is how psychological practitioners are using stress reduction techniques to address health issues. In addition to the traditional behavioral, cognitive, and psychodynamic psychotherapy approaches, psychoeducational approaches, meditation, and biofeedback are some of the other interventions found useful to reduce stress for health purposes.

Ethnicity, Race, and Immigration

Along with socioeconomic status, ethnicity, race, and immigration account for an appalling amount of the health disparity in our country. Disease after disease differentially affects our racial and ethnic minority populations, and the variables most often found to account for the health disparity are access, health dollar expenditure, and health risk behaviors.

The Committee on Capitalizing on Social Science and Behavioral Research to Improve the Public's Health (Institute of Medicine, 2000) piled research finding on research finding on research finding to document the relationship in the United States between socioeconomic status and racial and ethnic status to health. Although there are a few exceptions, disease by disease—heart, cancer, HIV/AIDS, asthma, and so forth—people of color have poorer health outcomes than do their White counterparts. Even when economic status and insurance coverage are controlled or minimized the discrepancy looms.

U.S. Surgeon General David Satcher unveiled his report on *Mental Health: Culture, Race, and Ethnicity* at the 2001 APA Convention in San Francisco. I was honored to introduce him. Dr. Satcher emphasized how mental health problems contribute significantly to the health of all. If disparities are present in access, utilization, and quality of mental health services, as Dr. Satcher's report identifies, it affects the health of the disfranchised groups (U.S. Department of Health and Human Services, 2001). The report contains data on the high rate of suicide, alcoholism, drug addiction, and violence-caused death and injury arising from the mental health needs that are being unmet in our country for African Americans, Hispanics, Asian American Pacific Islanders and American Indians.

And if the child is a person of color, the health care statistics are grim. Let me use but one example of hundreds of thousands. A Boston newspaper in the summer of 2002 carried a brief item buried in the back pages that should have been front-page headlines. The article highlighted the disparities in health care experienced by Hispanic children: 11% of U.S. children of Puerto Rican descent had asthma, double the rate of Black children and triple the rate of non-Hispanic White children; Hispanic children were 13 times more likely than non-Hispanic White children to have tuberculosis; when hospitalized with bone fractures, Hispanic children received lower doses of pain medication than non-Hispanic White children. The study concluded that Hispanic children receive inadequate health care due to cultural barriers, racial bias, and ignorance of their ethnicity-based needs. On the flip page of this same newspaper but receiving even more lines of coverage was an article with the headline "Cyclist Dies Under Bus Swerving to Avoid Door."

In the following studies there were no significant differences in the economic status of the participants, so the findings highlight the race and ethnicity effects: White men and women live longer than African American men and women; rates of infant mortality, low birthrate, cancer, high blood pressure, adolescent pregnancy, and psychiatric disorders increase for Hispanics the longer their stay in the United States (Vega & Amaro, 1994); heart disease kills proportionally more Native Hawaiians than any other racial group in the United States (Chen, 1993); Native American and Native Alaskans have the highest rate of suicide and alcohol deaths relative to their population proportions.

But it is not enough just to look at race and ethnicity to understand health disparities and to devise effective interventions for extending wellness and reducing the effects of illness. I was struck by the differences in life expectancy for American Indian or Alaskan Native males. For those living within a six-county cluster in South Dakota, the median life expectancy is 56.5 years. For those living in Los Angeles County, the median life expectancy is 92.3 years. As important as the influence of race, ethnicity, immigration status, and culture are on health status, it is difficult to separate their influence from the effect of socioeconomic status that is discussed next.

Poverty

The impact of poverty upon health is seen on the local, national, and world levels. There are disturbing global statistics about the role of poverty on world health. At first blush it may seem unnecessary to state that the world's wealthiest nations spend their health research dollars for diseases that impact their citizens. But this means that 90% of global health research funding goes for only 10% of the world's health problems (Global Forum for Health Research, 2002). Communicable diseases still represent a large share of the disease burden in low to middle income countries. In contrast, for the United States and developed countries, noncommunicable diseases such as cardiovascular, cancer, mental and behavioral problems, injuries, violence, and diabetes make up the vast preponderance of health issues.

In the United States on the community and individual level, poverty is increasingly connected to health with higher rates of death and illness being associated with lower socioeconomic status (Feinstein, 1993). One of the effects of low socioeconomic status is to limit access to health care, and without access acute illnesses become chronic. We are not talking about limited numbers of people even in America, the richest country in the world. More than 30 million Americans have no health insurance. The Kaiser Commission on Medicaid and the Uninsured's report found that the uninsured receive poorer care. For example, they have less preventive care and when they are sick and finally go for help, the disease is at a more advanced stage than in those patients with insurance who go to seek medical help earlier. Estimates are that if this population of uninsured had insurance, their mortality rate would be reduced by 10 to 15 percent.

For example, here in the states in 2000 there were 182,800 new cases of invasive breast cancer and 40,800 deaths. The incidence of breast cancer was greater among wealthier than lower income women; however, the wealthier women have lower rates of mortality (Schneider et al., 2001). A contributory factor to lower rates of mortality may be early and regular use of mammography. One study found that 33% of women with household incomes less than $15,000 had never even heard of mammography and 90% of the women did not obtain mammograms regularly (Michey, Durski, Worden, & Danigelis, 1995).

Looking at heart disease we find that poor men and women with heart disease die more frequently than men and women with higher incomes. The National Center for Health Statistics (2002) data indicated that men with heart disease and less than $10,000 annual income had two and a half times the risk of dying than men with incomes over $25,000. The poorest women are even worse off. Their risk of dying early is almost three and a half times that of women in the higher income category. Other statistics vary across disease categories, but the ratio is similar. The more income a person has, the less risk for illness and death than someone else with less income.

Poverty is so intertwined with high-risk behaviors for disease such as smoking, obesity, addiction, and violence that it seems a truism to assume that psychology will be an integral part of public health programs working to treat these problems. Community health psychology is a vital perspective for designing psychological research and interventions to combat the effects of poverty upon health. Psychology has developed multiple theories for guiding research and interventions in community health (see Pick, chap. 5, this volume; and Schneiderman, Speers, Silva, Tomes, & Gentry, 2001, for reviews of approaches found effective). And yet despite psychology's expertise and willingness to serve, despite the relevance of psychological research and the long history of psychology's involvement in public policy advocating for the poor, our nation has yet to integrate psychology fully into its national public health programs. This is an area of health care that demands increased multidisciplinary involvement and increased resources for the biopsychosocial model espoused in this chapter.

Violence and Injury

Violence and injuries are a major cause of death and disability, worldwide, and are routinely included in health statistics from the U.S. Centers for Disease Control and Prevention and the World Health Organization (National Center for Health Statistics, 2002; Institute for the Future, 2000; Institute of Medicine, 2000; U.S. Department of Health and Human Services, 2000). Violence and injury affect all ages, sexes, and cultures. Violence and injury, although reported in terms of individual statistics, are also family and community issues (Fox et. al., 1996). Roberts, Arias, Lutzker, Walker, and Wolfe (chap. 3, this volume) make the case that psychology as a behavioral science and practice has much to contribute to the study of injury and violence.

Authors in chapter 3 (Lutzker with Klevens and Shelley) comment on the difficulty in ascertaining intentional from unintentional injuries and how injuries to children may result in fatalities and lasting physical and psychological damage. Their intervention approach once again provides a strategy for the range of skill-based health behaviors for caretakers from prevention through changes in caretaking postinjury. David A. Wolfe (Roberts et al., chap. 3, this volume) indicates the extent of adolescent involvement in abuse, either as a perpetrator or as a victim, may be as high as 50%. It is beyond the scope of this chapter or book to report on the volumes of psychological research and interventions for child and teen physical abuse. The incidents are tremendous and the impact on lifelong health unmeasurable and need to be included in accounts of the psychosocial risk factors affecting health.

There is a cascade of research about violence toward women documented by Arias and Walker, internationally known experts in battered women (Roberts et al., chap. 3, this volume). Let me pick just one statistic from the hundreds documenting the extent of this problem in our nation alone. The estimate is that 22,254,037 women are physically assaulted by an intimate partner at some point in their lifetime and 7,753,669 are raped (Roberts et al., chap. 3, this volume). Worldwide, 1 in 5 women are physically or sexually abused by men at some point in their life. Men are murdered by other men. Through our awareness of elderly abuse and state laws enacted to protect older people, we find increasing numbers of reports of the aged being abused by family and strangers. And untold numbers of children have been sexually abused.

As the priests' sexual abuse scandals rocked our American society in 2002, the chapter by De La Cancela, Alpert, Wolff, and Dachs (chap. 6, this volume) on the prevalence of sexual abuse of children in our culture and the importance of reporting sexual abuse is ever timely. Supporting the importance of reporting sexual abuse, studies are providing data that suggest participation in primary prevention programs results in increased disclosure by children of sexual victimization (McIntyre & Carr, 1999). State after state enacted legislation requiring priests to join the list of legally mandated reporters of suspected child physical and sexual abuse. Again psychology has been a national leader in moving the prevention of child abuse agenda forward.

Gender

Biological differences obviously account for health differences between men and women; however, it is the social construction of gender that has most influenced health policy and the availability and delivery of services. Stanton and Courtenay (chap. 4, this volume) stress that gender effects are glaringly present across the disease spectrum, but the effects of gender are best understood within the complexity of other social cultural variables, socioeconomic status, ethnicity, race, and sexual orientation. Women's health has been neglected by research that focused on men's health issues and used only male subjects. Certain men's health issues, like prostate cancer, have not received the necessary prioritization and hence have not received funding commensurate with the increasing impact on men's lives.

Now it is recognized that women's health, at times, was jeopardized by the use of interventions based on generalizations from these flawed research programs, like the Framingham heart project. The emphasis on finding the genocodes for diseases has resulted in an under-funding of the cultural impacts on men's health and under-funding of interventions that address the risky behavior causes of men's major health problems. For many cultures being a man means you do not pay attention to the signals from your body that something is wrong, you just keep trucking. Men ages 30–50 are particularly vulnerable to ignoring symptoms of a health problem and delay seeking help until friends or family convince them that something is wrong.

Men's health is also compromised by their risky behavior. And men's risky behavior gets linked to more risky behavior: For example, alcohol or drug use frequently accompanies unprotected sex, higher automobile injury and death, and violent outbursts. Stanton and Courtenay (chap. 4, this volume) document how the messages society gives boys influence their adaptation of riskier behaviors that put their health and lives at risk.

APA's Women's Office in the Practice Directorate, under the outstanding direction of Dr. Gwen Keita, is a national leader on women's health. The Women's Office espouses interdisciplinary collaboration in designing research, interventions, and public policy to improve women's health. The APA-sponsored Women's Health Conference spotlights cutting edge research by psychosocial leaders in women's health. For example, it was reported that women's emotional reactions can lead to negative health sequelae through a combination of physiological, psychological, and behavioral mechanisms. Another discussion focused on female long-term cancer survivors' ongoing concerns about those they loved: For instance, that their children might "get" breast cancer or that their relationships with their spouses might be jeopardized.

Research suggests that health providers may place women at risk by minimizing women's reported symptoms (Chandra et al., 1998; Dracup et al., 1997; Marrugat et al., 1998; Martin, Gordon, & Lounsbury, 1998). Martin and Lemos (2002) found gender-biased stress discounting for women with heart disease, gallstones, and melanomas. They also found a differential pattern of support given by family and friends. Women are more likely to be diagnosed with depression than men and their health symptoms discounted because of a frequently false assumption that they are emotionally based and therefore not physical. When the health professional asks how a patient interprets her or his symptoms and what influence this has on the care he or she seeks and receives, then biases in reporting and interpretation of symptoms by the patient and by the health caretaker are reduced.

Men have increased health risks because of occupational hazards such as injuries and stress as well as masculinity-proving behaviors, such as unprotected sex, addictions, excessive smoking, and drinking. Men are more likely to commit suicide, whereas women are more likely to attempt suicide. Men are more likely to die of injuries, but women are more likely to die of injuries at home.

The Worldwide UNDP Human Development Report (1998) concluded that there are no societies where women are treated as equals. The reduced status of women places them in jeopardy of sexual abuse and violence within their society and within their intimate relationships. Psychology is one of the major disciplines contributing to research and interventions of sexual and physical abuse of women. And the abuse starts young. Research tells us that childhood sexual abuse, regardless of the extent of the abuse, is highly related to adult women's drug and alcohol dependency. A few statistics will illustrate how risky sexual behavior may jeopardize the future of our girls: Teen girls, ages 13–19 are the only age group in the U.S. where females exceed males in HIV, 64% versus 34%. Girls ages 15–19 have the highest rate of chlamydia and gonorrhea of any age group (Institute of Medicine, 2000). Men, women, girls, and boys have health needs that are better met if sex and gender variables are considered in the research and treatment interventions. Together with the other social, cultural, and behavioral variables, psychological knowledge of gender is vital for building a healthy world for everyone—not just the fortunate few.

USING TODAY'S PSYCHOLOGICAL RESEARCH AND PRACTICE TO LOOK INTO THE FUTURE

This book provides a look into the current state and future of health science and health care from the perspective of families, communities, and the workplace. As questions about the role of behavior, cognition, and social and cultural influences are increasingly investigated across the health spectrum, the contributors to this book put forward a stunning vision for the role of psychology research and practice in health promotion. And as effective psychological research is discussed across the range of wellness and illness, each chapter is a strong building block for a comprehensive, integrative approach to health that realizes the fallacy of continuing the false dichotomy of mind and body.

Psychology Builds a Healthy World: Opportunities for Research and Practice is the first book of its kind to use the biopsychosocial model to explore, in one text, the breadth of health issues today ranging from wellness and prevention, acute and chronic illnesses, to behavioral and social causes of death from the perspective of family, community, and workplace. The editors hope you enjoy the depth and breadth of this volume as much as we enjoyed working with the authors to forge this unique volume.

REFERENCES

Affleck, G., Urrows, S., Tennen, H., Higgins, P., Pav, D., & Aloisi, R. (1997). A dual pathway model in daily stressor effects on rheumatoid arthritis. *Annals of Behavioral Medicine, 19,* 161–170.

Anderson, B. L. (1992). Psychological interventions for cancer patients to enhance the quality of life. *Journal of Consulting and Clinical Psychology, 60,* 552–568.

Anderson, B. L. (2002). Biobehavioral outcomes following psychological interventions for cancer patients. *Journal of Consulting and Clinical Psychology, 70,* 590–610.

Andrews, J. A., Tildesley, E., Hops, H., & Fuzhong, L. (2002). The influence of peers on young adult substance abuse. *Health Psychology, 21,* 349–357.

Blumenthal, J. A., Wei, J., Babyak, M., Krantz, D. S., Frid, D., Coleman, R. E., et al. (1997). Stress management and exercise training in cardiac patients with myocardial ischemia: Effects on prognosis and on markers of myocardial ischemia. *Archives of Internal Medicine, 157,* 2213–2223.

Brockner, J., Siegel, P. A., Daley, J. P., Tyler, T., & Martin, C. (1997). When trust matters: The moderating effect of outcome favorability. *Administrative Science Quarterly, 42,* 558–583.

Cantor, D. W. (2000). *What do you want to do when you grow up?* New York: Little, Brown.

Chandra, N. C., Ziegelstein, R. C., Rogers, W. J., Tiefenbrunn, A. J., Gore, J. M., French, W. J., et al. (1998). Observations of the treatment of women in the United States with myocardial infarction: A report from the National Registry of Myocardial Infarction—I. *Archives of Internal Medicine, 158,* 981–988.

Chen, M. S. (1993). A 1993 status report on the health status of Asian Pacific Islander Americans: Comparisons with Healthy People 2000 objectives. *Asian American Pacific Islander Journal of Health, 1,* 37–55.

Clay, R. A. (2001). Research to the heart of the matter. *Monitor on Psychology, 32,* 42–45.

DeAngelis, T. (2001). How do mind–body interventions affect breast cancer? *Monitor on Psychology, 33*, 51–53.

DeLeon, P. H. (2002). Presidential reflections: Past and future. *American Psychologist, 57*, 425–430.

Dracup, K., Alonzo, A. A., Atkins, J. M., Bennett, N. M., Braslow, A., Clark, L. T., et al. (1997). The physician's role in minimizing prehospital delay in patients at high risk of acute myocardial infarction: Recommendations from the National Heart Attack Alert Program. *Annals of Internal Medicine, 126*, 645–651.

Engel, G. (1977). The need for a new medical model: A challenge for biomedicine. *Science, 196*, 129–136.

Feinstein, J. S. (1993). The relationship between socioeconomic status and health: A review of the literature. *The Millbank Quarterly, 71*, 279–322.

Fox, R. E., Walker, L. E., Norton, J. R., Courtois, C. A., Dutton, M. A., Geffner, R. A., et al. (1996). *Violence and the family*. Washington, DC: American Psychological Association.

Global Forum for Health Research. (2002). *10/90 Report 2001–2002*. Geneva, Switzerland: Global Forum for Health Research.

Haber, S. (1993). *Breast cancer: A psychological treatment manual*. Phoenix, AZ: American Psychological Association, Division of Independent Practice.

The Institute for the Future. (2000). *Health and health care 2010: The forecast, the challenge*. San Francisco: Jossey-Bass Publishers.

Institute of Medicine. (2000). *Informing the future: Critical issues in health*. Washington, DC: Author.

Januzzi, J. L., Stern, T. A., Pasternak, R. C., & DeSanctis, R. W. (2000). The influence of anxiety and depression on outcomes of patients with coronary artery disease. *Archives of Internal Medicine, 160*, 1921–1931.

Johnson, N. G. (1995, August). *Feminist frames of women's strength: Visions for the future*. Presidential address to the Division of the Psychology of Women presented at the annual convention of the American Psychological Association, New York.

Johnson, N. G. (2001). Building a healthy world: Addictions are a major health hazard. *Monitor on Psychology, 32*(6), 5.

Johnson, N. G., Roberts, M. C., & Worell, J. (1999). *Beyond appearance: A new look at adolescent girls*. Washington, DC: American Psychological Association.

LaPorte, R., Matsushima, M., & Chang, Y. (1995). Prevalence and incidence of insulin-dependent diabetes. In M. Harris (Ed.), *Diabetes in America, second edition* (NIH Publication No. 95-1468). Washington, DC: National Diabetes Data Group, National Institutes of Health, National Institute of Diabetes and Digestive and Kidney Diseases.

Marrugat, J., Sala, J., Masia, R., Pavesi, M., Sanz, G., Valle, V., et al. (1998). Mortality differences between men and women following first myocardial infarction. *Journal of the American Medical Association, 280*, 1405–1409.

Martin, R., Gordon, E. E. I., & Lounsbury, P. (1998). Gender disparities in the attribution of cardiac-related symptoms: Contribution of common sense models of illness. *Health Psychology, 17,* 346–357.

Martin, R., & Lemos, K. (2002). From heart attacks to melanoma: Do common sense models of somatization influence symptom interpretation for female victims? *Health Psychology, 21,* 25–32.

McIntyre, D., & Carr, A. (1999). Helping children to the other side of silence: A study of the impact of the Stay Safe Program on Irish children's disclosures of sexual victimization. *Child Abuse and Neglect, 23*(12), 1327–1340.

Michey, R. M., Durski, J., Worden, J. K., & Danigelis, N. L. (1995). Breast cancer screening and associated factors for low-income African-American women. *Preventive Medicine, 24,* 467–476.

Miller, T. Q., Smith, T. W., Turner, C. W., Guyarro, M. L., & Hallet, A. J. (1996). A meta-analytic review of research on hostility and physical health. *Psychology Bulletin, 119,* 322–348.

National Center for Health Statistics. (2002). *Health, United States, 2002 with urban and rural health chartbook.* Hyattsville, MD: Author.

Ottawa Charter for Health Promotion. (1986). *Health Promotion, 1*(4), iii–v.

Perkins, K. A., Broge, M., Gerlach, D., Sanders, M., Grobe, J. E., Cherry, C., et al. (2002). Acute nicotine reinforcement but not chronic tolerance, predicts withdrawal and relapse after quitting smoking. *Health Psychology, 21,* 332–339.

Pollack, W. S. (1999). *Real boys: Rescuing our sons from the myths of boyhood.* New York: Henry Holt.

Pollack, W. S. (2000). *Real boys' voices.* New York: Random House.

Presson, C. C., Chassin, L., & Sherman, S. J. (2002). Psychosocial antecedents of tobacco chipping. *Health Psychology, 21,* 384–383.

Resnick, M. D., Bearman, P. S., Blum, R. W., Bauman, K. E., Harris, K. M., Jones, J., et al. (1997). Protecting adolescents from harm: Findings from the national longitudinal study on adolescent health. *Journal of the American Medical Association, 278,* 828–832.

Rosch, P. J. (2001). The quandary of job stress compensation. *Health and Stress, 3,* 1–4.

Ryff, C. D., & Singer, B. (2002). From social structure to biology: Integrative science in pursuit of human health and well-being. In C. R. Snyder & S. J. Lopez (Eds.), *Handbook of positive psychology* (pp. 541–555). New York: Oxford University Press.

Salovey, P., Rothman, A. J., Detweiler, J. B., & Steward, W. T. (2000). Emotional states and physical health. *American Psychologist, 55,* 110–121.

Schneider, T. R., Salovey, P., Apanovitch, A. M., Pizarro, J., McCarthy, D., Zull, J., et al. (2001). The effects of message framing and ethnic targeting on mammography use among low-income women. *Health Psychology, 20*(4), 256–266.

Schneiderman, N., Speers, M. A., Silva, J. M., Tomes, H., & Gentry, J. H. (2001). *Integrating behavioral and social sciences with public health*. Washington, DC: American Psychological Association.

Seligman, M. E. P. (2002). Positive psychology, positive prevention and positive therapy. In C. R. Snyder & S. J. Lopez (Eds.), *Handbook of positive psychology* (pp. 3–9). New York: Oxford University Press.

Starr, D. (2002). *Blood: An epic history of medicine and commerce*. New York: Harper Collins.

Strader, T. N., Collins, D. A., & Roe, T. D. (2000). *Building healthy individuals, families, and communities: Creating lasting connections*. New York: Plenum Publishers.

Taylor, S. E. (2002). *The tending response*. New York: Holt.

Taylor, S. E., Kemeny, M. E., Reed, G. M., Bower, J. E., & Gruenewald, T. L. (2000). Psychological resources, positive illusions and health. *American Psychologist, 55*(1), 99–109.

Taylor, S. E., Klein, L. C., Lewis, B. P., Gruenewald, T. L., Gurung, R. A. R., & Updegraff, J. A. (2000). Biobehavioral responses to stress in females: Tend-and-befriend, not fight-or-flight. *Psychological Review, 107*, 411–429.

Twenge, J. M. (2000). The age of anxiety? Birth cohort change in anxiety and neuroticism, 1952–1993. *Journal of Personality and Social Psychology, 79*, 1007–1021.

U.S. Department of Health and Human Services. (2000). *Healthy people 2010: Understanding and improving health*. Washington, DC: Government Printing Office.

U.S. Department of Health and Human Services. (2001). *Mental health: Culture, race, and ethnicity. A supplement to mental health: A report of the Surgeon General* (Executive Summary). Rockville, MD: Author.

Vega, W. A., & Amaro, H. (1994). Latino outlook: Good health, uncertain prognosis. *Annual Review of Public Health, 15*, 39–67.

Westmaas, J. L., Wild, T. C., & Ferrence, R. (2002). Effects of gender in social control of smoking cessation. *Health Psychology, 21*, 368–376.

Worell, J., & Johnson, N. G. (1997). *Shaping the future of feminist psychology: Education, research, and practice*. Washington, DC: American Psychological Association.

World Health Organization. (1948). World Health Organization constitution. In *Basic documents*. Geneva, Switzerland: Author.

Worldwide UNDP Human Development Report. (1998). New York: United Nations Publications.

Woznick, L. A., & Goodheart, C. D. (2001). *Living with childhood cancer: A practical guide to help families cope*. Washington, DC: APA LifeTools.

Zager, K., & Rubenstein, A. (2002). *The inside story on teen girls*. Washington, DC: APA LifeTools.

Zautra, A. J., Burleson, M. H., Matt, K. S., Roth, S., & Burows, L. (1994). Interpersonal stress, depression, and disease activity in rheumatoid arthritis and osteoarthritis patients. *Health Psychology, 13,* 139–148.

I

BUILDING HEALTHY
FAMILIES

1

"REAL" BOYS, "REAL" GIRLS, "REAL" PARENTS: PREVENTING VIOLENCE THROUGH FAMILY CONNECTION

WILLIAM S. POLLACK

Parent of Orphans and Defender of widows.
God settles the solitary into a family,
Releases those bound in slavery;
Only the rebellious dwell in a parched land.

—Proverbs 68:7

While America's politicians debate the righteousness of their cause as to what a "real" boy or girl must be to gain support within our society; while religious and philosophical pundits regale us with their unique definitions of who a truly virtuous father or mother must aspire to as their role model; and while we ceaselessly debate the definition of what a "real" family is to be in this new century, we often lose sight of the growing body of psychological knowledge that can help the widest range of family units survive and prosper amongst us. We also lose the opportunity to not only support what we know to be "the psychological glue" that sustains family health, but also, and equally important, we often ignore that which will sustain families of all stripes and colors as central forces, as bulwarks, against the scourge of violence that threatens not only the vigor of our culture, but the very underpinnings of society as we know it. I will discuss this concept of violence as a means to understand what is and is not a healthy family.

Our so-called culture wars, which center around what constitutes a "real" family, have obscured the centrality of psychological connectedness or relationships as the bulwark of genuine "family values" and the ultimate creator of a "holding environment" that may subdue the very real threats of violence, while creating emotionally free climates of safety—havens of love and positive self-esteem (what I have referred to elsewhere as "shame-free zones")—within a myriad of healthy family structures. These "new," enlightened family environments may, in addition, affect our entire society. By sustaining parents and children alike they enhance genuine academic achievement and economic productivity as well. Indeed, I would suggest that the same factors for which our newly gained psychological knowledge can be of inestimable value in creating and supporting genuinely healthy families may lie at the heart of leveraging family connections to diminish both the threats and realities of fighting the growing specter of violence in our midst.

I will attempt to weave together the central components of large-scale data sets about children's and families' health; the pervasive fear that modern family structures are leading to decay and destruction; the realities of boyhood cultures of bravado, bullying, pain, and death; the new wave of girl violence; and the findings of my own work on the real voices of adolescents yearning for connection. Then I will connect these components with discoveries of the unique joint project of the U.S. Secret Service and Department of Education, Safe Schools Initiative—an initiative undertaken to understand the "tip of the iceberg" of violence in America, school-targeted shooting sprees—into a unique fabric of understanding. This will be a template for a new model that emphasizes our psychological knowledge of the ties that bind within healthy families of all types: human connectedness. Against this new foundation I will suggest what we can do to prevent violence, diminish our fears of it occurring, and enhance our positive well-being both as individuals and as members of tribes, clans, or families—natural groups that may now be viewed as the genuine glue that binds our society together. All this, in the hope that we may be set free from our violence-creating pain of aloneness, settle into connection, and leave the "parched land" of emotional disconnection that has laid waste to our society for far too long.

TRAGEDY AS KNOWLEDGE

Although school shootings are a genuinely rare occurrence, they have come to represent something that we take to be a growing insidious decay at the heart of our society, and a series of events that have raised fears of an emotional and mortal epidemic that no number of academic statistics cited, to date, have served to quell. Perhaps, then, the shedding of new psychological light where the heat, indeed the flames, of our social concerns lie may lead us toward new, more healthy solutions.

Kip Kinkel

In May 1998, at the age of 15, Kip Kinkel shot his father and mother to death and the next day opened fire on classmates in Springfield, Oregon, murdering two and injuring 25. For all intents and purposes, he appeared to be a boy from a solid, middle-class family who grew up in a good community. Yet, in retrospect, there were aspects of Kinkel's story even those most intimately involved in his life did not appear to know. Whereas school officials and counselors remembered Kip as a likeable teenager not identified as high risk, he soon after took the lives of those around him and may well have been contemplating sacrificing his own life as well. Many close to him, in his life, never noticed any warning signs that might indicate potentially self-destructive violent—or murderous—behavior. But there was a quiet terror and ordinary way in which Kip lost his way and those who cared about him lost touch with his eventually lethal pain. Small, easily unnoticed wounds shaped Kip's interior world: he was the awkward child in a family that prized athletic prowess, a boy with a learning disorder in a family of academic achievers, a boy whose self-esteem was plummeting. And Kip's parents struggled with his overtly growing signs of violence and emotional turmoil. He had become a teenage boy, now, not only in inner pain, but beginning to show outer signs that should have been of concern to all around him, as he turned into an adolescent who studied how to make bombs, set off small explosives, and became increasingly fascinated with firearms.

Ultimately, growing in an unresponded movement to despair, Kip was to write in his journal prior to the fateful day of the killings: "I am evil and want to kill and give pain without cost and there is no such thing. In the end, I hate myself for what I have become."

Am I suggesting that Kinkel is a prototype of all children across America, or his family necessarily typical? No, certainly not. I had the honor to consult with the United States Secret Service–Department of Education, Safe Schools Initiative. The final report findings (Vossekuil, Fein, Reddy, Borum, & Modzeleski, 2002) considered 41 current or recent student "attackers." In these cases of targeted lethal violence at schools reported from 1974 through the present, Kip is more typical than we would like to imagine.

The study found that although planning vicious violence in these teens' cases varied in its time frame or intricacy, almost all the tragic events had a "lead time" from days to months in which some preemptive action could have been taken. Indeed, in a large number of the cases the assailant-student "child" eventually broke his "code of silence" and told either a peer or an adult of his intent with little or no interventionary response forthcoming. Most of these tragedies were not only preventable early on through the type of family and community interactions I will describe in a moment, but they were, indeed, stoppable up to the last moment, if others had taken proper heed of the seriousness of those youths' communications. But, alas, this did not occur.

Most attackers, in retrospect, engaged in behaviors—not just thoughts—prior to the tragic events that caused others concern or indicated a need for intervention. Yet again, either no reasonable intervention on the part of adults vouchsafed with these children's and our children's safety occurred, or the intervention was not completely or properly monitored. Close to 70% of these so-called "killers" had been viciously teased or bullied for long periods prior to their violent attacks, and approximately 75% had either threatened suicide or attempted to kill themselves (Vossekuil et al., 2002). They were depressed and those closest to them, within the bosom of their families, did not appear to know. Many who used firearms in their attacks were able to purloin them from their own families' gun cabinets.

Again, I am not engaging in blame and shame in regard to family structure, for that is the "illness," not the cure. I am attempting to highlight the lack of genuine family *connection,* indeed the disconnect within these families, between the children and the adults who loved them; and perhaps the disconnect between these families and the families and institutions that surrounded them were an integral cause for the final enactment of violence. Violence we are learning, from our psychological perspective is, potentially, preventable through enhanced support for inter- and intra-family relationships. This is not to put the onus on the family, but rather to re-empower it as a unit of safety and succor, to recognize its myriad opportunities to not only vouchsafe psychological well-being, but, also, in doing so to prevent the very troubling aspects of youth violence we see around us.

Such an argument, I am well aware will anger the Left because, although it does not mean to suggest simpleminded, "old-fashioned" solutions, it may appear to support atavistic returns to nonrealistic "Ozzie and Harriet" worlds. It will, no doubt disappoint some of the political forces on the Right, for I do not blame "bad" or "evil" parents or children, nor believe that because we have new models of family structure we are doomed to societal decay. The facts as I interpret them support neither extreme position. Rather they argue for the centrality of a loving, sharing family unit, the definition of which includes a broad spectrum of relationship combinations. And they argue for the importance of the psychological glue that holds each individual family together by connecting elders with youth, and equally significantly undergirds the entire social fabric of our society. This "glue" thereby prevents violence and enhances psychological well-being. This occurs, in part, through the role families may play as "the emotional switchboards" of interpersonal connection. The potency of loving family relationships is much stronger than even the best (and potentially useful) antiviolence program, certainly greater than any simpleminded, required zero-tolerance curriculum, and more productive and less traumatic than any magnetometer or gun-sniffing dog.

Empirical Studies

One objection to be anticipated is, of course, the fact that up to this point I have used the most unusual and extreme forms of youth violence as my examples. How does that fit with so-called normal family life or even less egregious aspects of dysfunction? Here again, as I will argue in a moment, it is my contention that targeted school violence represents the "tip of an iceberg"—that is, the most extreme example of disconnection turned to violence—existing on a continuum all the way down to emotional teasing and psychologically induced blows to self-esteem. Looking at the same issues from a more positive perspective, it is the family that can make all the difference in this society as to whether our youths grow into happy, well-adjusted adults or become depressed, dysfunctional, or even violent and hateful. Beneath targeted school violence lurks all too much pain, heartache, and potential crime and violence that, I believe, the emotional glue of family love can ameliorate or eradicate.

Such belief is not mere speculation. There is both qualitative and interview data drawn from my own extensive interviews with youths (Pollack, 1999, 2000a), the growing wave of girl discontent, and a number of larger-scale research samples that point to this central role for the family in simultaneously sustaining societal health and reducing violence in our midst.

More than 90% of juvenile homicides in the United States are committed by boys, and although girls are catching up in bullying and gang-related assaults, teenage boys have, unfortunately, become the poster children for toxic violence around us. I have now begun to attempt to ameliorate this through a series of working models to enhance boys' relationships with their parents, teachers, and other responsible adults, and vice versa, exemplified in my newest book, *Real Boys Workbook* (Pollack, 2001). I believe that this is a societal phenomenon more than just a biological proclivity—more the impact of our unique nurture (or lack thereof) than mere nature. The messages we give to boys throughout our culture are to suppress their feelings of vulnerability and need, to go it alone when they most require our support and succor, and to keep silent about their pain—integral portions of what I have dubbed the *Boy Code*. Also, with the narrow limits of what we define as so-called normal masculinity—the *gender straitjacket*—put them at high risk to lose touch with their adult mentors and families when they need them most, and to fall prey to school failure, emotional despair, and violent enactment. The statistics support this painful contention.

Within the past 3 years, rates for less violent crime and gang behavior have risen for girls as well. The reasons for this are complex, but do interact in boys' plight. Many young women, who felt their "voices" would finally be heard, find themselves equally un-responded to and disconnected. Also the trend of "girl power" is a complex one. Is it to mean that female youth should and must have the same opportunity to succeed as males? Or has it become perverted into a form of negative power mimicry? Do the girls observe the boys and believe they have more privilege through their stance of bravado, "cool pose," and intimidation and take on these same characteristics as "role models?" If they do this, they then, of course, end up where their male predecessors have: more disempowered, disconnected, and in trouble.

Yet the results of our psychological research, if shared more widely, and in a more user-friendly model, can help point the way for most Americans to see that this conundrum does have a solution: the reinvigoration of family connection to forestall depression and violence in our youth and in our society.

CONNECTION CAN OVERCOME THE PROBLEMS OF VIOLENCE

I have found in my research with teenage boys (and I believe this is important for a large number of girls as well) that what they need most to survive the peer pressure, gender straitjacketing, and the other tribulations of adolescence is knowing that they have meaningful connections not only with their peers but also, and especially, with their parents and other family members. Although we are often taught that adolescents need or want to separate from their families, this is another dangerous, unsubstantiated myth. Certainly adolescents are struggling with issues of identity and growth and will push at us, even push away from us, at times. Certainly they wish to spend some time away from home and develop an individual sense of self. But our sons and daughters rarely wish to cut their ties, be on their own, or "separate." In fact, most children desperately need their parents, the family, and the extended family—coaches, teachers, ministers, rabbis—to be there for them, stand firm yet show flexibility, and form a living wall of love that they can lean on—and bounce off of—regularly. It is not separation, but rather individuation. It is becoming a more mature self in the context of loving relationships—stretching the psychological umbilical cord rather than severing it—that healthy adolescence is all about.

My research shows that our kids know this only too well. Fifteen-year-old Seth, in describing how he copes with the "separation" pain many boys experience, replied buoyantly:

> I think . . . [it's] just the *closeness* of my family. The way my parents have brought me up to want to be part of the family. I love going home and spending time with my mom or my dad. I'd have no problems going

and spending the whole weekend with my family than going to spend the weekend with my friends. Sometimes I'd rather be with my family. When I'm with my friends, sometimes I'd say I'd rather be home. (Pollack, 2000b)

For the adolescent, knowing that they have a loving home and that they can tap into the strength derived from positive family relationships—the "potency of connection"—is truly key to making it through adolescence. In my research, again and again, teens refer to the importance of family. I firmly believe that it is the potency of family connection that guards our adolescents from falling prey to violence or emotional harm and gives them the most reassurance in the adolescent world of "cool."

Other psychologists, too, have corroborated the central role of family connections during adolescence. Feldman and Wentzel (1995) from Stanford University found that the perception boys have of their parents' marital satisfaction directly affected their social adjustment during adolescence. Blake Bowden (Elias, 1997) of the Cincinnati Children's Hospital found that adolescents who shared dinners with their families five times a week were least likely to use drugs or be depressed, and most likely to excel at school and have a healthy social life. But perhaps the most striking data-based support for my thesis comes from the large-scale, University of Minnesota National Longitudinal Study on Adolescent Health.

Culled from a basic national survey of close to 100,000 adolescents from grades 7 through 12, Resnick and his colleagues (1997) found that what affected adolescent behaviors most was social contexts, but, again, most especially the family. According to the study, "parent–family connectedness" dramatically influences the level of emotional distress adolescents suffer, their level of suicidality, how much they abuse drugs and alcohol, and even to some extent how involved in violence they may become. The study also showed other important factors that affect these behaviors, such as whether an adolescent's parents are present during key periods of the day or whether the child's parents have high or low expectations of his or her academic performance. But these factors paled in significance to the connection factor. Such connection, according to the study, involves "closeness to mother and/or father," and a sense of caring emanating from them, as well as "feeling loved and wanted by family members" (Resnick et al., 1997, p. 831).

The family's protective value does not come from a sense of being a moral policeman or warden as some would have us believe nor from a laissez faire, "boys will be boys" and, therefore, boys will be gone attitude. Rather, it is the potency of family connection that guards adolescents from emotional harm and gives them succor from a world that is rough, a niche where a teen may express his most vulnerable and warm feelings in the open without fear of ridicule. In return for their protection from harm, we, in turn, are protected from being harmed by violence as their desperate adolescent's last-ditch efforts at connection or their despairing protest of disconnection.

ROLE MODELS: REAL HEROES FOR TEENS

For any parent or other family member who doubts the kind of positive influence he or she can have—for anyone who denies the potency of family connections—it is important to investigate exactly who our children say they look up to, who they claim their heroes really are. Despite the prevalent myth that children's heroes are distant Olympian figures such as sports stars, astronauts, and the muscle-bound stars of action-movies, my research reflects that, in reality, most teenage children find heroes closer to home: brothers, sisters, mothers, and fathers. In families with less-traditional structures, such as in single parent families or in families with parents that have separated or divorced, children often find these heroes in extended family members, such as aunts, uncles, and grandparents. These findings are buttressed by data from other research, such as the Horatio Alger Study that reports not only that the majority of teens respect their parents but that over 10% of them saw their parents as "heroes" (Horatio Alger Association of Distinguished Americans, 1998).

Listen to the voices of the children from our study when asked whom they emulate or see as a hero, and why. Curtis, a 16-year-old raised almost exclusively by his divorced mother, named her as his foremost model and inspiration: "My mom is everything to me. She's sacrificed so much so that I can go to good schools. She got me into art, which is what keeps me going, and what I hope will be my profession someday. She's opened a lot of doors for me. All the opportunities I have now are because of her."

Michael spoke of the male–male mentor bond he felt with his brother:

Who is my hero? My brother—*definitely* my brother. He is older so I always looked up to him. I try to emulate what he does in my life. There is no doubt in my mind when he came to Hillside School that I was going to come to Hillside School. Still I talk to him more than my parents do. He's at college and I call him more, he tells me more stuff. We're best friends and I've always looked up to him. He has really been my role model.

Harry was grateful to his mother: "Well my mother did everything. She put me in baseball. She took me everywhere. She worked all the time, but she did everything you could ask for—she was always around."

But for some of the boys in my study, moms or dads were around somewhat less, and the earlier family generation became the models to emulate, the heroes of the next generation: As one boy explained when I inquired who his hero was, "[W]hen my father wasn't around . . . [my grandfather] was the one who taught me how to pitch—he was . . . my father figure and I look up to him, like, even to this day. He is definitely my mentor . . . he's just like a great guy." One 14-year-old young woman published her homage to her grandmother who had taken on the role of her primary family connection. Sayyadina Thomas wrote to her great grandmother: "Dear Mama: I love you for deciding I would be your child. [You prepared] my young mind and soul for the complications you knew couldn't be avoided. I love you Mama for giving me a sense of character—loving me with no strings attached" (Franco, 2001).

Another adolescent reports,

> I adore my grandparents—they mean the world to me. I spend as much time as I can with them. I admire my grandfather . . . as well as my grandmother. I admire them for completely different qualities. My grandfather was a police officer. He is just like a brilliant man. He reads all the time. He is always cracking jokes just to lighten the situation up. He is a complete people-person and everyone seems to love him. He never seems to get on anyone's bad side or anything like that. He always used to take me to the park and play baseball with me and stuff like that. When I was having trouble in Little League he helped me out there and when I was having trouble in school he helped me there, too.

"My grandmother," he explained, "is completely different. She is extremely smart. She reads all the time too but she is always forcing me to read. She would always read books to me when I was really young—all types of novels. My grandmother is an amazing cook. Any time I go down there, they feed me like 6 or 7 times a day." And we can be certain that the sustenance this boy derived was greater than the culinary. It came from and went to the heart.

As the statements of these kids attest, adolescents look for role models close to home. By and large, they feel tremendous admiration for the mentors in their family, and more than any other category of people, they see these relatives as their heroes and heroines. So for any parent or other family members who wonder how much of an impact they can have on their quickly developing teen, much comfort should be derived from the fact they—and not somebody else—are the ones these kids look to most for guidance, love, and support.

As volatile as adolescence can be and as frustrating as it may be at times for the parents of children plodding their way through this trying period, I believe it is very important for parents to stay attuned to the voices of their adolescents and seek as many opportunities as possible to share the potency of connection. When parents do so, they lay the groundwork for a more meaningful relationship with their children, one that later, when their teens have grown into adults, is likely to flourish with a new kind of honesty and a new kind of closeness. In addition, in the *Sturm und Drang* of today's society they diminish the pulls toward despair and real violence, which the Secret Service Study so amply illustrates as a possible outcome to un-responded yearning for connection.

CONNECTING WITH OUR KIDS: CREATING GENUINE BONDS OF SAFETY AND ANTI-VIOLENCE HAVENS

In a heart-wrenching interview after the tragic school shootings at Columbine, one of the students who had barely escaped with his life from the midst of the melee, told me, in shock, "It is kind of terrifying that something like that could happen, *but I'm pretty sure it could happen again.*" Another, actually wounded by his fellow students, echoed this frightening, but prescient warning; "I think it could happen again, it could happen *anywhere*" (W. S. Pollack, personal communication, 1999).

What so many of the boys across this nation expressed so clearly in *Real Boys' Voices* (Pollack, 2000a) 3 years ago was that the fundamental pain, alienation and disconnection that is at the root of this violence, exists, not only in one community unlucky enough to see it erupt with severe consequences but all around us. They spoke poignantly of the scourge of bullying and teasing that adolescents are increasingly victim to, the growth of violence and violent images in our culture, but most significantly the lack of connection they felt with the adults who were supposed to guide and protect them. A "silent crisis" hidden behind the headlines of our more overt national crisis of violence.

It was as though these kids were saying, pleading, "Please listen to us, before it's too late." In fact in the tragedy in Sanatee, a boy broke his code of silence in what we can only surmise was a last desperate attempt to gain control, a cry for help. But no adults who could act, did so; and some who might have, never found out. The Secret Service Report corroborates this sense of tragic disconnect and suggests its remedy.

One of the largest difficulties for teenagers across America (boys and girls, alike) is that when they tell their parents and other adults still responsible for their care "Leave me alone," we do. Not because we do not love our boys and girls, but for a number of complex reasons that range from misguided advice from parts of the "expert community" that extol the virtues of "letting them go" to become independent, to caring parents overburdened with too many hours of work, to homes with fewer healthy adult role models present or emotionally available. We, still, more easily take aim at the media for its violent bath of images that immerse America's young, or poignantly argue against the all too easy availability of firearms for minors—two genuine societal elements integral to the rise of violence that I, too, decry. However, we have not yet found a reasonable and direct way to recognize and remedy the dangerous disconnect between our youth and their elders—without pointing critical, blaming fingers, on the one hand, or, denying the need for radical changes in our emotional lives with the boys and girls we love and wish to nurture, on the other.

As tragic and frightening as school shootings are, they are, as I have argued, the "tip of the iceberg" of a much larger ailment in our society. Boys make clear to all who will listen, everyday, that they cannot share their genuine pain, especially at times of emotional vulnerability, for fear of being called a "wuss" or a "fag" and are shamed into an emotional straitjacket of silence. Girls' voices of confusion and hurt too often go unheeded. And we love to pin everything on peer pressure. Of course, a kids' peers exert a strong influence, but much of our research shows, as I've demonstrated, that the greatest protection from harm, especially for adolescents, comes in the form of loving, openly sharing relationships with "clued-in" adults—especially family members or those acting in the expanded role of in loco parentis. It is we who do, and must, in greater numbers, continue to create the bridges necessary to the boys and girls closest to us, and to advocate for their needs in the society we create.

It is not just the perpetrators of homicidal violence who are in distress. The boys and girls "next door" are feeling a loneliness, often unassuaged by older mentors whose guidance they secretly long for with an intense hunger. If we were to imagine the umbilical cord as a metaphor for connection, then as our kids grow we should let the cord spread out appropriately, but never actually sever our ties. As a nation we have been hoodwinked into believing in a panacea of separation equals maturity. This has been particularly evident in the young male side of the equation, with our boy code of bravado and independence, our cultural myth that "boys will be boys" which has led to emotional distress, increased episodes of increasingly vicious bullying, climbing suicide rates, school failure, and severe violence. New models of "girl power" are equally confusing for we are not clear, nor are our daughters, whether we are supporting new female opportunity and strength or recreating the atavistic models of male power that are already psychologically crushing the boys we love behind a mask of false self-sufficiency.

So what's a parent (or other adult caregiver) to do? Our psychological data and clinical expertise can provide some useful and timely advice. Here is what we might tell a parent.

First and foremost maintain connections. Create an emotional "holding environment" early and do not relinquish it. That is not to say we should smother our kids, but you cannot—boy or girl—love them too much. This creates "shame-free zones" for talk and "emotional safety nets" of connection.

We need "human detectors" and protectors, not gun detectors to provide safety for our kids. *Listen*. That means don't lecture; and in the case of more reticent girls and a vast majority of preteen and adolescent boys, enlarge the wider panoply of skills to include "action talk and listening." Put simply, understand *behavior* as a form of reaching out, recognizing that even the most seemingly negativistic interaction is a moment to capture and transform to parent–child activity, and ultimately talk. Do not castigate yourself for not being perfect at parenting (be a "good-enough parent"), but never give up either. Blame-free environments at home are good for parent and child. Worry less about limits and focus on shared human frailty and joy with reality limitations that you and your child will both need to face.

Do not go it alone. That is exactly where your kids are getting stuck. Whether a traditional mother–father pair or a single parent or one of the myriad of new family constellations, reach out to neighbors, clergy, parents, and schools who are like-minded and can provide you with the support of connection. Mentors from outside the immediate family network are important additions for you and your children. Chaim Ginnott, the great parent educator, used to advise parents of teens that at times of turmoil, "Don't just do something, stand there" (C. Ginnott, personal communication, 1978). Being there is half of the story, and showing love, the other. Kids who have a connection to a caring adult, share meals with them, and feel loved and understood have higher self-esteem, higher success rates in life, and lower chance of violence. Do not feel like the weight of the world is all on your shoulders; but do recognize that the potency of parenting or caregiving has ten times the power of biology or peer culture—not only in making our kids' world safer but ultimately in making their lives and ours more joyful and meaningful.

So, work to reframe the small society of your home and the broader organizational surround into "cultures of connection" in which adults are willing to relate and listen. Then our kids will feel safe to talk, not just about impending danger to and from themselves or their peers—building a genuine anti-violence nexus—but, also, about all those deep yearnings for parental guidance. As one boy expressing a ray of hope in his then dark and saddened world told me: "A mother's love transcends all things, and now my dad also talks to me in a way I can talk to him." No list of warning signs, "profiles," or room checks can assure that level of genuine security for both generations, and our society as a whole.

REFERENCES

Elias, M. (1997, August 15). Family dinners nourish ties with teenagers. *The Wall Street Journal*.

Feldman, S. S., & Wentzel, K. R. (1995). Relations of marital satisfaction to peer outcomes in adolescent boys: A longitudinal study. *Journal of Early Adolescence,* 15(2), 220–237.

Franco, B. (2001). *Things I have to tell you: Poems and writings by teenage girls.* Cambridge, MA: Candlewick Press.

Horatio Alger Association of Distinguished Americans. (1998). *The state of our nation's youth survey 1998.* Alexandria, VA: Author.

Pollack, W. S. (1999). *Real boys: Rescuing our sons from the myths of boyhood.* New York: Henry Holt.

Pollack, W. S. (2000a). *Real boys' voices.* New York: Random House.

Pollack, W. S. (2000b). *Real boys' voices.* Unpublished monograph.

Pollack, W. S. (2001). *Real boys' workbook.* New York: Random House.

Resnick, M. D., Bearman, P. S., Blum, R. W., Bauman, K. E., Harris, K. M, Jones, L. H., et al. (1997). Protecting adolescents from harm: Findings from the National Longitudinal Study on Adolescent Health. *Journal of the American Medical Association, 278,* 823–832.

Vossekuil, B., Fein, R. A., Reddy, M., Borum, R., & Modzeleski, W. (2002). *The final report and findings of the safe school initiative.* Washington, DC: U.S. Secret Service and US Department of Education.

2

PSYCHOLOGISTS PROMOTE BIOPSYCHOSOCIAL HEALTH FOR FAMILIES

SUSAN H. McDANIEL, SUZANNE BENNETT JOHNSON, AND SAMUEL F. SEARS

Although Western health care systems are still organized primarily around a mind–body split, many health professionals and consumers are coming to understand these constructs as metaphors for human experience that, when integrated, can lead to a much more comprehensive approach to health and illness. Caring for people's health demands attention to all realms of experience. This idea led George Engel in 1977 to publish a paper in *Science* calling for a "new medical model" that expanded the biomedical model to include attention to other aspects of health. Engel called this the "biopsychosocial model." Although still not the dominant model in health care, the biopsychosocial model has had a profound effect on pockets of medical practice, including primary care internal medicine, pediatrics, and family medicine, and even on psychology practice (Belar, 1997; McDaniel, Hepworth, & Doherty, 1992). Many consumers of health care also report they want humane, comprehensive health care. All illnesses are biopsychosocial in nature, and all chronic or serious illnesses benefit from the involvement of family members or significant others in the assessment, decision making, and treatment of the illness (McDaniel, Hepworth, & Doherty, 1992).

Research continues to explicate the important associations between physical and mental health. For example, in the 6 months after a heart attack, patients with depression are twice as likely to die as those with the same severity of disease who are not depressed. In fact, depression is a greater risk factor for mortality than any biological factor following a heart attack (Frasure-Smith, Lesperance, & Talajic, 1993). This is just one health event that cries out for a biopsychosocial approach to assessment and treatment. Professional psychologists provide a variety of services that affect health status through many pathways—for example, management of pain, adherence to medical regimens, development of healthy habits, management of stressful medical procedures, and psychophysiology.

Mental health also benefits from a biopsychosocial conceptualization. Many patients with mental health problems seek help through physicians or nurse practitioners. Patients with mental disorders make up a large proportion of all primary care patients, about 20–25% (Spitzer et al., 1995). Over half of these patients are treated only in primary care (Shurman, Kramer, & Mitchell, 1985), but less than half of these mental health disorders are detected (Badger et al., 1994). Failures in biopsychosocial assessment and treatment can result in the delivery of substandard or inappropriate care. It may also influence costs of services because patients with mental disorders use more medical services and have increased disability, illness, and mortality than do other patients (Druss, Rohrbaugh, & Rosenheck, 1999; Olfson et al., 1997).

Simple medical or psychological problems may be handled by one kind of professional. But many health professionals and policy experts believe that complex, biopsychosocial problems often benefit from a health care team, including physicians, nurse practitioners, psychologists, and other health professionals, for comprehensive assessment and treatment (Belar, 1995; Cummings & Cummings, 1997; McDaniel, Campbell, & Seaburn, 1990; McDaniel, Hepworth, & Doherty, 1992). Psychologists have long been involved as innovators, researchers, clinicians, educators, and administrators for integrated health care programs. This chapter describes cutting edge examples of these programs, how psychologists function in them, and how patients, families, and other health professionals benefit from their involvement. We describe a range of illnesses, including myotonic dystrophy, childhood diabetes, and cardiac disease. We discuss prediction, management, and treatment. And we explore the psychological issues involved with new technologies such as genetic testing and implanted biomedical devices.

PREDICTION: GENETIC SCREENING FOR FAMILIAL ILLNESS
(Susan H. McDaniel)

Nowhere is the biopsychosocial model more applicable than with genetic, or familial illness. Whatever the quality or nature of family relationships, genetic illness means that family is implicated and affected by the results of an individual's illness experience. As with many issues, our technology in breaking the genetic code has far outstripped our understanding of the ethical, psychological, and social implications of these discoveries.

The so-called Genetic Revolution is fascinating because it raises questions such as: What is the essence of being human? How much will we try to control the sex, temperament, and genetic heritage of our children? What are the psychological and interpersonal implications of knowing one will have an illness at some time in the future? Psychologists are participating with geneticists, ethicists, and other health professionals to develop biopsychosocial approaches to the rapidly changing science involved in the human genomics (McDaniel & Campbell, 1999; McDaniel, Campbell, Hepworth, & Lorenz, in press).

Historically, clinical issues related to human genetics were primarily involved with prenatal testing for single gene disorders like Down syndrome, or adult testing for rare single gene, dominant disorders like Huntington disease. Evidence of these genetic mutations mean the person will inevitably develop the illness. More recently, cracking the genetic code has led to the discovery of the genetic component of more complex, multifactorial disorders, including cardiovascular disease, cancers, and mental illness. Mutations of these genes typically require some interaction of the mutations and the environment to develop the disorder; and a positive test for these mutations is not a definitive diagnosis, but rather an estimate of increased risk for the disease. To add to the complexity, different illnesses have different genetic versus environmental components.

Information about genetic risk is likely to become part of primary health care in the future. Already new diagnostic tests proliferate in the marketplace and predict, to a greater or lesser extent, the risk of adult disease. This raises the possibility that prevention and treatment can be tailored much more specifically to personal risk factors that depend on a patient's genetic blueprint and environmental situation.

Although all this does constitute a revolution in our health care, our identities, and even our family relationships, it is also true that "genohype" is very high. There is a pervasive belief that the secrets of life will be revealed by genetics. But DNA does *not* determine destiny. Much of the significance of the information in DNA sequences is largely unknown, and will take decades of study to understand (Acheson, 2001). At this point in time, many genetic tests do not lead to a clear recommendation about changing behavior once an outcome is known. And with any positive test it can be very difficult to tell just when a condition will occur, so a genetic predisposition may become known at birth for a condition that starts in old age.

Each of us carries several deleterious and several potentially beneficial genetic variations or mutations. Whether genetic variations are beneficial or harmful depends on the environmental circumstances. Lyman Wynne's research team studying schizophrenia (Wahlberg, Wynne, Oja, et al., 1997), for example, showed that the genes involved in schizophrenia are actually responsivity genes: Those with these genes who have a resource-filled environment do much better than those with the genes who have a very challenging environment. Those in the latter environment are at high risk for developing schizophrenia spectrum disorders.

Genetic illness is by definition a family issue. The tradition of health care targeting individuals is challenged with familial illness. What is the clinician's duty to inform first-degree relatives, for example, of a patient's genetic mutation for colon cancer? All of this information has the potential for radically altering family relationships by subdividing families and creating new family alignments. This means that it is very important for psychologists to participate in the research and clinical care involved with familial, or genetic illness. We need to bring our expertise in individual and family dynamics to help patients with decision making, disclosure, and the unforeseen repercussions of test results on the person and the family. Along with other health professionals, we must play a role in guiding and communicating with families as they work to understand the lifelong impact of genetic information on them and their relationships.

Some patients want this information whereas some do not. Information is most helpful when the identification of genetic risk can lead to a targeted intervention with presumed benefit. Even then, individuals, sometimes within the same family, may respond to the possibility of testing very differently. Additionally, testing can be very expensive; testing for the breast cancer genetic mutations 1 and 2 is about $2600 per test in 2001. Genome science raises serious ethical issues and concerns about potential discrimination in employment, for insurance, for people with disabilities, and so forth. All this in spite of the fact that people are 99.9% genetically identical.

What role will psychologists play in this unfolding drama? I would like to suggest an interdisciplinary team to respond to the clinical challenges of familial illness. This team should be composed of a primary care physician or nurse practitioner, a specialist to manage the genetic illness, a geneticist, a genetics counselor, and a family-oriented psychologist. The role of the psychologist has many different components, including providing a forum for more extensive discussions of whether to test or not, the meaning of test results, who to inform, as well as posttest services such as psychoeducational groups for patients and families who test positive (McDaniel & Speice, 2001). Psychologists help patients with lifestyle changes and surveillance behaviors that are likely to decrease their risk with multifactorial genetic illness. And, while the primary care physician or nurse practitioner provides long-term medical follow-up, psychologists may provide long-term psychological follow-up.

Systematic research is only beginning to be done on the effects of genetic testing on the psychological experience of people being tested. To understand more about the issues involved, examples have been taken from interviews with one family with a single gene disorder to illustrate the themes involved in psychological practice with patients with familial illness. These themes include understanding the experience of testing, the meaning of the mutations, the effect of testing on families, and what patients and families want from psychologists and other health professionals. The experience of patients testing for a multifactorial illness such as breast cancer does not have the certainty of illness that a family with a single gene disorder has. The ambiguity of the situation associated with multifactorial illness makes for a somewhat different psychological experience than for those with a single gene disorder. However, many of the individual and interpersonal themes described next are common to anyone testing for a genetic mutation.

A Single Gene, Dominant Disorder: One Family's Experience With Testing for Myotonic Dystrophy

Bob is a 63-year-old man with myotonic dystrophy, a muscular dystrophy that is progressive and has no cure or prevention.[1] He and his wife, Margaret, came to me referred by his neurologist because of fairly serious marital problems related to caregiving and Bob's denial of his disability. Figure 2.1 displays Bob's genogram and who in the family is positive for the myotonic dystrophy mutation. Note that Bob's mother and older brother had the illness. Bob already had his four children when he realized that there is a genetic illness in his family, and that he might have it. His children had a 50–50 chance of having the mutation and the illness. His two oldest children, Molly and Tim, tested negative; his two youngest children, Diana and David, tested positive. Molly and Tim are both married

---

[1] These family members have given their permission for their story to be told to train professionals about genetic illness. Their names have been changed, but the dialogue that follows was transcribed exactly from the videotaped interviews.

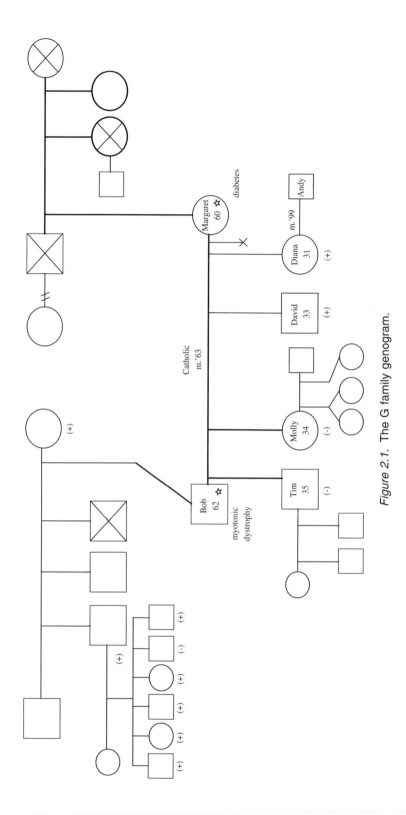

Figure 2.1. The G family genogram.

with children. Diana is married and would like to have children. David is mentally retarded, sometimes a feature of the illness, and is not married though he does live independently.

The Meaning of the Illness

Each patient and family develops an idiosyncratic explanation for the mutation and the illness. Sometimes the explanation given is religious, sometimes scientific, and sometimes superstitious. In any case, it is important for helping professionals to understand the meaning of the illness to the patient. Bob's family is quite religious, as is his explanation for his illness.

> *Dr. M.:* Why do you think you got the genetic mutation? Do you have personal theories about it?
>
> *Bob:* Well, um. You know some people get very angry at God. . . . And I wonder, "Well my God if I lived that sinful a life. . . ." Then you go through these phases of bargaining and realize that God didn't do it to me, he allowed it to happen. Um. Maybe, this is my route to heaven. If I offer this up, maybe I will go straight in there without any stops.

Do You Want to Be Tested? Do You Want to Know?

The issue of whether to get tested, who wants to know, and who does not can be a burden hanging over a patient and family. When preventive measures can help, the testing offers direction. However, with myotonic dystrophy and many other illnesses, there is no method to prevent or even treat the illness. Then the question arises about whether one wants to know, and why. For Bob, it was a psychologist who suggested he get tested in about 1980. Bob sought help for anxiety and the psychologist believed the underlying problem was Bob's concerns about whether he had the familial illness. Although clearly ambivalent, Bob did go for testing. In the interview, Bob first expressed his desire to deny and live fully for today. Then, when questioned again, he stated the opposite: that one has to find out about the illness. These contradictory feelings coexist in most people. Which side wins determines people's reaction to testing. Notice how the decision is most affected by feelings about other family members, especially children.

> *Dr. M.:* Some people want to know. Other people don't want to know.
>
> *Margaret:* He didn't want to know. It was [the psychologist] who made him . . . who said "Go."
>
> *Bob:* And I don't want to know what's going on down the road . . .
>
> *Dr. M.:* Uh huh. But you took his advice . . .

Bob:	You know, today is a good day. . . . I'm going to enjoy today.
Dr. M.:	Is there any reason you think that it makes sense for people not to get tested?
Bob:	You gotta know.
Margaret:	It's not a bad test.
Bob:	The symptoms will . . . will tell you. . . . As [the illness] gets worse, anybody with any kind of brains now knows that if it gets worse and worse. You got to find out what it is. And, can something be done about it?
Dr. M.:	Sure.
Bob:	Some diseases can be fixed. This can't.
Dr. M.:	What about that period for you or for your children when you knew that you had the damaged gene, but you really weren't very symptomatic? Was it useful still for you to know during that period, and why?
Bob:	I suppose we had to know, to have some sort of an understanding that this thing may progress. So you are not surprised. You are disappointed and sad, but you are not surprised.
Dr. M.:	Do you think you lived any differently knowing that?
Margaret:	No. Better I say. . . . Instead of worrying. And also if your children have it, you want to make sure they know because they cannot have a child.
Bob:	We didn't know [when we had our children]. We didn't know.
Margaret:	So I say "Get tested!"

Testing the Children

Testing the children for Bob and Margaret was much harder even than having Bob tested. Bob was unable to go accompany the children because he was so upset. Most experts strongly recommend against testing children unless they are symptomatic, as was the case with David and Diana.

Dr. M.:	How did [David] respond to the test results?
Margaret:	Well he didn't. See, when you are young you feel invincible, at 17 or 16.
Bob:	He didn't realize that it was going to be an awful thing, I think at first.

> Margaret: It is hard to get a 16 year old to think. I mean, they are like on top of the world. But I will tell you with Diana, it has been hard to have a beautiful girl like Diana shunned by boys that she's liked when they found out about the disease.

Blame, Responsibility, and Transgenerational Dynamics

Diana was the first to become concerned that she too had the illness at age 16. Her mother denied her symptoms, but finally her father insisted she be tested. She says, "I already knew," and described the "huge amounts of guilt" her father felt for passing on the mutation. She herself does not blame her father. "He didn't know he had it. If he had stopped after having two children, none of his children would have had it. . . . When I told him I tested positive, he said, 'Well, I'm still glad you were born.' It was not his fault."

"Survivor" Guilt

Several studies now show that so-called *non-affected* family members also have a strong and long-term reaction to testing. Clearly they *are* affected psychologically. Tim said, "Personally I felt, you know, just angry at the fact that Dad should have to have it, and David and Diana should have to have it. . . . At times, I have felt some amount of guilt that I don't have it."

Developmental Transitions and Familial Illness

As mentioned earlier, Diana had trouble when her boyfriends found out that she tested positive. She was engaged once and her fiancé broke it off when he found out about her future illness. When Diana became engaged to Arthur, the man who is her now-husband, her mother, Margaret, called the neurologist and asked him to write a letter to Arthur telling him the illness would not be that bad. The neurologist declined, but Margaret's request speaks to the challenges involved in having test information about single gene disorders. However, Arthur responded very differently than Diana's earlier fiancé. Even though he met Diana's father and saw his illness first-hand, he compared Diana's problem with his own uncle's deafness: "[Y]ou know, it's nothing. You just come to accept, you know, the flaws in people." Each person's family experience creates a template onto which this situation is mapped.

Diana also talked about how much knowledge of the mutation organizes her life. She said that some days when something bad happens, it is almost impossible not to blame the illness, whether it is related or not. Other days, she can focus on other aspects of her life. However, it is clear that it is at points of transition that it again can become an organizing force, whether it was when she and Arthur were planning to marry or at the time of the interview, when they wanted to have a child.

> Diana: We are now talking about having kids. . . . So, it is kind of playing a huge part of my life right now because I have been on the phone all month trying to find clinics that will, you know, do the embryonic testing. And insurance won't pay for it.

> Dr. M.: They don't do it here?

> Diana: I haven't found. . . . You know, there are places that have done it only once. Belgium—they have done it 20. And I would be willing to go to Belgium to get it.

The Role of the Psychologist

This couple and their family will undoubtedly use the services of a psychologist in the future. Along with primary care professionals, psychologists can provide these patients with useful support and secondary prevention, as well as conventional psychotherapy. Bob and Margaret said they had inadequate pretest counseling for themselves and the children 20 years ago. Bob now recognizes the he should have continued in psychotherapy at the time, and sought more information from his doctor about his condition. Margaret also wishes they had seen someone back then, individually and as a couple, to improve their coping skills and their communication. Diana talked about the need for families to receive test results as a group, so that the information is not filtered from one family member to another. Tim talked about the usefulness of "debriefing sessions" as well as family sessions about the testing and the illness:

> Tim: The only thing that I would add to what Diana said, is the option for families to be offered some sort of psychological or therapeutic support. I would think that, at a minimum, a kind of debriefing in a way. But for families that need it or want it, more . . . I mean, I felt like the [family] session that we had . . . was interesting and helpful, not only because of the marital problems that Mom and Dad were having, but also because of the [way] myotonic dystrophy was part of the marital problems, and . . . affected the whole family. In that session, there was [a huge] outpouring of feelings and information.

The road ahead of us promises massive change in the way health care is delivered because of advances in the science of genomics. Psychologists have important roles to play as researchers, clinicians, and educators working to understand the psychosocial ramifications of this information. Listening carefully to the experience of patients is a good place to start.

MANAGEMENT: CHILDHOOD DIABETES
(Suzanne Bennett Johnson)

Type 1 diabetes, also known as childhood diabetes, affects 120,000 children in the United States; 13,000 children are diagnosed with the disease each year, an incidence greater than all other chronic diseases of youth (LaPorte, Matsushima, & Chang, 1995). For every child living with Type 1 diabetes, there are one or two parents and often one or more siblings in some way affected. Disease prevalence estimates clearly underestimate the number of persons for whom Type 1 diabetes plays a significant role in their lives.

Diabetes is a family affair for a variety of reasons. First, the disease is usually diagnosed in childhood (LaPorte et al., 1995). Second, the disease is a genetically linked autoimmune disorder (Dorman, McCarthy, O'Leary, & Koehler, 1995). Third, it involves a complex daily management regimen requiring parental supervision. Insulin must be administered by injection multiple times a day, in a timed-relationship with meals. Small meals should be eaten frequently (three meals and two or three snacks are recommended) throughout the day; both concentrated sweets and high fat foods are to be avoided. Regular exercise is recommended as exercise improves insulin action. However, exercise should be coordinated with food intake so as to avoid hypoglycemia (blood glucose levels of 60 mg/dl). Because current treatment methods only approximate normal pancreatic functioning, patients are instructed to test their blood glucose several times per day (American Diabetes Association, 2001). Currently, home blood glucose testing is done almost exclusively by small, computerized meters. The patient places a small drop of blood on a reagent strip and inserts the strip into the meter. Within seconds the test result is displayed and the time and date of the test as well as the test result are stored in the meter's memory. This memory can be downloaded in the physician's office for review. These records assist the physician in determining the patient's appropriate insulin dose and serve as an estimate of the patient's glycemic control.

Family management of this disease is complicated by the changing needs of the child as the youngster grows and develops and by the changing nature of the disease as the years pass. Taking a developmental perspective means blending the child's age-related cognitive and social needs with the demands of the disease at each point in the disease's trajectory.

Changing Needs of the Developing Child

Infancy

Parents faced with the daily care of an infant with diabetes may experience considerable distress. Because the child is nonverbal, multiple finger sticks are required to closely monitor the infant's blood glucose levels. These, coupled with daily insulin injections, mean the parent must administer painful procedures repeatedly. Although these are necessary for the child's survival, the infant is only aware of the discomfort associated with such procedures. Because the parent cannot "explain" the reasons for the finger sticks and injections to the child, the parent may experience considerable guilt and anxiety when the child cries in response to these procedures. Fortunately, most infants readily adapt to the finger sticks and injections; any aversive reactions they may initially display dissipate with time.

Diabetes in infants can be difficult to manage because of the child's erratic eating and play behaviors. Babies are known for periods of high caloric intake followed by periods in which the child seems easily satiated. If the child is ill, the child may not want to eat at all. Introducing new foods (e.g., solids) and changing from a bottle to a cup may have a profound impact on caloric intake. Changing caloric consumption means changing insulin needs. For this reason, infants' blood glucose levels often fluctuate and need to be closely monitored.

Although maintenance of blood glucose levels in the near normal range is known to reduce or delay the serious long-term complications of diabetes (Diabetes Control and Complications Trial Research Group, 1993), "tight" (near normal) blood glucose control is not a realistic goal for children younger than 2 years. Efforts to maintain the infant's blood glucose levels in the near normal range place the child at increased risk for hypoglycemia. Hypoglycemia is associated with both cognitive and motor impairments and may have a particularly significant impact on the developing brain. Children diagnosed before age 5 are at increased risk for neuropsychological impairment. Although the mechanism underlying this effect is not well understood, hypoglycemia has been implicated as a potential cause (Ryan, 1990). For this reason, the American Diabetes Association recommends that tight control be attempted in youngsters ages 2–7 with extreme caution and should not be attempted at all in youngsters under 2 years of age (American Diabetes Association, 2001).

Parents of an infant with diabetes often find it difficult to set limits. Some parents may delay the transition from the bottle to a cup. Other parents continue to let the baby sleep in the parent's room, delaying the move to a crib in the child's own room. Mothers often complain that they are exhausted because the baby has never learned to sleep through the night. Most parents, including parents with a child who has diabetes, need time together or with other adults, away from the children. However, parents with an infant with diabetes may find locating appropriate child care particularly difficult.

Toddlers

Many of the concerns faced by parents of infants with diabetes are faced by parents of toddlers as well: parental distress over hurting the child with finger sticks or insulin injections, the toddler's erratic eating and activity patterns, the need for close monitoring because the child is unable to recognize and treat symptoms of hypoglycemia, changing insulin requirements, the parent's difficulty in setting limits, and problems locating appropriate child care. However, toddlers present additional challenges that are unique to this developmental period.

Toddlers are far more communicative than infants; they can make their needs known through words and gestures. They are also more physically active, providing new ways to express happiness as well as unhappiness. A parent whose toddler is newly diagnosed with diabetes may face a whole array of distress behaviors not possible from an infant. A toddler can scream, kick, bite, wriggle, run, give accusatory looks, and make angry or hurtful comments (e.g., "I hate you," "bad mommy"). Despite the toddler's increased communication skills, the child does not yet have the cognitive capacity to understand diabetes. Consequently, parents must conduct finger sticks and give injections to a child who does not understand the reasons for these procedures. Toddlers are also not yet capable of reliably informing the parent of impending hypoglycemia. The toddler's brain is still developing and may be particularly vulnerable to the effects of hypoglycemia. As with infants, attempts at tight control should be avoided.

Increased activity and picky eating habits seem to characterize this developmental period. These children are constantly moving, practicing and improving their newly acquired motor skills. Much of the time, they seem too busy to eat. They also begin to develop highly specific food preferences. Parents often marvel at their toddler's desire to eat the same foods over and over. Increased activity and erratic food consumption mean changing insulin requirements.

At ages 2 and 3, the child is busy developing a sense of self separate from other family members. The familiar "no" represents the child's beginning efforts at independence. Oppositional behavior of this sort can present problems for parents caring for a toddler with diabetes. When the response is "no" to a needed snack, the parent may become frantic, fearing an insulin reaction will ensue. Toddlers quickly learn what excites parents and may escalate this sort of behavior if it results in a great deal of parental attention.

Preschoolers

With preschoolers' increased verbal ability, their world becomes more social and interactive. For the first time, the youngster may realize that everyone does not have diabetes. Preschoolers are naturally curious; questions repeatedly surface about many aspects of diabetes care that may have been previously treated as routine by the toddler. The preschooler may want to help with diabetes care but does not yet have the cognitive ability, maturity, or motor skills to play a primary role. Their increasing verbal skills may enable some children of this age to begin to identify and communicate symptoms of impending hypoglycemia. Although children should be encouraged to tell a responsible adult if they are not feeling well, a blood glucose test needs to be done to confirm hypoglycemia.

For the first time, the child may be sent to day care or preschool. The parent must educate day-care workers and preschool teachers how to handle the child's diabetes. Assuring timely snack consumption and developing a response plan in cases of hypoglycemia are paramount. There may be an understandable hesitancy by day care staff to admit such a child to their preschool program. The public's fears about AIDS may surface with refusals to conduct blood glucose tests.

Although preschools offer new social and learning opportunities, they also expose the child to a wide variety of acute, infectious diseases. Ear infections, colds, flu, and stomach and intestinal disorders are all common and easily transferred from one child to another. Acute illness episodes present special problems for the child with diabetes. Illness can interfere with insulin action, raising blood glucose levels. Upset stomachs may make it difficult to assure sufficient caloric and fluid intake.

Elementary School Children

The transition to elementary school requires considerable planning. Parents need to meet with teachers and develop a school-based management plan that permits regular blood glucose testing, and rapid response to hypoglycemic episodes. Some schools may suggest home-schooling instead, potentially increasing the child's sense of isolation.

The elementary school child also faces a myriad of food choices, including easy access to sweets with little or no adult supervision. The child will be faced with telling others about diabetes and may be teased about some aspect of the disease. The child may want to spend time at a friend's home but other parents may be hesitant to take on the responsibility and the child's own parents may be fearful of this increased freedom. Both siblings and peers may feel the child gets special treatment because of diabetes, leading to teasing and rivalry.

Increased social interaction results in increased exposure to a wide variety of infectious diseases. Sick days are problematic for any child but present extra challenges for youngsters with diabetes.

Adolescents

Adolescence is a time of increased independence and exploration. Youngsters are increasingly concerned with fitting in and try to avoid being "different." Parental supervision declines as most parents view the adolescent as responsible for his or her own diabetes care (Ingersoll, Orr, Herrold, & Golden, 1986). Perhaps it is not surprising that medical regimen compliance is notoriously poor during this developmental period (Johnson, Freund, Hansen, & Malone, 1990; Johnson et al., 1992). Increased insulin resistance associated with pubertal development further complicates diabetes management, making appropriate insulin dose determination more difficult (Bloch, Clemons, & Sperling, 1987). Decreased exercise, often seen in adolescent girls, results in escalating blood glucose levels. Adolescents may be particularly concerned about their appearance and whether diabetes will diminish their attractiveness to members of the opposite sex.

Learning to drive is a rite of passage during the adolescent years. This milestone represents special challenges for the young person with diabetes and his or her family. A hypoglycemic episode is dangerous at any time but if it occurs when the teen is behind the wheel of a car, the danger increases not only for the adolescent but for others sharing the road.

Alcohol and tobacco are also the focus of considerable experimentation. These substances can prove particularly deadly for teens with diabetes. A hypoglycemic reaction may be misinterpreted as the effects of alcohol in an adolescent who has been drinking; peers may ignore important erratic behavior, leaving the teen's hypoglycemia untreated and risking seizures or death. Smoking is bad for all youngsters but places adolescents with diabetes at even greater risk for heart disease.

Despite the multiple dangers associated with this developmental period, adolescents often have a sense of invulnerability that can interfere with good diabetes management and may increase risk-taking behavior. This can lead to considerable tension between parents who recognize the multiple potential dangers and the adolescent who sees parents as overreacting and overcontrolling.

Young Adults

New issues arise during young adulthood. During this developmental period, the young person usually separates from the home, going to college or work and seeking some type of independent living arrangement. Family members are often concerned about who will be there if the young person has a diabetic crisis. The young person begins to consider marriage, career, and family planning, all of which can be profoundly affected by diabetes. Some careers are not available (e.g., armed services). Marriage to someone with diabetes means facing serious medical complications associated with diabetes at a relatively young age. Because the disease has a genetic component, it is likely the gene will be passed on to one's children. Medical insurance is often difficult to acquire because the young person has a preexisting condition; by age 21, most young people are no longer covered by their parents' insurance policies. Because the complications of diabetes begin to occur 10–15 years after diagnosis (Travis, Brouhard, & Schreiner, 1987), medical coverage is critical for young people with this disease.

Managing Diabetes: Family Challenges

Every family struggles with the myriad of needs and challenges presented by a developing child, but diabetes places additional demands on the family. At the time of diagnosis, parents are frequently stressed and anxious as they try to learn the many skills needed to manage the disease. They must establish a good working relationship with the diabetes care team, appropriately divide responsibility for diabetes care among family members, and assure adequate supervision of critical disease management tasks. Old family routines must be adjusted to incorporate diabetes care and parents must develop skills to cope with diabetes crises such as hypoglycemic reactions. Parents have to help the child navigate school, sports, and other family, social, or community activities in a manner that assures good diabetes care. At the same time, they have to be alert to the potential development of "sick-role" behavior; diabetes must be a focus of concern but not a means of manipulation by the child.

Transitioning responsibility for diabetes management from parent to child is one of the most difficult challenges. Although adolescents have the cognitive capacity to manage the disease, they often do not have the maturity. Usual parent–teen conflicts can have life-threatening implications for an adolescent with diabetes. Planning for the future can be particularly salient for parents of teens, although some years may pass before the adolescent is ready to face the challenge of planning for a life with diabetes. As parents watch their young adult move out of the house and face new career and social challenges, new anxieties may arise as parents recognize that their ability to help is now minimized.

Because managing diabetes is a family affair, it is no surprise that family environment has been linked to diabetes regimen adherence, glycemic control, and patient adjustment (Johnson & Rodrigue, 1997). A child's diabetes can also affect mothers, fathers, and sibling adjustment. The empirical literature suggests that mothers are most affected, with more variable findings in studies of fathers and siblings (Johnson & Rodrigue, 1997).

Summary

Managing childhood diabetes is clearly a family affair. Daily disease management places numerous demands on the family as parents, children, and siblings struggle to balance the needs of a developing child with the challenges of a serious and progressive disease. The importance of family context is confirmed by the research literature that has repeatedly documented links between family environment and diabetes regimen adherence, glycemic control, and patient adjustment. A child's diabetes can also take a toll on family members, with mothers particularly affected.

TECHNOLOGICAL INTERVENTION: IMPLANTABLE CARDIOVERTER DEFIBRILLATOR FOR CARDIAC DISEASE
(Samuel F. Sears and Jamie B. Conti)

The 1970s hit television show *The Six Million-Dollar Man* emphasized the expertise and benefits that people can receive from implantable biomedical devices. In fact, the show claimed that Steve Austin was made faster, stronger, and better as a result of bionics. In the real world, biomedical technology requires patients to accommodate and ultimately to accept the technology as a part of themselves. An episode that portrayed the "depressed bionic man" would demonstrate how both mind and body have to heal from damage. The interrelationship between psychological and physical health and recovery has been investigated for many years with cardiac patients. Some cardiac researchers have concluded that the current evidence implicating psychological variables and distress on health outcomes and quality of life is "clear and convincing" (Rozanski, Blumenthal, & Kaplan, 1999, p. 2192). Patients and health care professionals alike need to recognize that technology alone may never be able to mend the gap between a patient's premorbid functioning (what has been lost) and their postmorbid functioning (what has been gained). The purpose of this section is to describe the recent medical and psychological findings related to the use of implantable cardioverter defibrillator in the prevention of sudden cardiac death.

Incidence and Prevention of Sudden Cardiac Death

Sudden cardiac death due to ventricular tachyarrhythmias, or irregular, fast heartbeats, accounts for the majority of cardiovascular deaths in the United States, claiming more than 350,000 lives annually (Myerburg & Castellanos, 1997). The implantable cardioverter defibrillator (ICD) has emerged as an effective and life-saving biomedical device for potentially lethal ventricular arrhythmias. The ICD detects and attempts to correct potentially lethal ventricular arrhythmias by means of pacing, cardioversion, and defibrillation. The efficacy of the ICD in reducing mortality is now well established (Antiarrhythmics Versus Implantable Defibrillators Trial Investigators [AVID], 1997; Multicenter Automatic Defibrillator Implantation Trial [MADIT]; Moss et al., 1996; Multicenter Un-Sustained Tachyarrhythmia Trial [MUSTT]; Buxton, Lee, & Fisher, 1999). However, the ICD may prompt symptoms of anxiety and depression associated with the electrical shock necessary to complete defibrillation.

Psychosocial Aspects of the Implantable Cardioverter Defibrillator

Research examining the psychosocial impact of the ICD has yielded both positive and negative outcomes. On the positive side, ICD patient acceptance of the device and global quality of life have consistently been reported as desirable (Arteaga & Windle, 1995; Konstam, Colburn, & Butts, 1995). These findings are significant because the typical ICD patient is over the age of 65 and often has comorbid medical conditions that would likely negatively affect ratings of global quality of life. On the negative side, however, the impact of the ICD on psychological functioning may be significant across affective, behavioral, and cognitive processes. Specifically, the experience of aversive shock, the recognition of potential mortality, and the perceived lack of control or predictability over one's medical condition can lead to a state of "learned helplessness" that may make ICD patients vulnerable to anxiety and depressive disorders (Sears, Conti, et al., 1999). In fact, recent research highlighted ICD patients as "an appropriate risk population for a prospective study of the development of anxiety disorders" (Godeman et al., 2001, p. 231).

The development of symptoms of anxiety may be the most significant and common psychological consequence for the ICD recipient. A literature review found that 24–87% of ICD recipients experienced increased symptoms of anxiety after receiving an ICD, and diagnostic rates for clinically significant anxiety disorders ranged from approximately 13–38% (Sears, Todaro, Saia-Lewis, Sotile, & Conti, 1999). ICD-related fears are universal and may be the most pervasive psychosocial adjustment challenge ICD patients face. Psychological theory suggests that symptoms of fear and anxiety can result from a classical conditioning paradigm in which certain stimuli or behaviors are coincidentally paired with an ICD shock and are thereby avoided in the future. Due to fear of present or future discharges, some patients increasingly limit their range of activities and inadvertently diminish the benefits of the ICD in terms of quality of life. Pauli, Wiedemann, Dengler, Benninghoff, and Kuhlkamp (1999) examined the anxiety scores of ICD patients and found that anxiety was not related to ICD discharges but was highly related to a set of "catastrophic cognitions." Patients with high anxiety scores tended to interpret bodily symptoms as signs of danger and believed that they had heightened risk of sudden death. In addition, this cognitive style was associated with anxiety scores that were similar to the scores of panic disorder patients and different from the scores of a healthy volunteer control group. These results suggest that psychosocial interventions that utilize cognitive–behavioral protocols will likely prevent or reduce anxiety problems regardless of shock exposure by changing catastrophic thinking and overinterpretation of bodily signs and symptoms.

ICD patients may resort to a "sickness scoreboard" mentality, by which they view the frequency of ICD shocks as indicative of how healthy they are and as predictive of their future health (Sears, Todaro, et al., 1999). For example, the recently shocked patient concludes, "I was shocked twice this month and only once last month, so I must be getting worse." In general, outcomes based on the frequency of shocks alone are not a valid indicator of health. ICD shocks can be triggered by both appropriate indications (e.g., ventricular fibrillation) and inappropriate indications (e.g., supraventricular arrhythmias). The ICD is engineered to reduce and minimize the occurrence of inappropriate shocks. Moreover, most shocks are needed and appropriate and do not necessarily indicate declining health status. The ongoing appraisal of their own health by ICD patients may also be related to shock. Dunbar and colleagues (1999) conducted a prospective, longitudinal study of mood disturbance before implant and at 1, 3, 6, and 9 months post-implantation ($N = 176$). Results indicated that higher levels of mood disturbance at 1 and 3 months were independent predictors of subsequent arrhythmia events at 3 and 6 months, even after controlling for important cardiac variables such as ejection fraction. The authors concluded that "negative emotions were the cause, rather than a consequence, of arrhythmia events" (Dunbar et al., 1999, p. 163). Therefore, reducing negative emotions and psychological distress may also decrease the chances of receiving a shock.

Family Impact of the ICD

The impact of the ICD and its life-saving shock clearly transcends the patient and includes the patient's family. However, relatively few studies have fully included the family in the study of psychological impact. Sneed and Finch (1992) studied 15 ICD patients and their spouses 1 month to 3 years post-implantation, and noted that the major concerns of spouses were fear of patient death, family role changes, and being overprotective. Dunbar, Warner, and Purcell (1993) interviewed 22 ICD patients at 1, 3, and 6 months post-implantation, and found two primary areas of concern for their mates: (a) uncertainty regarding the appropriate course of action in the event of an ICD discharge; and (b) anxiety over the patient-spouse's loss of consciousness and need for administration of cardiopulmonary resuscitation. Perhaps the most clever study compared two groups of ICD patients and spouses: pairs who have not experienced an ICD shock (n = 10) and pairs who have experienced an ICD shock (n = 5; Dougherty, 1995). At 12-month follow-up, anxiety levels were significantly higher for patients who had experienced shock and their spouses. Both groups reported low levels of marital support and low marital satisfaction during the year following implantation. Although the sample size was very small, this study indicates that both the patient and the spouse are psychologically affected by the experience of the patient being shocked. Family and marital issues including sexual functioning are prominent for ICD patients and only extend the existing literature indicating the circular interplay between family systems operations and adjustment to illness from the general cardiac disease literature (Sotile, 1996).

Biological Aspects of Psychological Distress in Cardiac Patients

Multiple biological–behavioral mechanisms prompted by the experience of anxiety and depression may account for poor cardiac disease outcomes. Anxiety has been implicated in the provocation of electrical instability in the heart, the promotion of increased atherosclerotic processes, and the triggering of myocardial infarction (Kubzansky, Kawachi, Weiss, & Sparrow, 1998). Evidence suggests that depression affects cardiac health outcomes by altering neuroendocrine functioning, increasing sympathetic tone and decreasing vagal tone, and by increasing platelet aggregation (Carney, Freedland, Rich, & Jaffe, 1995). Anxiety and depression have also been associated with reduced adherence to the prescribed medical regimen (i.e., increasing self-care behaviors and decreasing health compromising behaviors) known to be important in the rehabilitation of cardiac patients (Januzzi, Stern, Pasternak, & DeSanctis, 2000). Many ICD patients report restricted activities primarily due to their fear that any elevated heart rate secondary to either physical or mental activity will prompt an ICD shock (Luderitz, Jung, Deister, & Manz, 1996). These "psychological activity restrictions" may go unrecognized by health care providers unless specific time and attention are paid to this part of patient functioning.

Quality of Life in ICD Patients

Health-related quality of life has emerged as an endpoint of interest because it reflects a patient's ability to function in a variety of life domains including physical, social, emotional, and work-related. As noted earlier, the ICD has demonstrated a significant survival benefit compared to anti-arrhythmic drugs for patients with potentially life-threatening arrhythmia (e.g., AVID Investigators, 1997; Moss et al., 1996). The quality of life benefit has not been as well studied, but the results regarding quality of life outcomes indicated that the ICD is at least equal to or better than anti-arrhythmic drugs on patient-reported and objective indicators of quality of life (Arteaga & Windle, 1995; Conti & Sears, 2001; Herbst, Goodman, Feldstein, & Reilly, 1999). The experience of ICD shock, psychological distress, and quality of life (QOL) has been investigated in a recent major clinical trial (Namerow et al., 1999). The CABG (Coronary Artery Bypass Graft) Patch Trial examined the value of prophylactic ICD implantation in patients undergoing coronary artery bypass graft surgery (n = 262) versus no ICD (n = 228) after CABG surgery. Data from this trial indicated that the quality of life outcomes (mental and physical) for the ICD patients were significantly worse compared with no-ICD patients. However, further analyses revealed that there was no difference in QOL for *non-shocked ICD* patients versus no-ICD patients. These results indicated that the ICD group who had received shocks was responsible for the significantly worse mental and physical QOL outcome scores between the groups. Collectively, these important data indicate that the experience of shock is strongly associated with psychological distress and diminished quality of life.

Treatment Approaches for ICD Patients and Families

ICD patients and families often do not receive comprehensive psychological intervention due to at least two sets of barriers that commonly exist within the health care system. First, health care providers may not be completely comfortable managing emotional issues in cardiology practices. A national survey of ICD health care providers, including both physicians and nurses, revealed the highest percentages of comfort handling traditional medical issues (e.g., 92% of the sample reported comfort in managing patient adherence concerns), and the least comfort in managing emotional well-being issues (e.g., only 39% of the sample reported comfort in managing depression and anxiety symptoms; Sears et al., 2000). These results are somewhat disconcerting when we consider that our previous work also showed that ICD patients were equally likely to seek discussion about emotional issues with health care providers (37%) as they were with family and friends (36%; Sears et al., 1999). The second barrier includes the relative lack of integration of psychologists in interdisciplinary teams in cardiac care settings. Despite the specific skills that psychologists could contribute, very few provide on-site and real-time consultation to cardiac treatment teams. Public policy and third party payers have also contributed to this barrier via inflexible or difficult processes to receive reimbursement for this type of clinic-based care. Nonetheless, psychological interventions appear indicated for the ICD patient and family. Initial research investigations using cognitive–behavioral therapies showed that active treatment patients reported less depression, less anxiety, and less general psychological distress than the no-treatment group at 9-month follow-up evaluations (Kohn, Petrucci, Baessler, Soto, & Movsowitz, 2000). These types of psychological interventions often incorporate multiple methods for symptom reduction including but not limited to ICD education, relaxation training, supportive therapy, cognitive reframing, family communication, social support engagement, and behavioral change strategies. Each of these techniques can result in a higher degree of confidence in the ICD patient's ability to cope and reduce patient and family distress.

Summary

The ICD is the treatment of choice for patients with potentially life-threatening cardiac arrhythmias. The life-saving effects of the ICD shock may be associated with increased psychosocial concerns. The psychosocial impact of the ICD is significant, with an estimated 13–38% of ICD patients experiencing diagnosable levels of depression and anxiety. Nonetheless, the ICD is well-tolerated by most recipients and family members. Multidisciplinary teams and family "teams" are critical aides to ICD patients. Ongoing research and clinical work focused on the resumption of quality of life allow ICD patients to truly benefit from the best of biomedical technology. If *The Six Million-Dollar Man* show ran today, the recovery of the Bionic Man would ideally include a surrounding team of health professionals, as well as his family, to maximize his quality of functioning. With increased understanding by health care professionals of the patients' challenges in adjusting to implantable devices, the science fiction of the 1970s may turn into a reality in the 2000s.

CONCLUSION

These three examples—genetic testing and myotonic dystrophy, childhood diabetes, and cardiac arrhythmias and implantable cardioverter defibrillators—demonstrate the powerful psychosocial issues associated with the assessment and treatment of serious chronic illness. With each illness, the family plays a central role in the success of managing the illness. In each case, the technology associated with assessment or treatment has serious psychological and interpersonal consequences, whether it be the family implications of genetic testing; a peer's reaction to a diabetic child's injections, glucose monitoring, or restricted diet; or the adult man's anxious reaction to being shocked by his ICD. These biopsychosocial illnesses call for biopsychosocial treatments, with psychologists as important team members working alongside physicians, nurses, and other health professionals. The three descriptions in this chapter are state-of-the-art examples of the teamwork necessary to provide comprehensive, biopsychosocial health care in the 21st century and how psychology and psychologists can contribute to building or restoring healthy families.

REFERENCES

Acheson, L. (2001, March 3). The family physician's perspective as part of the plenary. In L. Acheson, S. McDaniel, & J. Rolland (Speakers), *Does DNA determine destiny? Patient perceptions and family processes involving genetic information.* Presentation presented at the Family in Family Medicine: The 21st Annual Conference of the Society of Teachers of Family Medicine, Kiawah Island, South Carolina.

American Diabetes Association. (2001). Clinical practice recommendations 2001. *Diabetes Care, 24*(Suppl. 1).

Arteaga, W. J., & Windle, J. R. (1995). The quality of life of patients with life threatening arrhythmias. *Archives of Internal Medicine, 155,* 2086–2091.

AVID Investigators. (1997). A comparison of anti-arrythymic-drug therapy with implantable defibrillators in patients resuscitated from near-fatal ventricular arrhythmias. *New England Journal of Medicine, 337*(22), 1576–1583.

Badger, L. W., deGruy, F., Hartman, J., Plant, M. A., Leeper, J., Anderson, R., et al. (1994). Patient presentation, interview content and the detection of depression by primary care physicians. *Psychosomatic Medicine, 56,* 128–135.

Belar, C. D. (1995). Collaboration in capitated care: Challenges for psychology. *Professional Psychology: Research and Practice, 26,* 139–146.

Belar, C. D. (1997). Clinical health psychology: A specialty for the 21st century. *Health Psychology, 16,* 411–416.

Bloch, C., Clemons, P., & Sperling, M. (1987). Puberty decreases insulin sensitivity. *Journal of Pediatrics, 110,* 481–487.

Buxton, A. E., Lee, K. L., & Fisher, J. D. (1999). A randomized study of the prevention of sudden death in patients with coronary artery disease. *New England Journal of Medicine, 341,* 1882–1890.

Carney, R. M., Freedland, K. E., Rich, M. W., & Jaffe, A. S. (1995). Depression as a risk factor for cardiac events in established coronary heart disease: A review of possible mechanisms. *Annals of Behavioral Medicine, 17,* 142–149.

Conti, J. B., & Sears, S. F. (2001). Understanding and managing the psychological impact of the implantable cardioverter defibrillator. *Cardiac Electrophysiology Review Journal, 5,* 129–133.

Cummings, N. A., & Cummings, J. L. (Eds). (1997). *Behavioral health in primary care: A guide for clinical integration.* Madison, CT: International Universities Press, Plenum Press.

Diabetes Control and Complications Trial Research Group. (1993). The effect of intensive treatment of diabetes on the development and progression of long-term complications in insulin-dependent diabetes mellitus. *The New England Journal of Medicine, 329,* 977–986.

Dorman, J., McCarthy, B., O'Leary, L., & Koehler, A. (1995). Risk factors for insulin-dependent diabetes. In M. Harris (Ed.), *Diabetes in America* (2nd ed.). (NIH Publication No. 95-1468). Bethesda, MD: National Diabetes Data Group, National Institutes of Health, National Institute of Diabetes and Digestive and Kidney Diseases.

Dougherty, C. M. (1995). Psychological reactions and family adjustment in shock versus no shock groups after implantation of internal cardioverter defibrillator. *Heart and Lung, 24,* 281–291.

Druss, B. G., Rohrbaugh, R. M., & Rosenheck, R. A. (1999). Depressive symptoms and health costs in older medical patients. *American Journal of Psychiatry, 156,* 477–479.

Dunbar, S. B., Kimble, L. P., Jenkins, L. S., Hawthorne, M., Dudley, W., Slemmons, M., et al. (1999). Association of mood disturbance and arrhythmia events in patients after cardioverter defibrillator implantation. *Depression and Anxiety, 9,* 163–168.

Dunbar, S. B., Warner, C. D., & Purcell, J. A. (1993). Internal cardioverter defibrillator discharge: Experiences of patients and family members. *Heart and Lung, 22,* 494–501.

Engel, G. (1977). The need for a new medical model: A challenge for biomedicine. *Science, 196,* 129–136.

Frasure-Smith, N., Lesperance, F., & Talajic, M. (1993). Depression following myocardial infarction: Impact on 6-month survival. *Journal of the American Medical Association, 270,* 1819–1825.

Godeman, F., Ahrens, B., Behrens, S., Berthold, R., Gandor, C., Lampe, F. et al. (2001). Classical conditioning and dysfunctional cognitions in patients with panic disorder and agoraphobia treated with an implantable cardioverter defibrillator. *Psychosomatic Medicine, 63,* 231–238.

Herbst, J. H., Goodman, M., Feldstein, S., & Reilly, J. M. (1999). Health related quality of life assessment of patients with life-threatening ventricular arrhythmias. *PACE, 22,* 915–926.

Ingersoll, G., Orr, D., Herrold, A., & Golden, M. (1986). Cognitive maturity and self-management among adolescents with insulin-requiring diabetes mellitus. *Journal of Pediatrics, 108,* 620–623.

Januzzi, J. L., Stern, T. A., Pasternak, R. C., & DeSanctis, R. W. (2000). The influence of anxiety and depression on outcomes of patients with coronary artery disease. *Archives of Internal Medicine, 160,* 1921–1931.

Johnson, S. B., Freund, A., Hansen, C. A., & Malone, J. (1990). Adherence health status relationships in childhood diabetes. *Health Psychology, 6,* 606–631.

Johnson, S. B., Kelly, M., Henretta, J. C., Cunningham, W. R., Tomer, A., & Silverstein, J. H. (1992). A longitudinal analysis of adherence and health status in childhood diabetes. *Journal of Pediatric Psychology, 17,* 537–553.

Johnson, S. B., & Rodrigue, J. (1997). Health related disorders in children. In E. Mash & L. Terdal (Eds.), *Behavioral assessment of childhood disorders* (3rd ed., pp. 481–519). New York: Guilford Press.

Kohn, C. S., Petrucci, R. J., Baessler, C., Soto, D. M., & Movsowitz, C. (2000). The effect of psychological intervention on patients' long-term adjustment to the ICD: A prospective study. *PACE, 23,* 450–456.

Konstam, V., Colburn, C., & Butts, L. (1995). Psychosocial adaptation of automatic implantable cardioverter defibrillator recipients: Implications for the rehabilitation counselor. *Journal of Applied Rehabilitation Counseling, 26,* 19–22.

Kubzansky, L. D., Kawachi, I., Weiss, S. T., & Sparrow, D. (1998). Anxiety and coronary heart disease: A synthesis of epidemiological, psychological, and experimental evidence. *Annals of Behavioral Medicine, 20,* 47–58.

LaPorte, R., Matsushima, M., & Chang, Y. (1995). Prevalence and incidence of insulin-dependent diabetes. In M. Harris (Ed.), *Diabetes in America* (2nd ed., pp. 37–46, NIH Publication No. 95-1468). Bethesda, MD: National Diabetes Data Group, National Institutes of Health, National Institute of Diabetes and Digestive and Kidney Diseases.

Luderitz, B., Jung, W., Deister, A., & Manz, M. (1996). Quality of life in multiprogrammable implantable cardioverter-defibrillator recipients. In S. Saksena & B. Luderitz (Eds.), *Interventional electrophysiology: A textbook* (pp. 305–313). Armonk, NY: Futura Publishing.

McDaniel, S. H., & Campbell, T. L. (Eds.). (1999). Genetic testing and families. *Families, Systems, and Health, 17,* 1–144.

McDaniel, S. H., Campbell, T. L., Hepworth, J., & Lorenz, A. (in press). *Family-oriented primary care* (2nd ed.). New York: Springer-Verlag.

McDaniel, S. H., Campbell, T. L., & Seaburn, D. (1990). *Family-oriented primary care: A manual for medical providers.* New York: Springer-Verlag.

McDaniel, S. H., Hepworth, J., & Doherty, W. (1992). *Medical family therapy: A biopsychosocial approach to families with health problems.* New York: Basic Books.

McDaniel, S. H., & Speice, J. (2001). What family psychology has to offer women's health: The example of conversion, somatization, infertility treatment, and genetic testing. *Professional Psychology, 32,* 44–51.

Moss, A. J., Hall, W. J., Cannom, D. S., Daubert, J. P., Higgins, S. L., Klien, H., et al. (1996). Improved survival with an implanted defibrillator in patients with coronary disease at high risk for ventricular arrhythmia. *New England Journal of Medicine, 335,* 1933–1940.

Myerburg, R. J., & Castellanos, A. (1997). Cardiac arrest and sudden cardiac death. In E. Braunwald (Ed.), *Heart disease: A textbook of cardiovascular medicine* (pp. 742–779). Philadelphia: W. B. Saunders.

Namerow, P. B., Firth, B. R., Heywood, G. M., Windle, J. R., Parides, M. K., et al. (1999). Quality of life six months after CABG surgery in patients randomized to ICD versus no ICD therapy: Findings from the CABG patch trial. *PACE, 22,* 1305–1313.

Olfson, M., Fireman, B., Weissman, M. M., Leon, A. C., Sheehan, D. V., Kathol, R. G., et al. (1997). Mental disorder and disability among patients in a primary group practice. *American Journal of Psychiatry, 154,* 1734–1740.

Pauli, P., Wiedemann, G., Dengler, W., Benninghoff, G. B., & Kuhlkamp, V. (1999). Anxiety in patients with an automatic implantable cardioverter defibrillator: What differentiates them from panic patients? *Psychosomatic Medicine, 61,* 69–76.

Rozanski, A., Blumenthal, J., & Kaplan, J. (1999). Impact of psychological factors on the pathogenesis of cardiovascular disease and implications for therapy. *Circulation, 99,* 2192–2217.

Ryan, C. (1990). Neuropsychological consequences and correlates of diabetes in childhood. In C. Holmes (Ed.), *Neuropsychological and behavioral aspects of diabetes.* New York: Springer-Verlag.

Sears, S. F., Conti, J. B., Curtis, A., Saia-Lewis, T. L., Foote, R., & Wen, F. (1999). Affective distress and implantable cardioverter defibrillators: Cases for psychological and behavioral interventions. *PACE, 22,* 1831–1834.

Sears, S. F., Eads, A., Marhefka, S., Sirois, B., Urizar, G., Todaro, J. F., et al. (1999). The U.S. national survey of ICD Recipients: Examining the global and specific aspects of quality of life [Abstract]. *European Heart Journal, 20,* 232.

Sears, S. F., Todaro, J. F., Saia-Lewis, T. L., Sotile, W., & Conti, J. B. (1999). Examining the psychosocial impact of implantable cardioverter defibrillators: A literature review. *Clinical Cardiology, 22,* 481–489.

Sears, S. F., Todaro, J. F., Saia, T. L., Urizar, G., Sirois, B., Wallace, R., et al. (2000). Assessing the psychosocial impact of the ICD: A national survey of implantable cardioverter defibrillator health care providers. *PACE, 20,* 939–945.

Shurman, R. A., Kramer, P. D., & Mitchell, J. B. (1985). The hidden mental health network: Treatment of mental illness by nonpsychiatrist physicians. *Archives of General Psychiatry, 42,* 89–94.

Sneed, N. V., & Finch, N. J. (1992). The effects of psychosocial nursing intervention on the mood state of patients with implantable cardioverter and their caregivers. *Progress in Cardiovascular Nursing, 12*(2), 4–14.

Sotile, W. M. (1996). *Psychosocial interventions for cardiopulmonary patients.* Champaign, IL: Human Kinetics.

Spitzer, R. L., Kroenke, K., Linzer, M., Hahn, S. R., Williams, J. B., deGruy, F. V., et al. (1995). Health-related quality of life in primary care patients with mental disorders: Results from the PRIME-MD 1000 study. *Journal of the American Medical Association, 274,* 1511–1517.

Travis, L., Brouhard, B., & Schreiner, B. (1987). *Diabetes mellitus in children and adolescents*. Philadelphia, PA: W. B. Saunders.

Wahlberg, K. E., Wynne, L. C., Oja, H., et al. (1997). Gene–environment interaction in vulnerability to schizophrenia: Findings from the Finnish adoptive family study of schizophrenia. *American Journal of Psychiatry, 154,* 355–362.

3

FAMILY HEALTH THROUGH INJURY AND VIOLENCE PREVENTION AT HOME

MICHAEL C. ROBERTS, ILEANA ARIAS, JOHN R. LUTZKER,
LENORE E. A. WALKER, AND DAVID A. WOLFE

Violence and injury appear to be an unfortunate common element of American life, as witnessed in news reports, in personal experiences, and in others' experiences in the community, or within families. Violence includes acts of physical assault and abuse, sexual abuse, and psychological maltreatment. Injuries may occur through intentional actions such as violent behavior, or without such intentionality, through what have been called "accidents."

Feeling an important gap in the psychological literature, the authors of this chapter focus on the research and psychological interventions appropriate to the prevention of injuries and violence *in the home*. This consideration is of particular interest because in American society the home is

The order of authorship is alphabetical after the first author. This chapter is composed of sections authored by individual professionals who were responsible for the contents of the sections. The merging of the sections into a single chapter was reviewed by the authors. Contributions to the Child Maltreatment section were also made by Joanne Klevens and Gene Shelley.

idealized as a sanctuary, a safe place where family members are nurtured and protected. Americans consider violations of these ideal assumptions as tragedies, such as when injury occurs, whether accidental or deliberate. The focus on the home is especially important because the residence is a primary setting for much injury and violence. The interpersonal relationships of those residing therein lend more legal and psychological complexity to the home situation as compared to injury-causing and assaultive behavior outside the home.

Coupled with the view that the home has an esteemed position in the American perspective are personal and political beliefs that intrusions into one's home life by government (or by anybody for that matter) should be minimized. Prominent in the United States Constitution is the clause that homes are protected or immune from invasion by the government. This view includes that Americans have rights to behave in ways other than how people think they should, even if well-intentioned. Such perspectives have historically constrained government and nongovernmental organizations from intervening in the home for the prevention of violent or unintentional injuries.

The concepts and methods of psychology would seem to be well formed and applicable to injury and violence in terms of improving understanding about the etiological causes, risk factors, and situational characteristics of injuries, whether intentional or unintentional. Additionally, psychologists have designed interventions to prevent interpersonal injuries or ameliorate the effects of physical and psychological injuries. Finally, psychological techniques are employed in the evaluation of preventive intervention efforts for injury and violence. Thus, psychology has much to offer in creating a healthy world in this domain.

The devastating consequences of physical and psychological injuries are also seen in clinical cases by psychologists, psychiatrists, social workers, and other professionals in social service agencies. The complexity of violence and injury, because of the multiple determinants, behaviors, and outcomes, makes scientific study and professional intervention more difficult, but ever more important. Inevitably, behavior is involved in violence and injury.

Thus, the science and practice of psychology comes to bear because it inherently deals with behavior. Psychology has taken particular interest in violence in American society, specifically as it involves children (American Psychological Association Commission on Violence and Youth, 1993) and families (American Psychological Association Task Force on Violence and the Family, 1996) through activities of the American Psychological Association. The formal organizations of psychology have been less involved in unintentional injuries, although the Society of Pediatric Psychology created a Task Force on Children's Injuries that prepared a fairly comprehensive report (Finney et al., 1993).

A number of professions and scientific disciplines have been involved in various aspects of injury and violence, often leading to prevention efforts. Although each discipline lends its particular expertise to the topic, sometimes terminology, conceptualizations, and approaches have conflicted. Injury and violence are both considered public health problems, and as such, attempts to prevent injury and violence from a public health perspective originally and primarily have entailed the application of epidemiological methods. However, the public health approach is interdisciplinary, and empirically supported research and interventions increasingly are making significant contributions and finding merit in the public health approach to injury and violence prevention. As exemplified by the concepts outlined in this chapter's sections, psychology, as a science of behavior and as a health care profession, is making significant contributions to creating a healthy world for the human inhabitants, for the very young to the very old. Distinctions are typically made between intentional and unintentional injuries. The presumed intent of the commission of injury-producing actions or the omission of injury-preventing actions is recognized by the Codes for the International Classification of Diseases (ICD): unintentional, homicidal, and suicidal. Not all researchers consider the distinctions useful (Peterson & Gable, 1998), but much of the research, conceptualization, and intervention programs follow these lines. Although the inclusion of both unintentional injury and intentional violence in the same chapter may seem like a difficult combination, the latest version of the federal report establishing health objectives for the nation, currently entitled *Healthy People 2010* (U.S. Department of Health and Human Services [USDHHS], 2000), includes a section combining injury and violence prevention. As noted in *Healthy People 2010*, "although the events leading to an unintentional injury and an intentional injury differ, the outcomes and extent of the injury are similar" (chapter 15, paragraph 4). The report also stated "many of the factors that cause unintentional injuries are closely associated with violent and abusive behavior" (chapter 15, paragraph 9). Each of the following sections prepared by different authors illustrates aspects of conceptualizing and preventing injury and violence in the complexity of the numerous factors and considerations.

Family health psychology inherently involves both psychological health and physical health of all members of the group identified as a family. The ultimate goal of the psychology of positive family health is the application of psychological knowledge and techniques to the understanding, limitation, or reversal of problems that limit the full enjoyment of physical and psychological health (Roberts & McElreath, 1992).

Broadening the definition of family health to include psychosocial phenomena inevitably brings in psychological knowledge of injuries (both intentional and unintentional) and violence. The range of injuries and violence includes that which occurs among family members or intimate partners, which will be the focus of this chapter. Using a developmental perspective this chapter will span the breadth of the injury and violence field including risks in infancy, childhood, adolescence, and adulthood. Because of the expertise of the authors each segment integrates current psychological research in this complicated area with psychological interventions. Each segment of this chapter will first define and give the incidences of a specific category of injury or violence. Then each segment will provide examples of research-based interventions.

Too long we have looked at injuries and violence as separate phenomena and yet together they rank in the top 10 health hazards in the United States. This chapter provides a unique, first look at the range from prevention to treatment on the individual, family, and community level for injuries and violence.

UNINTENTIONAL INJURIES AND PREVENTION

Definition and Incidences

The issues of injury prevention are illustrative of ways to improve family health because unintentional injuries remain the single largest threat to the health and well-being of humans (Finney et al., 1993). Injuries result from behavioral and environmental factors that interact in such a way as to result in harm to an individual. Each year, countless people experience trauma, disability, and death as a result of an unintentional injury. In childhood and adolescence, as well as in early, middle, and late adulthood, injury is one of the leading causes of death and disability when it is not *the* leading cause for a particular age group (USDHHS, 2000). These unintentional injuries and deaths due to injury significantly affect the lives of children, adolescents, adults, and their families in all ways of functioning. Injuries are costly for society, health care institutions, families, and those who receive the injuries—in terms of dollar costs to society; in terms of financial burdens to families; and in terms of the psychological toll. Although there are special risk factors associated with childhood, adolescent, and adult injuries, the inescapable fact is that everybody is at risk for injuries.

Before discussing injury prevention, three important foundational points need to be presented. First, the term *injuries* is now emphasized, not the terms *accidents* or *accidental injury*, because "accidents" implies that chance factors or fate play a role in injuries. If injuries did result from uncontrollable elements, then there would be no place for a scientific approach to understanding of how injuries develop and to prevention or controlling of injuries. However, injuries are open to scientific study and are preventable.

Second, the terms *unintentional* or *unintentional injuries* are used to signify a difference with the types of injuries described in the other sections of this particular chapter. Although a perpetrator of interpersonal violence might say he or she did not "mean" or "intend" to cause injury or harm in those situations of family violence, for example, intent or knowledge that an action will result in harm are features distinguishing violence from unintentional injuries (Wilson, Baker, Teret, Shock, & Garbarino, 1991). As we noted earlier, not all injury researchers believe the distinction is useful (Peterson & Gable, 1998). Nonetheless, injuries occur "neither randomly nor capriciously but rather in predictable patterns" (Widome, 1991, p. v).

A third premise is that psychology, as the science of behavior, has a strong contribution to make in the injury prevention field and to create a healthier world. These contributions include (a) gaining a better understanding of how injuries develop, (b) developing injury prevention efforts, and (c) evaluating the effectiveness of injury control activities. Protecting health and safety inherently involves actions related to environment, behavior, and lifestyles. What people do is the realm of psychology. This point needs to be emphasized because there are relatively few psychologists currently working in injuries, despite its universal risk and impact. This is an area in which psychologists can expand both research and practice in exceptional ways to build a healthier world. The first aspect of enhancing an understanding of how injuries develop is exemplified by research on risk factors and situational elements, and epidemiology of injuries (e.g., incidence, prevalence). Psychologists have identified such considerations as parental supervision characteristics, behavioral actions of children and adults leading to injuries, and the interaction of a hazardous environment and humans (Alexander & Roberts, 2003; Roberts & Brooks, 1987; Roberts, Brown, Boles, & Mashunkashey, in press). For the second and third contributions, psychologists have devised a number of effective interventions using behavioral techniques and intensive instructional strategies; they have also evaluated many of these intervention programs to determine successes, failures, and limitations (Finney et al., 1993; Roberts, Fanurik, & Layfield, 1987).

Prevention

There are three very general ways to prevent unintentional injuries. In this section we will combine contributions of several disciplines on the basis of a conceptualization that these pieces interact in the production of injuries and in the prevention of them.

Target the Environment and Make Structural Changes to Be Safer

Structural or environmental change comes about because public policy decision makers are persuaded to take action or because somebody fears getting sued in case a person gets hurt under their liability. Structural changes are frequently referred to as passive prevention. There is no or minimal individual action required, the injury control is built-in so that it occurs regardless of the individual's behavior. Empirical support is strong for environmental changes to create a safer world: refrigerator construction, packaging of poisons and medicines, crib design, eliminating choking hazards on children's toys, power equipment with safeguards, softer playground materials for landings, and putting up berms and bridges to separate pedestrians from traffic (Alexander & Roberts, 2003). Sometimes safer environments mean rules and regulations on human behavior such as safety seat and safety belt laws, airbag requirements, bicycle helmet laws, and gun control laws, all of which have demonstrated reductions in injuries and deaths (National Committee for Injury Prevention and Control, 1989; Wilson et al., 1991). Of course, in these types of prevention interventions somebody has to take some action: first, to require some preventive improvement for the environment and second, to implement the changes necessary to gain safety benefit. Some health advocates assert that environmental changes are best because protection is afforded to everyone. Others acknowledge that this type of prevention is often hard to implement given the political realities of Americans' dislike for being intruded upon, and there are limitations on what structural change can accomplish (Peterson & Roberts, 1992). This takes a strong will and commitment to safety to overcome the political and business objections to such interventions.

Target People Themselves to Engage in Safer Behaviors

A second major approach to increasing safety is to target people to take the necessary actions to protect themselves from injuries. This idea has strong appeal to many Americans who historically believe in individual responsibility. Consequently, programs to encourage people to take responsibility for safer behaviors have proliferated. Although most fail to show demonstrable effects (and many have not evaluated effectiveness based on educational efforts), some programs that utilized behavioral principles and intensity of intervention have empirical support: for example, community-wide, school-based programs for increasing seatbelt use; teaching emergency skills; teaching pedestrian skills; and teaching people, children, and adults self-protective strategies has some support (Roberts et al., 1987).

Unfortunately, the most ubiquitous safety education program, driver's education in high school, does not appear to reduce motor vehicle crashes (Vernick, Li, Ogaitis, MacKenzie, Baker, & Gielen, 1999). There are certainly limitations on what safety behaviors can be taught. Also, the question arises over the issue of whether some aspects of safety should be the responsibility of children or adolescents. It is also questionable whether all aspects of the environment are under enough of an individual's control to make appropriate safety decisions and engage in safe behaviors even if known.

Target the Caregivers to Teach Safer Behaviors and Make the Environment Safer

The last approach has been to improve caregivers' preventive actions on behalf of children, but could be expanded to include caregivers' responsibility for older people or for politicians and rule makers to make safety decisions for their constituents. This effort is based on three *faulty* assumptions: (a) parents have the appropriate knowledge to make decisions about safe environments and allowing unsafe behavior, (b) they are motivated to take action, and (c) they have effective control over their children's situations.

There is evidence to show that parents do not have adequate information about safety and there is little consensus among parents (much less among professionals) about what are safe behaviors and how to motivate change (Peterson, Ewigman, & Kivlahan, 1993; Peterson & Saldana, 1996). To a large degree, parents have functionally, but perhaps unwillingly, conceded control over their children's environments—others are making the decisions for them. In general, giving health and safety information to parents has not been found effective whether that information is given in the media or by pediatricians or some other professional. Some evidence exists that parents can be rewarded for taking safety actions, such as placing babies in car seats, and they will increase that behavior (Roberts, Layfield, & Fanurik, 1991). Similarly, punishment or threat of punishment seems to work as well to decrease unsafe behaviors. Research tends to indicate that parents lack knowledge of what their children are getting into, especially parents of adolescents who are engaging in health-risky behavior (Young & Zimmerman, 1998).

Still, everyday, caregivers do make numerous decisions about safety behaviors; thus psychology needs to gain a better understanding about the process and content. The ability of parents to provide appropriate supervision is a critical factor in children's injury rates: being distracted, use of alcohol, large families, stress, and cognitions about injuries and safety decrease the amount of supervision parents apply. In addition, a significant problem for parents is just knowing when a hazard exists and, therefore, knowing whether to provide more supervision or intervene in some way.

Parents struggle to raise healthy, autonomous individuals, but must also provide sufficient supervision to ensure their children's well-being.

Psychologists can assist by helping define the differences between encouraging appropriate independence and providing inadequate supervision. The scientific discipline and applied profession can do more than they have to improve family health psychology through injury prevention (Roberts & McElreath, 1992). Safe and unsafe behaviors are in the family health psychology bailiwick, not just an issue for the public health profession. Injury prevention is one way that psychologists can involve themselves in building a healthy world.

CHILD MALTREATMENT

Definition and Incidence

In 1999, about 826,000 children across the United States suffered maltreatment, and 1,100 died from abuse or neglect (U.S. Department of Health and Human Services, Administration on Children, Youth, and Families, 2001). Eighty-six percent of these deaths were children under age 6, and 42.6% were less than 1 year old. Depending on the definition, many more children could be identified as maltreated. Over half the cases of maltreatment are attributed to neglect, mainly physical neglect, whereas physical abuse is the most common cause of abuse. Children of low income, single parents, or in large families are at the highest risk of maltreatment (Sedlak & Broadhurst, 1996).

In addition to the deaths and injuries directly caused by abuse or neglect, there are many other short- and long-term consequences, which include failure to thrive, cognitive and intellectual deficits, problematic school performance, poor interpersonal skills, early physical aggression and antisocial behavior, juvenile delinquency, running away, poor mental health, and drug use (National Research Council, 1993). The effects of child maltreatment are not limited to childhood. Many adult health problems such as heart disease, obesity, smoking, and others stem from childhood experiences such as abuse, neglect, witnessing partner violence between their caretakers, and mental illness of a parent (Felitti et al., 1998).

The Federal Child Abuse Prevention and Treatment Act (CAPTA), as amended in October 1996, defines child abuse and neglect as any recent act or failure to act on the part of a parent or caretaker that results in death, serious physical or emotional harm, sexual abuse or exploitation, or which presents an imminent risk of serious harm, which is defined differently by each state such that a child might be identified as maltreated in one state and not another.

Many unintentional injuries may also be cases of abuse or neglect. About a third of unintentional injuries may actually be cases of abuse or neglect and another third could be considered possible cases (Ewigman, Kivlahan, & Land, 1993). Differentiating cases of intentional and unintentional injuries among children is not clear-cut. Peterson and Gable (1998) suggested that for prevention purposes, the intentionality of inflicted injury or neglect might best be viewed as a continuum.

Unintentional and intentional child injuries share similar risk factors and circumstances, resulting from a lack of parental knowledge of potential hazards and developmental stages. Others can be attributed to the lack of resources, which may cause parents to leave children unattended or be financially unable to attend to their child's health and safety matters. It is difficult to say that such harm to children due to parental inadequacies is intentional. Efforts to prevent injuries would benefit from a combination of behavior change strategies and skill building with environmental changes in a more holistic approach.

Interventions to Treat and Prevent Child Maltreatment

The ecobehavioral model represents an example of such an approach, using multifaceted assessment and skill-building strategies to treat and prevent child maltreatment (Lutzker, 1984). Although standardized "indirect" assessments can be used with the ecobehavioral model, reliable direct observation methods are the preferable means of data collection. Skills are taught that have been validated by relevant professionals. Performance criteria for staff and parent training are developed such that being trained is an outcome that can be directly measured. "Fidelity" measures are conducted during and after intervention to ensure that the program is being delivered as prescribed and that parents are performing the skills that they are taught.

Since 1979, the ecobehavioral model has been delivered in rural southern Illinois through Project 12-Ways (Lutzker, 1984). Program evaluation data have shown that families who participate in this program have a lower risk of recidivism than families who receive other services in the same region (Lutzker, 1984; Lutzker & Rice, 1984). Project SafeCare (PS) was a systematic replication of Project 12-Ways, the goal of which was to provide similar services in an urban environment that were culturally responsive to a primarily Latina clientele, and could be delivered in a succinct manner (Lutzker, Bigelow, Doctor, Gershater, & Greene, 1998). Thus, PS taught young parents parent–child interaction skills, home safety, and child health care skills in packages of five training sessions for each component.

Single-case experimental data documented that the skills building strategies produced individual behavior change in parents' interaction skills with their children (Lutzker, Bigelow, Doctor, & Kessler, 1998), in reducing the number of safety hazards in homes (Metchikian, Mink, Bigelow, Lutzker, & Doctor, 1998), and in parents' abilities to identify, treat, or report the illnesses of their children, birth to 5 years (Bigelow & Lutzker, 2000). It was also found that some of the interventions could be delivered through videotape (Bigelow & Lutzker, 1998; Mandel, Bigelow, & Lutzker, 1998) and by nurses and caseworkers (Lutzker, Bigelow, Doctor, & Kessler, 1998), and that the protocols were effective in Spanish (Cordon, Lutzker, Bigelow, & Doctor, 1998).

Program evaluation data from PS have been striking, showing significant group reductions in safety hazards, and significant increases in parenting skills and child health care skills (Gershater-Molko, Lutzker, & Wesch, 2002). There were large differences in survival rates between the PS sample of 41 completed families and a matched comparison of families who received Family Preservation Services (Gershater-Molko et al., 2002). Eighty-five percent of PS families showed no recidivism after 2 years, whereas 54% showed recidivism in the comparison group.

There are numerous promising and model programs aimed at child maltreatment. The important elements of successful programs such as PS are that they are scientifically sound. The standards of validity and reliability need to be met, there should be programmatic fidelity, and there should be clear outcome data measured in a variety of ways. Program and outcome evaluation data are essential and should minimally use comparison groups, preferably randomized control groups, though the latter are especially difficult to construct in child maltreatment. Programs should be replicable.

Families at risk or substantiated for child maltreatment have higher rates of home safety problems. A common referral for child neglect is for home safety hazards. The Home Accident Prevention Inventory (HAPI) was developed by having safety experts validate which household hazards should be kept out of reach and access of young children (Tertinger, Greene, & Lutzker, 1984). The HAPI was revalidated (HAPI-R) for use in an urban area (Mandel et al., 1998) so that observers can calculate the number of accessible hazards in homes.

Three kinds of interventions have shown clear and dramatic effects in reducing the safety hazards in the homes served by Projects 12-Ways and SafeCare: (a) counselor education about safety hazards presented directly to the families in their homes, (b) a slide-tape presentation with a manual that was delivered in five sessions to families in their homes, and (c) a four-part video showing how to reduce home safety hazards. Medical personnel validated the child health care skills that young parents should possess to be able to identify, report, self-treat, or bring to medical services their children's illnesses. Skills were taught by counselors providing modeling and flowcharts of tasks to learn such as taking a temperature, and requiring role-playing by the young parents. It was shown that a nurse and caseworker could successfully teach these skills in addition to research assistants (Bigelow

& Lutzker, 2000). Additionally, these skills were successfully taught in Spanish to Spanish-speaking parents (Cordon et al., 1998).

Interventions should also go beyond preventing injury to promoting healthy child development. Hart and Risley (1995) identified five aspects of this interaction that appeared to make a meaningful difference in child development: talking to the child often, being nice, explaining things, giving choices and listening, and responding to the child. The bonding component of PS is an example of an intervention aimed at teaching parents to engage their children as a means of preventing behaviors that require other more forceful disciplinary techniques.

Behavioral antecedents are the focus of Planned Activities Training (PAT), the primary teaching tool of the bonding component of PS. PAT teaches parents to plan for engagement with their children and anticipating their needs. Parents are further taught to explain activities to children, state the rules of an activity, explain the consequences for following and not following the rules of activities, use of incidental teaching during activities, and to provide feedback after the activity. Although many planned activities are "leisure" activities such as some kind of structured play, many also are daily living activities such as shopping, going to the mall or dentist, or visiting a friend or relative.

Strategies must be developed to extend these programs to children in greatest need. Even parents in difficult circumstances may be able to use a range of planfully implemented parenting strategies to achieve goals, protect their children, instill values, and correct misbehavior (Brodsky & DeVet, 2000). However, there is a need to explore the factors that support competent parenting in adverse circumstances.

EARLY INTERVENTION IN ADOLESCENT RELATIONSHIP VIOLENCE

Definition and Incidence

Adolescence offers an ideal opportunity for education and skills that promote healthy romantic relationships. The formation of romantic relationships typically begins in early to mid-adolescence, and the initiation of dating calls for the development of important relationship skills, including methods for handling unfamiliar conflict and emotions. However, early and mid-adolescence are also periods of high frequency, high intensity conflict, especially with parents (Laursen, Coy, & Collins, 1998) and dating partners (Wekerle & Wolfe, 1999). Fortunately, as teens seek to develop intimate relationships, motivation to learn about healthy relationships and positive conflict resolution alternatives is strong, although such interest may be compromised unless they are provided with a balanced perspective that includes them as partners in healthy decision making.

Abusive or violent behavior in mid-adolescent dating relationships is typically defined as acts of physical aggression, intimidation, or coercion, which range from threats, pushes, and slaps to beatings and forced sex. Considering only the more severe forms of physical aggression and sexual coercion resulting in harm, approximately 1 in 10 high school-aged teens report ever being involved in an abusive relationship (Centers for Disease Control and Prevention, 2000; Coker et al., 2000). However, studies often place the true estimate of abuse much higher (about 50% of all youth report being a victim, perpetrator, or both), based on a broader definition that includes verbal and psychological intimidation as well (Molidor & Tolman, 1998: O'Keefe & Treister, 1998). Either way, these figures suggest that a considerable number of youths engage in acts with romantic partners that may be far from harmless, and point to the need for education and guidance during adolescence.

Many adolescents (estimated to be 25–30%) have experienced or witnessed violence in their family while growing up, which has a profound impact on their subsequent intimate relationships. A recent study conducted by our team found that high school students with histories of maltreatment had significant adjustment and emotional problems, compared with students without such maltreatment experiences. For female students, risk of clinically significant anger and depression problems was seven times greater among those with a history of maltreatment, and risk of anxiety and posttraumatic stress (PTS) problems was more than nine times greater. For male students, risk of using physical abuse against their partners was over three times greater among those with a history of maltreatment (Wolfe, Scott, Wekerle, & Pittman, 2001).

Psychological Interventions and Prevention of Adolescent Relationship Violence

Psychologists are actively involved in adolescent dating violence prevention by incorporating the latest theoretical understanding of this issue into research projects that can be implemented and evaluated. Early intervention in adolescent relationship violence involves assisting adults in empowering youth to end violence in relationships (their own and that of their peers) through education, skill development, and social competence.

Because adolescence is a critical time in the development of intimate relationships, educating youth about relationships and violence holds promise as a viable prevention strategy. Over the past few years, a dating violence prevention program for at-risk youth, known as the Youth Relationships

Program (YRP), was developed and evaluated at the University of Western Ontario (Wolfe et al., 1996). This program was developed from feminist, social learning, and empowerment theory, and has three main components: (a) education about woman abuse, sexual assault, violence, and date rape; (b) conflict resolution and communication skills development; and (c) social action. The program was originally designed for adolescents 14–17 years of age who had experienced maltreatment while growing up, with the intention of providing them with more positive, nonviolent relationship skills and awareness. The YRP takes teens through a process of learning about the issue and about themselves, and then expands their efforts to affect change within their peer groups, the teen culture, and the broader community. It reflects an incremental strategy aimed at self-awareness and social change by involving peers, school personnel, social institutions, and cultural influences.

The research team recently completed an evaluation of this program that involved more than 200 adolescents. The 2-year follow-up results indicate that this approach is successful in reducing threatening behavior toward dating partners, as well as physical and emotional abuse perpetration. In addition, the program was found to show growth in healthy relationship skills and in related areas of emotional support, conflict resolution, assertion, and self-disclosure (Wolfe et al., 2003). Intervention participants also reported fewer symptoms of emotional distress over time, suggesting that the intervention was of benefit to youth with background experiences of maltreatment and current symptoms of maladjustment. If the profession wished to focus solely on preventing dating violence or woman abuse, then the approach just mentioned has several strengths. If the profession wants to expand its thinking to include a greater emphasis on developing healthy, nonviolent relationships, however, there are several areas in which this program can be further developed. As a funded research project comprising the U.S. National Institutes of Health's Youth Violence Consortium, the research team is collaborating with researchers in Houston, Texas (led by Drs. Ernie Jouriles and Renee McDonald) to redefine the Youth Relationships Program and make it more compatible with school-based implementation. This new prevention initiative will consider a more holistic view of healthy adolescent intimate relationships, incorporating issues such as alcohol and drug use, safe sexual practices and behavior, sexism, violence, abuse of power and control, and decision making. For example, assumptions are often made by partners regarding their relationship, such as the level of commitment, how much time will be spent together, and whether sexual activity will be a part of the relationship. Expectations regarding use of alcohol and drugs are also seldom discussed. Teaching communication and negotiation skills around the hopes and expectations of the relationship will assist in preventing dangerous assumptions from being made, and perhaps prevent risky behaviors from developing.

The revised and expanded program is a violence prevention and health promotion curriculum aimed at Grade 9 students (ages 13–14) as part of their health requirements. The program has been designed for classroom-based instruction, but it offers a number of different teaching styles and learning opportunities, involving discussion groups, activities, guest speakers, videos, and so forth. Teachers administer the program with the assistance of small-group facilitators who may come from university or community settings. This universal prevention initiative addresses the issues of sexism, dating violence, abuse of power and control, substance use and abuse, decision making, and onset of sexual activity and safe sex practices in the context of forming healthy, nonviolent relationships. Because adolescence is a time when developing intimate romantic relationships begin to emerge, the research team decided to focus on adolescent dating relationships; however, the skills and knowledge gained from this program are intended to be transferable to other relationships as well.

Prevention programs to address adolescent dating violence and the formation of healthy relationships must consider the health and well-being of adolescents in its entirety. Although some areas have not yet been adequately researched, such as the link between alcohol and adolescent interpersonal violence, risk behaviors often develop and occur concurrently (Capaldi, Crosby, & Stoolmiller, 1996). At a time when youth are beginning to develop more autonomy from family and greater attachment to peers, guidance, information and assistance with decision making need to be offered.

Encouraging youth to set goals and objectives is usually focused on the context of education and career aspirations; however, an opportunity to consider values and choices regarding healthy lifestyles should be just as important. Making choices and goal setting for issues such as onset of sexual intercourse, safe sex practices, alcohol and drug use, as well as choices regarding dating partners and dating relationships will provide youth with an opportunity to explore how these choices and goals may influence other goals and aspirations, and hence have a greater impact on their decision making and behavior. Youth need to understand that they always have choices, and that they can and do have control over many situations.

Help-seeking and information-seeking skills should also be promoted in prevention programs aimed at teens. Of benefit to youth are programs that teach about resources available in the community and how to access them, which provides a vehicle for community-wide collaboration in the prevention program (i.e., agencies are made aware of the program and open their doors to the youth involved to learn more about their services). In addition, an opportunity to develop social action skills is of benefit to youth. Standing up and making a difference through advocacy, fund raising for organizations and charities, and so forth affirms choices and commitments made by youth to avoid risky behaviors.

Because peers and dating partners become the central focus of teen lives, developing prevention skills that focus on these relationships provides a natural conduit for discussion and applicability to their lives. Long-term, sustained prevention programs are needed. Programs that are offered on a continuing basis and are open to repeat visitors may have greater impact, especially because some youth may require longer time and more practice to develop skills or explore choices and make decisions. Greater flexibility and comprehensiveness is required in prevention to address the needs of the many versus the needs of the few. In sum, it is important for initiatives in this area to consider ways to

- create a climate that makes disclosures of abuse and violence safe;
- help schools and students become part of the solution to relationship violence;
- encourage skill development as alternatives to violence such as problem solving, anger management, mediation, and conflict resolution;
- integrate effective interventions across multiple risk areas: for example, substance abuse, violence, safe sex, and healthy sexuality; and
- tailor the information to the needs of the community, such as age and cultural differences.

INTIMATE PARTNER VIOLENCE

Definition and Incidence

Intimate partner violence (IPV) refers to the use of actual or threatened physical or sexual violence, or psychological and emotional abuse, by current or former spouses, boyfriends, or girlfriends (including heterosexual or same-sex partners). Some of the terms commonly used to describe IPV include domestic violence, courtship violence, marital rape, and date rape. IPV is a major public health problem in the United States, with serious consequences and costs for individuals, families, communities, and society (Gelles, 1997; Kernic, Wolf, & Holt, 2000; Rennison & Welchans, 2000; Sorensen & Saftlas, 1994). Men may be victims of their partners' physical and psychological violence. However, women are 2–3 times more likely than men to report that they had been pushed, shoved, or grabbed; and 7–14 times more likely to report that they had been beaten up, choked, or that their partners had threatened or actually used weapons, or attempted to drown them (Tjaden & Thoennes, 1998). Women are more likely than men to require medical attention, take time off from work, and spend more days in bed as a result of their victimization (Stets & Straus, 1990). Accordingly, the focus herein will be on female victims of IPV.

Women experiencing ongoing IPV report deteriorating physical and emotional health over time (Sutherland, Bybee, & Sullivan, 1998). Non-lethal IPV has been conservatively estimated to result in financial losses of approximately $150 million per year (Greenfeld et al., 1998). Medical costs accounted for approximately 40% of these costs, property loss for another 44%, and lost pay for the remainder. Although women are the primary and direct victims of IPV, children of battered women suffer similar consequences (Felitti et al., 1998; Straus, 1992) and violence against women by an intimate partner is a significant risk factor for child abuse (Straus & Gelles, 1990; Straus, Gelles, & Steinmetz, 1980).

Definitions of IPV and research methods often vary across studies. There is no standardized measurement strategy, and surveys differ in their methodologies and populations. Sample sizes employed typically are not large enough or representative enough of the United States population to be able to generate reliable estimates of the prevalence of IPV. To address some of these deficiencies, the National Center for Injury Prevention and Control (NCIPC) at the Centers for Disease Control and Prevention (CDC), through a collaboration with the National Institute of Justice (NIJ), provided funding to design and conduct a survey, to provide reliable estimates of the prevalence and incidence of physical assault and rape by intimate partners; related injuries; and medical costs including costs for mental health services.

The National Violence Against Women Survey (NVAWS; Tjaden & Thoennes, 1998) was conducted from November 1995 to May 1996, and consisted of a national probability sample of 8,000 women and 8,000 men age 18 and older. Physical assault was defined as any behavior that threatens, attempts, or actually does inflict physical harm, such as throwing something at the victim; pushing, grabbing, or shoving; pulling hair; slapping or hitting; kicking or biting; choking or trying to drown; hitting with objects; beating up; threatening with gun or knife. Rape was defined as the use of force (without the victim's consent) or threat of force to penetrate the victim's vagina or anus by penis, tongue, fingers, or object, or the victim's mouth by penis.

The lifetime prevalence of physical assault of women by an intimate partner was 22.1% and 7.7% for rape. Accordingly, it was estimated that 22,254,037 women are physically assaulted by their intimate partners at some point in their lifetime and 7,753,669 are raped. The 12-month prevalence rates were 1.3% for physical assault and 0.2% for rape, suggesting that 1,309,061 women are physically assaulted and 201,394 are raped annually by an intimate partner. Women who were physically assaulted reported an average of 3.4 victimizations annually; those who were raped reported an average of 1.6 rapes.

Among women who were physically assaulted, 41% were injured during the most recent victimization, and 36% of the women who were raped by an intimate partner sustained an injury (other than the rape itself). The majority of women who were injured during the most recent IPV episode sustained relatively minor injuries, such as scratches, bruises, and welts. Relatively few women sustained more serious types of injuries, such as lacerations, broken bones, dislocated joints, head or spinal cord injuries, chipped or broken teeth, or internal injuries. Twenty-eight percent of the women who were injured during their most recent intimate partner physical assault received some type of medical treatment (e.g., ambulance or paramedic services, treatment in a hospital emergency facility, or physical therapy).

A comparable proportion (31%) of rape victims who were injured by an intimate partner received some type of medical treatment. Twenty-six percent of physical assault victims and 33% of rape victims reported they consulted with a mental health professional. Among these women, physical assault victims averaged 12.9 visits and rape victims averaged 12.4 visits.

Analysis of NVAWS data yielded a lifetime prevalence of psychological victimization by an intimate partner of 27% of women. This may have occurred in the context of physical or sexual victimization as well. The lifetime prevalence of psychological victimization alone (no other form of intimate partner violence) was 14%. Four percent of women reported psychological-only violence by a current intimate partner. As was true of the mental health consequences of physical violence, analysis of data from the NVAWS suggested that women who were victims of psychological violence only were also at higher risk for depression, alcohol use, and medication use including antidepressants, tranquilizers, pain killers, and, unlike victims of physical violence, recreational drugs. Victims of psychological abuse were at higher risk for developing posttraumatic stress disorder (PTSD) symptoms.

When all forms of violence were considered, only psychological abuse and sexual assault were significant risk factors for PTSD—not physical abuse. Psychological abuse is emerging as an important focus for prevention of IPV. Psychological violence appears to be a precursor to physical violence; physical violence rarely occurs in the absence of psychological violence; psychological abuse appears to be related to negative outcomes equally or more so than physical assault, and some women are only psychologically abused (Arias & Pape, 1999; Ronfeldt, Kimerling, & Arias, 1998).

Prevention and Intervention of Intimate Partner Violence

Prevention, especially primary prevention, of IPV is a high public health priority. Past and current efforts typically include secondary and tertiary prevention with an individual focus. Existing programs frequently target victims and perpetrators of IPV and attempt to prevent revictimization and recidivism, or, among victims, focus on recovery from the effects of victimization. These efforts are necessary but limited because they require "waiting" for victims and the identification of perpetrators and victims. Additionally, it is not clear the extent to which the effects of these programs are maintained in the absence of contextual support. For individuals to change and maintain those changes over time, professionals need to achieve contextual changes. Specifically, social norms that support domestic violence need to be addressed.

Social norms are statements that regulate behavior (Hechter & Opp, 2001). Individuals attempt to conform to perceived norms (Prentice & Miller, 1993). Social norms interventions for domestic violence would attempt to change norms in order to influence an individual's own perpetration and victimization, and the response (confronting versus acceptance) to others' perpetration and victimization.

The applicability and effectiveness of a social norms approach to behavior change has been illustrated by research and prevention of college student alcohol use (cf. Haines, 1996). Those successful efforts were based on the assessment of misperceptions with respect to the target behavior (i.e., discrepancy between perceptions of college student drinking and actual drinking behavior of college students), the prevalence of adherence to such misperceptions, the effect of the misperception on behavior, and predicted changes resulting from correction of misperceptions. Media campaigns are frequently used to influence social norms.

The CDC is currently conducting a project to address social norms related to IPV. The project consists of a 2-year plan encompassing formative research and communications planning. The objectives of the research component are to identify target audiences, dissemination techniques, and promotion strategies. Based on these results, a communications plan will be developed to identify appropriate messages and develop dissemination tools that can be implemented both nationally and locally. On the basis of the existing literature focusing on modifiable risk factors, protective factors, and consequences of IPV, this effort will focus on primary prevention among male and female adolescent perpetrators or potential perpetrators of less severe forms of violence.

The focus will be on perceptions and misperceptions of others and strategies for coping with anger and violent feelings. Specifically, the project proposes to address factors such as own and others' use of verbal or physical aggression in intimate relationships; acceptance of myths about domestic violence; justification of violence as a function of the situation; willingness to identify and report IPV; use of sexist and violent language; alcohol as a coping strategy; support seeking; and taking responsibility for relationships and relationship problems.

Families Torn Apart by Domestic Violence

Families where domestic violence has occurred are often torn apart by the consequences that follow the actual or alleged abuse of any member in that family. The most common consequence is either permanent or temporary separation of a battered woman from her abusive husband, battered children from the abusive parent or parents, battered elderly person from the family member or caretaker who has been abusive. Whereas some families can repair themselves after abuse has been reported, others have been unable to survive the intense legal and psychological scrutiny. Psychologists who work with these families may have the opportunity to assist them in rebuilding the original family or building a new family that is healthy and violence-free.

Family Violence and the Legal System

When violence occurs within the family, the legal system is often notified. If it is child abuse, then the criminal and juvenile justice systems may both become involved, particularly because medical or psychological providers are responsible for mandatory reporting of suspected child abuse cases. In some cases the divorce courts may also become involved particularly if there is a question about whether access to the alleged abuser is in the best interests of the child. If it is a marital partner, such as the battered woman, then the divorce court and criminal courts may become involved. Remedies such as a temporary "stay-away" or "protective" order or even civil personal injury claims against the abuser may also bring the family issues into the legal arena. Each of these legal courts may make demands on the family members that can further destroy the family unit or help it to rebuild itself in a new and healthy way.

Psychotherapy Interventions and Prevention of Reoccurring Family Violence

Domestic violence intervention programs are typically run by or supervised by the legal system, often the department of probation. Batterers' intervention groups follow a model of short-term psychoeducation rather than psychotherapy in most jurisdictions, although some programs such as the Denver-based AMEND (Abusive Men Exploring New Directions) program combine both 2–5 years of psychotherapy with the psychoeducational model. Evaluation of these programs suggests that in some cases it helps batterers to stop their physical abuse and treat their partners better, but in others it makes a meaner psychological batterer (Harrell, 1991).

The focus on physical abuse, which relegates the psychological abuse to the background (and often ignores sexual abuse), may be partly responsible for giving an impression that psychological abuse is less damaging than the physical. Interestingly, in many other countries, where family violence programs are centered in the public health ministries, the health needs of all the family members get more attention than in the criminal justice system in the United States (Walker, 1999).

Family or couple's therapy is not recommended when there is violence in the family for several reasons. First, it is important for the batterer to take total responsibility for his or her abusive behavior. This can rarely happen in couple's therapy where each person's behavioral impact on the system is the focus of attention. Second, it is important to permit the victim to have time to decide what to do about the relationship. It may be more important to rebuild a new family than attempt to repair the old one. Third, legal restraining orders may make it impossible to meet together, even with one or two therapists in the room because the couple is told not to have any contact with each other. If the therapist attempts to overturn this order, it may place the victims in greater jeopardy, especially if emotions get stirred up during the therapy session. Fourth, it is almost impossible for a victim to perceive neutrality: victims of violence believe that a professional is either with them or against them! The following outlines a modality of therapy for survivors of domestic violence.

Intervention to assist victims in surviving physical, sexual, and psychological abuse has been termed "survivor therapy" by some (Walker, 1994, 1996, 2000). It is important to attend to the special issues raised by the abuse for both victims and perpetrators in any treatment program. Although there are those who do not like to use labels, mostly to avoid stigmatization, the argument to use them suggests that it is critical to normalize the experience to avoid the shame and self-blame that creates resistance to treatment. Although victims should not be ordered into treatment, intervention with a psychologist who is sensitive to abuse issues can assist the survivor's quest for health.

Safety planning is critical before attempting any further intervention. The homicide and suicide rate is highest at the point of separation so it is important to institute a safety plan that includes taking a time-out when emotions get too intense and other protection of the victims, especially women and children who have the highest risk of becoming the victim of a man's violence. Safety plans should also anticipate the need for shelter or protection at some point. Contact information for the local shelters, law enforcement, and attorneys are all part of safety planning and should be given to the abuse victim.

The second stage in survivor therapy includes a comprehensive assessment period where a standard clinical evaluation is performed and relevant social histories are obtained. It is important to evaluate developmental competencies in children, including social, intellectual, behavioral, and emotional issues. Records should be reviewed such as those from school, parents, other observers, medical, mental health, and the like. In adults, it is important to learn details about family, friendship, and love relationships, school and work histories, and any other abuse in their lives. Medical and mental health records and any court records should be reviewed. Problems with alcohol and other drugs need to be assessed along with the relationship, if any, with abuse. Psychological and neuropsychological standardized testing may be done along with a very careful abuse history from this current relationship. Impact from abuse such as PTSD, Battered Woman Syndrome, Rape Trauma Syndrome, and Battered Child Syndrome, including Child Sexual Abuse Accommodation Syndrome, should be assessed. Other mental health problems often associated with abuse such as affective disorders including depression and bipolar moods, chronic serious mental illness such as various forms of schizophrenia, and personality disorders should also be assessed.

The third phase of treatment calls for the validation of the person's experiences. This phase requires the psychologist to listen to the client and accept what he or she describes as part of the experience. Although it is not important to assess for the "truth" of what is being said in therapy relationships, it may be helpful for legal purposes to help assess for credibility by comparing the client's descriptions with what is known about victims' or perpetrators' experiences in the literature. For forensic evaluators, it is important to check for reliability and validity of statements that are made. Sometimes the mental health symptoms make it difficult to assess for credibility. However, validation of the client's experience is more important for the client's health needs than accuracy. The fourth stage in the survivor therapy model is helping regain cognitive clarity or thinking clearly without undue interference from strong emotions. Victims of abuse may use a variety of ways to avoid dealing directly with the impact from violence. Alcohol and other drug abuse is a common way to avoid thinking or feeling. Mental health symptoms, including depression, anxiety, dissociation, delusions, and hallucinations, may also possibly cloud one's cognitive abilities and judgment. New research suggests that there are biochemical secretions within the subcortical brain regulated by the autonomic nervous system that affect the ability to think, feel, and behave during and after trauma experiences. It is important to understand these interactions for each client as they move toward health and recovery. Intervention must focus on assisting clients in regaining the ability to think and make good judgments so that cognitive clarity occurs.

Around 3–6 months after treatment is begun, the trauma victim begins to focus on the symptoms that are associated with PTSD. This includes high levels of anxiety such as exhibited in physiological behaviors, hypervigilant and startle responses, generalized nervousness, and panic disorders. Clients can also be helped to learn how to control intrusive memories that may just pop into their minds or that are associated with a symbol or similar experience. Therapy methods such as relaxation training, systematic desensitization, thought stopping, and cognitive restructuring may be helpful here.

Violence in the family affects people across all demographic groups including those who have a variety of other mental health problems. These issues should be dealt with once the violence issues are being addressed. Unfortunately most of the court-ordered or supervised treatment programs for both offenders and victims do not have trained psychologists who can use methods appropriate for the complexities raised by most of their clients. Today's batterers may well have been yesterday's battered children. Many battered women are multiple abuse victims, having been sexually abused as children or even sexually assaulted by another man as a teen or adult. As behavior is often multidetermined and especially affected by early environment, after the PTSD symptoms are controlled it is important to look at those long-term psychological issues. The APA Task Force on Violence and the Family (APA, 1996) reported that when one form of violence is found in the family, it is important to look for other forms of violence if there has not been any treatment.

The process of restoration to psychological health is implicit in most psychotherapy treatment even though it is not always stated in such a way. Health, which is often defined as "absence of disease" is a physical and mental state that most people strive to meet. Absence of health may be episodic or may be continuous, depending on what causes a disruption to the individual's and family members' system. In some cases, there is a breakdown of the immunological system causing major disease. In other cases, there are episodic breakdowns followed by reconstitution of health. Psychologists who work with victims and perpetrators in treatment programs are in a position to assist the clients in learning how to restore their own health. Prevention programs that focus on children who have been exposed to domestic violence are also important in restoring the family to health— whether the family stays together or splits up.

Most domestic violence relationships do terminate. In fact, some research indicated that the average battering relationship lasted as long as the average marriage, which was 6 years (Walker, 2000). Thus, it is important to assist both the offender and the victim in making new relationships.

Battles over the custody of children, visitation, and where to live are common in relationships where domestic violence has occurred. In some small number of cases, the allegations of domestic violence may be made to gain advantage during these custody battles, which often revolve around lowering child support payments rather than genuine interest in parenting. Psychologists who work with families may be able to resolve some of these battles before they get too entrenched. It is important to find ways to avoid such conflicts as they take a tremendous toll on the relationships between parents and the children and on the future health of the children (Drozd, 2001).

As noted here, there are a variety of points where the attempt to protect victims of violence can be destructive to families. Many of these families will be torn apart before the offender can learn to stop the violence or the victim can be restored to health. Sometimes this occurs because of the rules and regulations in the legal system that help protect victims. Other times it occurs because of the emotional stress associated with the experience of or exposure to trauma. Psychologists are in positions to assist the victims and perpetrators in terminating relationships without the angst and struggles currently seen. Psychologists are also able to assist clients in healing from the effects of the traumatic abuse and rebuilding new relationships where appropriate. As indicated in the previous sections, new intervention and therapy methods are available to assist victims in becoming survivors.

CONCLUDING REMARKS

The section presentations in this chapter make clear that the issues and impact of interpersonal violence and unintentional injury are significant concerns in modern life. Additionally evident is that the discipline of psychology, through its empirical and applied activities, is contributing to finding solutions to these enormous problems. Psychologists and related professions should focus further energy on empirical research to direct and evaluate preventive interventions. Program evaluations are essential to establish interventions for violence and injury that are evidence-based, replicable, and attentive to the cultural, economic, and developmental diversity that makes up the world. In doing so, the focus should not just be on researching prevention of injury or violence per se, but also on enhancing development of humans and their relationships. Thus, further attention is needed to establish the roles of resilience, competence, skills development, and problem solving to increase human functioning as well as reduce exposure to hazards. Eventually, integrated and empirically supported interventions will be complementary in various situations and behaviors for a comprehensive approach to prevention of injury and violence and health promotion.

Each of the sections in this chapter demonstrates psychological approaches to different aspects to the overall theme. The coverage has been illustrative, at best, and not at all exhaustive, because of the limitations placed on section authors. Nonetheless, in combination in the area of injury and violence in the home, much more empirical work needs to be conducted to complete a professional understanding of the issue and to lead to effective prevention efforts aimed at creating a healthy world for its inhabitants.

REFERENCES

Alexander, K., & Roberts, M. C. (2003). The prevention of unintentional injuries in childhood. In T. Gullota & M. Bloom (Eds.), *The encyclopedia of primary prevention and health promotion* (pp. 615–621). New York: Kluwer.

American Psychological Association Commission on Violence and Youth. (1993). *Violence and youth: Psychology's response* (Volume I: Summary Report). Washington, DC: American Psychological Association.

American Psychological Association Task Force on Violence and the Family. (1996). *Violence and the family*. Washington, DC: American Psychological Association.

Arias, I., & Pape, K. T. (1999). Psychological abuse: Implications for adjustment and commitment to leave violent partners. *Violence and Victims, 14*, 55–67.

Bigelow, K. M., & Lutzker, J. R. (1998). Using video to teach planned activities training to parents reported for child abuse. *Child and Family Behavior Therapy, 20*, 1–14.

Bigelow, K. M., & Lutzker, J. R. (2000). Training parents reported for or at risk for child abuse and neglect to identify and treat their children's illnesses. *Journal of Family Violence, 15*, 311–330.

Brodsky, A .E., & DeVet, K. A. (2000). "You have to be real strong": Parenting goals and strategies of resilient, urban, African American single mothers. *Journal of Prevention and Intervention in the Community, 20*, 159–178.

Capaldi, D. M., Crosby, L., & Stoolmiller, M. (1996). Predicting the timing of first sexual intercourse for at-risk adolescent males. *Child Development, 67*, 344–359.

Centers for Disease Control and Prevention. (2000, June 9). Youth Risk Behavior Surveillance—United States 1999. *Morbidity and Mortality Weekly Report, 49*(5), 1–96.

Coker, A. L., McKeown, R. E., Sanderson, M., Davis, K. E., Valois, R. F., & Huebner, E. S. (2000). Severe dating violence and quality of life among South Carolina high school students. *American Journal of Preventive Medicine, 19*, 220–227.

Cordon, I. M., Lutzker, J. R., Bigelow, K. M., & Doctor, R. M. (1998). Evaluating Spanish protocols for teaching bonding, home safety, and health care skills. *Journal of Behavior Therapy and Experimental Psychiatry, 29*, 41–54.

Drozd, L. (2001, August). *Psychology and hot media issues: Child custody in domestic violence allegations.* Invited presentation at the annual meeting of the American Psychological Association, San Francisco.

Ewigman, B., Kivlahan, C., & Land, C. (1993). The Missouri Child Fatality Study: Underreporting of maltreatment fatalities among children under five years of age, 1983–1986. *Pediatrics, 91,* 330–337.

Felitti, V. J., Anda, R. F., Nordenberg, D., Williamson, D. F., Spitz, A., Edwards, V., et al. (1998). Relationship of childhood abuse and household dysfunction to many of the leading causes of death in adults: The Adverse Childhood Experiences (ACE) study. *American Journal of Preventive Medicine, 14,* 245–258.

Finney, J. W., Christophersen, E. R., Friman, P. C., Kalnins, I. V., Maddux, J. E., Peterson, L., et al. (1993). Society of Pediatric Psychology Task Force: Pediatric psychology and injury control. *Journal of Pediatric Psychology, 18,* 499–536.

Gelles, R. J. (1997). *Intimate violence in families* (3rd ed.). Thousand Oaks, CA: Sage.

Gershater-Molko, R. M., Lutzker, J. R., & Wesch, D. (2002). Using recidivism to evaluate Project SafeCare: Teaching "bonding," safety, and health care skills to parents. *Child Maltreatment, 7,* 277–285.

Greenfeld, L., Rand, M. R., Craven, D., Klaus, P. A., Perkins, C. A., Ringel, C., et al. (1998). *Violence by intimates: Analysis of data on crimes by current or former spouses, boyfriends, and girlfriends* (NCJ-167237). Washington, DC: U.S. Department of Justice.

Haines, M. P. (1996). *A social norms approach to preventing binge drinking at colleges and universities.* Newton, MA: The Higher Education Center for Alcohol and Other Drug Prevention.

Harrell, A. (1991). *Batterer treatment programs.* Washington, DC: The Urban Institute.

Hart, B., & Risley, T. R. (1995). *Meaningful differences in the everyday experience of young American children.* Baltimore, MD: Paul H. Brooks.

Hechter, M., & Opp, K. (Eds.). (2001). *Social norms.* New York: Russell Sage Foundation.

Kernic, M. A., Wolf, M. E., & Holt, V. L. (2000). Rates and relative risk of hospital admission among women in violent intimate partner relationships. *American Journal of Public Health, 90,* 1416–1420.

Laursen, B., Coy, K. C., & Collins, W. A. (1998). Reconsidering changes in parent–child conflict across adolescence: A meta-analysis. *Child Development, 69,* 817–832.

Lutzker, J. R. (1984). Project 12-Ways: Treating child abuse and neglect from an ecobehavioral perspective. In R. F. Dangel & R. A. Polster (Eds.), *Parent training: Foundations of research and practice* (pp. 260–291). New York: Guilford Press.

Lutzker, J. R. (1987). Using recidivism data to evaluate Project 12-Ways: An ecobehavioral approach to the treatment of child abuse and neglect. *Journal of Family Violence, 2,* 283–290.

Lutzker, J. R., Bigelow, K. M., Doctor, R. M., Gershater, R., & Greene, B. F. (1998). An ecobehavioral model for the prevention and treatment of child abuse and neglect: History and applications. In J. R. Lutzker (Ed.), *A handbook of child abuse research and treatment* (pp. 239–266). New York: Plenum.

Lutzker, J. R., Bigelow, K. M., Doctor, R. M., & Kessler, M. L. (1998). Safety, health care, and bonding within an ecobehavioral approach to treating and preventing child abuse and neglect. *Journal of Family Violence, 13,*163–185.

Lutzker, J. R., & Rice, J. A. (1984). Project 12-Ways: Measuring outcome of a large-scale in-home service for the treatment and prevention of child abuse and neglect. *Child Abuse and Neglect: The International Journal, 8,* 519–524.

Mandel, U., Bigelow, K. M., & Lutzker, J. R. (1998). Using video to reduce home safety hazards with parents reported for child abuse or neglect. *Journal of Family Violence, 13,* 147–162.

Metchikian, K. L., Mink, J. M., Bigelow, K. M., Lutzker, J. R., & Doctor, R. M. (1998). Reducing home safety hazards in the home of parents reported for neglect. *Child and Family Behavior Therapy, 3,* 23–34.

Molidor, C., & Tolman, R. M. (1998). Gender and contextual factors in adolescent dating violence. *Violence Against Women, 4,* 180–194.

National Committee for Injury Prevention and Control. (1989). *Injury prevention: Meeting the challenge.* New York: Oxford University Press.

National Research Council. (1993). *Understanding child abuse and neglect.* Washington, DC: Author.

O'Keefe, M., & Treister, L. (1998). Victims of dating violence among high school students: Are the predictors different for males and females? *Violence Against Women, 4,* 195–223.

Peterson, L., Ewigman, B., & Kivlahan, C. (1993). Judgments regarding appropriate child supervision to prevent injury: The role of environmental risk and child age. *Child Development, 64,* 934–950.

Peterson, L., & Gable, S. (1998). Holistic injury prevention. In J. Lutzker (Ed.), *Handbook of child abuse research and treatment* (pp. 291–318). New York: Plenum Press.

Peterson, L., & Roberts, M. C. (1992). Complacency, misdirection, and effective prevention of children's injuries. *American Psychologist, 47,* 1040–1044.

Peterson, L., & Saldana, L. (1996). Accelerating children's risk for injury: Mothers' decisions regarding common safety rules. *Journal of Behavioral Medicine, 19,* 317–331.

Prentice, D. A., & Miller, D. T. (1993). Pluralistic ignorance and alcohol use on campus: Some consequences of misperceiving the social norm. *Journal of Personality and Social Psychology, 64,* 243–256.

Rennison, C. M., & Welchans, S. (2000). *Intimate partner violence* (NCJ-178247). Washington, DC: U.S. Department of Justice.

Roberts, M. C., & Brooks, P. (1987). Children's injuries: Issues in prevention and public policy. *Journal of Social Issues, 43*(2), 1–12.

Roberts, M. C., Brown, K. J., Boles, R. E., & Mashunkashey, J. O. (in press). Prevention of injuries: Concepts and interventions for pediatric psychology in the schools. In R. Brown (Ed.), *Handbook of pediatric psychology in school settings*. Mahwah, NJ: Lawrence Erlbaum Associates.

Roberts, M. C., Fanurik, D., & Layfield, D. (1987). Behavioral approaches to prevention of childhood injuries. *Journal of Social Issues, 43*(2), 105–118.

Roberts, M. C., Layfield, D., & Fanurik, D. (1991). Motivating children's use of care safety seats. In M. Wolraich & D. Routh (Eds.), *Advances in developmental and behavioral pediatrics* (Vol. 10, pp. 61–88). Philadelphia: Jessica Kingsley.

Roberts, M. C., & McElreath, L. H. (1992). The role of families in the prevention of physical and mental health problems. In T. J. Akamatsu, M. A. P. Parris, S. E. Hobfall, & J. H. Crowther (Eds.), *Family health psychology* (pp. 45–65). Washington, DC: Hemisphere.

Ronfeldt, H. M., Kimerling, R., & Arias, I. (1998). Relationship power satisfaction and perpetration of dating violence in the context of paternal marital violence. *Journal of Marriage and the Family, 60*, 70–78.

Sedlak, A. J., & Broadhurst, D. D. (1996). *Executive summary of the Third National Incidence Study of Child Abuse and Neglect*. Retrieved February 26, 2002, from www.calib.com/nccanch/pubs/statinfo/nis3.cfm

Sorensen, S. B., & Saftlas, A. F. (1994). Violence and women's health: The role of epidemiology. *Annals of Epidemiology, 4*, 140–145.

Stets, J. E., & Straus, M. A. (1990). Gender differences in reporting marital violence and its medical and social consequences. In M. A. Straus & R. J. Gelles (Eds.), *Physical violence in American families: Risk factors and adaptations to violence in 8,145 families* (pp. 151–166). New Brunswick, NJ: Transaction Publishers.

Straus, M. A. (1992). Children as witnesses to marital violence: A risk factor for lifelong problems among a nationally representative sample of American men and women. In D. F. Schwartz (Ed.), *Children and violence: Report of the Twenty-Third Ross Roundtable on Critical Approaches to Common Pediatric Problems* (pp. 98–109). Columbus, OH: Ross Laboratories.

Straus, M. A., & Gelles, R. J. (Eds.). (1990). *Physical violence in American families: Risk factors and adaptations to violence in 8,145 families*. New Brunswick, NJ: Transaction Publishers.

Straus, M. A., Gelles, R. J., & Steinmetz, S. K. (1980). *Violence behind closed doors: Violence in the American family*. New York: Doubleday/Anchor.

Sutherland, C., Bybee, D., & Sullivan, C. (1998). The long-term effects of battering on women's health. *Women's Health: Research on Gender, Behavior and Policy, 4*, 41–70.

Tertinger, D. A., Greene, B. F., & Lutzker, J. R. (1984). Home safety: Development and validation of one component of an ecobehavioral treatment program for abused and neglected children. *Journal of Applied Behavior Analysis, 17*, 159–174.

Tjaden, P., & Thoennes, N. (1998). Prevalence, incidence, and consequences of violence against women: Findings from the National Violence Against Women

Survey. *National Institute of Justice and Centers for Disease Control and Prevention, research in brief.* Washington, DC: U.S. Department of Justice.

U.S. Department of Health and Human Services. (2000). *Healthy People 2010: Understanding and improving health.* Washington, DC: U.S. Government Printing Office.

U.S. Department of Health and Human Services, Administration on Children, Youth and Families. (2001). *Child Maltreatment 1999.* Retrieved February 26, 2002, from www.acf.dhhs.gov/programs/cb/publications/cm99/index.htm

Vernick, J. S., Li, G., Ogaitis, S., MacKenzie, E. J., Baker, S. P., & Gielen, A. C. (1999). Effects of high school driver education on motor vehicle crashes, violations, and licensure. *American Journal of Preventive Medicine, 16,* 40–46.

Walker, L. E. A. (1994). *Abused women and survivor therapy: A practical guide for the psychotherapist.* Washington, DC: American Psychological Association.

Walker, L. E. A. (1996). *The abused woman: A survivor therapy approach: A video.* New York: Newbridge Communications.

Walker, L. E. A. (1999). Psychology and domestic violence around the world. *American Psychologist, 54,* 21–29.

Walker, L. E. A. (2000). *The battered woman syndrome.* New York: Springer.

Wekerle, C., & Wolfe, D. A. (1999). Dating violence in mid-adolescence: Theory, significance, and emerging prevention initiatives. *Clinical Psychology Review, 19,* 435–456.

Widome, M. D. (1991). Foreword. In M. H. Wilson, S. P. Baker, S. P. Teret, S. Shock, & J. Garbarino (Eds.), *Saving children: A guide to injury prevention* (pp. v–vii). New York: Oxford University Press.

Wilson, M. H., Baker, S. P., Teret, S. P., Shock, S., & Garbarino, J. (Eds.). (1991). *Saving children: A guide to injury prevention.* New York: Oxford University Press.

Wolfe, D. A., Scott, K., Wekerle, C., & Pittman, A. (2001). Child maltreatment: Risk of adjustment problems and dating violence in adolescence. *Journal of the American Academy of Child and Adolescent Psychiatry, 40,* 282–298.

Wolfe, D. A., Wekerle, C., Gough, B., Reitzel-Jaffe, D., Grasley, C., Pittman, A., et al. (1996). *The Youth Relationships Manual: A group approach with adolescents for the prevention of woman abuse and the promotion of healthy relationships.* Thousand Oaks, CA: Sage.

Wolfe, D. A., Wekerle, C., Scott, K., Straatman, A., Grasley, C., & Reitzel-Jaffe, D. (2003). Dating violence prevention with at-risk youth: A controlled outcome evaluation. *Journal of Consulting and Clinical Psychology, 71,* 279–291.

Young, T. L., & Zimmerman, R. (1998). Clueless: Parental knowledge of risk behaviors of middle school students. *Archives of Pediatric and Adolescent Medicine, 152,* 1137–1139.

4

GENDER, STRESS, AND HEALTH

ANNETTE L. STANTON AND WILL COURTENAY

When asked to address the intersections of gender, stress, and health for the 2001 Presidential Miniconvention of the American Psychological Association and this book, we agreed that the task was both exciting and daunting. The rapid expansion of research in these areas in recent years provided a rich foundation for approaching these topics and necessitated that we be selective in our points of focus. Our charge was not to provide a broad overview of the field, but rather to highlight exciting new developments that carry implications for research and practice. We agreed that we would not adopt a traditional approach to women's and men's health focused on discrete, major diseases (e.g., cardiovascular disease and cancer) and their psychosocial concomitants for women and men. We refer the reader to good sources that do so (e.g., Blechman & Brownell, 1998; Gallant, Keita, & Royak-Schaler, 1997; Stanton & Gallant, 1995). Instead, we agreed to allow individual latitude in selecting the most exciting developments in the areas of men's and women's health and hence the very distinct approaches represented in each section of this chapter.

Developed by Dr. Courtenay, the section on men's health emphasizes the roles that men's beliefs and behaviors play in their health and the grounding of those beliefs and behaviors in the social environment. It outlines a model for working with men to promote their health and well-being. Written by Dr. Stanton, the next section illustrates contributors to women's health in several domains with the goal being to emphasize the point that determinants of women's health are located not solely within the individual but also within the environmental and social context and to describe exciting new research and conceptual initiatives that carry implications for the next generation of biopsychosocial research and practice in women's health.

Within each section, we focus more on within-sex parameters than on differences between women and men. We acknowledge, however, that any discussion of gender and health-related variables often invites gender comparisons, and we believe it important to cite related cautions. Specifically, gender comparisons often mask important within-group heterogeneity and between-group similarities. For example, Costa, Terracciano, and McCrae (2001) recently reported findings regarding the major personality dimensions in over 20,000 participants across more than 20 cultures, concluding that within-gender variability was of greater magnitude than were gender differences in personality attributes. A health-relevant example comes from the frequently cited finding that women live an average of 6 years longer than men in the United States. However, the three leading causes of death (i.e., diseases of the heart, malignant neoplasms, and cerebrovascular diseases) are identical for men and women. Further, within women, life expectancy for European American women is an average of 5 years longer than their African American counterparts (Hoyert, Arias, Smith, Murphy, & Kochanek, 2001). We also caution against using sex or gender as explanatory variables when a difference is found between women and men. Gender differences in cardiovascular disease morbidity and mortality, for example, may result from biological, behavioral, and environmental factors, and determinants are likely to be multifaceted. Until mechanisms are investigated, the finding of a gender difference reveals nothing about what produced the difference. Research on health- or stress-related gender differences is useful to the extent that it increases understanding of contributors to health and disease and to effective interventions for women and men.

ENGENDERING MEN'S HEALTH: AN EVIDENCE-BASED PSYCHOSOCIAL AND BEHAVIORAL MODEL

There is a gap between the life span of women and that of men, a gap that has widened steadily over the past century. Today in the United States, men die, on average, more than 6 years younger than women. For 14 of the 15 leading causes of death (the exception being Alzheimer's disease), and in every age group, men and boys have higher death rates than women and girls (U.S. Department of Health and Human Services

[USDHHS], 2000). Men's age-adjusted death rate for heart disease, for example, is nearly 2 times higher than women's rate, and the death rate for cancer is 1.5 times higher (USDHHS, 2000). Men also suffer more fatal chronic diseases than women (Verbrugge, 1988). One in four men age 18 to 64 years has been diagnosed with at least one of five chronic health conditions: hypertension, heart disease, diabetes, arthritis, or cancer (Sandman, Simantov, & An, 2000).

The health and well-being of men varies significantly with their ethnicity and age. Death rates are highest for economically disadvantaged men and for men of color. African American men die 7 years younger than European American men (USDHHS, 2000). The age group with the greatest gender disparity in mortality is 15- to 24-year-olds. Three out of every four deaths in this age group are men (USDHHS, 2000). The number of 15- to 24-year-old men who died in the United States in any 28-month period of the 1990s is equivalent to the 58,000 American men who died during the 11 years of the Vietnam War. By any definition, this represents a health crisis.

EXPLAINING MEN'S HEALTH RISKS: MEN'S ATTITUDES, HEALTH, BELIEFS, AND BEHAVIORS

The explanatory power of biological factors in predicting gender differences in morbidity and mortality is comparatively small (Krantz, Grunberg, & Baum, 1985; Verbrugge, 1989). The 6-year gender gap in longevity is explained largely by men's health beliefs and behaviors. For example, despite their high risks, 70% of men nationally consider their health to be either "excellent" or "very good" (USDHHS, 1998b) and rate their health as better than women do (Ross & Bird, 1994; USDHHS, 1998a)—even if they are found to be equally healthy as women and if they are matched for a variety of socioeconomic factors (Jenkins, 1985). Similarly, men are less likely than women to believe that personal behaviors contribute to good health (Verbrugge, 1989; Wilson & Elinson, 1981), or to accept personal responsibility for their health (Walker, Volkan, Sechrist, & Pender, 1988). Men are also less emotionally expressive than women—except when it comes to expressing anger (Balswick, 1982; Friedman, 1991; Hyde, 1986; Snell, 1989; Tannen, 1990; Williams, 1985). Furthermore, men manage their emotions—including anger and aggression—in less healthy ways than women do (Friedman, 1991). Similarly, men respond to stress in less healthy ways than women do. They are more likely than women to use avoidant coping strategies, such as denial, distraction, and increased alcohol consumption, and are less likely to employ healthy, vigilant coping strategies and to acknowledge that they need help (Friedman, 1991; Kopp, Skrabski, & Szedmak, 1998; Weidner & Collins, 1993). Compounding their unhealthy behavioral responses to stress, men exhibit greater psychophysiological responses during acute behavioral stress than women do, and men are slower to recover from stress (Matthews, Gump, & Owens, 2001; Polefrone & Manuck, 1987; Stone, Dembroski, Costa, & MacDougall, 1990; Stoney, Davis, & Matthews, 1987). All of these health beliefs and coping strategies increase men's risks.

Men's behaviors contribute greatly to their risks. Men are more likely than women to engage in over 30 behaviors that are associated with a greater risk of disease, injury, and death (Courtenay, 2000a; Courtenay, McCreary, & Merighi, in press). For example, men consume more meat, fat, and salt than women do, and consume less fiber and fewer fruits and vegetables. Contrary to popular belief, national data indicate that men are adopting increasingly less healthy exercise habits than women (Caspersen & Merritt, 1995). They are also less likely than women to engage in the types of exercise that experts now agree are the healthiest, such as walking and aerobics (Courtenay, 2000a). As a result of these factors, 59% of men—compared with 51% of women—are overweight (National Institutes of Health, 1998).

Automobile crashes are one of the leading causes of death for men, and the death rate for automobile crashes is more than twice as high for men as it is for women (USDHHS, 2000). Several behavioral factors help to explain this disparity. Men are less likely than women to wear safety belts, obey speed limits, stop at stop signs, or signal for turns (Courtenay, 2000a). Men also constitute 96% of all those charged with drunk driving (U.S. Department of Justice, 1994). As this evidence suggests, men's behaviors also increase the health risks of women and children. In California, men are at fault in nearly 8 of 10 fatal crashes and are responsible for twice as many injury crashes as women (California Highway Patrol, 1994). This example illustrates how women's health and men's health are relational and interdependent. They cannot be fully understood in isolation from each other.

The Influence of Gender

There are a variety of possible explanations for why men adopt beliefs and behaviors that undermine their own health and that of others. One explanation is the attitudes and beliefs about manhood that men adopt (Courtenay, 1998b, 2000b, 2000c). There is strong agreement among North Americans as to what constitute typically masculine characteristics: a man should be tough, robust, self-reliant, and assertive; and he should take risks and never cry (Golombok & Fivush, 1994; Martin, 1995; Williams & Best, 1990). Men who strongly endorse these beliefs increase their health risks. Research indicates that men with traditionally masculine beliefs about manhood have less healthy habits; experience higher levels of anxiety, depression, psychological stress; and adopt more maladaptive coping patterns than their less traditional peers (Eisler, Skidmore, & Ward, 1988; Good, Dell, & Mintz, 1989; McCreary, Newcomb, & Sadava, 1999; Neff, Prihoda, & Hoppe, 1991; O'Neil, Good, & Holmes, 1995). These men are also at greater risk of death (Lippa, Martin, & Friedman, 2000). Furthermore, there is broad support for these traditional beliefs. Among young men nationally, 86% agree that "a guy should be completely sure of himself"; 62% think that "a young man should be physically tough even if he is not big"; and 82% are "bothered when a guy acts like a girl" (Courtenay, 1998a). Men who agree with statements like these are more likely to engage in a variety of risky behaviors, such as smoking; alcohol and drug use; and unhealthy behaviors related to safety, diet, sleep, and sexual practices (e.g., Copenhaver & Eisler, 1996; Courtenay, 1998a; Eisler, 1995).

The resources available to men to demonstrate that they are men by and large involve unhealthy attitudes and behaviors. Some of the ways that boys prove their manhood in the United States include not backing down from fights, driving fast, drinking heavily, engaging in frequent sexual activities, denying pain, and playing risky sports. In fact, these behaviors are all more common among men than they are among women, and each of them increases men's health risks (Courtenay, 2000a). These behaviors also illustrate how masculinity and health risk occur in social and relational contexts. Mental health professionals generally locate masculinity and health behavior not in these contexts, but in men's individual psychologies. However, masculinity and risk taking are not simply inherent, psychological "traits." Boys are *taught* that it is manly to risk danger, that getting hurt is inevitable, and that bravely sustaining injury is admirable (Courtenay, 2000c). Risky behaviors then become ways for men to prove that they are "real" men—that they are fearless, strong, and invincible.

Another way that men prove their manhood is by delaying needed medical care and then bragging about it. If a woman were to say, "I haven't been to the doctor in years," her friends would be incredulous. But men often flaunt the statement like a badge of honor. Part of what a man is communicating when he says this is "I'm a *real* man, because I don't need a doctor!" The effects of demonstrating gender in this particular way can be devastating to men's health. Twice as many men (20%) as women (10%) have no regular source of medical care (Centers for Disease Control and Prevention [CDC], 1998), and 70% of those who have not visited a physician in more than 5 years are men (USDHHS, 1998b). Indeed, one in four men says that he would wait as long as possible before consulting a physician if he felt sick, experienced pain, or was concerned about his health (Sandman et al., 2000). Delays in obtaining timely health care can have profound consequences for men's health; early detection is often critical for preventing disease and premature death (USDHHS, 1998a). Nearly half of men with either prostate cancer or testicular cancer have advanced forms of these diseases when they are finally diagnosed (Gerber, Thompson, Thisted, & Chodak, 1993; Roth, Nichols, & Einhorn, 1993).

Although ethnicity and socioeconomic status are strongly associated with health and health care utilization, these factors do not explain gender differences in utilization rates. Among African Americans and Latinos, women make 1.5 times more physician visits than men do (Solis, Marks, Garcia, & Shelton, 1990; USDHHS, 1990). Even when there is no fee for those services—or when care is paid for through insured health plans—men still use fewer health services than women (Stockwell, Madhavan, Cohen, Gibson, & Alderman, 1994; Wells, Manning, Duan, Newhouse, & Ware, 1986). These findings indicate that factors other than socioeconomic status and ethnicity are influencing men's health care utilization. Indeed, research consistently indicates that men are less likely than women to have any *intention* to seek help, regardless of access—and that men with traditional beliefs about masculinity are even less likely to seek care (e.g., Ashton & Fuehrer, 1993; Good et al., 1989; Rule & Gandy, 1994).

Men and boys learn a variety of unhealthy attitudes and behaviors while they are growing up. Research consistently indicates that girls and boys are raised very differently, and that this has serious consequences for their health. Boys, even as infants, are handled more roughly than girls; male infants are perceived as firmer and less vulnerable physically than female infants, despite being more vulnerable; boys are discouraged from seeking help, and are often punished if they do; boys are exposed to more violence, both inside and outside the home; boys are exposed to less social interaction than girls; and boys, unlike girls, are encouraged to engage in risky games and activities (for a review see Courtenay, 2001). Society teaches boys many of the beliefs and behaviors that increase their risks. The health effects of these gender differences in socialization are seen early. Research indicates that boys are less likely than girls to talk about their symptoms, to show their feelings, to admit to being sick, or to use their school health services (for reviews see Kilmartin, 1994; Tinsley, 1992; Verbrugge, 1985).

Conflicting Messages

The messages men and boys receive about health often conflict with the messages they receive about manhood. Aggression provides one example. Health education campaigns attempt to teach men that violence is wrong and that it is inappropriate to be aggressive with their partners or on the road, yet they are encouraged to use aggressive force in sports, the military, and business (Courtenay, 1999). Three out of four Americans actually believe that it is important for a boy to have a few fistfights while he is growing up (Gelles & Straus, 1988). Not surprisingly, half of all young men get into a fight each year (Courtenay, 2000a). Physical fighting, however, is the very thing that most often leads to homicide among young men (Courtenay, 2000a). This example illustrates how a relational perspective on health must address not only relationships between women and men, but also relationships among men.

Men receive a variety of conflicting messages about health and manhood. Public health officials try to encourage men not to drink or use tobacco. However, *Sports Illustrated*—the magazine read most by men—has more alcohol and tobacco advertisements than any other magazine (Klein et al., 1993). Not surprisingly, both the quantity and the frequency of alcohol consumption are higher among men than women (Courtenay, 2000a; McCreary et al., 1999). Research consistently reveals greater problem and heavy drinking among men, and a higher prevalence of alcohol abuse and dependence (Courtenay, 2000a). Among adults nationally, men are three times more likely than women to binge drink (binge drinking is typically defined as consuming five or more drinks in one sitting) and seven times more likely to report chronic drinking (Powell-Griner, Anderson, & Murphy, 1997). Frequent binge drinkers are up to 10 times more likely than their nonbinging peers to have unprotected sex or to get injured. Men's smoking habits are also more dangerous than those of women. One in four men smokes, compared with one in five women (CDC, 2001a). Men are also less likely to quit, and they smoke more cigarettes per day, inhale more deeply, smoke fewer filter-tipped cigarettes, and smoke more high-tar and nicotine cigarettes than women do (see Courtenay, 2000a).

Improving Men's Health: The Six-Point HEALTH Plan

The good news is that even simple changes in lifestyle can postpone an estimated 4 out of 10 deaths (Louis Sullivan, as cited in Goldberg, 1993). In fact, changing unhealthy behaviors is one of the most effective ways to prevent disease. It is estimated, for example, that behavioral change can reduce the risk of cancer by half (Winawer & Shike, 1995). Furthermore, an estimated one half of all of men's deaths each year are preventable (U.S. Preventive Services Task Force [USPSTF], 1996). However, because masculinity is a unique contributor to men's risks, it is essential that gender be addressed in any interventions that are intended to improve men's health (Courtenay, 2002; Courtenay & Keeling, 2000). The Six-Point HEALTH Plan provides gender-specific clinical guidance for health professionals who work with men.

With a basis in hundreds of biopsychosocial and behavioral research studies, the Six-Point Plan summarizes Dr. Courtenay's clinical practice guideline for working with men (Courtenay, 2001). This guideline identifies behavioral and psychosocial factors that affect the onset, progression, and management of men's health problems; reviews evidence demonstrating the effectiveness of various interventions; and outlines specific recommendations for addressing these factors when working with men in clinical practice. Psychologists and other mental health professionals are ideally suited to apply these best practices to improve men's health, because, as indicated previously, men's greatest health risks are the result of modifiable psychosocial and behavioral factors. Because men make infrequent health care visits, it is important for health professionals to use the Six-Point Plan. Any encounter a health professional has with a man—particularly a young or middle-aged man—may be the only opportunity for assessment and intervention that any health professional will have with that man for a very long time. It is essential that we make the most of these opportunities.

The plan includes specific communication strategies for clinicians who work directly with men. The American Medical Association has referred to the lack of effective clinician–patient communication as a health hazard for men (AMA, 1991a). Poor communication is associated with inaccurate diagnoses, poor compliance and outcomes, and low knowledge and knowledge retention (Davis & Fallowfield, 1991). Conversely, effective patient and clinician communication has been found to be associated with improved compliance and better patient health status, as measured physiologically, behaviorally, and subjectively (Cramer & Spilker, 1991; Hall, Roter, & Katz, 1988; Kaplan, Greenfield, & Ware, 1989; Meichenbaum & Turk, 1987). Because the learning patterns and conversational styles of women and men in this society differ distinctively, and because women and men respond to and accept information differently (Golombok & Fivush, 1994; Tannen, 1990), if these interventions are to be effective it is imperative that health professionals incorporate what is currently understood about these gender differences into their interventions with men.

Each point represents one of six types of interventions discussed in the clinical practice guideline. Together, the titles of the six points form an acronym that spells HEALTH: Humanize, Educate, Assume the worst, Locate supports, Tailor a plan, and Highlight strengths. Whether a health professional is treating men in a clinical setting, developing gender-specific programming for men, or designing health education materials, the same basic principles of the Six-Point Plan hold true.

Humanize

The first step in working with men is to humanize. Humanizing is a technique in patient counseling that validates, legitimizes, or normalizes their health problems and concerns. Conveying to patients that their feelings and experiences are understandable or legitimate—and that other people would probably feel the same way—is considered essential to effective communication with patients (Gruninger, 1995). Humanizing is especially important with men. Attending to health matters has historically been socially sanctioned and encouraged among women, but not men (Courtenay, 2000b, 2000c; Oakley, 1994). Consequently, many men associate health matters with womanly matters, and men receive strict social prohibitions against doing anything that women do (Courtenay, 2000c). Because disease, disability, and behavioral responses to illness are antithetical to traditional meanings of manhood, men can experience embarrassment and shame when they do have health problems (Charmaz, 1995; Courtenay, 2000c).

Specific aspects of men's experience that should be humanized include help-seeking, illness and vulnerability, pain, rest and recovery, and sexuality (Courtenay, 2001). Clinicians need to convey to patients that they are not lesser men if they experience these things. Needing help, being ill, and experiencing pain are not unmanly; they are human. Compared with women, men report less pain for the same pathology, less severe pain, greater tolerance of pain and higher pain thresholds, and shorter duration of pain (Miaskowski, 1999; Unruh, Ritchie, & Merskey, 1999). Although hormones may play some role in mediating the experience of pain (Miaskowski, 1999), it is clear that psychosocial factors do, too. Men have been found to report less pain in front of female health professionals than male health professionals (Levine & DeSimone, 1991; Puntillo & Weiss, 1994). A man may need to experience literally intolerable pain before he can acknowledge to himself or to others that he is hurting. The reluctance to acknowledge or report physical or emotional distress can have far-reaching implications for men's health; it can influence help-seeking decisions, delay intervention, and undermine diagnosis and treatment planning. In humanizing pain, clinicians should label conditions known to be painful as such and express surprise if a man claims that he does not experience any discomfort. It may also be necessary to humanize the need for pain medication.

Men also often need permission to rest. When they are ill, men are less likely than women to restrict their activities or stay in bed for both acute and chronic conditions (Courtenay, 2000a). Some men consider staying in bed to rest or recover to be pampering, and by traditional standards, men should not pamper their bodies (Courtenay, 2000c). It is also important to humanize sexuality. Masculinity presumes perfect sexual functioning at all times, so it can be threatening for a man to acknowledge a sexual problem. At least three out of four men with sexual concerns report not discussing those concerns with their physician, and report that they are deterred from doing so by embarrassment (AMA, 1991b; Metz & Seifert, 1990). Humanizing sexuality gives men permission to discuss their concerns by normalizing sexual problems or fears among men. Finally, because male patients typically think that men should be self-sufficient and not need help, when a man does attend an appointment the clinician should reframe his getting help as a positive step. Reframing a man's help-seeking as an act of strength, courage, and self-determination may decrease any embarrassment or self-doubt that he may experience in asking for help. A clinician can reconceptualize help-seeking by saying, for example, "Getting in here today was the best thing you could have done!"

Educate

The second point is to educate. For many men, health care is simply a conundrum. Men are not socialized into health care as women are. Unlike most adolescent girls, boys do not receive annual exams and are not taught how to listen to, talk about, and take care of their bodies. Historically, for example, health education generally and cancer education specifically have been directed primarily at women (Oakley, 1994; Reagan, 1997). One consequence of this differential socialization is the fact that men and boys are far less knowledgeable than women and girls about health in general and about specific diseases in particular (see Courtenay, 1998b, 2000c). To make matters worse, men are provided with fewer and briefer explanations— as well as less information overall—from clinicians during medical examinations (for a review see Roter & Hall, 1997a). Furthermore, although men engage in more unhealthy behaviors, they are less likely than women to be counseled by clinicians about changing those behaviors (Friedman, Brownson, Peterson, & Wilkerson, 1994). For example, only 29% of physicians routinely provide age-appropriate instruction on performing self-exams for testicular cancer, compared to 86% who provide age-appropriate instruction to women on performing breast self-exams (Misener & Fuller, 1995).

There is a wealth of evidence indicating that health education can help to reduce risks, improve compliance, facilitate change, and promote health (see McCann & Blossom, 1990; USPSTF, 1996). In fact, research indicates that it is essential that men be educated if they are to change their unhealthy behaviors (see Courtenay, 1998a). A good way to start educating a man is by saying, "You know, most of the things that have the biggest impact on your health are completely within your control."

When educating men, clinicians need to include even very basic knowledge—such as whom to call for an appointment—because many men have had relatively little experience with the health care system. Clinicians should keep the information simple, provide written materials, and make statements and written materials both clear and direct (Meichenbaum & Turk, 1987; USPSTF, 1996). They should also provide alternative responses to unhealthy behaviors, assess the patient's comprehension, and discuss with him whatever was explained (Courtenay, 2001; Meichenbaum & Turk, 1987). Having a patient restate the information is the only way a clinician can really tell whether a man understands what he was told. For similar reasons, it is important that a patient demonstrate any task that he has been shown (Kacmarek, 1994; Meichenbaum & Turk, 1987). If a man does not understand instructions, it is unlikely that he will ask for clarification. It is also important that clinicians encourage questions. Men ask health professionals fewer questions than women do (e.g., Kaplan, Gandek, Greenfield, Rogers, & Ware, 1995; Waitzkin, 1985). All of these intervention strategies are associated with improved outcomes.

Assume the Worst

The third point is to assume the worst. Men often deny their physical or emotional distress, and attempt to conceal their illnesses or disabilities (Charmaz, 1995; Courtenay, 2000c, 2001; Sutkin & Good, 1987). Compared with women, men are less likely to confide in friends, express vulnerability, disclose their problems, or seek help or support from others (see Courtenay 1998b, 2000b, 2000c). One in five men nationally says that he is not comfortable discussing his feelings with a doctor (Sandman et al., 2000). Among people with depression, men are more likely than women to rely on themselves, to withdraw socially, or to try to talk themselves out of it (see Courtenay, 2000b). In a recent national survey, one in four men reported a high level of depressive symptoms; another one third reported a moderate level (Sandman et al., 2000). The same survey found that although 1 man in 10 nationwide thought he needed to consult with a health professional because he felt depressed or anxious, only half of those men actually saw one. As a result of these factors, it is essential for clinicians to assume the worst, and to remember that a man may not verbalize his need for help.

An additional reason for assuming the worst is that health professionals can also be blinded by gender stereotypes. Depression provides one example. Research consistently indicates that clinicians are less likely to diagnose depression correctly in men than in women (Borowsky et al., 2000; Potts, Burnam, & Wells, 1991). This in turn contributes to suicide rates that are up to 12 times higher for men (USDHHS, 1993). Assuming the worst compensates for this tendency among clinicians to overlook or underestimate men's vulnerability.

Health professionals also need to help men to start assuming the worst about themselves. Research consistently indicates that men are less likely than women to perceive themselves as being at risk for illness, injury, and a variety of health problems for which they are in fact at greater risk, including automobile crashes; HIV; skin cancer; and the risks associated with smoking, drug and alcohol use, and dangerous sports (Courtenay, 1998b, 2000a; Cutter, Tiefenbacher, & Solecki, 1992; DeJoy, 1992; Gustafson, 1998; Savage, 1993; Weissfeld, Kirscht, & Brock, 1990). Men's perceived invulnerability can prevent them from practicing preventive care or changing unhealthy behavior, such as not using sunscreen or performing self-testicular exams, thus actually increasing their health risks (Janz & Becker, 1984; Kreuter & Strecher, 1995; Mermelstein & Riesenberg, 1992; Reno, 1988; Rosenstock, 1990; Taylor, 1986; Weinstein, 1987). Perceived invulnerability has also been linked with poor compliance (Friedman & DiMatteo, 1989).

Locate Supports

The next point is to locate supports. Men are taught to value independence, autonomy, and self-sufficiency in themselves (Courtenay, 2000c). It is not surprising then that men have fewer friendships and smaller social networks than women do, and that they tend not to use the support that they do have (Courtenay, 2000a). This limited social support threatens men's lives. There is overwhelming evidence that social relationships are strongly associated with health and longevity (Courtenay, 2000a). Consequently, single men have greater health risks than any other group. Being a single man is associated with the poorest health behavior; the most drinking and smoking; the greatest STD risk; and the fewest health care visits (Courtenay, 2000a).

It is essential that men recognize and make use of the friends and family that are available to them. Health professionals can help them to identify these people, as well as support groups and social activities—such as church and organized sports—which can be valuable sources of social support. Clinicians should ask each male patient, "Who are the people you're most comfortable asking to give you a hand?" It is important to encourage men to reach out to these people, because often they will not do so of their own accord. Clinicians should also keep in mind that they too are an important source of support, particularly for single men. One effective, low-cost means of providing support to men is through follow-up phone contact, which is associated with a variety of positive outcomes (Meichenbaum & Turk, 1987; USPSTF, 1996).

Tailor a Plan

The next point is to tailor a plan. This means devising a health maintenance plan, like a maintenance schedule for a car. A man is more likely to have a maintenance plan for his car than for himself. Developing and implementing such a plan is associated with improved treatment follow-through and behavioral change (see Courtenay, 2001; Meichenbaum & Turk, 1987; Prochaska, Norcross, & DiClemente, 1994). Some of the items that a health maintenance plan might include are a vitamin or medication regimen, a list of relevant self-care techniques and self-examinations, including dates or times for carrying them out, a diet plan, and a schedule of physicals and screenings. Regular physicals are especially important. They are one of the most consistent ways that people get screened for cancer, for example (Bostick, Sprafka, Virnig, & Potter, 1993; Polednak, 1990). Diet and exercise are also critical. Poor diet and a lack of regular exercise are significant contributors to both heart disease and cancer, which are the leading causes of death for men (USDHHS, 1998a).

"Tailoring" the plan means individualizing it to the patient's needs, age, intellectual capacity, attitudes, cultural background, and circumstances; this is considered essential both in establishing a plan and in fostering adherence (Meichenbaum & Turk, 1987). For the plan to be successful it must be realistic; it must be broken down into attainable steps; and the patient must have the skills necessary to carry it out (Meichenbaum & Turk, 1987; Prochaska et al., 1994; USPSTF, 1996). Clinicians should invite the patient's own input and suggestions, and help him to identify potential obstacles (McCann & Blossom, 1990). He may know, for example, that if he drinks he is not likely to use a condom. It is also beneficial to develop a verbal or written contract, with dates for achieving specific goals (Meichenbaum & Turk, 1987). All of these factors are associated with improved outcomes.

Highlight Strengths

The last point of the Six-Point Plan is to highlight strengths. Health professionals who identify and emphasize the strengths of their patients increase their motivation, improve their follow-through, and foster behavioral change (Meichenbaum & Turk, 1987). The fact is that whereas many traditionally masculine behaviors do hurt men, some of those same behaviors can be turned to a health advantage. For example, being intellectual, logical, and rational are highly valued coping mechanisms among men (Eisler, 1995; Meth, 1990). This can create problems when a partner wants to know what is in a man's heart, not in his head, but it can be an asset when a man is learning about his health. So clinicians should emphasize the intellectual aspects of health education, and in general, draw on men's strengths when trying to interest them in their health. Setting goals and keeping score are popular male pastimes in this society. In fact, men engage in more action-oriented, problem-solving, and goal-setting coping than women do (see Courtenay, 2001). Goal setting is also an effective way to modify behavior and improve health (Little, Stevens, Severson, & Lichtenstein, 1992; Meichenbaum & Turk, 1987), so clinicians can frame health goals as targets to shoot for. Similarly, they can capitalize on a man's talent for keeping baseball scores when he is tracking cholesterol, blood pressure, or behavioral change.

A crucial part of highlighting men's strengths is empowering them to be engaged in their own health care. For most men, health care is something that is done to them; it is not something in which they see themselves as active participants. Clinicians need to invite a man's active involvement and emphasize teamwork. Men are often most comfortable engaging in relationships through action and by doing things, such as projects, together (see Courtenay, 2001). A relationship with a health professional can be ideal for a man, if it is approached as teamwork. This kind of patient-clinician collaboration has also been found to increase treatment follow-through (McCann & Blossom, 1990; Meichenbaum & Turk, 1987; O'Brien, Petrie, & Raeburn, 1992). A good way to begin is for a clinician to ask, "Where do you want to start?" This communicates to a male patient that successful treatment will require his participation.

Conclusion

In this section Dr. Courtenay provided an overview of the psychosocial and behavioral factors that influence men's health and outlined the Six-Point Plan, which summarizes the findings and recommendations of a clinical practice guideline for working with men. Men are subject to serious health risks, which are compounded by their gendered health behaviors and beliefs—including their beliefs about manhood. If health professionals take these six steps, their male patients are likely to live longer, healthier lives.

PSYCHOSOCIAL AND STRESS-RELATED CONTRIBUTORS TO WOMEN'S HEALTH

Underlining the point that health is not located within the individual woman, but also in her surrounding context, this section will offer examples in three domains of contributors to the health of women: the environmental context, the interpersonal context, and the personal context. The goal is not to provide a broad overview, but rather to highlight empirical developments and emerging perspectives that promise to contribute to our understanding of women's health.

The Environmental Context and Women's Health

Illustrations of important environmental contributors to women's health include sociodemographic factors, traditions within the medical system of care for and research on women, and social role occupancy. With regard to demographic parameters, socioeconomic status is a well-known correlate of morbidity and mortality (Adler & Coriell, 1997). Because women are more likely to live in poverty, this relation is of particular concern. Health-related differences among women as a function of ethnicity highlight the importance of attending to within-group diversity. For example, the 5-year survival rate for breast cancer is considerably lower in African American women (71%) than in White women (86%; American Cancer Society, 2001). Explanations for this difference are multifaceted and include such factors as access to medical care, delay in diagnosis, and estrogen receptor status of the breast tumor (see Meyerowitz, Richardson, Hudson, & Leedham, 1998, for a review). Another example of the diversity among women is in smoking prevalence. In this case, Native American women are particularly at risk, with a 34% smoking rate, as compared with 24% White, 22% African American, 14% Latina, and 11% Asian American/ Pacific Islander women (CDC, 2001b). Lesbians also are more likely to smoke than are heterosexual women (Institute of Medicine, 1999). Rates of smoking in adolescent girls also are cause for concern. Obesity, another important risk factor for morbidity and mortality, also evidences significant ethnic differences, with a 38% age-adjusted rate of obesity (Body Mass Index > 30) in Black, non-Hispanic women, a 26% rate in Hispanic women, and a 19% rate in White women (National Center for Health Statistics, 2000). Accompanying differences in socioeconomic status account only in part for these differences.

Another contributor to women's health that can be considered part of the environmental context involves the tradition of medical care and research for women. A recent report (Brett & Burt, 2001) documented that women are twice as likely as men to attend medical appointments unrelated to illness. This is likely good news, in that such appointments most often are for regular or preventive care. The work of Roter and others also suggests that women are likely to receive more information during medical appointments, although physician gender appears to be a more potent factor than patient gender in determining the nature of the interaction (Roter & Hall, 1997b). Consistent evidence exists that a strong predictor of several health-related behaviors (e.g., mammography use) is the physician's recommendation (e.g., Royak-Schaler, Stanton, & Danoff-Burg, 1997). Unfortunately, considerable research documents under-referral of women for particular procedures (e.g., mammogram and cardiac diagnostic testing), treatments (e.g., cardiac rehabilitation), and health-enhancing behaviors (e.g., exercise and quitting smoking; e.g., Shumaker & Smith, 1995). For example, a recent study revealed that less than 30% of women report that their physicians ever discuss heart disease with them (Mosca et al., 2000).

Although women's health is gaining more empirical attention, discrepancies remain. For example, a recent report of the United States General Accounting Office (2001) revealed that the Food and Drug Administration still is failing to oversee gender-specific analyses of medication effects in applications for new medications. Furthermore, although 43% of myocardial infarctions are incurred by women, of participants in recent randomized, controlled trials of treatments for myocardial infarction or angina, only 25% were women (Yee, Alexander, Hammill, Pasquali, & Peterson, 2001). This under-attention to women's health in some realms within the medical sphere is a barrier to optimal health for women.

A third aspect of the environmental context that contributes to the health of women is their role occupancy. A body of research suggests that women's engagement in multiple, valued roles is protective for their health (e.g., Barnett & Hyde, 2001). However, particular aspects of roles also can confer risk. For example, Frankenhauser's research (1994) with business managers suggested that men are likely to unwind physiologically (e.g., norepinephrine and blood pressure) when they return home from work, whereas women are more prone to wind up, particularly if they have young children. Over the long run, such prolonged arousal may take a physical toll.

As demonstrated in a meta-analysis of gender differences in self-reported stress involving over 80,000 participants in 119 studies (Davis, Matthews, & Twamley, 1999), women are likely to report higher stress exposure and appraisal than men in both work and interpersonal roles. The difference is stronger for interpersonal stress, with an obtained 9% disadvantage for women with regard to interpersonal roles. In general the 141 effect sizes were relatively small and heterogeneous, however, suggesting that it is important to identify the specific conditions under which women are likely to experience greater stress. One interpersonal role that may be particularly challenging is the caregiver role. Although this role can bring many rewards, it may also carry burdens. In reporting stressful events, women report more events pertinent to their social networks. They also are likely to be the primary caregivers for ill or elderly loved ones. For example, women are at least twice as likely as men to care for sick or disabled relatives, and they can expect to spend 18 years caring for a parent (see Donelan, Falik, & DesRoches, 2001). Research such as Kiecolt-Glaser's (e.g., Kiecolt-Glaser, Glaser, Gravenstein, Malarkey, & Sheridan, 1996) on spousal caregiving for individuals with Alzheimer's disease documents the negative health consequences for the caregiver (e.g., immune compromise). In addition to being shaped by the environmental and cultural context, the caregiver role also could be considered part of the interpersonal context, pointing to the interrelations of the major domains of contributors to women's health. It is to the more specific interpersonal context that we now turn.

The Interpersonal Context and Women's Health

Any treatment of contributors to women's health needs to acknowledge the profound effects of violence on the health of women. Violence toward women, particularly by their partners, is a significant contributor to morbidity and mortality, and estimates of lifetime prevalence of male partner violence exceed 20% (see Koss, Ingram, & Pepper, 2001, for a review). These sobering data remind us that to promote women's health, we often need to consider interventions directed toward men.

Interactional processes in intimate relationships also are important contributors to women's health. In an important recent paper, Kiecolt-Glaser and Newton (2001) reviewed 64 investigations of the relations between marriage and physiological processes or other markers of health conducted in the past decade. A consistent finding over many years is the association of being married with better health, both with regard to morbidity and mortality and acute and chronic conditions. This relation between marital status and health, however, is stronger for men than women. For example, Ross, Mirowsky, and Goldstein (1990) found that unmarried women had 50% greater mortality than married women, whereas unmarried men had 250% greater mortality than married men.

Kiecolt-Glaser and Newton (2001) focused attention on the mechanisms for the relationship between marriage and health, and their review yielded several intriguing conclusions. First, they postulated a direct pathway from marital functioning to physiological functioning. A study by Zautra and colleagues (1998) of women with rheumatoid arthritis offers an example of the link between marital functioning and specific disease parameters. In this longitudinal study, disease activity increased following interpersonal stress, but positive marital interaction buffered this relation. Specifically, women who reported more positive marital interactions or fewer criticisms by their husbands were protected from the increase in disease activity following interpersonal stress. Kiecolt-Glaser and Newton cited consistent evidence that marital conflict behaviors produce greater and more prolonged physiological reactivity in women than men in the realms of cardiovascular, endocrine, and immune functioning. These findings conflict with those in studies that manipulate stress in the laboratory, for example through achievement-related tasks, for men or women individually, which typically suggest that men demonstrate greater physiological reactivity than women. In an interesting study, Smith, Gallo, Goble, Ngu, and Stark (1998) manipulated both communal (i.e., disagreement) and achievement-related stressors in marital dyads discussing topics unrelated to their marriage. Disagreement elicited stronger cardiovascular responses in women, and the achievement challenge prompted greater reactivity in men. Thus, women may be particularly sensitive physiologically to their intimate, interpersonal context, whereas men may react more strongly to agentic challenge. Kiecolt-Glaser and Newton also cited data suggesting that physiological responses to marital conflict may be amplified for women when their husbands are high in trait hostility, whereas men's physiological reactivity appears more responsive to their own hostility than to that of their partners. Continued study is necessary to determine whether physiological alteration of the magnitude and duration invoked through marital parameters is sufficient to determine ultimate health outcomes; however, Kiecolt-Glaser and Newton made a good case for the contention that such physiological processes indeed may be sufficient to produce clinically relevant health consequences.

Marital functioning also may influence health indirectly, through its association with depressive symptoms. Depressive symptoms are a demonstrated risk factor for negative health consequences such as cardiovascular morbidity and mortality (e.g., Barefoot et al., 2000), perhaps through their association with physiological compromise or poor health habits. Finally, partners may influence each other's health habits, in both positive and negative directions. Evidence suggests that women attempt to influence men's health behaviors more than the reverse and that positive influence attempts can be effective in changing health behaviors (e.g., Lewis & Rook, 1999).

Kiecolt-Glaser and Newton's (2001) review clearly demonstrates the importance of considering the interpersonal context as a contributor to health outcomes. Interactions within intimate relationships may be a potent catalyst of health-related outcomes in women, both for better and for worse. The authors suggested that women's self-construals and personality attributes, as well as normative inequities in marital and familial roles between women and men, may explain the stronger link between relational processes and health for women than for men. Clearly, sustained research on the impact of the interpersonal context on health for women is essential, as is translation of this knowledge into effective interventions.

The Personal Context and Women's Health

A number of personal attributes have been linked to health outcomes in women, including factors such as conscientiousness, optimism, positive and negative affectivity, and hostility (for reviews, see Friedman, 2000; Smith & Gallo, 2001). For example, a recent study (Danner, Snowden, & Friesen, 2001) demonstrated that positive emotions expressed in written essays by nuns in young adulthood predicted longevity 6 decades later. We recently found that coping through emotional expression predicted better self-reported health and fewer medical appointments for cancer-related morbidities in a longitudinal study of breast cancer patients (Stanton et al., 2000). Such links between personal attributes and health outcomes may be mediated through direct physiological pathways, health behaviors, or other processes.

Of course, an understanding of women's biology with reference to health outcomes also is important. For example, the protective effects of estrogen with regard to heart disease, in part through influences on the arterial wall and on lipid profiles, are well documented. This section highlights a provocative new conceptualization suggesting that women may have distinct biobehavioral responses to threat.

In their exciting contribution, Taylor and colleagues (2000) pointed out that existing models of the stress response focus on activation of the sympathetic-adrenal-medullary system and the hypothalamic-pituitary-adrenal axis in prompting an evolutionarily adaptive flight, fight, or freeze response. They argued that these models obscure potentially important behavioral and biological gender differences and point out that women are under-represented in experimental investigations of physiological and neuroendocrine responses to acute stress. Acknowledging that men and women are similar in the basic core of the stress response, Taylor and colleagues proposed a tend-and-befriend model to characterize stress responses that are more uniquely female. Drawing evidence from hundreds of studies of humans and other animals, they suggested that adaptive responses to stress in females are likely to involve efforts to tend, that is to nurture the self and others, and to befriend, that is to create and maintain social networks to provide protection from external threats. The authors suggested that these behaviors are likely to be prompted by the biobehavioral attachment and caregiving system, which depends in part on hormonal mechanisms. They focused particularly on the putative role of oxytocin and endogenous opioids in downregulating the stress response in women. These mechanisms may be sensitive to environmental input and individual differences. For example, Turner, Altemus, Enos, Cooper, and McGuinness (1999) found that oxytocin increased in response to positive emotions only in women who were involved in intimate relationships and that oxytocin depletion in response to negative emotions was related to greater interpersonal distress.

Taylor and colleagues also acknowledged potentially important roles for higher-order cortical and social mechanisms in women's stress responses, as well as the importance of considering the nature of the particular stressor. Although they focused on biobehavioral underpinnings of the model, they cautioned against reductionism and the assumption that a biological mechanism produces behavioral inflexibility. As they pointed out,

> Biology is not so much destiny as it is a central tendency, but a central tendency that influences and interacts with social, cultural, cognitive, and emotional factors that result in substantial behavioral flexibility. . . . Rather than viewing social roles and biology as alternative accounts of human behavior, a more productive theoretical and empirical strategy will be to recognize how biology and social roles are inextricably interwoven to account for the remarkable flexibility of human behavior. (p. 423)

The tend-and-befriend model will require a broadening of our research agenda to consider unique facets of the stress response and its health consequences for women and men. Although many of its propositions currently rely on evidence from animal models and require testing in humans, it has the potential to promote a greater understanding of the place of stress in behavioral and health-related outcomes. It also may foster the development of gender-sensitive interventions for managing stress and promoting the health of women.

Implications for Promoting the Health of Women

Clearly, the foregoing demonstrates that we are in the midst of an exciting time in women's health research and that researchers are considering the joint and reciprocal influences of environmental, interpersonal, and individual contexts of stress-related processes and health outcomes. In addition, several exciting empirical and applied developments are underway, including the Women's Health Initiative (WHI; e.g., Matthews et al., 1997), which promise to advance this area further. For example, the WHI randomized, controlled trial of estrogen plus progestin versus placebo for coronary heart disease prevention was halted in 2002 because the health risks were determined to exceed the benefits in 16,608 postmenopausal women with an intact uterus at baseline (Rossouw et al., 2002). The federally established National Centers of Excellence in Women's Health also will promote treatment and research.

The burgeoning empirical foundation on women's health and stress-related processes poses a formidable task for those of us who are health psychologists or who wish to expand practice in this area. Clinicians' ethical obligation to maintain current knowledge in their areas of expertise is challenged when a knowledge base is expanding rapidly. An excellent paper first-authored by Cynthia Belar, the executive director of the American Psychological Association's Education Directorate (Belar et al., 2001), suggested a strategy for self-assessment to maintain competence in the practice of clinical health psychology.

The growing empirical foundation also points the way to exciting opportunities for intervention at multiple levels to improve women's health. System-level interventions are necessary to enhance women's health through decreasing barriers to health care, ethnic disparities, caregiver and other role burdens, and violence toward women. Reduction of caregiver burden through provision of systemic supports, for example, is likely to be more effective than interventions directed toward the individual caregiver. Collaborative interventions with other health care providers also are essential to address multilevel contributors to women's health.

Although some couples-level interventions to promote health have not yielded strong results, we have not yet tapped the promise of approaches directed toward couples that are sensitive to relationship and individual dynamics pertinent to particular health issues. Research by Keefe and colleagues (1996, 1999) on spouse-assisted coping skills training for participants experiencing pain from osteoarthritis is an example of an effective couples-directed approach.

Certainly, many effective interventions are directed toward the individual woman. For example, interventions are available or in development to aid women making decisions about hormone replacement therapy (Bastian et al., 1999), to reduce menopausal symptoms in breast cancer survivors (Ganz et al., 2000), and to decrease women's risk behaviors for HIV infection (e.g., Hobfoll, Jackson, Lavin, Britton, & Sheperd, 1994). Such interventions often share effective ingredients (e.g., Exner, Seal, & Ehrhardt, 1997; Rimer, McBride, & Crump, 2001). The provision of multiple contacts or sources of intervention, as well as training in specific skills, often are helpful. Another useful approach involves embedding consideration of the environmental and interpersonal context within the intervention and tailoring the intervention to women's unique life circumstances. For example, HIV risk behavior reduction is more beneficial for women if it promotes skills relevant to relationships and negotiation (Exner et al., 1997).

An integrated approach to addressing stress- and health-related concerns of women requires consideration of the environmental, interpersonal, biological, and personal contexts of women's lives, as well as acknowledgment of within-group diversity. Only through the integration of cutting-edge research with evidence-based interventions will we address complex biopsychosocial contributors and thereby most effectively promote the health of both women and men.

REFERENCES

Adler, N. E., & Coriell, M. (1997). Socioeconomic status and women's health. In S. J. Gallant, G. P. Keita, & R. Royak-Schaler (Eds.), *Health care for women: Psychological, social, and behavioral influences* (pp. 11–23). Washington, DC: American Psychological Association.

American Cancer Society. (2001). *Cancer facts and figures 2001.* Atlanta, GA: American Cancer Society.

American Medical Association. (1991a, October). *Lack of doctor–patient communication hazard in older men* [News release]. Chicago, IL: Author.

American Medical Association. (1991b, October). *Results of 9/91 Gallup survey on older men's health perceptions and behaviors* [News release]. Chicago, IL: Author.

Ashton, W. A., & Fuehrer, A. (1993). Effects of gender and gender role identification of participant and type of social support resource on support seeking. *Sex Roles, 28*(7/8), 461–476.

Balswick, J. O. (1982). Male inexpressiveness: Psychological and social aspects. In K. Solomon & N. B. Levy (Eds.), *Men in transition: Theory and therapy* (pp. 131–150). New York: Plenum Press.

Barefoot, J. C., Brummett, B. H., Helms, M. J., Mark, D. B., Siegler, I. C., & Williams, R. B. (2000). Depressive symptoms and survival of patients with coronary heart disease. *Psychosomatic Medicine, 62,* 790–795.

Barnett, R. C., & Hyde, J. S. (2001). Women, men, work, and family: An expansionist theory. *American Psychologist, 56,* 781–796.

Bastian, L., McBride, C., Halabi, S., Fish, L., Skinner, C., Kaplan, E., et al. (1999). Attitudes and knowledge associated with being undecided about hormone replacement therapy: Results from a community sample. *Women's Health Issues, 9,* 330–337.

Belar, C. D., Brown, R. A., Hersch, L. E. Hornyak, L. M., Rozensky, R. H., Sheridan, E. P., et al. (2001). Self-assessment in clinical health psychology: A model for ethical expansion of practice. *Professional Psychology: Research and Practice, 32,* 135–141.

Blechman, E. A., & Brownell, K. D. (Eds.). (1998). *Behavioral medicine for women: A comprehensive handbook.* New York: Guilford Press.

Borowsky, S. J., Rubenstein, L. V., Meredith, L. S., Camp, P., Jackson-Triche, M., & Wells, K. B. (2000). Who is at risk of nondetection of mental health problems in primary care? *Journal of General Internal Medicine, 15*(6), 381–388.

Bostick, R. M., Sprafka, J. M., Virnig, B. A., & Potter, J. D. (1993). Knowledge, attitudes, and personal practices regarding prevention and early detection of cancer. *Preventive Medicine, 22,* 65–85.

Brett, K. M., & Burt, C. W. (July, 2001). Utilization of ambulatory care by women: United States, 1997–98. *Vital and Health Statistics* (Series 13, No. 149; DHHS Publication [PHS] 2001-1720). Hyattsville, MD: U.S. Department of Health and Human Services.

California Highway Patrol. (1994). *1993 annual report of fatal and injury motor vehicle traffic accidents.* Sacramento, CA: Author.

Caspersen, C. J., & Merritt, R. K. (1995). Physical activity trends among 26 states, 1986–1990. *Medicine and Science in Sports and Exercise, 27*(5), 713–720.

Centers for Disease Control and Prevention. (1998). Demographic characteristics of persons without a regular source of medical care—Selected states, 1995. *Morbidity and Mortality Weekly Report, 47*(14), 277–279.

Centers for Disease Control and Prevention. (2001a). Cigarette smoking among adults—United States, 1999. *Morbidity and Mortality Weekly Report, 50*(40), 869–873.

Centers for Disease Control and Prevention. (2001b). *Women and smoking: A report of the Surgeon General—2001.* Atlanta, GA: Author.

Charmaz, K. (1995). Identity dilemmas of chronically ill men. In D. Sabo & D. F. Gordon (Eds.), *Men's health and illness: Gender, power and the body* (pp. 266–291). Thousand Oaks, CA: Sage.

Copenhaver, M. M., & Eisler, R. M. (1996). Masculine gender role stress: A perspective on men's health. In P. M. Kato & T. Mann (Eds.), *Handbook of diversity issues in health psychology* (pp. 219–235). New York: Plenum.

Costa, P. T., Terracciano, A., & McCrae, R. R. (2001). Gender differences in personality traits across cultures: Robust and surprising findings. *Journal of Personality and Social Psychology, 81*, 322–331.

Courtenay, W. H. (1998a). Better to die than cry? A longitudinal and constructionist study of masculinity and the health risk behavior of young American men (Doctoral dissertation, University of California at Berkeley, 1998). *Dissertation Abstracts International, 59*(08A). (Publication number AAT 9902042)

Courtenay, W. H. (1998b). College men's health: An overview and a call to action. *Journal of American College Health, 46*(6), 279–290.

Courtenay, W. H. (1999). *Youth* violence? Let's call it what it is. *Journal of American College Health, 48*(3), 141–142.

Courtenay, W. H. (2000a). Behavioral factors associated with disease, injury, and death among men: Evidence and implications for prevention. *Journal of Men's Studies, 9*(1), 81–142.

Courtenay, W. H. (2000b). Constructions of masculinity and their influence on men's well-being: A theory of gender and health. *Social Science and Medicine, 50*(10), 1385–1401.

Courtenay, W. H. (2000c). Engendering health: A social constructionist examination of men's health beliefs and behaviors. *Psychology of Men and Masculinity, 1*(1), 4–15.

Courtenay, W. H. (2001). Counseling men in medical settings. In G. R. Brooks & G. E. Good (Eds.), *The new handbook of psychotherapy and counseling with men: A comprehensive guide to settings, problems, and treatment approaches* (Vol. 1, pp. 59–91). San Francisco: Jossey-Bass.

Courtenay, W. H. (2002). A global perspective on the field of men's health. *International Journal of Men's Health, 1*(1), 1–13.

Courtenay, W. H., & Keeling, R. P. (2000). Men, gender, and health: Toward an interdisciplinary approach. *Journal of American College Health, 48*(6), 1–4.

Courtenay, W. H., McCreary, D. R., & Merighi, J. R. (in press). Gender and ethnic differences in health beliefs and behaviors. *Journal of Health Psychology.*

Cramer, J. A., & Spilker, B. (Eds.). (1991). *Patient compliance in medical practice and clinical trials.* New York: Raven Press.

Cutter, S. L., Tiefenbacher, J., & Solecki, W. D. (1992). En-gendered fears: Femininity and technological risk perception. *Industrial Crisis Quarterly, 6*(1), 5–22.

Danner, D. D., Snowden, D. A., & Friesen, W. V. (2001). Positive emotions in early life and longevity: Findings from the nun study. *Journal of Personality and Social Psychology, 80*, 804–813.

Davis, H., & Fallowfield, L. (1991). Counseling and communication in health care: The current situation. In H. Davis & L. Fallowfield (Eds.), *Counseling and communication in health care* (pp. 3–22). New York: John Wiley & Sons.

Davis, M. C., Matthews, K. A., & Twamley, E. W. (1999). Is life more difficult on Mars or Venus? A meta-analytic review of sex differences in major and minor life events. *Annals of Behavioral Medicine, 21*, 83–97.

DeJoy, D. M. (1992). An examination of gender differences in traffic accident risk perception. *Accident Analysis and Prevention, 24*(3), 237–246.

Donelan, K., Falik, M., & DesRoches, C. M. (2001). Caregiving: Challenges and implications for women's health. *Women's Health Issues, 11*, 185–200.

Eisler, R. M. (1995). The relationship between masculine gender role stress and men's health risk: The validation of a construct. In R. F. Levant, & W. S. Pollack (Eds.), *A new psychology of men* (pp. 207–225). New York: Basic Books.

Eisler, R. M., Skidmore, J. R., & Ward, C. H. (1988). Masculine gender-role stress: Predictor of anger, anxiety, and health-risk behavior. *Journal of Personality Assessment, 52*(1), 133–141.

Exner, T. M., Seal, D. W., & Ehrhardt, A. A. (1997). A review of HIV interventions for at-risk women. *AIDS and Behavior, 1*, 93–124.

Frankenhauser, M. (1994). A biopsychosocial approach to stress in women and men. In V. J. Adesso, D. M. Reddy, & R. Fleming (Eds.), *Psychological perspectives on women's health* (pp. 39–56). Washington, DC: Taylor & Francis.

Friedman, C., Brownson, R. C., Peterson, D. E., & Wilkerson, J. C. (1994). Physician advice to reduce chronic disease risk factors. *American Journal of Preventive Medicine, 10*(6), 367–371.

Friedman, H. S. (Ed.). (1991). *Hostility, coping, and health*. Washington, DC: American Psychological Association.

Friedman, H. S. (2000). Long-term relations of personality and health: Dynamisms, mechanisms, tropisms. *Journal of Personality, 68*, 1189–1107.

Friedman, H. S., & DiMatteo, M. R. (Eds.). (1989). *Health psychology*. Englewood Cliffs, NJ: Prentice Hall.

Gallant, S. J., Keita, G. P., & Royak-Schaler, R. (Eds.). (1997). *Health care for women: Psychological, social, and behavioral influences*. Washington, DC: American Psychological Association.

Ganz, P. A., Greendale, G. A., Petersen, L., Zibecchi, L., Kahn, B., & Belin, T. R. (2000). Managing menopausal symptoms in breast cancer survivors: Results of a randomized controlled trial. *Journal of the National Cancer Institute, 92*, 1054–1064.

Gelles, R. J., & Straus, M. A. (1988). *Intimate violence*. New York: Simon & Schuster.

Gerber, G. S., Thompson, I. M., Thisted, R., & Chodak, G. W. (1993). Disease-specific survival following routine prostate cancer screening by digital rectal examination. *Journal of the American Medical Association, 269*(1), 61–64.

Goldberg, K. (1993). *How men can live as long as women: Seven steps to a longer and better life*. Fort Worth, TX: The Summit Group.

Golombok, S., & Fivush, R. (1994). *Gender development*. Cambridge, MA: Cambridge University Press.

Good, G. E., Dell, D. M., & Mintz, L. B. (1989). Male role and gender role conflict: Relations to help seeking in men. *Journal of Counseling Psychology, 36*(3), 295–300.

Gruninger, U. J. (1995). Patient education: An example of one-to-one communication. *Journal of Human Hypertension, 9*(1), 15–25.

Gustafson, P. E. (1998). Gender differences in risk perception: Theoretical and methodological perspectives. *Risk Analysis, 18*(6), 805–811.

Hall, J. A., Roter, D. L., & Katz, N. R. (1988). Meta-analysis of correlates of provider behavior in medical encounters. *Medical Care, 26*(7), 657–675.

Hobfoll, S. E., Jackson, A. P., Lavin, J., Britton, P. J., & Sheperd, J. B. (1994). Reducing inner city women's AIDS risk activities. *Health Psychology, 13*, 397–403.

Hoyert, D. L., Arias, E., Smith, B. L., Murphy, S. L., & Kochanek, K. D. (2001). Deaths: Final data for 1999. *National Vital Statistics Reports, 49*(8), 1–114.

Hyde, J. S. (1986). Gender differences in aggression. In J. S. Hyde & M. C. Linn (Eds.), *The psychology of gender* (pp. 51–66). Baltimore, MD: Johns Hopkins University Press.

Institute of Medicine. (1999). *Lesbian health: Current assessment and directions for the future*. Washington, DC: National Academy Press.

Janz, N., & Becker, M. (1984). The health belief model: A decade later. *Health Education Quarterly, 11*(1), 1–47.

Jenkins, R. (1985). Sex differences in minor psychiatric morbidity [Monograph]. *Psychological Medicine* (Suppl. 7).

Kacmarek, R. M. (1994). Make discussion. *Respiratory Care, 39*(5), 579–583.

Kaplan, S. H., Gandek, B., Greenfield, S., Rogers, W., & Ware, J. E. (1995). Patient and visit characteristics related to physicians' participatory decision-making style: Results from the Medical Outcomes Study. *Medical Care, 33*(12), 1176–1187.

Kaplan, S. H., Greenfield, S., & Ware, J. F. (1989). Assessing the effects of physician–patient interactions on the outcomes of chronic disease. *Medical Care, 27*(Suppl. 3), S110–S127.

Keefe, F. J., Caldwell, D. S., Baucom, D., Salley, A., Robinson, E., Timmons, K., et al. (1996). Spouse-assisted coping skills training in the management of osteoarthritic knee pain. *Arthritis Care and Research, 9*, 279–291.

Keefe, F. J., Caldwell, D. S., Baucom, D., Salley, A., Robinson, E., Timmons, K., et al. (1999). Spouse-assisted coping skills training in the management of knee pain in osteoarthritis: Long-term follow-up results. *Arthritis Care and Research, 12*, 101–111.

Kiecolt-Glaser, J. K., & Newton, T. L. (2001). Marriage and health: His and hers. *Psychological Bulletin, 127*, 472–503.

Kiecolt-Glaser, J. K., Glaser, R., Gravenstein, S., Malarkey, W. B., & Sheridan, J. (1996). Chronic stress alters the immune response to influenza virus vaccine in older adults. *Proceedings of the National Academy of Sciences, USA, 93,* 3043–3047.

Kilmartin, C. T. (1994). *The masculine self.* New York: Macmillan Publishing.

Klein, J. D., Brown, J. D., Childers, K. W., Oliveri, J., Porter, C., & Dykers, C. (1993). Adolescents' risky behavior and mass media use. *Pediatrics, 92*(1), 24–31.

Kopp, M. S., Skrabski, A., & Szedmak, S. (1998). Why do women suffer more and live longer? *Psychosomatic Medicine, 60,* 92–135.

Koss, M. P., Ingram, M., & Pepper, S. L. (2001). Male partner violence: Relevance to health care providers. In A. Baum, T. A. Revenson, & J. E. Singer (Eds.), *Handbook of health psychology* (pp. 541–557). Mahwah, NJ: Erlbaum.

Krantz, D. S., Grunberg, N. E., & Baum, A. (1985). Health psychology. *Annual Review of Psychology, 36,* 349–383.

Kreuter, M. W., & Strecher, V. J. (1995). Changing inaccurate perceptions of health risk: Results from a randomized trial. *Health Psychology, 14*(1), 56–63.

Levine, F. M., & DeSimone, L. L. (1991). The effects of experimenter gender on pain report in male and female patients. *Pain, 44,* 69–72.

Lewis, M. A., & Rook, K. S. (1999). Social control in personal relationships: Impact on health behaviors and psychological distress. *Health Psychology, 18,* 63–71.

Lippa, R. A., Martin, L. R., & Friedman, H. S. (2000). Gender-related individual differences and mortality in the Terman longitudinal study: Is masculinity hazardous to your health? *Personality and Social Psychology Bulletin, 12,* 1560–1570.

Little, S. J., Stevens, V. J., Severson, H. H., & Lichtenstein, E. (1992). Effective smokeless tobacco intervention for dental hygiene patients. *Journal of Dental Hygiene, 66*(4), 185–190.

Martin, C. L. (1995). Stereotypes about children with traditional and nontraditional gender roles. *Sex Roles, 33*(11/12), 727–751.

Matthews, K. A., Gump, B. B., & Owens, J. (2001). Chronic stress influences cardiovascular and neuroendocrine responses during acute stress and recovery, especially in men. *Health Psychology, 20*(6), 403–410.

Matthews, K. A., Shumaker, S. A., Bowen, D. J., Langer, R. D., Hunt, J. R., Kaplan, R. M., et al. (1997). Women's Health Initiative: Why now? What is it? What's new? *American Psychologist, 52,* 101–116.

McCann, D. P., & Blossom, H. J. (1990). The physician as a patient educator: From theory to practice. *Western Journal of Medicine, 153*(1), 44–49.

McCreary, D. R., Newcomb, M. D., & Sadava, S. W. (1999). The male role, alcohol use, and alcohol problems: A structural modeling examination in adult women and men. *Journal of Counseling Psychology, 46,* 109–124.

Meichenbaum, D., &, Turk, D. C. (1987). *Facilitating treatment adherence: A practitioner's guidebook.* New York: Plenum Press.

Mermelstein, R. J., & Riesenberg, L. A. (1992). Changing knowledge and attitudes about skin cancer risk factors in adolescents. *Health Psychology, 11*(6), 371–376.

Meth, R. L. (1990). The road to masculinity. In R. L. Meth and R. S. Pasick (Eds.), *Men in therapy: The challenge of change* (pp. 3–34). New York: Guilford Press.

Metz, M. E., & Seifert, M. H. (1990). Men's expectations of physicians in sexual health concerns. *Journal of Sexual and Marital Therapy, 16*(2), 79–88.

Meyerowitz, B. E., Richardson, J., Hudson, S., & Leedham, B. (1998). Ethnicity and cancer outcomes: Behavioral and psychosocial considerations. *Psychological Bulletin, 123*, 47–70.

Miaskowski, C. (1999). The role of sex and gender in pain perception and responses to treatment. In R. J. Gatchel & D. C. Turk (Eds.), *Psychosocial factors in pain: Critical perspectives* (pp. 401–411). New York: Guilford Press.

Misener, T. R., & Fuller, S. G. (1995). Testicular versus breast and colorectal cancer screen: Early detection practices of primary care physicians. *Cancer Practice, 3*(5), 310–316.

Mosca, L., Jones, W. K., King, K. B., Ouyang, P., Redberg, R. F., & Hill, M. N. (for the American Heart Association's Women's Heart Disease and Stroke Campaign Task Force). (2000). Awareness, perception, and knowledge of heart disease risk and prevention among women in the United States. *Archives of Family Medicine, 9*, 506–515.

National Center for Health Statistics. (2000). *Early release of selected estimates from the National Health Interview Survey* [Data file]. Retrieved on June 27, 2003, from Centers for Disease Control Web site: www.cdc.gov/nchs/about/major/ nhis/earlyrelease2000.htm

National Institutes of Health. (1998). *Clinical guidelines on the identification, evaluation, and treatment of overweight and obesity in adults: The evidence report* (NIH Publication No. 98-4083). Bethesda, MD: Author.

Neff, J. A., Prihoda, T. J., & Hoppe, S. K. (1991). "Machismo," self-esteem, education and high maximum drinking among Anglo, Black, and Mexican-American male drinkers. *Journal of Studies on Alcohol, 52*, 458–463.

Oakley, A. (1994). Who cares for health? Social relations, gender, and the public health. *Journal of Epidemiology and Community Health, 48*(5), 427–434.

O'Brien, M. K., Petrie, K., & Raeburn, J. (1992). Adherence to medication regimens: Updating a complex medical issue. *Medical Care Review, 49*(4), 435–454.

O'Neil, J. M., Good, G. E., & Holmes, S. (1995). Fifteen years of theory and research on men's gender role conflict: New paradigms for empirical research. In R. F. Levant & W. S. Pollack (Eds.), *A new psychology of men*. New York: Basic Books.

Polednak, A. P. (1990). Knowledge of colorectal cancer and use of screening tests in persons 40–74 years of age. *Preventive Medicine, 19*, 213–226.

Polefrone, J. M., & Manuck, S. B. (1987). Gender differences in cardiovascular and neuroendocrine response to stressors. In R. Barnett, L. Biener, & G. K. Baruch (Eds.), *Gender and stress* (pp. 13–38). New York: Free Press.

Potts, M. K., Burnam, M. A., & Wells, K. B. (1991). Gender differences in depression detection: A comparison of clinician diagnosis and standardized assessment. *Psychological Assessment, 3,* 609–615.

Powell-Griner, E., Anderson, J. E., & Murphy, W. (1997). State- and sex-specific prevalence of selected characteristics: Behavioral Risk Factor Surveillance System, 1994 and 1995. *Morbidity and Mortality Weekly Report, 46*(3), 1–31.

Prochaska, J., Norcross, J., & DiClemente, C. (1994). *Changing for good: The revolutionary program that explains the six stages of change and teaches you how to free yourself from bad habits.* New York: William Morrow.

Puntillo, K., & Weiss, S. J. (1994). Pain: Its mediators and associated morbidity in critically ill cardiovascular surgical patients. *Nursing Research, 43,* 31–36.

Reagan, L. J. (1997). Engendering the dread disease: Women, men, and cancer. *American Journal of Public Health, 87*(11), 1779–1787.

Reno, D. R. (1988). Men's knowledge and health beliefs about testicular cancer and testicular self-exam. *Cancer Nursing, 11*(2), 112–117.

Rimer, B. K., McBride, C. M., & Crump, C. (2001). Women's health promotion. In A. Baum, T. A. Revenson, & J. E. Singer (Eds.), *Handbook of health psychology* (pp. 519–539). Mahwah, NJ: Erlbaum.

Rosenstock, I. M. (1990). The Health Belief Model: Explaining health behavior through expectancies. In K. Glanz, F. M. Lewis, & B. K. Rimer (Eds.), *Health behavior and health education: Theory, research and practice.* San Francisco: Jossey-Bass.

Ross, C. E., & Bird, C. E. (1994). Sex stratification and health lifestyle: Consequences of men's and women's perceived health. *Journal of Health and Social Behavior, 35,* 161–178.

Ross, C. E., Mirowsky, J., & Goldstein, K. (1990). The impact of the family on health: The decade in review. *Journal of Marriage and the Family, 52,* 1059–1078.

Rossouw, J. E., Anderson, G. L., Prentice, R. L., LaCroix, A. Z., Kooperberg, C., Stefanick, M. L., et al. (2002). Risks and benefits of estrogen plus progestin in healthy postmenopausal women: Principal results from the Women's Health Initiative randomized controlled trial. *Journal of the American Medical Association, 288,* 312–333.

Roter, D. L., & Hall, J. A. (1997a). *Doctors talking with patients/patients talking with doctors: Improving communication in medical visits.* Westport, CT: Auburn House.

Roter, D. L., & Hall, J. A. (1997b). Gender differences in patient–physician communication. In S. J. Gallant, G. P. Keita, & R. Royak-Schaler (Eds.), *Health care for women: Psychological, social, and behavioral influences* (pp. 57–71). Washington, DC: American Psychological Association.

Roth, B. J., Nichols, C. R., & Einhorn, L. H. (1993). Neoplasms of the testis. In J. F. Holland, E. Frei, & R. C. Basett (Eds.), *Cancer medicine* (Vol. 2, 3rd ed., pp. 1592–1619). Philadelphia: Lea & Febiger.

Royak-Schaler, R., Stanton, A. L., & Danoff-Burg, S. (1997). Breast cancer. In S. J. Gallant, G. P. Keita, & R. Royak-Schaler (Eds.), *Health care for women: Psychological, social, and behavioral influences* (pp. 295–314). Washington, DC: American Psychological Association.

Rule, W. R., & Gandy, G. L. (1994). A thirteen-year comparison in patterns of attitudes toward counseling. *Adolescence, 29*(115), 575–589.

Sandman, D., Simantov, E., & An, C. (2000). *Out of touch: American men and the health care system.* New York: Commonwealth Fund.

Savage, I. (1993). Demographic influences on risk perceptions. *Risk Analysis, 13,* 413–420.

Shumaker, S. A., & Smith, T. R. (1995). Women and coronary heart disease: A psychological perspective. In A. L. Stanton & S. J. Gallant (Eds.), *The psychology of women's health: Progress and challenges in research and application* (pp. 25–49). Washington, DC: American Psychological Association.

Smith, T. W., & Gallo, L. C. (2001). Personality traits as risk factors for physical illness. In A. Baum, T. A. Revenson, & J. E. Singer (Eds.), *Handbook of health psychology* (pp. 139–173). Mahwah, NJ: Erlbaum.

Smith, T. W., Gallo, L. C., Goble, L., Ngu, L. Q., & Stark, K. A. (1998). Agency, communion, and cardiovascular reactivity during marital interaction. *Health Psychology, 17,* 537–545.

Snell, W. E. (1989). Development and validation of the Masculine Behavior Scale: A measure of behaviors stereotypically attributed to males vs. females. *Sex Roles, 21,* 749–767.

Solis, J. M., Marks, G., Garcia, M., & Shelton, D. (1990). Acculturation, access to care, and use of preventive services by Hispanics: Findings from HHANES 1982–84. *American Journal of Public Health, 80*(Suppl.), 11–19.

Stanton, A. L., Danoff-Burg, S., Cameron, C. L., Bishop, M. M., Collins, C. A., Kirk, S. B., & Twillman, R. (2000). Emotionally expressive coping predicts psychological and physical adjustment to breast cancer. *Journal of Consulting and Clinical Psychology, 68,* 875–882.

Stanton, A. L., & Gallant, S. J. (Eds.). (1995). *The psychology of women's health: Progress and challenges in research and application.* Washington, DC: American Psychological Association.

Stockwell, D. H., Madhavan, S., Cohen, H., Gibson, G., & Alderman, M. H. (1994). The determinants of hypertension awareness, treatment, and control in an insured population. *American Journal of Public Health, 84*(11), 1768–1774.

Stone, S. V., Dembroski, T. M., Costa, P. T., & MacDougall, J. M. (1990). Gender differences in cardiovascular reactivity. *Journal of Behavioral Medicine, 13*(2), 137–156.

Stoney, C. M., Davis, M. C., & Matthews, K. A. (1987). Sex differences in physiologic responses to stress and in coronary heart disease: A causal link? *Psychophysiology, 24*(2), 127–131.

Sutkin, L., & Good, G. E. (1987). Therapy with men in health-care settings. In M. Scher, M. Stevens, G. Good, & G. A. Eichenfield (Eds.), *Handbook of counseling and psychotherapy with men* (pp. 372–387). Thousand Oaks, CA: Sage Publications.

Tannen, D. (1990). *You just don't understand: Women and men in conversation*. New York: Ballantine.

Taylor, S. E. (1986). *Health psychology*. New York: Random House.

Taylor, S. E., Klein, L. C., Lewis, B. P., Gruenewald, T. L., Gurung, R. A. R., & Updegraff, J. A. (2000). Biobehavioral responses to stress in females: Tend-and-befriend, not fight-or-flight. *Psychological Review, 107*, 411–429.

Tinsley, B. J. (1992). Multiple influences on the acquisition and socialization of children's health attitudes and behavior: An integrative review. *Child Development, 63*, 1043–1069.

Turner, R. A., Altemus, M., Enos, T., Cooper, B., & McGuinness, T. (1999). Preliminary research on plasma oxytocin in normal cycling women: Investigating emotion and interpersonal distress. *Psychiatry, 62*, 97–113.

Unruh, A. M., Ritchie, J., & Merskey, H. (1999). Does gender affect appraisal of pain and pain coping strategies? *Clinical Journal of Pain, 15*(1), 31–40.

U.S. Department of Health and Human Services. (1990). *Health, United States, 1989* (DHHS publication number [PHS] 90–1232). Washington, DC: U.S. Government Printing Office.

U.S. Department of Health and Human Services. (1993). *Vital and health statistics: Health promotion and disease prevention, United States, 1990* (DHHS Publication No. [PHS] 93-1513). Hyattsville, MD: Public Health Service.

U.S. Department of Health and Human Services. (1998a). *Health, United States, 1998: Socioeconomic status and health chartbook* (DHHS publication number [PHS] 98-1232-1). Hyattsville, MD: National Center for Health Statistics.

U.S. Department of Health and Human Services. (1998b). *Vital and health statistics: Current estimates from the National Health Interview Survey, 1995* (DHHS Publication No. PHS 98-1527). Hyattsville, MD: Author.

U.S. Department of Health and Human Services. (2000). Deaths: Final data for 1998 (DHHS Publication No. [PHS] 2000-1120). *National Vital Statistics Reports, 48*(11). Hyattsville, MD: National Center for Health Statistics.

U.S. Department of Justice. (1994). *Sourcebook of criminal justice statistics—1993* (Publication No. NCJ-148211). Washington, DC: U.S. Government Printing Office.

U.S. General Accounting Office. (July, 2001). *Women's health: Women sufficiently represented in new drug testing, but FDA oversight needs improvement* (GAO-01-754). Washington, DC: Author.

U.S. Preventive Services Task Force. (1996). *Guide to clinical preventive services* (2nd Ed.). Baltimore, MD: Williams & Wilkins.

Verbrugge, L. M. (1985). Gender and health: An update on hypotheses and evidence. *Journal of Health and Social Behavior, 26*, 156–182.

Verbrugge, L. M. (1988). Unveiling higher morbidity for men: The story. In M.W. Riley (Ed.), *Social structures and human lives* (pp. 138–160). Newbury Park, CA: Sage.

Verbrugge, L. M. (1989). The twain meet: Empirical explanations of sex differences in health and mortality. *Journal of Health and Social Behavior, 30*(3), 282–304.

Waitzkin, H. (1985). Information giving in medical care. *Journal of Health and Social Behavior, 26*(2), 81–101.

Walker, S. N., Volkan, K., Sechrist, K. R., & Pender, N. J. (1988). Health promoting life-styles of older adults: Comparisons with young and middle-aged adults, correlates and patterns. *Advances in Nursing Science, 11*, 76–90.

Weidner, G., & Collins, R. L. (1993). Gender, coping, and health. In H. W. Krohne (Ed.), *Attention and avoidance* (pp. 241–265). Seattle, WA: Hogrefe and Huber.

Weinstein, N. D. (1987). Unrealistic optimism about illness susceptibility: Conclusions from a community-wide sample. *Journal of Behavioral Medicine, 10*(5), 481–500.

Weissfeld, J. L., Kirscht, J. P., & Brock, B. M. (1990). Health beliefs in a population: The Michigan Blood Pressure Survey. *Health Education Quarterly, 17*(2), 141–155.

Wells, K. B., Manning, W. G., Duan, H., Newhouse, J. P., & Ware, J. E. (1986). Sociodemographic factors and the use of outpatient mental health services. *Medical Care, 24*(1), 75–85.

Williams, D. G. (1985). Gender, masculinity-femininity, and emotional intimacy in same-sex friendship. *Sex Roles, 12*(5/6), 587–600.

Williams, J. E., & Best, D. L. (1990). *Measuring sex stereotypes: A multination study.* Newbury Park, CA: Sage.

Wilson, R. W., & Elinson, J. (1981). National survey of personal health practices and consequences: Background, conceptual issues, and selected findings. *Public Health Reports, 96*(3), 218–225.

Winawer, S. J., & Shike, M. (1995). *Cancer free: The comprehensive cancer prevention program.* New York: Simon & Schuster.

Yee, P. Y., Alexander, K. P., Hammill, B. G., Pasquali, S. K., & Peterson, E. D. (2001). Representation of elderly persons and women in published randomized trials of acute coronary syndromes. *Journal of the American Medical Association, 286*, 708–713.

Zautra, A. J., Hoffman, J. M., Matt, K. S., Yocum, D., Potter, P. T., Castro, W. L., et al. (1998). An examination of individual differences in the relationship between interpersonal stress and disease activity among women with rheumatoid arthritis. *Arthritis Care and Research, 11*, 271–279.

II

BUILDING HEALTHY
COMMUNITIES

5

HEALTHY SEXUALITY FOR ALL: THE ROLE OF PSYCHOLOGY

SUSAN PICK

There is nothing so useful as a good theory.

—K. Lewin, 1951

Theories represent a high level of abstract thinking. They represent a world of ideas and possibilities. However, it is only in the application of their tenets that theories take on life and meaning. This potential for application can only be realized through human effort and skill. We, as psychologists, have a unique opportunity to act as mediators for the application of the theories that serve as the basis for our academic and professional lives. By using the practical tools of program development, evaluation systems, and instrument development, we are able to apply our theories about human nature and behavior in ways that address the very practical needs of the populations we serve. Unfortunately, the psychological community has not yet maximized our potential in this respect. In particular, we have not yet realized our potential to contribute to the well-being of both individuals and societies by joining forces with public policymakers as they address issues central to the common constituencies we serve.

Our professional and academic associations and universities have been slow in transforming our theoretical beliefs into applicable curricula and practices that accommodate the needs of our populations. The movement toward translating our ideas into public policies has been even slower. We are at a critical moment. Now, more than ever before, there is a recognition of the importance of strengthening human capital as a means of strengthening economic and social development. This recognition provides us with a unique opportunity and obligation to lend our knowledge and skills to improve the human psychological, economic and social condition through assisting in the development of appropriate and effective public policies.

This chapter presents a "theory to action model" developed by psychologists at the Instituto Mexicano de Investigación de Familia y Población (IMIFAP—Educación, salud y vida; Pick, Givaudan, & Poortinga, in press; Pick, Poortinga, & Givaudan, in press). The issues dealt with in this model are related to sexual and reproductive health in the context of a healthy world and can serve as an example of how we can build a healthy world. To clearly and thoroughly walk the reader through the theory to action process, this chapter is divided into the following sections: Psychological aspects of gender inequalities in human sexuality, theoretical framework for interventions, research to action strategies, and examples of IMIFAP programs that have used this process to address the needs of Mexicans and Latin Americans since 1985.

PSYCHOLOGICAL ASPECTS OF GENDER INEQUALITIES AND HUMAN SEXUALITY

Healthy sexuality implies a sense of volition in sexual relations. It implies a sense of control over one's body. Sexual autonomy plays a key role in healthy sexuality. Autonomy can only be achieved if an individual is empowered to make informed and responsible decisions. Autonomous decision making cannot take place under coercive circumstances. Unfortunately, gender inequalities often create coercive sexual situations, making healthy and responsible decisions about sexuality difficult (Reproductive Health in Developing Countries, 1997).

One of the psychological constructs contributing to gender inequalities, particularly in sexual situations, is power. In many cultures, gendered power structures that support male superiority complexes inhibit women from deciding or insisting on the use of contraception during intercourse. Women often do not have the right to insist on contraception and, likewise, if a man chooses not to use a condom, a woman does not have the right to refuse sex. This lack of women's power results in an inability to control fertility and makes her vulnerable to sexually transmitted infections (Pick, 1986). Imbalanced power dynamics are also evident in patterns of partner selection and role expectations. In many cultures, men have the power to select the number of sexual partners they will have throughout a lifetime. Even in cultures where monogamy is the standard social norm, male adultery is a more common and socially acceptable occurrence. This gendered power imbalance fosters sexual situations wherein women have little autonomy to refuse sex with polygamous men who may expose them to dangerous diseases or unwanted pregnancies. A final example of power imbalances in sexual scenarios is rooted in role expectations. Sexual role expectations refer to a gendered continuity ranging from self-reliance in sexual behavior, which is expected of men, to submissiveness in sexual encounters, which is expected of women. Role expectations also reflect an imbalance in emotional display, wherein "strong" men are not expected to display emotion and the expectation of women's propensity toward emotional responses is viewed as weak. The power imbalance inherent in role expectations presents a psychological obstruction to women's autonomous decision-making abilities in sexual situations.

One of the most dangerous, physical manifestations of psychological power imbalances among the sexes is gender-based violence. Both the fear and practice of violence inhibit a woman's control over her sexual health. Fear of violence makes women unable to negotiate for contraceptive use. Violence and pain are positively associated with sexuality in many cultures, particularly for women. Women are often chastised for taking pleasure in sexual behaviors and are viewed as prostitutes or "loose" women if they do so. The correlation between women's sexuality and pleasure and pain is analogized by Nobel prize winning author Octavio Paz. In his writing, Paz draws a parallel between women and machine guns; commenting on the notion that women, like machine guns, should be "charged" (impregnated) to prevent promiscuity and left in a corner (Paz, 1961). It can only be assumed that pleasure's opposite, pain (or at best, indifference) is considered the acceptable and preferred manifestation of women's position in sexual situations. The taboo against women's sexual pleasure combined with psychological power imbalances breeds sexual violence.

These psychological incongruities in power between the sexes, and their physical manifestations, beg a series of questions regarding women's sexual rights. Does only the male partner have the right to refuse sex or do both partners have the right to say no? Is lack of pain or pleasure rights inherently associated with sexuality? And, perhaps most urgently, in what ways might political or social rights regarding sexuality help to bridge the power imbalances that impede women from making autonomous, healthy sexual decisions? To answer this final question, we will need to consider a theoretical framework that will enable us to support policy suggestions based on psychological understandings of gender inequalities and sexuality.

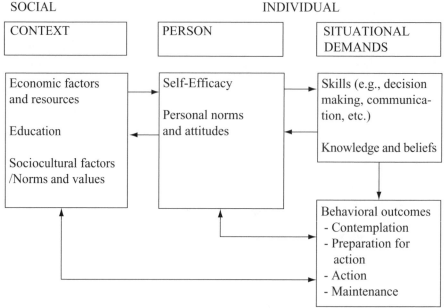

SOCIAL   INDIVIDUAL

Figure 5.1. A theoretical framework developed by the Mexican Institute for the Study of Family and Population to support practical intervention efforts.

A THEORETICAL FRAMEWORK FOR UNDERSTANDING GENDER INEQUALITIES AND SEXUALITY

On the basis of almost 18 years of experience conducting research and programs in the field of sexual health, women's empowerment and education, the Mexican Institute for the Study of Family and Population (IMIFAP) has developed a theoretical framework, outlined and explained in Figure 5.1, to support practical intervention efforts.

Context

The *social context* in which one lives constitutes the active backdrop in this theoretical framework. Context refers to the economic, educational, and sociocultural aspects that determine one's initial opportunities in life. Economic factors include available resources such as access to food, available subsidies, watering systems, and the degree to which the production and distribution of goods is possible. Education refers to the number and quality of schools available for children as well as to adult enhancement opportunities. Sociocultural factors include social expectations regarding behaviors among society members in both public and private social settings.

According to Mary Bateson (1990), social context, including economic, educational, and sociocultural factors, is organized along gender lines. In terms of *economics*, men are traditionally responsible for the productive, out-of-home activities within a family, whereas women traditionally take charge of productive and reproductive responsibilities within the household. This gendered division of labor leaves many of the world's women with few independent resources. In 1995, USAID reported that of the 1.3 people surviving on less than one dollar a day that year, 75% were women (USAID, 2000). Lack of economic resources feeds into the power imbalances between men and women that affect sexual autonomy. In terms of *education*, the same division of labor that is evident from an economic standpoint also affects the educational levels of boys and girls. Often girls are responsible for taking on household tasks that either prevent them from attending school or limit the time they have to study and achieve in an educational environment. The direct correlation between education and future opportunities and decision making suggests that lack of education for girls may have significant consequences in terms of knowledge, skills, and beliefs related to sexuality (Pick, 1985). In terms of *sociocultural factors*, traditional normative standards perpetuate gender-based expectations of men and women. Men are expected to reign in the public sphere where they are encouraged to act as community leaders and family breadwinners. They are rewarded, in particular, for their sexual prowess. Women, on the other hand, are expected to live in the privacy of their own homes. They are expected to maintain a silent, repressed relationship to their bodies, sexuality, and needs (Pick, Givaudan, & Aldaz, 1996). As one woman from Oaxaca, Mexico explains, "Bearing burden and sickness is part of being a woman." This sociocultural discrepancy, which is intimately tied to both economic and educational factors, creates the context within which women make sexual choices.

Situational Demands

Situational demands refer to the beliefs that inform an individual's knowledge and the skills such as communication and decision making. It is at this level that small-group or face-to-face interventions take place with the purpose of modifying erroneous beliefs and providing the person with the necessary skills and knowledge to be able to change his or her behaviors. Many of the changes we as psychologists need to focus on occur at this situational demand level.

Erroneous beliefs about sexuality tend to dominate individuals' perceptions of sex and reproductive health. Common beliefs that IMIFAP has found in its work with women include the following: If I seek information about sexuality, people will think I'm a prostitute; If I masturbate, I will have hair in my hands; If I act confident in sexual situations, people will think I am arrogant (Pick de Weiss & Andrade, 1989; Pick et al., 1996). These types of beliefs influence an individual's behavior and decisions in sexual scenarios (Pick de Weiss, Atkin, Gribble, & Andrade-Palos, 1991). IMIFAP interventions are designed to strengthen skills and knowledge, facilitate the removal of erroneous beliefs and, in so doing, to contribute to changes in individuals by positively affecting their behavior patterns (Pick de Weiss, Andrade-Palos, Townsend, & Givaudan, 1994). Examples of skills that are fostered during interventions and that have had a notable impact on behaviors include: substituting blind obedience with educated decision making; substituting indirect communication with direct, open, assertive communication; substituting nonexpression of feelings with the open expression of feelings (Fawcett, Heise, Isita, & Pick, 1999; Givaudan, Ramón, Camacho, & Pick, 1997). Examples of knowledge and facts that are imparted during interventions that have had a notable impact on behaviors include: sexual and reproductive rights information, advantages and disadvantages of different contraceptives, safe sex practices, and the legal status of abortion (country-specific).

Behavioral Outcomes

To explain the relationship that we have found between changes in skills and knowledge and positive modifications in intentions and behaviors we have borrowed from Ajzen and Fishbein's Theory of Reasoned Action (1980) as well as Prochaska and DiClemente's Transtheoretical Model of Behavior Change (1982). These theories hold that when an individual starts to observe that he or she can achieve levels of behavior that make him or her feel good and that are not socially punished (or are occasionally even socially rewarded), he or she will begin to contemplate taking further steps toward overall and consistent behavior change. The steps laid out for behavior change in Prochaska and DiClemente's work include contemplation of change, getting prepared to make a change, making the change, and maintaining the changed behavior. At each step of this process, social context, skills, and knowledge contribute to an individual's realization of behavioral change. The following example illustrates this model.

A rural Mexican woman who has faced domestic violence has grown up in a social context wherein men have been the main economic providers, educational opportunities have been limited, and her social role has been largely relegated to the household domain. This social context has in turn influenced a set of specific beliefs about gender and violence. Most likely, this belief consists of a passive acceptance of male power and violence. For such a woman to begin the first step toward a behavioral change (in this case, removing oneself from a violent situation), she must have an impetus to contemplate change. This impetus may come from a psychologist, a friend, an extremely harsh violent episode, or a targeted intervention for rural women. Once this impetus takes effect, a woman may think to herself

"Maybe I should leave. . . ." This thought represents the step of contemplation. As she begins to plan ways to leave or possibilities for securing a different life she moves toward the second step, preparing for action. Once she is prepared, the action is taken. In this case, the action may involve leaving the home, discussing the problem with her spouse, seeing a social worker, or doing anything in her power to prevent the violence. The ultimate step is to maintain the behavior that prevents the violence. It is important to note that this cycle may be repeated numerous times before a healthy behavior is maintained. For example, our woman may leave her home, decide to come back, realize the violence has not ended, and repeat the cycle once again. To ensure that maintenance of healthy behaviors is achieved, it is important that interventions occur over a long period of time to stabilize the targeted behavior and achieve long-term success.

Personal

The personal domain of our theoretical framework works through a feedback mechanism. We have found that attitudes, personal norms, and feelings of self-esteem and self-efficacy are modified when behavioral change is observed (Givaudan, Pick, Aldaz, & Saldívar, 1996; Givaudan et al., 1997). This positive correlation between improved behavioral outcomes and personal psychosocial characteristics speaks to one of the biggest questions and challenges that psychologists face: How does an individual become empowered to maximize his or her personal potential?

The majority of the world has developed with high economic poverty and authoritarian systems where strict rules and regulations determine acceptable personal norms. There is often little acceptance of experimentation and meeting social expectation is more highly valued than personal development. Such a context makes it difficult to support and maintain individual development (i.e., decision making and open communication) in many countries, including Mexico. Education systems, which should foster individual empowerment, instead are based on rule obedience, submissiveness, guilt, and threats as a means of social control. These characteristics make it difficult to directly affect individual development in the developing world.

The correlation that we have found between behavior and personality change provides an exciting opportunity to affect individuals' self-esteem, self-efficacy, attitudes, and norms in developing countries by providing them with the skills and knowledge to change their daily and sexual behaviors. A change in sexual behaviors may be conducive to changes in other spheres of life as well. For example, we have found an increased willingness to take on new challenges and experiences (i.e., starting a business, participating more in class discussions, talking to health personnel, and making eye contact during conversations; Venguer & Givaudan, 2001).

In this theoretical model, then, a person is empowered not through a direct therapeutic intervention, but through a taught and self-applied model of skill development, knowledge acquisition, and behavioral change.

FROM THEORY TO ACTION

Using our theoretical framework as a guide, psychologists at IMIFAP have developed effective intervention strategies for improving the sexual, reproductive, and mental health of Mexican women, men, children, and adolescents. These interventions take into consideration the social context and situational demands of targeted individuals and attempt to provide them with a psychologically founded, skills-based approach to empowerment and healthy behaviors. Examples of interventions include an empowerment program for women who have been the subjects of domestic violence, coupled with a small grant to build and run bakeries as a means of economic survival; a life skills and health education curriculum for rural women in Oaxaca; and a peer education program that teaches high school students about attitudes and knowledge related to HIV/AIDS and empowers them to educate their friends (www.imifap.org.mx). These types of programs address contextual and situational demands to achieve behavioral and personal change.

To move from theoretical visualization to the actualization of interventions, several logistical steps must be followed. The first of these steps is the *detection of needs*. Clinical psychologists most often see patients who seek them out or who are assigned to them; in both cases, the psychologist is not a proactive need-seeker. This may require a change of emphasis for some in our field. To detect larger needs, statistics, government, nongovernment, and ethnographic reports, surveys, and census materials may be useful. In addition, psychologists can utilize their skills to hold focus groups, conduct in-depth interviews, and develop questionnaires that will assess the needs of individuals and communities.

After the need is detected, *program development* begins. Program development involves the selection of contents (i.e., skills, knowledge, and beliefs) that will be addressed and methodology (i.e., participatory workshops, training sessions, community campaign, mass media campaigns, etc.) that will be used. Program development should be tied to a theoretical framework, like the one outlined previously, which will guide the move from concepts to practical action and ensure that the program approach is well thought out and effective at addressing the detected need.

Once the program has been developed, it must be *piloted and revised*. A pilot is a small-scale implementation of the program that has been developed. The pilot assesses the adequacy of contents, methodology, acceptance, and short-term effectiveness. For example, if the need detected was prevention of sexually transmitted infections and the program developed aimed at increasing condom use, a pilot study would examine questions such as the following: Are people using condoms more? Are they talking to their children more about safe sex and sexuality? In what ways are people communicating about safe sex? On the basis of the answers to these questions, the program can be revised and improved before it is implemented on a larger scale.

A program that has been piloted and revised must then be made public through a *publicity strategy*. To have a successful program, a multilevel strategy must be developed to advocate and disseminate program information. There are a variety of techniques that may be included to publicize the program to target populations, communities, and government officials. These techniques may include opinion surveys, Web pages, press conferences, and television and radio programs. Meetings with local groups, educational groups, and health authorities are an essential part of any publicity strategy for health education programming. Once the public and relevant authorities are informed and in support of the program, it is ready to be implemented on a larger scale.

Upscaling refers to the extensive application of the program with close follow-up to maximize the number of people reached. The upscaling process involves the training of trainers, distribution of materials, and the measurement of effectiveness. To effectively train program replicators (or trainers), it is essential to imbue those being trained with the knowledge, ability, and enthusiasm for replicating the program with target populations. Comfort with program contents and support of program goals by those directly involved in replication is essential for large-scale success.

All of IMIFAP's programs have been developed and implemented using this need detection through upscaling model. Examples of these programs include:

1. *Planning Your Life* (Planeando tu vida): A basic training program in sexuality and life skills (Pick de Weiss et al., 1988).
2. *I Want, I Love, I Can* (Yo quiero, yo puedo): An integrated life-skills education program for children in preschool through 9th grade (Pick & Givaudan, 1996).
3. *Learning to Be a Mom and a Dad* (Aprediendo a ser papá y mama): A life-skills education program for parents with children under the age of 12 (Pick, Givaudan, & Martinez, 1995).
4. *Let Your Adolescent Fly and He or She Will Be a Great Adult* (Deja volar a tu adolescente . . . y sera un gran adulto): A life-skills education program for parents and adolescents (Fernández, Pick, & Givaudan, 2002).

5. *If I Am Okay, My Family Is, Too* (Si yo estoy bien, mi familia también): A health and empowerment program for rural and indigenous women and their children (Venguer, Quezada, et al., 1999).

6. *A Pharmacist, a Friend* (Un farmaceuta, un amigo): An HIV/AIDS prevention program for pharmacists and their customers (IMIFAP-SOMARC Futures Group, 1993).

7. *The Role of Health Personnel: A Humanist Approach* (El rol del personal de salud: un enfoques humanista): A program to enhance focus on health, communication, and showing of empathy and knowledge during doctor–patient interactions about sexual and reproductive health and rights (Venguer, Givaudan, Reyes, & Miranda, 1999).

8. *Faces and Masks of Violence* (Rostros y mascaras de la violencia): A program for adolescents to help them identify and prevent the precursors of violent behavior in dating scenarios (Ruiz & Fawcett, 1999).

9. *We Break the Chain of Violence* (Rompamos la cadena de la violencia): A program that facilitates the formation of self-help groups among women (Fawcett & Isita, 2000).

RESULTS

The following illustrations from selected IMIFAP programs indicate how our theoretical framework has guided the selection of target populations, informed the development of program goals, and resulted in positive outcomes.

The first set of results, presented in Figure 5.2, are drawn from a program that IMIFAP participated in as part of a larger consortium of sexual and reproductive health organizations throughout the world (PATH). Based on considerations of social context in three Central American countries (Mexico, Nicaragua, and Guatemala), IMIFAP developed and implemented mass media campaigns aimed at reducing the contextual constraints that keep health personnel from disseminating information about emergency contraception. By airing information about emergency contraception, doctors and pharmacists, as demonstrated below, were able to communicate more freely with clients about protecting themselves from pregnancy through the use of emergency contraceptives.

The second set of results, presented in Figure 5.3, are drawn from an implementation of IMIFAP's *Yo quiero, yo puedo* (I Want, I Love, I Can) curriculum in Mexico City, Mexico. This curriculum is based on the theoretical premise that fostering basic life skills in elementary school-age children

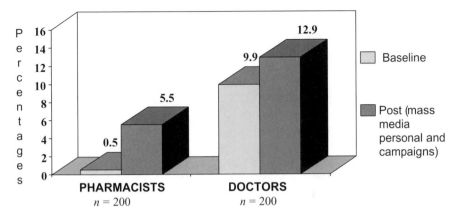

Figure 5.2. Increases in the percentage of respondents who have recommended the use of emergency contraception in the last year.

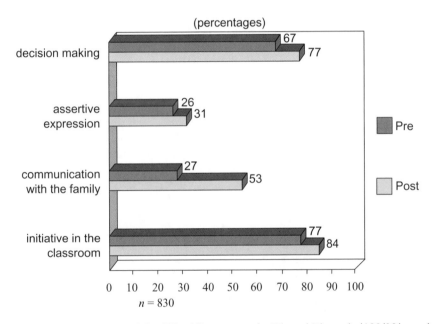

Figure 5.3. "I Want, I Love, I Can" life skills program for 5th and 6th grade (120/60 hours).

will positively affect their present and future, daily and sexual behaviors. The results in Figure 5.3 show the life skills that were improved upon among 5th and 6th grade students during the course of the program.

The third set of results are taken from an evaluation of IMIFAP's *Un farmaceuta, un amigo* (A Pharmacist, a Friend) program. It also focuses on the development of a skill. This program trains pharmacists to take the

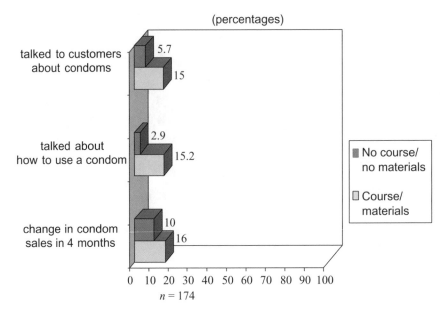

Figure 5.4. Communication with customers and condom sales by pharmacy workers (40 hours, after 3 months).

initiative in discussing HIV/STI related issues and advocating for condom use with pharmacy clientele. The results, shown in Figure 5.4, reflect the program's significant impact among a group of Mexico City pharmacists.

The final set of results, shown in Figure 5.5, reflect a behavioral change seen among rural women who participated in IMIFAP's *Si yo estoy bien, mi*

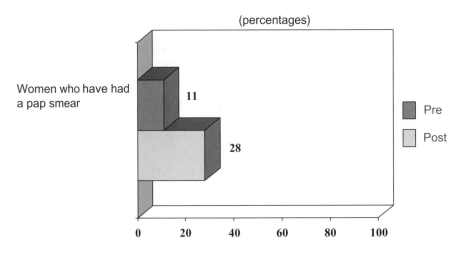

Figure 5.5. "If I Am Okay, My Family Is, Too" health and empowerment for rural women (160/30 hours).

familia también (If I Am Okay, My Family Is, Too) health and empowerment program. The *Si yo estoy bien, mi familia también* program, like all of IMIFAP's projects, takes into account the social context of its target audiences, young rural women, and utilizes a skills and knowledge-building approach to behavioral change. The increase in incidence of pap smears among participating women provides a concrete example of positive behavior change as a result of a contextually sensitive, skills- and knowledge-based intervention.

In addition to the positive results indicated in the illustrations, we are particularly proud of the results IMIFAP work has produced at the political level. Indicators such as the ones just mentioned have been used to convince federal education authorities in Mexico to reform national education policies (Pick, Givaudan, & Brown, 2000). A Civic and Ethic Formation curriculum, which is based on a life-skills education model, is now a requirement in Grades 7–9 throughout the Republic. IMIFAP wrote official textbooks that are now used to teach the curriculum in all of Mexico.

Overall, IMIFAP's programs have trained more than 30,000 teachers, health personnel, and community members as reproductive health promoters in 11 different countries. Our work has reached more than 11 million children, adolescents, and parents. We have distributed more than 7.5 million books and more than 1 million posters and pamphlets regarding gender, health, and empowerment. Currently, IMIFAP programs are being implemented in 9 countries throughout Latin America and with Latinos in the United States.

CONCLUSION

The results of IMIFAP's research in the field of gender and reproductive health indicate that psychology and theory can be combined to create interventions that successfully address the practical needs of women, adolescents, and health care personnel. These interventions can then be used as tools for advocating on behalf of larger-scale policy changes. By developing theory-based programs that address practical mental health needs, we as psychologists have a unique opportunity to contribute to improving the day-to-day lives and health of individuals as well as to impact the ways in which our leaders develop public policies that affect our own communities and communities around the world.

REFERENCES

Ajzen, I., & Fishbein, M. (1980). *Understanding attitudes and predicting social behavior*. Englewood Cliffs, NJ: Prentice-Hall.

Bateson, M. C. (1990). *Composing a life*. New York: Penguin Putnam.

Fawcett, G., Heise, L., Isita, L., & Pick, S. (1999). Changing community responses to wife abuse: A research and demonstration project in Iztacalco, Mexico. *American Psychologist, 54*(1), 41–49.

Fawcett, G., & Isita, L. (2000). *Rompamos la cadena de la violencia: Un taller para mujeres sobre violencia en la relación de parejas* [We break the chain of violence: A workshop for women on violence in partner relationships]. Mexico: Editorial IDEAME, S.A. de C.V.

Fernández, F., Pick, S., & Givaudan, M. (2002). *Deja volar a tu adolescente y sera un gran adulto* [Let your adolescent fly and he or she will be a great adult]. Mexico: Editorial IDEAME, S.A. de C.V.

Givaudan, M., Pick, S., Aldaz, E., & Saldívar, A. (1996). Creencias y normas que influyen las conductas sexuales de las mujeres respecto a la prevención del SIDA [Beliefs and norms that influence sexual conduct in women, with respect to AIDS]. *La Psicología Social en México, VI,* 187–192.

Givaudan, M., Ramón, J., Camacho, D., & Pick, S. (1997, September 26). *Qualitative evaluation of the Yo Quiero, Yo Puedo program for 5th and 6th grades.* Report presented to the World Bank by IMIFAP—Educación, salud y vida, Washington, DC.

IMIFAP-SOMARC Futures Group (Developer). (1993). *Video: Un Farmaceuta, Un Amigo* [A pharmacist, a friend]. Mexico.

Lewin, K. (1951). *Field theory in social science*. New York: Harper Row.

Paz, O. (1961). *The labyrinth of solitude: Life and thought in Mexico*. New York: Grove Press.

Pick, S. (1985, November). *Psychological components of research in sexual health in Mexico.* Presentation at the Third Colombian Congress of Sexology, Bogota, Colombia.

Pick, S. (1986, February). *Research, education, and services in sexual and reproductive health: The case of Mexico.* Paper presented at the First Latin American Congress of the World Mental Health Federation, Mexico City, Mexico.

Pick, S., & Givaudan, M. (1996). *Yo Quiero, Yo Puedo* [I want, I love, I can]. Mexico: Editorial IDEAME, S.A. de C.V.

Pick, S., Givaudan, M., & Aldaz, E. (1996, June 28). *Adolescent sexuality: A qualitative study in Mexico City.* Report presented to the Rockefeller Foundation by IMIFAP—Educación, salud y vida, New York.

Pick, S., Givaudan, M., & Brown, J. (2000). Quietly, working for school-based sexuality education in Mexico: Strategies for advocacy. *Reproductive Health Matters, 8*(16), 92–102.

Pick, S., Givaudan, M., & Martinez, A. (1995). Aprendiendo a ser papá y mamá: de niñas y niños desde el nacimiento hasta los 12 años [Learning to be a mom and dad for girls and boys from birth to 12 years old]. Mexico: Editorial Planeta.

Pick, S., Givaudan, M., & Poortinga, Y. (in press). Sexuality and life skills education: Multi-strategy interventions in Mexico. *American Psychologist.*

Pick, S., Poortinga, Y., & Givaudan, M. (in press). Integrating intervention theory and strategy in culture-sensitive health promotion programs. *Professional Psychology: Research and Practice.*

Pick de Weiss, S., Aguilar, J., Rodriguez, G., Reyes, J., Collado, M. E., Pier, D., et al. (1988). *Planeando tu vida: Nuevo programa de educacion sexual para adolescentes* [Planning your life: A new program of sexual education for adolescents]. Mexico: Editorial Planeta (7th edition, 1997; 14th printing, 2002).

Pick de Weiss, S., & Andrade, P. (1989, May 31). *Development and longitudinal evaluation of comparative sex education courses.* Report presented to the Agency for International Development by IMIFAP—Educación, salud y vida, Washington, DC.

Pick de Weiss, S., Andrade-Palos, P., Townsend, J., & Givaudan, M. (1994). Evaluación de un programa de educación sexual sobre conocimientos, conducta sexual y anticoncepción en adolescentes [Evaluation of a sexual education program about knowledge, sexual conduct, and contraception in adolescents]. *Salud Mental, 17*(1), 25–31.

Pick de Weiss, S., Atkin, L. C., Gribble, J. N., & Andrade-Palos, P. (1991). Sex, contraception and pregnancy among adolescents in Mexico City. *Studies in Family Planning, 22*(2), 74–82.

Prochaska, J., & DiClemente, C. (1982). Transtheoretical therapy: Toward a more integrative model of change. *Psychotherapy: Theory, Research and Practice, 19*(3), 276–287.

Reproductive Health in Developing Countries: Expanding Dimensions, Building Solutions. (1997). In A. O. Tsui, J. N. Wasserheit, & J. G. Haaga (Eds.), *Panel on reproductive health.* Washington, DC: National Academy Press.

Ruiz, M. G., & Fawcett, G. (1999). *Rostros y máscaras de la violencia: Un taller sobre amistad y noviazgo para adolescentes* [Faces and masks of violence: A workshop for adolescents on friendships and dating]. Mexico: Editorial IDEAME, S.A. de C.V.

USAID. (2000). Economic growth and poverty reduction. In *Women 2000: Beijing Plus Five.* Retrieved June 17, 2003, from http://www.genderreach.com/pdfs/pubs/Beijing-section-5.pdf

Venguer, T., & Givaudan, M. (2001, September 15). *Multiplication of an integral health education program for young women in the Oaxaca region of Mexico.* Report presented to GlaxoSmithKline by IMIFAP—Educación, salud y vida, Mexico City.

Venguer, T., Givaudan, M., Reyes, J., & Miranda, L. (1999). *El rol del personal de salud en la sociedad: Un enfoque humanista* [The role of health care providers in society: A humanist approach]. Mexico: Editorial IDEAME, S.A. de C.V.

Venguer, T., Quezada, M., Pick, S., Cabral, J., Montero, G. N., Morales, N., et al. (1999). *Programa de educacion integral para la salud de la mujeres en el medio rural: "Si yo estoy bien, mi familia tambien"* [Integral health education program for rural women: "If I am fine, so is my family"]. Mexico: IMIFAP—Educacion, salud y vida.

6

PSYCHOLOGICAL APPROACHES TO COMMUNITY HEALTH: COMMUNITY HEALTH PSYCHOLOGY

VICTOR DE LA CANCELA, JUDITH L. ALPERT, TOM WOLFF, AND SHOSHANA L. DACHS

The community health psychology perspective emphasizes the community as the unit of intervention and psychological principles as the units of analysis. Its biopsychosocial approach is systemic, ensuring that individuals are treated in their family, cultural, economic, and community context. Its roots lie in clinical community psychology and public health orientations and a commitment to social activism among its proponents. Community health psychologists have historically advocated for social justice, human rights, access to quality health and human services, systems change, collaboration among practitioners and consumers, partnerships of cultural equity, and empowerment at the individual, family, and community level (Chin, De La Cancela, & Jenkins, 1998). It has been suggested that for this approach "to be truly effective, psychology as a field must reinvent itself and fully embrace this perspective in order to lead other providers, consumers, and policymakers in this crucial social movement" (Kuramoto, 1998).

Indeed, community health psychologists believe diversification of the psychologist's (and psychology's) role is paramount to promote the overall health and well-being of underserved communities. Role diversification of psychologists expands opportunities for the profession to impact progressively relevant policy development, outreach, management, and practice (Jenkins, De La Cancela, & Chin, 1998). It is the intent of this chapter to illustrate how community health psychologists are meeting this objective in varied community settings by playing a change agent role in enabling others to take ownership and promote changes. The three sections of this chapter reflect both the diversity of perspectives and backgrounds and shared vision of a community health model. Section one describes how psychologists can improve the prevention of child sexual abuse by educating the parents and the wider community of the importance of disclosure and creating environments in which disclosure will be forthcoming. Section two reflects how psychologists involved in or interested in the training of family medicine residents can contribute through development of community health and cultural competency curricula. The final section delineates how psychologists are involved in macro efforts to improve the quality of life for various communities. Each section identifies some research and practice opportunities for psychologists interested in promoting the development of healthy communities. Each also identifies how psychologists can remain relevant and contribute to the profession by pioneering and reinventing praxis responsive to social change.

In an age of technology and rapid social change, individuals and communities are seeking ways to integrate all aspects of life and to empower themselves by taking control of their health and environments. Psychologists can integrate these perspectives in clinical practice and fashion new roles for the profession in the public interest, community health, and public health systems. The approaches described in each section emphasize health and prevention within community contexts or developmental challenges within traumatic situations that can move clients, patients, psychologists, and communities toward restoration of well-being and improved quality of life. To do so, psychologists need to reexamine and recommit to their roles as change agents, and embrace multidisciplinary and culturally competent perspectives to forge collaboration across diverse groups.

SECTION I: DISCLOSURE AND CHILD SEXUAL ABUSE PREVENTION

A major problem in our society is the sexual abuse of children and youth. A widely used estimate is that 20% of the female population and 5–10% of the male population are victims of child sexual abuse (Finkelhor, 1994). There is little disclosure of child sexual abuse, yet benefits can result from disclosure provided the recipients of the disclosure respond with support. Psychology can help by educating adults to hear and children and youth to tell about their own or others' abuse. Psychologists need to help people *to want to know, to know how to know, and to know what to do once they do know.* Furthermore, they need to help children and youth to want to tell.

We present an abbreviated case of child sexual abuse that impacted on an entire community. Although it is a fictionalized version of a true account, the case illustrates why the victim may not tell and why people may not hear.

Sexual Abuse on a Bus

One bus driver sexually abused a group of children from a predominantly White, middle-class community almost every day over several years. It took place in parking lots and in the back of the bus while the bus driver's friend drove. The children ranged in age from 5 to 10 years old at the time of the abuse. The abuse involved fondling, oral sex, and sodomy. Although every child may not have been involved in all of these acts, every child was involved in some way and every child was a witness to sexual abuse for 1–3 years. Many of the children returned from school with rectal bleeding and they reported pain when urinating and defecating. Parents found bruises, abrasions, and imprints on the children's thighs and buttocks. They found bloodstains on the children's underwear. Despite such physical evidence, dramatic psychological symptoms, and disguised communications, many children were exploited over several years. Approaches common to perpetrators of extrafamilial child sexual abuse were used. The bus driver gained the children's confidence by befriending their parents, giving the children gifts and candy and promising them prized meetings with their athletic heroes, playing nonsexual games initially, turning nonsexual games into sexual games, and eventually ensuring secrecy by means of threats. Houses would be burned. Parents would be killed. Siblings would be kidnapped.

The legal case initiated by the families of these 18 children never went to trial. Rather, it was settled out of court. At the time of settlement, the bus driver was already serving a 20–60-year prison term for the rape, sodomy, and sexual abuse of 20 other children.

How could this happen? The bus driver was friendly. He had kids about the ages of their children. Many of the parents had known him since grade school. The sexual abuse on the bus was denied. Some of the children attempted to tell about the ongoing abuse. One child tried to tell the adults as best she could. The adults did not hear. The child used a vocabulary based on her level of development as well as shame and the adults were operating out of disbelief and ignorance about sexual abuse, a desire not to know about evil, and a primitive understanding about child sexual trauma.

Problem

Although disclosure can be therapeutic, victims often do not disclose. Victims and witnesses remain silent about abuse for a variety of reasons. In a study of adults who were victims of childhood abuse, the most common reasons identified for not disclosing were fear of the abuser (85%) and fear of negative reactions from other family members (85%; Palmer, Brown, Rae-Grant, & Loughlin, 1999). Other reasons for nondisclosure include self-blame, difficulty in talking about the abuse, concern that they would not be believed, and lack of knowledge that the abuse was inappropriate. Victims are frequently not believed, which can have a deleterious impact on the victim. The disclosure, which may involve recantations and vague, partial, confused, and vacillating comments, may seem unbelievable.

Disclosure Can Be Therapeutic

To receive the full benefits of disclosure and to minimize its adverse effects, the child must be the recipient of a positive reaction to the disclosure (Gries et al., 2000). Keeping an abuse secret is associated with the negative effects of child sexual abuse (Hanson et al., 1992; Hoefnagels & Baartman, 1997; Waller & Ruddock, 1993). It is generally acknowledged that healing from sexual abuse trauma is related to having at least one significant other hear the abuse story in a way that communicates belief, understanding, and capacity for prevention of further trauma (Gries, Goh, & Cavanaugh, 1996; Gries et al., 2000). For example, there was less emotional and behavioral disturbance in those victims who received support from adults on whom they depend (Adams-Tucker, 1982; Tufts, 1984) and children who disclosed in court reported feeling good about disclosing (London Ontario Family Court Clinic, 1995). Clearly disclosing can have the following positive effects: It can result in the victim (a) being protected from further abuse, (b) receiving treatment for the abuse, and, possibly, (c) being helped simply by being heard and learning that the abuse was not his or her fault. Moreover, it can prevent revictimization of that child or the victimization and revictimization of other children.

Statistics on disclosure of child sexual abuse indicate that most children do not disclose (Gonzalez, Waterman, Kelly, McCord, & Oliveri, 1993; Lawall, 1993; Palmer et al., 1999) and, when they do, it is usually decades later (Finkelhor, 1979; Russell, 1983; Wyatt, 1985). Sometimes there is disclosure. There are two types: accidental (revealed by chance) and purposeful (child consciously decides to tell). Based on their research, Sorenson and Snow (1991) noted that accidental disclosure is the most common type (74% of their sample). Furthermore, Sorenson and Snow (1991) found that disclosures by preschoolers are more likely to be accidental. In contrast, disclosures by older children and adolescents are more likely to be purposeful

(Sorensen & Snow, 1991; Mian, Wehrspan, Klajner, LeBaron, & Winder, 1986). Also, the type of abuse seems to be related to the type of disclosure. Purposeful disclosure, for example, is more frequent in cases of extrafamilial abuse than in intrafamilial abuse (Gomes-Schwartz, Horowitz, & Cardarelli, 1988). The child victim is more likely to disclose if she or he was not threatened or coerced by the abuser (Butler, 1978; Conte & Berliner, 1987). The length of abuse is related to the type of disclosure with lengthier abuses associated with disclosure. In one study, purposeful disclosures occurred in the situation in which sexual abuse had been ongoing for 24 months or more (Farrell, 1988).

There has been research on the person to whom a child makes a disclosure. It has been found that if disclosures are made, they are directed to a nonabusive parent, another relative, a neighbor or friend, and, less frequently, to professionals or others (Gries et al., 1996; Palmer et al., 1999). In addition, there has been research on the impetus to disclose (Sorenson & Snow, 1991), process of disclosure (Gonzalez et al., 1993; Gries et al., 2000; Palmer et al., 1999; Sorenson & Snow, 1991), responses to disclosure (Everson, Hunter, Runyon, Edelsohn, & Coulter, 1989; Gries et al., 2000; Sirles & Franke, 1989) and the effects of disclosure (Gries et al., 2000; Palmer et al., 1999).

What is crucial is how the recipient accepts disclosures. Research seems to indicate that children are at risk for developing problems from the social reaction following abuse disclosure. Victim disclosure can have a positive, neutral, or negative effect. What seems to make a difference is the response that results from the victim's disclosure. If it is negative, the effects on the victim are usually negative, and if it is positive, the effects on the victim can be positive (Conte & Schuerman, 1987; James, 1989; Palmer et al., 1999; Peters, 1988; Roberts & Taylor, 1993). Palmer and colleagues (1999) reported a relation between the reactions children receive to their disclosure and their levels of self-esteem and family functioning. Other research (De-Francis, 1969; Fromuth, 1983; Wyatt & Mickey, 1988) indicates that the relationship between the victim and the person to whom he or she discloses may not be as important as the person's response to the disclosure.

It appears that full support is not often given to the disclosing child. Full support includes believing the child, offering emotional support, and taking action such as removing or reporting the offender (Palmer et al., 1999; Everson et al., 1989; Sirles & Franke, 1989). On the basis of Lawall's (1993) summary of 12 studies concerned with child abuse disclosure, she concluded that children receive little, if any support in their disclosures. Responses to disclosure include inaction (Palmer et al., 1999), the minimization of abuse, and the blaming or rejection of the child (Roberts & Taylor, 1993). Factors that are related to degree of support directed to the victim include whether the mother was an abuse victim and type of abuse (intrafamilial or extrafamilial). Lawall (1993) cautioned that it is difficult to derive conclusions given the paucity of research. Nevertheless, she noted that the research points to an age difference with respect to response to child disclosure, with preschoolers more likely to be believed than teenage victims and teenage victims more likely to be blamed for the abuse than victims of other ages. Although there is some discrepancy in the literature, the research seems to indicate that parents and others need help in providing more support to victimized children both before and after disclosure.

In the most comprehensive study of disclosure, Gries and colleagues (2000) made accommodations for (a) levels of disclosure (no, partial, full, had recanted but disclosed partially, had recanted but fully re-disclosed, had recanted but not re-disclosed, and had recanted repeatedly); (b) degrees of support and nonsupport (adverse, full support, partial support, nonsupport, and mixed); (c) and a miscellany of potentially significant people (offender, nonoffending parent, caseworker, foster parent, and other relative). They found significant behavior differences between those children who actively disclosed and those who were non-disclosing or non-redisclosing. Children who addressed the past trauma openly exhibited less externalizing behavior and were less dissociative than the recanters. Furthermore, it was found that fully supportive reactions by foster parents were related to healthy emotional functioning in those children who were in foster care. The investigators indicate that their study suggests that the disclosure response by the person who spends the most time with the child who was abused can have a significant impact.

What Psychologists Can Do

First, psychologists can further develop child sexual abuse prevention programs in a way that places more emphasis on disclosure. School-based prevention programs primarily address core safety concepts such as body ownership, the distinction between good touch and bad touch, finding the courage to say "no," and learning skills for escape. In addition, programs may emphasize that children learn to discern which types of secrets should not be kept, as well as identify those adults to whom children can turn for help. Child sexual abuse programs as well as those that stress assertiveness and personal rights are a major impetus for disclosure especially for primary school-age children. Schools that implemented programs aimed at preventing child sexual abuse received significantly more abuse disclosures during the following year (Hoefnagels & Baartman, 1997).

Psychologists can engage in empirical validation regarding the impact of these programs on disclosure. Whereas detection of ongoing sexual abuse has been defined as one of the primary goals of these prevention initiatives, relatively few evaluation studies have employed disclosure rates as a measure of prevention program success or provide empirical information regarding the relationship between disclosures and prevention programs. In a comprehensive review of 30 studies focusing on the efficacy of child sexual abuse prevention programs (McIntyre & Carr, 2000), only 4 out of 30 program evaluations used disclosure rates as a measure of program efficacy.

Clearly, the data from these few preliminary studies provide ample evidence that children who participate in these primary prevention programs and receive safety skills training are significantly more likely to disclose past or current sexual victimization (McIntyre & Carr, 1999). Until the recent evaluation of the Stay Safe Program by McIntyre and Carr (1999), no empirical study had been conducted with the basic goal of identifying the percentage of children who disclose in response to a child sexual abuse prevention program.

Second, professionals need to work to create environments in which disclosure will be forthcoming. Abuse may be disclosed in supportive environments, which can include counseling and therapy situations and schools and consultation rooms (Hoefnagels & Baartman, 1997) or by means of a brief evaluation protocol for eliciting information about prior sexual abuse in children (Gries, Goh, & Cavanaugh, 1996).

One creative intervention designed to increase disclosures on a national scale (in the Netherlands) could serve as a model. Hoefnagels and Baartman (1997) ran a high intervention density campaign that involved, for example, billboard advertisements, television programs for children, announcements about an abuse-line to which children were invited to phone, documentaries, articles, and education for teachers around listening to and believing children and reporting. The results indicated that mass media communication influenced the process of disclosure. The investigators reported that there were three times as many calls to the Child Line Services as there were preintervention.

Third, it has been found (McIntyre & Carr, 2000) that sexual abuse prevention programs are particularly effective if children are not the only targeted program recipients. Programs are more effective if such significant others as parents and teachers are trained as well.

Thus, psychologists can educate the general community about the importance of the response to disclosure, the process of disclosure, and the importance of certain educational programs that are an impetus for disclosure.

Perhaps most important in the discussion of facilitating disclosure is educating mental health providers regarding the process of disclosure. Sorenson and Snow (1991) studied the process of child sexual abuse disclosure in more than 100 children ages 3–17. The sexual abuse of these children was confirmed. They found that the majority of the victims (79%) initially denied the abuse. Active disclosure followed denial in only 7% of the children. Most of the children (78%) made tentative disclosures. Recantations of allegations were common as well (22%). The disclosures were frequently vague, partial, confused, and inaccurate. Often the children vacillated from disclosure to denial. Their work supports that disclosure is a process rather than a one-time event or a simple statement. The public must understand this process.

When young children disclose, they are more likely to disclose accidentally. Because many accidental disclosures involve children "telling" by means of sexualized behavior and inappropriate statements, it is important that professionals and others be knowledgeable about sexual acting out behaviors in children and other ways that young children may disclose. Although sexual acting out behaviors do not identify sexual abuse, they can serve as a red flag.

Finally, peer influence can be an impetus for adolescent disclosure of child sexual abuse (Sorenson & Snow, 1991). Thus, professionals need to think about developing programs for sexual abuse identification and prevention that model those used for the identification and prevention of suicide or drug abuse by means of peer support.

Conclusion

Both primary and secondary prevention efforts are needed. Disclosures enable both. Disclosures of past or current abuse can prevent victimization (primary prevention) or revictimization of the victim or revictimization of other children (secondary prevention). We need to educate children and their parents in order to prevent child sexual abuse and we need to educate parents and other significant adults to recognize child sexual abuse, enable disclosures, and respond constructively to disclosures. Disclosure plays a dual role in prevention by preventing both new instances of abuse as well as preventing revictimization in those who were abused in the past.

SECTION II: DEVELOPING A COMMUNITY HEALTH CURRICULUM IN FAMILY MEDICINE

Clinical, counseling, health, and medical psychologists are increasingly expanding their role as educators, clinicians, and collaborators in primary care. Family medicine and practice settings have historically been friendly to psychology, social work, and other behavioral sciences. In the late 1970s and early 1980s, most behavioral scientists in family practice were family physicians, psychiatrists, or nonclinical academics. Currently, over 90 percent of behavioral science faculty consists of psychologists, family therapists, social workers, psychiatric nurses, and anthropologists (McCutchan,

Sanders, & Vogel, 1999). The role of the behavioral scientist in primary care sites can include teaching team competencies; conducting clinical studies of outcomes of care to modify practice behavior; use of various patient satisfaction measures; development of valid, reliable measures of achievement of specific competencies; and emphasizing practical behavioral change counseling for health promotion and disease prevention in busy clinical practices (Association of Family Practice Residency Program Directors, 1999).

Traditionally, psychologists in these settings work as program managers, providers, consultants, or psychosocial faculty members whose expertise lies in patient–family systems interactions. They provide education to residents using seminars, video review, and direct observation. Some provide mental health services to patients and precept residents in clinics. Others co-teach with family physicians and engage in cross-disciplinary discussions with medical doctors introducing residents to collaborative discourse and multi-disciplinary problem solving. Many co-counsel with residents, do home visits with them, and conduct psychosocial rounds. Psychologists also give feedback to residents on their interviewing skills, and on interpersonal dynamics in interactions (McCutchan et al., 1999).

The psychologist's role in fostering the residents' development of essential skills in providing family-oriented comprehensive care is best appreciated by noting Residency Review Committee for Family Practice Program Requirements. Behavioral counseling is a required curricular element in the individual patient area. Family structure and dynamics, family development, child rearing, end of life issues, the role of the family in illness care, and family counseling are required curricular elements in the family area. Didactic and clinical curricular program requirements in Human Behavior and Mental Health include: diagnosis and management of psychiatric disorders in children and adults, emotional aspects of non-psychiatric disorders, psychopharmacology, alcoholism and other substance abuse, the physician–patient relationship, patient interviewing skills, counseling skills, normal psychosocial growth and development in individuals and families, and stages of stress in a family life cycle.

Curricular requirements also include sensitivity to gender, race, age, and cultural differences in patients; family violence including child, partner, and elder abuse (physical and sexual), as well as neglect, and its effect on both victims and perpetrators; medical ethics, including patient autonomy, confidentiality, and issues concerning quality of life; and factors influencing patient compliance.

Program requirements for the general medical care of women include addressing domestic violence, rape, and sexual abuse; women's changing role in society; preventing teenage pregnancy, eating disorders, and postassault sequelae. Required curricular elements for care of the older patient include preventive aspects of health care, psychological changes of senescence, social-cultural parameters, proper use of all members of the health care team, and functional assessment of elderly patients.

Community medicine program requirements include occupational medicine, disability assessment, employee health, community and public health resources, environmental health, disease prevention and health promotion, health assessment, health education, and healthful lifestyles.

In the 21st century practice of psychology, curriculum development within primary care internships and residencies can inform community-oriented primary care practice with patients, families, and communities. An important role for the psychologist is to both be an organizational change agent, stimulating critical thinking and social change, and to teach health professionals in training about their own change agent role by providing them with opportunities for dialogue on and skill attainment in the critical areas of cross-cultural communication, conflict resolution, and health care team building, including providers, administrators, and consumers.

Recently, professional psychologists on the cutting edge in these settings offer community psychology orientations, organizational change perspectives, and advocacy for culturally competent clinical service delivery that is population-based. Examples abound of how psychologists have become more population- or community-needs focused in AIDS/HIV care and domestic violence interventions. The American Psychological Association HIV Office for Psychology Education (HOPE) Training Resource Package 2000 provides an entirely modular, flexible, "non-curriculum-based" didactic and experiential components resource that includes epidemiological, primary, and mental health care integration and biopsychosocial-spiritual assessment and prevention information designed to be built-upon and updated as needed. Blending of traditional clinical psychology approaches with public and community health-oriented practice and research has led to innovative health promotion, disease prevention, and service delivery that addresses the complex sociopolitical issues of power and change in communities facing critical issues of health care, behavioral health, violence, aging, and racism in United States society (De La Cancela, Chin, & Jenkins, 1998).

Developing a longitudinal, multidisciplinary community health and cultural competency curriculum requires institutional support, collaboration, and cooperation between course coordinators and residency program family physicians, as well as highly motivated residents. Such a curriculum recognizes that health care professionals are frequently asked to lead discussion and ameliorative efforts in their communities, workplaces, and schools related to issues of concern such as health disparities or youth violence. Thus, it promotes agendas for change by developing strategies to decrease disparities from the grass roots up; improve knowledge and skills for individual and organizational leadership, development, and training; and provide practical applications that residents can use to address community demands for information, access, equitable treatment, integrative primary health care, and cultural competency.

The following aspirational curriculum, a work in progress based on one psychologist's experiences, can be used to generate ideas for discussion, to provide a format for planning instruction, and to identify best practices and evidence-based resources. Although written from the perspective of the psychologist physician faculty in a family practice residency program, the curriculum is adaptable for use in other primary care internship and residency programs. Psychologists working in these programs both teach others to model their interventions and demonstrate their ability to (a) influence community health through involvement in community education projects, (b) collaborate with other health professionals in delivering community-oriented primary care, and (c) integrate care for the underserved and diverse communities in their postdoctoral practice (Association of Family Practice Residency Program Directors, 1999).

Goals of a Community Health Curriculum

A community health curriculum provides residents with greater exposure to Community Oriented Primary Care (COPC), the use of behavioral sciences in promoting community health and in individual, family, and community health. It also provides residents with opportunities for personal growth and self-understanding (Association of Family Practice Residency Program Directors, 1999).

COPC is defined as "[t]he provision of primary care services to a defined community, coupled with systematic efforts to identify and address the major health problems of that community through effective modifications in both the primary care services and other appropriate community health programs" (Nutting, Wood, & Conner, 1985, p. 1763). In a 1999 "Action Plan for the Future of Residency Education in Family Practice" the Association of Family Practice Residency Program Directors (AFPRD) suggests that residencies define community as the population of patients they serve. The intent being to identify one or more subgroups of patient populations to target in the development of COPC and population-based projects, as well as communities, which are geographically near Family Practice Centers (FPC). FPCs are an integral component in educating family physicians, serving as the laboratory in which residents develop skills necessary to provide continuous, comprehensive care within a team-based setting (Association of Family Practice Residency Program Directors, 1999). The Action Plan clearly states that residents should develop two community competencies: Community-oriented primary care, and service to vulnerable and underserved populations (Association of Family Practice Residency Program Directors, 1999).

AFPRD specifically encourages family practice residencies to incorporate service to vulnerable and underserved populations in their mission and to include consideration of interest in caring for underserved populations in resident applicant acceptance criteria. Their definition of underserved and vulnerable populations includes people who lack access to care not only because they are poor or live in health professional shortage areas but also because of diagnosis, sexual orientation, race, ethnicity, gender, or language (Association of Family Practice Residency Program Directors, 1999). Another identification of routinely underserved populations includes the uneducated and mentally retarded, pregnant adolescents and their partners, men of color, migrant workers, recent immigrants, and residents of rural areas (Jenkins et al., 1998).

The National Center for Cultural Competence (NCCC) has identified the goal of eliminating long-standing disparities in the health status of people of diverse racial, ethnic, and cultural backgrounds as a key reason for incorporating cultural competence into institutional change efforts. NCCC reached this conclusion on review of the fact that nowhere are the divisions of race, ethnicity, and culture more sharply drawn than in the health of the U.S. population. The center posits that cultural competence has to be inextricably linked to the definition of specific health outcomes and to an on ongoing system of accountability that is committed to reducing health disparities (NCCC, 1998). Current focus on elimination of health disparities has extended to age, sexual orientation, and other variables, and ways in which varied organizations, communities, schools, and business can collaborate toward this end.

Establishing New Community Health Learning Opportunities

The psychologist reaches out to community institutions to enhance family medicine residents' exposure to community health issues throughout the life span (preschool, senior centers, hospices) and to expand services to underserved populations (abused women and children, and people living with substance abuse, developmental delay and mental retardation, serious and persistent mental illness). These settings allow family medicine residents to develop collaboration skills working both as team members and leaders. Although many of these settings lack physician or nurse practitioner supervisors, they are highly interested in residents providing preventive public health or community health interventions and request residents rotating through their sites to deliver health education and related patient education workshops. Others seek residents to sit on their health advisory committees.

For example, a community-based organization (CBO) involved in providing housing for the homeless requests a long range collaboration with a residency program involving community health education, health system advocacy, and organizing with youth. Another CBO requests a resident to be involved in the organization and coordination of community health care resources to sponsor an annual health fair as part of his or her rotation at the program.

Allied health care programs, colleges, universities, and government agencies are contacted for possible collaboration in providing community projects for residents to complete as part of their professional development. Research, teaching, and mentoring opportunities for residents in community-based training of future health professionals who intend to work in underserved communities are arranged in collaboration with local area health education centers. Doctoral training programs in clinical psychology and master in public health (MPH) programs in community health agree to place their students in family practice–affiliated, school-based health centers at nearby high schools. Public health schools also seek to place MPH students in community health education to complete required field placement at FPC under the supervision of a resident-faculty team.

Psychologist, resident, nurse practitioner, nurse, social worker, and clerk collaborate in conducting health fairs and national disease prevention, screening, and education activities (Anxiety Recognition and Smoking Cessation campaigns) and provide needed education and outreach to consumers working and living within the community. Illustrative is a managed long-term care plan that provides a unique opportunity for residents to plan and coordinate comprehensive, interdisciplinary, biopsychosocial care for adults living with physical disability in collaboration with disabled consumers. Such settings also afford residents a degree of exposure to complex social and medical pathology that simply is not available in the confines of a hospital or FPC.

Teaching Methods

Residents are placed or rotate through community agencies (health care, worksite, school, and university), select a specific community project that they will make a formal presentation on to the residency program, or are given a structured outreach, linkage, or needs assessment assignment related to an identified area of need in the community. Conferences, grand and psychosocial rounds, and resident precepting use guest faculty and community presenters, featuring prominent psychologists. Community assessments, small group activity, debate or dialogue, video review, and participatory teaching occur (Bell, Kozakowski, & Winter, 1997). Topics are chosen from among the following:

I. Community Health Knowledge (Doyle & Ward, 2001)
   A. Community-oriented primary care
   B. Epidemiological approaches in the community
   C. Historical and life span perspectives
   D. Health status of ethnic communities
   E. Planning and implementing health programs
      1. Social marketing
      2. Locating funds and grants
      3. Models of collaboration
      4. Community coalitions
      5. Coordinating health events
   F. Communicating health and health education needs
      1. Health advocacy
      2. Communication strategies and principles
      3. Health education and health educators
      4. Code of ethics for health educators
   G. Healthy People 2010 objectives, effective models, opportunities
   H. Health education in the Internet age (distance learning, social marketing)
   I. Program evaluation (new approaches to qualitative and quantitative research)
   J. Behavioral health care roles in HIV primary care
   K. Domestic violence identification/intervention in family practice
   L. School health (adapted from *Recommended Curriculum Guidelines for Family Practice Residents, Adolescent Health* [American Academy of Family Physicians, 1999])
      1. Behavioral disabilities
      2. Screening (ADHD, dyslexia)
      3. Gang, family, and sexual violence and harassment
      4. Eating disorders
      5. Effects of peer pressure and peer support
      6. Child and adolescent gender and sexual identity issues
      7. Medico-legal issues of consent and confidentiality in the school physician–pediatric patient interaction
      8. Avoidance of recreational drug use and smoking; alcohol cessation
      9. Safe sexual practices and pregnancy prevention
      10. Suicide and homicide
      11. Cultural, class, ethnic, and gender differences that affect school health care
      12. Effects of family, school, community, cultural, and societal

environment on growth and development (parents, siblings, teachers, media, poverty, firearm availability, spirituality)

II. Community Health Skills
   A. Assessing community health issues
   B. Needs assessment strategies (focus groups, surveys)
   C. Community participation and capacity building (Henley & Williams, 1999)
   D. Using the PRECEDE–PROCEED model of health promotion planning to assess Predisposing, Reinforcing, and Enabling Constructs in the Educational Diagnosis and Evaluation, and the Policy, Regulatory, and Organizational Constructs for Educational and Environmental Development (Green & Kreuter, 1991)
   E. Community-oriented primary care assessment (Williams, Crabtree, O'Brien, Zyzanski, & Gilchrist, 1999)
   F. Advocacy in health policy and education
   G. Health policy development with local boards of health
   H. Communicating with local legislators

III. Learning Objectives in Community Health: To individualize their learning residents will select from the following learning objectives as they prepare for their community health rotations, electives, and community projects and will demonstrate the ability
   A. To collaborate with CBOs, and public health resources
   B. To collaborate with other health care professionals (psychologists, nurse educators, certified health education specialists, social workers, pharmacists)
   C. To participate in the formation of an FPC COPC committee composed of residents, faculty, staff, patients, and members of the community
   D. To conduct a qualitative COPC community assessment
   E. To implement COPC projects
   F. To develop patient and community education materials
   G. To integrate consumer perspectives in understanding, assessing, and planning for health care needs
   H. To learn principles of COPC as applied to specific populations
   I. To integrate care for the underserved in their postresidency practices

Community Health Competencies

Community Health Projects involve self-directed scholarship in which the residents relate their interests to the residency program's COPC goals, designing projects that satisfy both curricular requirements and their own professional objectives, learning with faculty in an educational partnership that stimulates critical thinking, specialized knowledge, and social change relating to the unique health problems of communities (Harper, Baker, & Rief, 2000).

Key American College of Graduate Medical Education (ACGME) competencies that residents can develop from conducting community health projects and participating in community medicine rotations are (a) appreciation and recognition of the community as the primary context for promoting healthy behaviors and reducing health risks, (b) responsiveness to the need of patients and society that supercedes self-interest, (c) awareness that health care is provided in the context of a larger system and the ability to call on system resources to support the care of patients, and (d) advocacy for quality patient care and assisting patients in dealing with system complexities (Murray, 2000).

At the end of each training year residents will be evaluated in terms of their progress in achieving the following AFPRD Strategic Planning Working Group Recommended Community Competencies (Association of Family Practice Residency Program Directors, 1999).

1. Understands COPC and the practice of population-based medicine (Henley & Williams, 1999).
2. Capable of assessing the health needs of a community, developing interventions and assessing the outcomes.
3. Recognizes the importance of interventions beyond the level of the individual patient and her or his family to improve overall health status.
4. Actively participates in the design, implementation, and evaluation of COPC programs.
5. Understands the role of community in the lives of patients.
6. Learns the role family physicians play in meeting the health care needs of underserved and vulnerable populations.
7. Analyzes the economics of the U.S. health care system, including the history of financing health care to the poor, charity care, Medicaid and Medicare, and problems of the uninsured.
8. Identifies health problems prevalent in the poor, homeless, and populations of color compared with the general population.
9. Possesses clinical experience working in sites that serve underserved and vulnerable populations.

Because residency programs must provide educational experiences for the residents to develop their competencies in these areas, an interdisciplinary COPC team consisting of a clinical-community psychologist, family medicine faculty physician, FPC social worker, family nurse practitioner, and resident interacts with a variety of community organizations, with a focus on those potentially relevant for COPC projects that residents could later develop (Thompson et al., 1997). The interdisciplinary team models teamwork, which is a central tenet of COPC, in choosing themes relevant to both community health and primary care such as access to care, youth violence, or chemical dependency to guide the search for appropriate community projects. To increase the success of such a team, it must be consistently supported and reinforced by all faculty clinicians. Family practice faculty, including those not directly involved in teaching community health, should be role models advocating for COPC principles in comprehensive health care. The best role models are those attendings that use community resources, work in community settings, and provide residents guidance in arranging supervised projects in a community setting that complement their professional goals (Thompson et al., 1997; Association of Family Practice Residency Program Directors, 1999).

A primary role of the community health psychologist is to be a resident advisor, mentor, and role model in promoting the development of leadership potential among residents. The psychologist emphasizes the knowledge and skills necessary to take a leadership role in local, community health policy development and the residency or focus on issues of importance to the health of underserved populations. Talented residents who have shown their potential in work experience and community activities receive support to increase their leadership capability, increase understanding of current key health policy issues, develop innovative solutions to critical issues in public health services affecting underserved or vulnerable populations, and develop a network with local and community experts in health policy and public health careers—for example, lobbyists and members of state legislature health committees.

In accordance with AFPRD recommendations, the COPC curriculum is taught in conjunction with the multicultural curriculum whenever possible (Association of Family Practice Residency Program Directors, 1999). An aspirational community health curriculum aims to foster cultural competency among family medicine residents and faculty. It also attempts to address the concern raised by recent findings that physicians who work with patients of color lack involvement in three of the four distinct activities through which physicians interact with their communities (Garr & Rhyne, 1998; Pathman, Steiner, Williams, & Riggins, 1998).

But how can multicultural competence be developed within the time constraints of an already intense residency education taxed by ever expanding and changing curricular requirements? Additionally, which cross-cultural curricula of the many that are being developed should be used? Noting that many of these have taken a categorical and potentially stereotyping approach that ties patients of specific cultures to a set of unifying characteristics, or overlooks the importance of social factors on cross-cultural encounters, Carrillo, Green, and Betancourt (1999) offered a patient-based, cross-cultural curriculum that provides an analytic framework to working with the individual patient's social context and cultural health beliefs and behaviors.

The curriculum consists of five thematic modules taught in both the intern and senior year of residency in four weekly 2-hour sessions that build on the existing focused and problem-oriented learning style of medical doctors. The modules include basic concepts, core cross-cultural issues, meaning of the illness, social context, and doctor–patient negotiation. The curriculum includes interview questions that are selectively used to obtain a social context "review of systems" and teaching activities that develop skills through 10–15 minute interviews with medical actors. This curriculum moves beyond looking at patients to health professionals as another source of diversity affecting care (Plotnikoff & Barnes, 2000).

Health providers coming from different ethnic groups or nationalities may differ over patient autonomy, quality of life, what patients can be told, and who makes decisions, suggesting that Western-oriented biomedical training does not obliterate the provider's cultural beliefs about health, illness, and the doctor–patient relationship. Another set of clinically relevant and concise, practical guidelines on culturally sensitive and competent health care that have been widely used and modified have been provided by Like, Steiner, and Rubel (1996). Elements of both these curricula have informed the development of key learning goals and objectives that psychologists can use.

1. To teach practical skills for analyzing the individual patient rather than teaching about cultural characteristics that can lead to stereotyping
2. To integrate a cross-cultural focus into residents' standard approach to patients rather than as "add on" to patient care
3. Clinicians will use a cross-cultural, primary care patient-based approach.

Methodology

The psychologist conducts an "Introduction to cross-cultural communication workshop" geared to interns. Guest presentations by 2nd and 3rd year residents are included to model physician skill development. Residents discuss relevant cultural aspects of patients' presentation and chief complaints. Preceptors routinely include such inquiries in their precepting in a manner similar to how they include psychosocial considerations. Interns and residents select outreach, linkage, needs assessment, placement, and related field experience in areas identified as having great diversity.

Video review, vignettes, and popular music videos provide realistic portrayals of how cultural factors can impact on health and quality of life. Clips are shown during weekly teaching activities to expand awareness of diverse lifestyles and trigger discussion of cultural competency issues pertaining to patient care. Popular songs with insightful lyrics familiar to community residents are examined to increase empathy toward patients. Curricula include short research and practice presentations, case studies, panel, debate, small group activity, and participatory learning (Bell, Kozakowski, & Winter, 1997; McCutchan et al., 1999).

Medical Spanish Rotation

The purpose of this 4-week rotation is to learn basic conversational Spanish, with an emphasis on medical communication to facilitate interaction with patients in the clinical setting. General and hospital related topics are developed, such as giving directions, working with interpreters, increasing familiarity with Latino cultures, and issues involved in ensuring linguistic access in primary care settings. Language skills are measured by faculty observation of an interview of a bilingual Spanish–English speaking patient, video review and discussion of interviews, and accompanying resident during a patient session. Pertinent videos, CD-ROMs, online resources, and journal articles are used in class.

Culturally Competent Community Oriented Primary Care

This month-long rotation provides residents with a clinical experience in a primary care health center serving an indigent and culturally diverse population in an urban setting. Residents provide health care and preventive services in the office, home, and diverse community settings. Residents learn about different health professional cultures by participating in interdisciplinary collaborative care team meetings. They are precepted in Culturally Competent Community Oriented Primary Care, conduct patient interviews that elicit health beliefs, conduct bilingual interviews with an interpreter, and use a team approach to patient care. They research a topic that integrates cultural competency and COPC aspects of their experience and present it to medical and other health professionals. Residents master use of various mnemonics with patients and share their experience during an interdisciplinary team meeting.

Clinical Practice Mnemonics

The Cross-Cultural SMARTS Model provides a mnemonic for hot topics or core areas in which physician–patient differences may emerge in cross-cultural encounters (Carrillo et al., 1999):

Sexual and gender issues
Mistrust and prejudice
Authority, autonomy, and family dynamics
Role of physician and biomedicine
Traditions and customs
Styles of communication

Betancourt, Carrillo, and Green's (1999) Medication Adherence *ESFT* model seeks to improve doctor–patient communication and cooperation in delivering health care to diverse populations:

Explanatory model
Social and financial barriers
Fears and concerns about medication
Therapeutic Contracting/Playback

Following is Carrillo, Green, and Betancourt's Determining the Patient's Social Context *TELL* (Pine, 1999) mnemonic:

Tension accounts for the patient's social support and social stressors
Environmental change relates to patient's previous experiences with health care providers
Language and literacy as factors in communication breakdown
Life control refers to subjective and objective factors that affect patient's sense of stability

SECTION III: HEALTHY COMMUNITIES: BUILDING COMMUNITIES FROM THE GROUND UP

From Europe to South America; from South Carolina to California; from the tiny hill towns of the Berkshires in Massachusetts to 21 different neighborhoods in the city of Boston communities are mobilizing around local issues and finding ways to create exciting new solutions. They are demonstrating the capacity of communities to rally together to solve their own problems. These broad-based initiatives are wonderful illustrations of the international healthy communities movement.

The goals of these community initiatives are ambitious: Nothing short of achieving radical measurable improvement in the health and long-term quality of life in U.S. communities (Norris, 1997). The movement has many names including "sustainable communities," "community building," and even "loveable communities." Some use the phrase "healthy communities," in which the term *health* is a metaphor for a much broader approach to building community.

The healthy communities movement emerged from the World Health Organization in 1986 and has quickly spread across the globe. A cornerstone of the healthy communities movement is the Ottawa Charter for Health Promotion (1986), which describes the prerequisites for health as peace, shelter, education, food, income, a stable ecosystem, sustainable resources, social justice, and equity. This broader definition of health allows the movement to address the needs of the whole community, to be responsible to whatever issues the community identifies, and to be comprehensive in its definition of community and health.

To produce a healthy community in addition to redefining the way we look at health, we also look at new mechanisms of community problem solving. These mechanisms rely on collaborative, multisectoral approaches that incorporate the promotion of citizen leadership while building on community strengths and empowering local citizens.

How would we know a healthy community if we saw one? Hancock and Duhl (1986) define the characteristics of a healthy community as including

- a clean, safe physical environment
- an ecosystem that is stable and sustainable
- a strong, mutually supportive, and nonexploitative community
- a high degree of participation and control by the public over decisions affecting their lives, health, and well-being
- meeting basic needs
- access to a wide variety of experiences and resources
- a diverse, vital, and innovative local economy
- encouragement of connectedness with the past
- an optimum level of appropriate public health and sick-care services
- and high levels of positive health and low levels of disease

There are ten commonly agreed-on core elements of healthy community efforts (Norris & Howell, 1999; Norris & Pittman, 2000; Wolff, 1995):

1. They employ a broad definition of health as noted in the Ottawa Charter (1986).
2. They build on a shared community vision and shared values. To accomplish this the community must create visioning processes that engage a broad spectrum of the community and identify shared values and hopes for the future.
3. They create shared ownership by involving the community in defining the issues and being part of the solution.

4. Relationships are the core of the process. The building of relationships across sectors, between the grassroots and the formal sectors, and within sectors is central to the healthy community process.

5. Membership is multisectoral, which means that those engaged in the healthy community process come from government, education, public safety, health services, faith-based organizations, neighborhoods, and grassroots organizations.

6. The process is citizen-driven. A core belief is that those most affected by the issues are central to the decision making.

7. Issues are addressed by collaborative problem solving. Himmelman (2001) has defined collaboration as a complex interorganizational relationship in which each party tries to enhance the capacity of the other. This is the high level of community functioning that healthy communities initiative strive for.

8. The community uses an assets-based approach. Kretzmann and McKnight (1993) have defined a way of looking at communities that builds on its assets not deficits. This is another critical building block for healthy communities.

9. Healthy communities initiatives move toward systems change. They always have a view beyond individual programs and solutions, and look to create systems change that can make a long-term difference.

10. Community initiatives develop clear measures of progress with indicators.

The content of healthy communities initiatives can vary enormously. Some are focused on traditional health indicators such as reducing the incidence of specific diseases or promoting specific preventive practices around a wide range of community identified health issues such as asthma, teen pregnancy, or substance abuse. Another set of healthy community initiatives address social problems such as community violence, domestic violence, and child abuse. A vibrant wing of healthy communities initiatives are focused on environmental issues promoting sustainable communities and fighting for environmental justice. And yet another form of healthy communities focuses on civic engagement dealing with what Robert Putnam in *Bowling Alone* (2000) has talked about as the United States' crisis of the decline of civic engagement. In this case the communities initiatives work to increase the involvement of citizens in community life.

Research on the impact of healthy community initiatives is just beginning to emerge. Berkowitz and Cashman (2000) noted that many healthy communities initiatives fail to engage in evaluation processes for a wide range of reasons including lack of time, lack of knowledge, lack of resources, and lack of qualified outside help.

Roussus and Fawcett (2000) reviewed the factors affecting the capacity of coalitions (like healthy community coalitions) to create community change. Looking across a wide number of studies they identified seven variables:

1. Having a clear vision and mission
2. Action planning for community and systems change
3. Developing and supporting leadership
4. Documentation and ongoing feedback on programs
5. Technical assistance and support
6. Securing financial resources for the work
7. Making outcomes matter

In Massachusetts, 16 years of long-term commitment have allowed community coalitions to grow and prosper (Wolff, 2001). Over time, these groups have successfully tackled many difficult community issues. Some of these healthy community coalitions have made the engagement of the grassroots their top goal. They have achieved this through devotion of resources and the application of successful techniques such as the development of mini-grants, neighborhood organizing, community health outreach workers, and leadership developments. Illustrative is how when the Northern Berkshire Community Coalition began to engage the grassroots they struggled with how to start. Finally, one neighborhood asked for help with absentee landlords and invited the coalition to a meeting. The coalition attended the meeting and began to focus on the neighborhoods. They began to rebuild neighbor associations across the city, and even build new neighborhood organizations. Soon, the city was celebrating its neighborhoods. Neighbor associations became an avenue for the city to reengage its communities through community policing, public health, arts, and recreation.

The Massachusetts coalitions have also been able to tackle larger systems issues. The Lower Outer Cape Community Coalition brought data on the livable wage to its residents. The livable wage or self-sufficiency standard measures the real costs of living, working, and paying taxes without subsidies. The coalition showed residents that according to the livable wage statistics the average Cape worker with one child needs to be earning $15 an hour to just survive. When the coalition presented this information to the Chamber of Commerce, Chambers members looked at the justification for the high wages and expressed concern about the lack of affordable child care and housing in the area. They noted that these issues were hurting worker retention and agreed to work together with the coalition on these issues. A unique new partnership aimed at systems change emerged in which the coalition and the business community work hand-in-hand on developing affordable housing and child care.

The same Massachusetts coalitions have made a real impact on the quality of life. In North Quabbin, a rural mill town area, residents faced significant transportation problems that prevented people from having access to work, health appointments, and higher education. The coalition tried for 10 years to find a solution. Finally a group of grassroots advocates, working from the local literacy project in partnership with coalitions, decided to tackle the problem. They began a ride pool, engaged the local transportation authorities, and advocated for change. A local Congressman became involved. Soon, a new transportation system with fixed routes and connecting rides was implemented. The coalitions also began a campaign to encourage ridership on the new buses. In the first year the new system provided more than 44,000 rides. This systems change, which affects education, health, and the economy, emerged as a result of the coalitions' collaboration, grassroots engagement, and advocacy.

Formal evaluations of these coalitions (Stein, 2001a, 2001b) have confirmed their effectiveness in enhancing the capacity of helping systems to collaborate on problems and their success in creating new solutions to community problems. The Lower Outer Cape Community Coalition has been the catalyst for the creation of programs that annually contribute $2.3 million of programming and 25 staff positions to the community.

So what are the opportunities for psychologists in healthy communities? David Chavis (Chavis, Florin, & Felix, 1992) has described the role of what he calls enabling systems that provide the supports for healthy communities initiatives in communities. The factors identified by Roussus and Fawcett (2000) that lead to successful coalitions are ones that many psychologists have the skills to contribute to: action planning, developing leadership, documentation and feedback, technical assistance, and making outcomes matter. Many community psychologists are presently providing the support systems for these healthy communities initiatives, as technical assistance and trainers, consultants, and evaluators.

The most critical role for psychologists can be to contribute to understanding of the issues and systems change possibilities inherent in healthy community efforts. The skills of psychologists, specifically community psychology skills, can be of great assistance to these efforts. These skills include (a) taking an ecological view of the issues, one that incorporates the context along with the individual; (b) understanding prevention programming, both what are the effective programs and of the key issues implementation; (c) understanding the critical steps in program development that lead to success; (d) developing the capacity to bring qualitative and quantitative evaluation and documentation skills to complex community interventions; and (e) specific group skills including group process facilitation and consultation. The healthy communities movement provides a world of opportunity for psychologists, especially those with the skills of a community psychologist, to find valuable ways to contribute to the future of America's communities.

COMMUNITY HEALTH PSYCHOLOGY AND SOCIAL CHANGE

This chapter has referred to social change repeatedly because we believe that all psychologists are accountable to the public and that our profession flourishes when it works for the public good. Community health psychology, like all health service disciplines, has a necessary relationship with economics, politics, and social change whenever it advocates for access to health care for all (Stephens, 2001). Similar to family practice, community health psychology has a generalist primary health orientation serving rural and urban underserved and vulnerable populations, emphasizing coordination, comprehensiveness and continuity of care, and the importance of behavioral sciences in health (Stephens, 2001). Community health psychologists appreciate the underlying socioeconomic, legal, political, and psychological determinants of health and illness that include court decisions, voter initiatives, health insurance coverage, economic security and income inequality, health provider characteristics and geographic distribution, and the psychosocial stresses of social hierarchies, social oppression, racism, changing family structure, and changing gender roles (South-Paul & Grumbach, 2001).

Health disparities in the United States have been described as the "hallmark of inequities" in the nation's medical system (Candib & Gelberg, 2001). Psychologists as health professionals have multiple opportunities to teach others to recognize and address these problems through training, education, and by role-modeling commitment, action, participation, and leadership as service providers, academics, researchers, and "community change agents" (Candib & Gelberg, 2001).

For example, the posttraumatic sequela of child sexual abuse addressed in section one provides us with an opportunity to help others recognize that although families can be nurturing, they can also be dangerous to the victimized if families are blinded through ignorance, reluctance, fear, bias, or denial to the abuse conducted by trusted male figures (Candib & Gelberg, 2001). It raises the question of how physical symptoms were confronted regularly yet not recognized. It augurs the need for interventions at the individual, family, and community level given research indicating that child sexual abuse survivors disproportionately are diagnosed with somatization, irritable bowel disorders, chronic pelvic pain, obesity, and fibromyalgia (Candib & Gelberg, 2001).

With vulnerable patients with child sexual abuse backgrounds, family practitioners in both medicine and psychology need to both learn and teach culturally competent community health skills, as outlined in section two, to consciously frame the doctor–patient relationship and communication within it, given the dynamics of patients having been touched against their will by an adult and the reparative task of partnering with patients to put them in control of what happens to them (Candib & Gelberg, 2001). Integration of mental health, behavioral health, women's health, men's health, primary care, and social services, and collaboration between providers is necessary to more cost-effectively treat and prevent the impaired subjective health, chronic illness, and somatic symptoms that the sexually victimized manifest in their greater consumption of medical care and increased office visits (Candib & Gelberg, 2001). Practitioners from all these sectors can also serve as a resource to community leaders to fashion more effective child sexual abuse prevention efforts, toward changing the context of health in the family and health in the community to an improved quality of life as described in section three.

REFERENCES

Adams-Tucker, C. (1982). Proximate effects of sexual abuse in childhood: A report on 28 children. *American Journal of Psychiatry, 139,* 1252–1256.

American Academy of Family Physicians. (1999). Recommended curriculum guidelines for family practice residents. *Adolescent Health,* AAFP Reprint No. 278. Retrieved June 17, 2003, from http://www.aafp.org/x16525.xml

Association of Family Practice Residency Program Directors. (1999). *Action plan for the future of residency education in family practice.* Retrieved June 17, 2003, from http:www.afprd.org/actplan/

Bell, H. S., Kozakowski, S. M., & Winter, R. O. (1997). Competency-based education in family practice. *Family Medicine, 29*(10), 701–704.

Betancourt, J. R., Carrillo, J. E., & Green, A. R. (1999). Hypertension in multicultural and minority populations: Linking communication to compliance. *Current Hypertension Reports, 1,* 482–488.

Berkowitz, W., & Cashman, S. (2000). Building healthy communities: Lessons and challenges. *Community, 3*(2), 1–7.

Butler, S. (1978). *Conspiracy of silence: The trauma of incest.* San Francisco: Volcano.

Candib, L. M., & Gelberg, L. (2001). How will family physicians care for the patient in the context of family and community? *Family Medicine, 33*(4), 298–310.

Carrillo, J. E., Green, A. R., & Betancourt, J. R. (1999). Cross-cultural primary care: A patient-based approach. *Annals of Internal Medicine, 130*(18), 829–834.

Chavis, D. M., Florin, P., & Felix, M. R. J. (1992). Nurturing grassroots initiatives for community development: The role of enabling systems. In T. Mizrahi &

J. Morrison (Eds.), *Community and social administration: Advances, trends, and emerging principles*. Binghamton, NY: Haworth Press.

Chin, J. L., De La Cancela, V., & Jenkins, Y. M. (1998). Community-oriented health service delivery: A systemic approach. In V. De La Cancela, J. L. Chin, & Y. M. Jenkins (Eds.), *Community health psychology: Empowerment for diverse communities* (pp. 89–114). New York: Routledge.

Conte, J., & Berliner, L. (1987). The impact of sexual abuse on children: Empirical findings. In L. Walker (Ed.), *Handbook on sexual abuse of children: Assessment and treatment issues*. New York: Springer.

Conte, J., & Schuerman, J. R. (1987). Factors associated with an increased impact of child sexual abuse. *Child Abuse and Neglect, 11*, 201–211.

DeFrancis, V. (1969). *Protecting the child victim of sex crimes committed by adults*. Denver, CO: American Humane Association.

De La Cancela, V., Chin, J., & Jenkins, Y. (Eds.). (1998). *Community health psychology: Empowerment for diverse communities*. New York: Routledge.

Doyle, E., & Ward, S. (2001). *The process of community health education and promotion*. California: Mayfield Publishing.

Everson, M. D., Hunter, W. M., Runyon, D. K., Edelsohn, G. A., & Coulter, M. L. (1989). Maternal support following disclosure of incest. *American Journal of Orthopsychiatry, 59*, 197–207.

Farrell, L. T. (1988). Factors that affect a victim's self-disclosure in father–daughter incest. *Child Welfare, 67*, 463–469.

Finkelhor, D. (1979). *Sexually victimized children*. New York: Free Press.

Finkelhor, D. (1994). Current information on the scope and nature of child sexual abuse. *The Future of Children, 4*, 31–53.

Fromuth, M. E. (1983). *The long-term psychological impact of childhood sexual abuse*. Unpublished doctoral dissertation, Auburn University, Auburn, AL.

Garr, D. R., & Rhyne, R. L. (1998). Primary care and the community. *The Journal of Family Practice, 46*(4), 291–292.

Gomes-Schwartz, B., Horowitz, J. M., & Cardarelli, A. P. (1988). *Child sexual abuse victims and their treatment*. Washington, DC: U.S. Government Printing Office.

Gonzalez, L. S., Waterman, J., Kelly, R. J., McCord, J., & Oliveri, M. K. (1993). Children's patterns of disclosures and recantations of sexual and ritualistic abuse allegations in psychotherapy. *Child Abuse and Neglect, 17*(2), 281–289.

Green, L. W., & Kreuter, M. W. (1991). *Health promotion planning: An educational and environmental approach*. Mountain View, CA: Mayfield.

Gries, L. T., Goh, D. S., Andrews, M. B., Gilbert, J., Praver, F., & Stelzer, D. N. (2000). Positive reaction to disclosure and recovery from child sexual abuse. *Journal of Child Sexual Abuse, 9*(1), 29–51.

Gries, L. T., Goh, D. S., & Cavanaugh, J. (1996). Factors associated with disclosure during child sexual abuse assessment. *Journal of Child Sexual Abuse, 5*(3), 1–19.

Hancock, T., & Duhl, L. (1986). Healthy cities: Promoting health in the urban context. *World Health Organization, Healthy Cities Papers No. 1.* Copenhagen: FADL Publishers.

Hanson, R. F., Resnick, H. S., Kilpatrick, D. G., Saundars, B. E., Lipovsky, J. A., & Best, C. (1992, August). *What factors are predictive of reporting of childhood sexual assault: Are we just studying the tip of the iceberg?* Paper presented at the Ninth International Congress on Child Abuse and Neglect, Chicago, IL.

Harper, P., Baker, N., & Rief, C. (2000). Implementing community-oriented primary care projects in an urban family practice residency program. *Family Medicine, 32*(10), 683–690.

Henley, E., & Williams, R. L. (1999). Is population-based medicine the same as community-oriented primary care? *Family Medicine, 31*(7), 501–502.

Himmelman, A. (2001). On coalitions and the transformation of power relations: Collaborative betterment and collaborative empowerment. *American Journal of Community Psychology, 29*(2), 277–284.

Hoefnagels, C., & Baartman, H. (1997). On the threshold of disclosure: The effects of a mass media field experiment. *Child Abuse and Neglect, 21*(6), 557–573.

James, B. (1989). *Treating traumatized children.* Lexington, MA: Lexington Books.

Jenkins, Y. M., De La Cancela, V., & Chin, J. L. (1998). Culturally competent community health psychology: A systemic approach. In V. De La Cancela, J. L. Chin, & Y. M. Jenkins (Eds.), *Community health psychology: Empowerment for diverse communities* (pp. 119–135). New York: Routledge.

Kretzmann, J., & McKnight, J. (1993). *Building communities from the inside out: A path toward finding and mobilizing the community's assets.* Chicago: ACTA Publications.

Kuramoto, F. H. (1998). Commentary. In V. De La Cancela, J. L. Chin, & Y. M. Jenkins (Eds.), *Community health psychology: Empowerment for diverse communities* (pp. 115–117). New York: Routledge.

Lawall, S. L. (1993). Child sexual abuse disclosure: Research findings and implications for research and practice. *Critical Issues: The Journal of GSO-SEHNAP, NYU, 1*(1), 123–134.

Like, R. C., Steiner, R. P., & Rubel, A. J. (1996). Recommended core curriculum guidelines on culturally sensitive and competent health care. *Family Medicine, 28*(4), 291–297.

London Ontario Family Court Clinic. (1995). *Tipping the balance to tell the secret: The public discovery of child sexual abuse.* (Available from London Family Court Clinic, 254 Pall Mall Street, London, ON N6A 5P6)

McCutchan, F. C., Sanders, D. E., & Vogel, M. E. (1999). *Society of Teachers of Family Medicine Group on Behavioral Science resource guide for behavioral science educators in family medicine.* Leawood, KS: Society of Teachers of Family Medicine.

McIntyre, D., & Carr, A. (1999). Helping children to the other side of silence: A study of the impact of the Stay Safe Program on Irish children's disclosures of sexual victimization. *Child Abuse and Neglect, 23*(12), 1327–1340.

McIntyre, D., & Carr, A. (2000). Prevention of child sexual abuse: Implications of programme evaluation research. *Child Abuse Review, 9,* 183–199.

Mian, M., Wehrspan, W., Klajner, D. H., LeBaron, D., & Winder, C. (1986). Review of 125 children 6 years of age and under who were sexually abused. *Child Abuse and Neglect, 10,* 223–229.

Murray, J. L. (2000). Family medicine: Return to counterculture. *Family Medicine, 32*(2), 129–130.

National Center for Cultural Competence. (1998). *Why is there a compelling need for cultural competence?* Retrieved June 17, 2003, from http: www.athealth.com/practitioner/particles/compellingneed

Norris, T. (1997). America's best kept secret: The healthy communities movement. *National Civic Review, 86*(1).

Norris, T., & Howell, L. (1999). *Healthy people in healthy communities: A dialogue guide.* Chicago: Coalition for Healthy Cities and Communities.

Norris, T., & Pittman, M. (2000). Healthy communities principles. *Public Health Reports, 115*(2&3), 122.

Nutting, P. A., Wood, M., & Conner, E. M. (1985). Community oriented primary care in the United States: A status report. *Journal of the American Medical Association, 253,* 1763–1766.

Ottawa Charter for Health Promotion. (1986). *Health Promotion, 1*(4), iii–v.

Palmer, S. E., Brown, R. A., Rae-Grant, N. I., & Loughlin, M. J. (1999). Responding to children's disclosure of familial abuse: What survivors tell us. *Child Welfare, 78*(2), 259–282.

Pathman, D., Steiner, B., Williams, E., & Riggins, T. (1998). The four community dimensions of primary care practice. *The Journal of Family Practice, 46*(4), 293–303.

Peters, S. D. (1988). Child sexual abuse and later psychological problems. In G. Wyatt & G. Powell (Eds.), *The lasting effects of child sexual abuse* (pp. 119–123). Newbury Park, CA: Sage.

Pine, J. T. (1999). *A lesson plan for teaching cultural competence, multiethnic healthcare.* Retrieved June 17, 1999, from http://www./closing-the-gap.Comments/culturalCompetence/teachcomp2.htm

Plotnikoff, G. A., & Barnes, L. L. (2000). Cross-cultural primary care. *Annals of Internal Medicine, 1132,* 164–165.

Putnam, R. (2000). *Bowling alone.* New York: Simon & Schuster.

Roberts, J., & Taylor, C. (1993). Sexually abused children and young people speak out. In L. Waterhouse (Ed.), *Child abuse and child abusers: Protection and prevention* (pp. 13–37). London: Jessica Kingsley.

Roussos, S., & Fawcett, S. (2000). A review of collaborative partnerships as a strategy for improving community health. *Annual Review of Public Health, 21,* 369–402.

Russell, D. E. H. (1983). The incidence and prevalence of intrafamilial and extra-familial sexual abuse of female children. *Child Abuse and Neglect, 7,* 133–146.

Sirles, E. A., & Franke, P. J. (1989). Factors influencing mother's reactions to intrafamilial sexual abuse. *Child Abuse and Neglect, 13*, 131–139.

Sorenson, T., & Snow, B. (1991). How children tell: The process of disclosure in child sexual abuse. *Child Welfare, Jan–Feb LXX(1)*, 3–15.

South-Paul, J. E., & Grumbach, K. (2001). How does a changing country change family practice? *Family Medicine, 33(4)*, 278–285.

Stein, C. (2001a). *Moving from issues to solutions: An evaluation of 13 years of coalition work.* Amherst, MA: AHEC/Community Partners.

Stein, C. (2001b). *Moving from issues to solutions: An evaluation of 17 years of coalition work.* Amherst, MA: AHEC/Community Partners.

Stephens, G.G. (2001). Family practice and social and political change. *Family Medicine, 33(4)*, 248–251.

Thompson, R., Haber, D., Chambers, S., Fanuiel, L., Krohn, K., & Smith, A. J. (1997). Orientation to community in a family practice residency program. *Family Medicine, 30(1)*, 24–28.

Tufts New England Medical Center, Division of Child Psychiatry. (1984). *Sexually exploited children: Service and research project* (Final report for the Office of Juvenile Justice and Delinquency Prevention). Washington, DC: U.S. Department of Justice.

Waller, G., & Ruddock, A. (1993). Experiences of disclosure of childhood sexual abuse and psychopathology. *Child Abuse Review, 2*, 185–195.

Williams, R., Crabtree, B., O'Brien, C., Zyzanski, S., & Gilchrist, V. (1999). Practical tools for qualitative community-oriented primary care community assessment. *Family Medicine, 31(7)*, 488–494.

Wolff, T. (2001). A practitioner's guide to successful coalitions. *American Journal of Community Psychology, 29(2)*, 173–191.

Wolff, T. (1995). Healthy Communities Massachusetts: One vision of civic democracy. *Municipal Advocate, 14(2)*, 22–24.

Wyatt, G. E. (1985). The sexual abuse of Afro-American and White-American women in childhood. *Child Abuse and Neglect, 9*, 507–519.

Wyatt, G. E., & Mickey, M. R. (1988). The support by parents and others as it mediates the effects of child sexual abuse. In G. E. Wyatt & G. J. Powell (Eds.), *Lasting effects of child sexual abuse* (pp. 211–226). Beverly Hills, CA: Sage.

7

USING PSYCHOLOGY FOR INJURY AND VIOLENCE PREVENTION IN THE COMMUNITY

DAVID A. SLEET, W. RODNEY HAMMOND, RUSSELL T. JONES, NINA THOMAS, AND BILLY WHITT

Psychologists make a wide range of contributions to developing and sustaining healthy communities. Among those are contributions to practice and research in injury prevention and control. Community and health psychologists have traditionally been involved in issues related to chronic disease rather than in injury and violence prevention. But as this chapter demonstrates, the profession has much to contribute. From healing individual scars left by burns, fire-related injuries, and youth violence to healing nations traumatized by war, psychologists bring tools and techniques to assist in recovery but also in prevention.

This chapter consists of sections authored by different professionals, who were responsible for the content and accuracy of their material. The merging of sections into a single chapter was reviewed and accepted by all the authors. The views represented in individual sections do not necessarily represent the official views of the Centers for Disease Control and Prevention, the U.S. Department of Health and Human Services, or any other agency of the U.S. Federal Government. This chapter was authored or coauthored by an employee of the United States government as part of official duties and is considered to be in the public domain.

Injury prevention is a new way to think about trauma. Many psychologists identify trauma with mental health only. Yet trauma in the community ranges from physical injury to psychological and social harm. Each manifestation presents opportunities for psychologists to bring their tools of assessment and health behavior change to reduce injuries and their impact in the community.

Whether by violent or unintentional means, injury exacts a large toll on individuals, families, workplaces, and the community. Nearly 150,000 people die each year from injuries; another 3 million are hospitalized or treated in emergency departments. It is estimated that injuries cost society more than 260 billion dollars annually. Injuries cause more years of potential life lost than cancer, heart disease, or stroke combined and are the leading cause of death during the first 4 decades of life. These health burdens are not trivial (National Research Council, Committee on Trauma Research, 1985; Institute of Medicine, 1999).

This enormous burden on the health care system is shared by practicing psychologists and social workers who see the aftermath of trauma on patients. Patients are helped by psychologists to manage posttraumatic stress disorders. Families shattered by the loss of loved ones from an automobile crash or a child drowning are assisted by social workers and family therapists. Psychologists help communities to manage the fear and grief that results from a school shooting, child abuse, fire in a housing complex or nightclub, a teenage suicide, or a terrorist attack.

These threats to community health pose a real challenge for the field. Trauma from injury, whether self-inflicted, inflicted by others, or unintentional, is largely preventable. Behaviors that give rise to injury and violence are amenable to preventive interventions, just as are many diseases.

Psychologists too often limit their involvement in injury and trauma to the post-injury phase of assessment and treatment, and neglect psychology's role in prevention. Behavioral and social sciences are needed to document behavioral and social risk factors, and to develop interventions that influence social norms and shape individual and community preventive behavior. This chapter highlights the significance of the growing problem of injuries in public health and demonstrates how psychologists can be—and are—involved. As examples, we address community health promotion for injury control, reducing youth violence, improving children's response to fire emergencies, and recovering from collective violence in war-torn countries. These are but a few examples of how psychology has relevance to injury prevention, and it is our hope that it will motivate other psychologists to see a role for themselves in injury prevention.

COMMUNITY HEALTH PROMOTION
FOR INJURY CONTROL

Injury is one of the leading causes of death and disability for all age groups in the United States, and the leading cause of death from ages 1–44 (Table 7.1). Each year, nearly 150,000 people die from injuries, including 41,000 deaths from motor vehicle crashes; 30,500 from suicide; 28,000 deaths from fires, drowning, falls, and poisonings; and 25,500 from homicide (Centers for Disease Control and Prevention [CDC], 2003).

In addition, injuries result in 3.3 million potential years of life lost prematurely before age 65. This is compared with only 3 million potential years of life lost each for cancer and heart disease and 400,000 each for AIDS and stroke (CDC, 2003).

Nonfatal injuries result in 114 million physician contacts every year, and more than one-quarter of all emergency room visits are for the treatment of injuries. Injuries are the leading cause of hospital admissions for people under age 45 and one in four Americans will suffer a potentially preventable injury serious enough to require medical attention this year (National Center for Injury Prevention and Control, 2001).

Injuries remain a critical public health priority. Many disciplines and professions play a role in controlling and preventing injuries. The financial, social, and emotional consequences of injuries point particularly to the importance of psychology in reducing these burdens through programs and policies aimed at injury prevention and control.

Accidents, Injuries, and Trauma

The term *accident* implies an unavoidable event. Its use in public health and community psychology is waning. Even the prestigious *British Medical Journal* has "banned" the use of the word "accident" in the articles it publishes (Davis & Pless, 2001). The term has largely been substituted by the term *injury* or *trauma* to reflect the public health consequences and preventability of the problem (National Committee for Injury Prevention and Control, 1989; Sleet & Rosenberg, 1997).

In psychology, trauma is often used as a term to reflect the psychological impact of negative events, particularly stress that affects individual and family life. Trauma also refers to the physical consequences of these events. We know that injuries, trauma, and the events that cause them are not random events—they are predictable and preventable. Psychology can refocus its efforts to include interventions that prevent trauma and injuries,

TABLE 7.1.
Ten Leading Causes of Death, United States, 2000, All Races, Both Sexes

Rank	Under 1	1–4	5–9	10–14	15–24	25–34	35–44	45–54	55–64	65+	All ages
1	Congenital Anomalies 5,743	Unintentional Injury 1,826	Unintentional Injury 1,391	Unintentional Injury 1,588	Unintentional Injury 14,113	Unintentional Injury 11,769	Malignant Neoplasms 16,520	Malignant Neoplasms 48,034	Malignant Neoplasms 89,005	Heart Disease 593,707	Heart Disease 710,760
2	Short Gestation 4,397	Congenital Anomalies 495	Malignant Neoplasms 489	Malignant Neoplasms 525	Homicide 4,939	Suicide 4,792	Unintentional Injury 15,413	Heart Disease 35,480	Heart Disease 63,399	Malignant Neoplasms 392,366	Malignant Neoplasms 553,091
3	SIDS 2,523	Malignant Neoplasms 420	Congenital Anomalies 198	Suicide 300	Suicide 3,994	Homicide 4,164	Heart Disease 13,181	Unintentional Injury 12,278	Chronic Low. Respiratory Disease 10,739	Cerebro-vascular 148,045	Cerebro-vascular 167,661
4	Maternal Pregnancy Comp. 1,404	Homicide 356	Homicide 140	Homicide 231	Malignant Neoplasms 1,713	Malignant Neoplasms 3,916	Suicide 6,562	Liver Disease 6,654	Cerebro-vascular 9,956	Chronic Low. Respiratory Disease 106,375	Chronic Low. Respiratory Disease 122,009
5	Placenta Cord Membranes 1,062	Heart Disease 181	Heart Disease 106	Congenital Anomalies 201	Heart Disease 1,031	Heart Disease 2,958	HIV 5,919	Cerebro-vascular 6,011	Diabetes Mellitus 9,186	Influenza & Pneumonia 58,557	Uninten-tional Injury 97,900
6	Respiratory Distress 999	Influenza & Pneumonia 103	Benign Neoplasms 62	Heart Disease 165	Congenital Anomalies 441	HIV 2,437	Liver Disease 3,371	Suicide 5,437	Uninten-tional Injury 7,505	Diabetes Mellitus 52,414	Diabetes Mellitus 69,301

Rank											
7	Unintentional Injury 881	Septicemia 99	Chronic Low. Respiratory Disease 48	Chronic Low. Respiratory Disease 91	Cerebro-vascular 199	Diabetes Mellitus 623	Homicide 3,219	Diabetes Mellitus 4,954	Liver Disease 5,774	Alzheimer's Disease 48,993	Influenza & Pneumonia 65,313
8	Bacterial Sepsis 768	Perinatal Period 79	Influenza & Pneumonia 47	Cerebro-vascular 51	Chronic Low. Respiratory Disease 190	Cerebro-vascular 602	Cerebro-vascular 2,599	HIV 4,142	Nephritis 3,100	Nephritis 31,225	Alzheimer's Disease 49,558
9	Circulatory System Disease 663	Benign Neoplasms 53	Septicemia 38	Influenza & Pneumonia 40	Influenza & Pneumonia 189	Congenital Anomalies 477	Diabetes Mellitus 1,926	Chronic Low. Respiratory Disease 3,251	Suicide 2,945	Unintentional Injury 31,051	Nephritis 37,251
10	Intrauterine Hypoxia 630	Chronic Low. Respiratory Disease 51	Two Tied 25	Benign Neoplasms 37	HIV 179	Liver Disease 415	Influenza & Pneumonia 1,068	Viral Hepatitis 1,894	Septicemia 2,899	Septicemia 24,786	Septicemia 31,224

Note. SIDS = Sudden infant death syndrome. From Centers for Disease Control and Prevention, National Center for Injury Prevention and Control. Retrieved January 1, 2003, from www.cdc.gov/ncipc/wisqars. In the public domain.

even reinjury, as a way of reducing posttraumatic sequelae, and improving treatment and rehabilitation.

Community Health Promotion Approaches to Injury Control

Taking a health promotion approach to injury prevention is a recent phenomenon (Sleet & Gielen, 1998). In 1982, injury prevention was not even considered an area of importance in textbooks on community psychology or health promotion (Taylor, Ureda, & Denham, 1982). This may have been partly due to the way the U.S. Public Health Service had categorized injuries as "accidents" and placed them in the "health protection" category, along with other environmentally oriented problems considered to be beyond individual control (U.S. Public Health Service, 1979). Inevitably, as injury prevention and health promotion have become more closely aligned, the potential benefits of injury prevention behavior change strategies have become more widely accepted (Gielen & Sleet, 2003).

Health promotion is traditionally defined as "any planned combination of educational, organizational, economic, political, and regulatory supports for actions and conditions of living conducive to the health of individuals, groups and communities" (Green & Kreuter, 1999, p. 44). This widely recognized definition acknowledges the importance of taking a behavioral, environmental, *and* policy approach to the prevention of disease and injury. Evaluations of the effects of health education on injury prevention have not usually included these broader efforts (Towner, 1995; Dowswell, Towner, Simpson, & Jarvis, 1996). As behavioral and social scientists become more involved in research in public health (Holtgrave, Doll, & Harrison, 1997), we are seeing the general acceptance of their contributions to preventive psychology, community health, and clinical preventive services (Snider & Satcher, 1997). Counseling and patient education are two promising approaches in injury prevention (Gielen, 2002) but are enhanced if delivered within a broader mix of health promotion strategies in the community. The immediate objects of health promotion for injury control include (a) modifying individual risk factors, (b) reducing exposure to hazardous environments, and (c) removing or modifying harmful products. Individual and community actions are required to succeed in these efforts, and are fostered by education, stimulated by social and organizational change, and encouraged through public policy, legislation, and enforcement.

Selecting Community Injury Prevention Strategies

Changing human behavior, modifying products, and changing environments present three key opportunities for reducing injuries in the community.

Using terms such as *injury prevention* rather than *accident prevention* helps make clear the potential for preventing such events.

There are three generally accepted strategies in injury prevention: (a) education and behavior change; (b) legislation and enforcement, and (c) engineering and technology. Strategies involving education and behavior change usually target reduction of host risk behaviors. Legislation and enforcement strategies usually effect changes in the legal environment. Engineering and technology strategies usually effect changes in the design and manufacture of safer products. Community health promotion allows us to use all three strategies in efforts to reduce community injury problems. Strategies are usually selected after a thorough community needs assessment. The strategy mix also takes into consideration local standards and the public acceptability of various behavioral, environmental, or engineering and infrastructural changes necessary to reduce injuries.

Strategies often overlap, so that education and behavior change strategies can also be used to affect legislation and environmental safety by changing the behavior of lawmakers, product designers, and environmental engineers and planners in the community (Gielen & Girasek, 2001).

Using Education and Behavior Change Strategies for Injury Control

One key area for involvement of psychology is in education and behavior change. These strategies have the potential to change injury risk behaviors and to bring about new social expectations and social norms, such as reducing the acceptability of drinking and driving or intimate partner violence. Yet, behavioral science applications to injury prevention have lagged behind other approaches during the past half-century (Gielen & Sleet, 2003).

Whereas some early research using educational strategies in injury prevention showed that education makes no difference in preventing injuries (Pless, 1978; O'Conner, 1982) other more recent research has shown important changes in risk behaviors for violence (Lonsway, 1996; Shechtman, 1999) and unintentional injuries (Bablouzian, Freedman, Wolski, & Fried, 1997; Clamp & Kendrick, 1998; Wilson, Dwyer, & Bennett, 2003). Changes in injury outcomes have also been reported for violence (Orpinas et al., 2000) and unintentional injury (Towner & Dowswell, 2002). Variations in the effectiveness of education and behavior change strategies from various studies can be attributed to a number of factors, including lack of control groups, use of different methods of education, the absence of theory-based approaches in designing interventions, poorly designed measures of change, and inadequate educational dosing, among others. The effectiveness of an intervention in a particular setting depends not just on whether it's been demonstrated to work in the past, but on the quality and fidelity of its implementation (Mercy & Hammond, 2001).

Behavior change methods designed and carried out by behavioral and social scientists (especially those using applied behavioral analysis techniques) have produced more positive results. Behavioral methods have been successfully used to prevent violence and aggressive behaviors among youth (Thornton, Craft, Dahlberg, Lynch, & Baer, 2002; U.S. Department of Health and Human Services, 2001) and children and adolescents (Fields & McNamara, 2003; Scheckner, Rollin, Kaiser-Ulrey, & Wagner, 2002) and to increase protective behaviors for unintentional injuries (Geller et al., 1990; Roberts, Fanurik, & Layfield, 1987; Streff & Geller, 1986; Williams, Wells, & Farmer, 2002). Behavioral approaches employ the use of incentives, social modeling, feedback, rewards, skills development, cognitive rehearsal, and competition to improve injury prevention behaviors (DeTurch, Chih, & Hsu, 1999; Farrell, Meyer, & Dahlberg, 1996; Jones, Van Hasselt, & Sisson, 1984; Huesmann, Guerra, Miller, & Zelli, 1992). These approaches have been especially successful and widely adopted in traffic safety (Geller, Elder, Hovell, & Sleet, 1991; Sleet, Hollenbach, & Hovell, 1986; Sleet & Lonero, 2002) and occupational safety (Geller, 1998; Krause, 1997). Behavior change methods can be targeted to change one person's behavior (such as a juvenile's fire-starting behavior), a group at risk (such as victims of domestic violence), or the behavior of an entire community (such as dialing the emergency 9-1-1 number).

In clinical health care settings, use of brief interventions in counseling (Hungerford & Pollock, 2002), motivational interviewing (Johnston, Rivara, Droesch, Dunn, & Copass, 2002), and patient education (Gielen, 2002) have also been found effective in reducing injury risk, although not equally effective across risk domains (Dunn, DeRoo, & Rivara, 2001). Evidence reviewed by the U.S. Preventive Services Task Force (1996) recommends counseling for injury prevention, and in their latest report, education is recommended in combination with other approaches, such as legislation and enforcement, for reducing injuries to motor-vehicle occupants (Zaza & Thompson, 2001). Education and behavior change approaches can also affect those who make laws and design products, and those who enforce laws or sell products, in ways that ultimately protect whole populations.

Combining Strategies

A good example of combining education and behavior change, engineering and technology, and legislation and enforcement strategies to reduce injuries is the successful effort to reduce injuries from alcohol-impaired driving. Legislation controlling access of young drivers to alcohol was combined with policies that lower blood alcohol concentration limits and heavy penalties for drunk driving. These efforts were accompanied by widespread public education on the dangers of drunk driving, including risks and penalties. Efforts were further enhanced through engineering and the development of sophisticated alcohol sensing devices for use in breathalyzer testing, and vehicle-use-deterrent-systems, such as ignition interlocks fitted to the vehicles of repeat drunk drivers.

Psychologists can influence the use and success of all three strategies in a community setting and can employ many methods to implement each. Use of all three strategies can help practitioners design specific interventions targeted to specific populations and can be used effectively to design comprehensive community-based approaches to injury prevention. Key areas for further research by psychologists include behavioral methods for motivating behavior change, the role of risk perception, developmental aspects of childhood and elderly injuries, stages of change research, applications of social learning and protection-motivation theory, and psychological factors in assessment and treatment of trauma and factors leading to success in rehabilitation. Many of these themes, with specific subtopics, are described in the recent CDC research agenda on injury prevention (CDC, 2002a)

REDUCING YOUTH VIOLENCE

Across the nation, urban and rural communities, prosperous and poor communities all struggle to keep their children safe—safe from adults and from each other. Although youth violence has declined significantly in recent years, many indicators of violent youth behavior suggest that much work remains.

The World Health Organization (Krug, Dahlberg, Mercy, Zwi, & Lozano, 2002) defined violence as

> The intentional use of physical force or power, threatened or actual, against oneself, another person, or against a group or community, that either results in or has a high likelihood of resulting in injury, death, psychological harm, mal-development or deprivation. (p. 5)

Traditionally the purview of the criminal justice system, violence entered the public health arena in the 1970s as public health professionals recognized the significant and growing health consequences of interpersonal and self-directed violence. This early development led to increased interest and resources in public health devoted to the study of violence and violence prevention.

Viewing violence prevention as a part of public health draws attention to the measurable health consequences of assault related injuries, highlights the role of the health sector in identifying and reducing violence, and highlights the potential of epidemiology and behavioral science tools in identifying risk factors and designing effective interventions. Many of these tools and solutions lie outside the usual sphere of crime prevention and control. In this way the perspective and methods of public health complement the perspective and methods of criminal justice in understanding and responding to violence.

Prevalence of Lethal and Nonlethal Violence

Homicide is the second leading cause of death among 15- to 24-year-olds. Within this age group, homicide is the leading cause of death for African Americans, the second leading cause of death for Hispanics, and the third leading cause of death for Native Americans. In 2000, homicide rates for males ages 15 to 24 years were highest for African Americans (85.3 per 100,000) followed by American Indians and Alaska Natives (20.8 per 1000,000), White Americans (10.1), and Asian Americans (8.9). For women ages 15 to 24, African Americans had the highest rates (10.9 per 1000,000) followed by White Americans (2.6), American Indians (2.2), and Asian Americans (1.8; CDC, 2003). Low socioeconomic status is a consistent risk factor for violence among youth (U.S. Department of Health and Human Services, 2001).

Violence need not be lethal to greatly impact individuals and communities. Violence is also a leading cause of nonfatal injuries among young people. In the year 2000, there were 932,700 violence related visits to hospital emergency departments by people under age 24 (CDC, 2003). Findings from the 2001 Youth Risk Behavior Survey, a nationally representative sample of students in grades 9 through 12, revealed that a significant portion of young people in grades 9–12 are involved in violent behavior. In the 30 days preceding the survey, 17.4% of students reported carrying a weapon, 6.4% carried a weapon on school property. In the 12 months preceding the survey, almost 9% of high school youth reported being threatened or injured with a weapon on school property. Almost 7% of students reported missing 1 day or more of school during the past 30 days because they felt unsafe at school or on their way to or from school (CDC, 2002b).

Cost data represent an additional means of studying the national impact of violence. Although very little research of this type has been done, one study estimated the cost of intentional injury (excluding suicide) for ages 1–19 in 1995 at $149,500,000, including estimates for medical costs, lost income, and reduced quality of life (Miller, Covington, & Jensen, 1997).

Risk and Protective Factors

The concepts of risk and protection are integral to public health. A risk factor is anything that increases the probability that a person will suffer harm. A protective factor is something that decreases the potential harmful effect of a risk factor. In terms of youth violence, risk factors increase the probability that a young person will become violent or be violently victimized, whereas protective factors buffer the young person against those risks. Risk and protective factors are generally categorized in five domains: individual and psychological; family; school; peer; and community and neighborhood (U.S. Department of Health and Human Services, 2001).

Among the significant gains in understanding the influence of risk and protective factors is the evidence that the impact of these factors varies with the developmental stage of the child (Sleet & Mercy, 2003). For example, the family plays a greater role in preventing injury during childhood than in adolescence. As children develop into adolescents, peer group influence on injury risks increases in importance. Such findings have strong implications for intervention design in developmental studies (Hawkins et al., 1998; Lipsey & Derzon, 1998). Additionally, promising research on school and peer factors, especially protective factors, is under way (Kellam, Rebok, Ialongo, & Mayer, 1994; Meyer & Farrell, 1998). As research has expanded to include focus on protective factors more emphasis has been given to the additive effects and interaction among multiple risk or protective factors.

Prevention and Intervention

Although youth violence prevention and intervention strategies are used in nearly all communities, many have not been rigorously evaluated. Fortunately, the information concerning effective strategies is growing rapidly. Recent reports from the U.S. Department of Health and Human Services, Office of the Surgeon General, Department of Justice, and the Centers for Disease Control and Prevention (Injury Center) inform policymakers, practitioners, and prevention researchers about science-based strategies that hold the most promise (U.S. Department of Health and Human Services, 2001; Thornton et al., 2002; Thornton, Craft, Dahlberg, Lynch, & Baer, 2000; Wasserman, Miller, & Cothern, 2000).

Some of these strategies include home visiting-nurse programs for at-risk children from birth to age 2; programs aimed at improving parental monitoring and discipline for families with 5- to 12-year-old children; mentoring programs for children and youth who lack appropriate adult role models; and programs that teach prosocial and cognitive skills that are incompatible with violence (Thornton et al., 2002).

Developing skills in implementing effective violence prevention programs is also important. Successful implementation involves careful attention to planning and evaluation through a series of steps. These include

- describing the specific problem or type of youth violence in a community;
- identifying intended participants for an intervention;
- setting goals and objectives;
- selecting interventions that will most appropriately address the goals and objectives in addition to meeting the needs of participants;
- involving the community in the effort;
- using activities that are supported by well-organized implementation materials or manuals, if possible;
- providing trained staff;
- monitoring the intervention's progress; and
- evaluating impact.

Because of the cultural diversity present within most high-risk populations, acceptability is an important component of successful violence prevention programs in ethnic minority youth. An example is Positive Adolescent Choices Training, which includes prosocial skills development and anger management interventions uniquely adapted for African American youth (Yung & Hammond, 1995). Similar prevention programs have been developed and implemented in recent years. Recent declines in intentional injury and homicide rates among ethnic minority youth may reflect, in part, the widespread adoption of successful programs like these (Hammond & Prothrow-Stith, 2001).

Table 7.2 provides a framework to identify effective and ineffective strategies. The Surgeon General's report (U.S. Department of Health and Human Services, 2001) used several criteria in rating these strategies as effective or ineffective. Effective strategies were culled from published studies that used rigorous experimental design, found evidence of significant deterrent effects on violence, and replicated these effects at multiple sites. Similarly, the Surgeon General's report specified ineffective strategies based upon the absence of positive effects or the presence of negative effects affecting violence prevention.

The Surgeon General's report also distinguished between prevention and intervention approaches. *Prevention* typically includes programs and strategies that target general (i.e., universal) populations of youth who are not currently involved in violence or do not exhibit specific risk factors for violence. The report defined *intervention* as those approaches that target high risk or already violent youth. The Surgeon General noted some overlap between prevention and intervention efforts. However, the report cautioned

TABLE 7.2.
Effective and Ineffective Strategies to Prevent Youth Violence

Effective strategies	Ineffective strategies
Primary prevention: Universal	**Primary prevention: Universal**
Skills training	Peer counseling, peer mediation, peer
Behavior monitoring and reinforcement	leaders
Behavioral techniques for classroom	Nonpromotion to succeeding grades
management	Secondary prevention: Selected
Building school capacity	Gun buyback programs
Continuous progress programs	Firearm training
Cooperative learning	Mandatory gun ownership
Positive youth development programs	Redirecting youth behavior
	Shifting peer group norms
Secondary prevention: Selected	
Parent training	**Tertiary prevention: Indicated**
Home visitation	Boot camps
Compensatory education	Residential programs
Social problem solving	Milieu treatment
Thinking skills	Behavioral token programs
	Waivers to adult court
Tertiary prevention: Indicated	Social casework
Social perspective taking, role	Individual counseling
taking	
Multi-modal interventions	
Behavioral interventions	
Skills training	
Marital and family therapy by clinical	
staff	
Wraparound services	

Note. From *Youth Violence: A Report of the Surgeon General,* by the U.S. Department of Health and Human Services, 2001, Rockville, MD. In the public domain.

that effective programs used with general populations are not always effective with seriously offending youth (p. 105). An important consideration for future violence prevention policy and research will be to assure the quality of implementation, the cultural acceptability, and cost benefits of various prevention approaches (Mercy & Hammond, 2001)

Using a Public Health Approach to Youth Violence Prevention

The Centers for Disease Control and Prevention (CDC) has helped conceptualize and institutionalize a public health approach to violence prevention in the United States since the early 1980s. The approach has been to combine analysis and action to develop, implement, and evaluate effective interventions. Within the CDC, the National Center for Injury Prevention and Control (Division of Violence Prevention [DVP]) is dedicated specifically to the study of interpersonal and self-directed violence. DVP staff studies the problem of youth violence with the same kinds of public health tools that are applied to the study of infectious diseases, chronic diseases, and occupational hazards. DVP supports both intramural and extramural projects and activities to prevent violence. These activities focus on primary prevention of violence through a public health approach that complements traditional approaches used by other disciplines such as criminal justice, education, and social services. Projects have included programs that intervene at the individual, family, or social setting levels. They have been implemented in school, hospital, community center, prison, and home-care settings. All projects include a major emphasis on evaluation. The CDC's DVP has three branches active in youth violence prevention: The Etiology and Surveillance Branch collects data on the prevalence and incidence of violence in multiple areas in addition to examining multilevel causal factors in violence, the Prevention Development and Evaluation Branch promotes internal and external research that identifies and develops promising approaches to violence prevention, and the Program Implementation and Dissemination Branch assists in the diffusion of effective approaches to numerous community-based settings including state health departments and schools.

Prevention Research Priorities

Many prevention research priorities remain for violence prevention. Some are described in the CDC injury center research agenda (CDC, 2002a). Among them are (a) identification of risk and protective factors that are specific to violent outcomes, (b) understanding the associations between youth violence and other forms of violence (e.g., dating violence and suicide), (c) the role of social factors such as exposure to violence in the media on youth violence, (d) the role of illegal weapon carrying in youth violence, (e) the efficacy of promising strategies that have not been rigorously evaluated, (f) the effectiveness of strategies to prevent firearm injuries among youth, (g) the cost-effectiveness and relative influence of specific intervention components in strategies demonstrated to be effective (e.g., social development programs and parenting programs), (h) strategies to maintain the benefits of efficacious programs when implemented in real-world settings, and (i) research that improves our understanding of how best to disseminate proven youth violence prevention strategies. Each of these areas or research themes is appropriate for community psychologists and many cut across multiple themes. For example, efforts to prevent school shootings and to reduce disparities in access to and outcomes of youth violence prevention programs can be enhanced by progress within each of these research themes.

In conclusion, youth violence prevention remains an important public health priority in the United States. It is clear that psychologists are needed to advance our understanding of the causes and effective interventions to reduce youth violence. Opportunities also exist to consult with schools, families, and communities regarding effective strategies to prevent violence and to investigate new interventions. Of critical importance will be the training and involvement of psychologists with skills in addressing the disproportionate impact of violence within ethnic minority and economically disadvantaged communities.

IMPROVING CHILDREN'S RESPONSES TO FIRE EMERGENCIES

Both environmental and behavioral variables contribute to burn injuries in children. Public health and psychology often work together to identify these risks and to develop complementary and appropriate prevention strategies. Jones and McDonald (1986) developed a prevention model for childhood injuries that provides an example of how tools from psychology can be used to address cognitive and behavioral risk factors associated with childhood injuries and yield guidelines for prevention. This model combines prevention and cognitive–behavioral and community psychology frameworks together to aid in the conceptualization of problems related to childhood trauma. These practical, empirically derived guidelines consist of (a) documenting the need for intervention, (b) deciding what behaviors to modify and what skills to perfect, (c) deciding how best to teach the skills, (d) determining when to teach the skills, (e) selecting change agents and training settings, and (f) obtaining community-wide involvement. These guideline components are likely to be helpful in designing many different behavioral interventions. Planning strategies to manage behavior in emergencies and mass trauma events have attracted a much larger audience since September 11th and the opportunities to combine expertise in psychology with public health have never been greater. These approaches to research have been conducted to develop and maintain fire evacuation skills, identify steps to be taken in the event of future emergencies, validate these approaches using experts, and improve the acquisition and frequent practicing of prevention steps. However, the application of these strategies to behavioral responses in other emergencies seems warranted (Jones, Kazdin, & Haney, 1981b; Leslie, 2001).

Consequences of Fire

Almost a fifth of all families in the United States will experience a house fire. More than 5,000 people die each year in residential fires (Greenberg & Keane, 1997). Children and adolescents are at particular risk for fire-related injury, especially those from low-income families (Tarnowski, 1994). Residential fires account for 80% of all fire deaths (National Fire Protection

Association, 1999), with burn injuries from residential fires being the third leading cause of death for children in the United States (Tarnowski, 1994).

The past few decades have resulted in important progress in burn survivability. Before the 1970s, victims who had been burned on at least a third of their bodies almost always died from burn shock or wound sepsis. Today, medical technology has made it possible to survive the first few critical weeks following a serious burn (Sheridan et al., 2000).

Recent research has documented that those who have been severely burned (on more than 70% of the body) may recover quite well, despite the disfiguring physical problems that often persist throughout life. In a recent study, researchers followed 80 people who were treated for massive burns at Boston Hospital and followed up with them approximately 15 years later. Results showed that from the 80 people, 27 were employed, 27 were full-time students, and 22 had spouses or significant others (Sheridan et al., 2000). Only 4 of them had no job, were not in school, and did not have a spouse. The study concluded that most children who are severely burned can nevertheless have a satisfying quality of life in adulthood.

Along with the physical trauma associated with severe burns, there is often psychological trauma. Many individuals do not recover well psychologically. Sheridan and colleagues (2000) reported that 12 individuals in the Boston burn study just mentioned became unemployed, 8 reported chemical or alcohol dependence, and 1 spent time in prison following the fire.

Psychological Study of Fire Trauma

Unfortunately, research on psychological reactions to fire and fire-related injury is minimal. We still do not know the full range and intensity of the psychological consequences of burn injuries. We do know, however, that residential fire is a unique form of disaster emergency in that fires occur suddenly, cause major property and financial losses, and often force a family to relocate or become homeless. Additionally, a serious fire typically triggers a series of other stressful life events, ranging from changes in the schools children attend to the death of family members and pets. Consequently, survivors experience isolation in their suffering, unlike environmental or natural disasters where the whole community suffers together. This isolation can contribute to even greater psychological distress (Kaniasty, Norris, & Murrell, 1990), not unlike the experiences of survivors of collective violence described later in this chapter.

Most research has focused on general distress reactions following residential fire. Krim (1983) described the reactions of poor, urban fire victims, which includes separation anxiety, sleep disorders, illness, withdrawal, and other social and psychological problems. Keane et al. (1994) studied the psychological pain and suffering that victims experience over an extended period. They concluded that victims experience significant amounts of distress over an extended period of time.

Research by Jones and Ribbe (1991) focused on 20 fire survivors. They documented that surviving children, adolescents, and adults expressed varying levels of distress and symptoms related to posttraumatic stress disorder (PTSD). Using a similar methodology, they found elevated levels of PTSD symptomatology in a group of children whose homes had been destroyed by fire compared with a group of children whose homes were unaffected. One of the important mediators of adverse outcome, or a protective factor, appeared to be social support.

In a more recent effort, Jones and Ollendick (2002) examined the impact of residential fire on children, adolescents, and their parents. The team interviewed families from several states following house fires, and then, employing a multimethod assessment procedure, they obtained the short- and long-term consequences of this event. On the basis of a theoretical model, assessment in the following four areas is being carried out: (a) characteristics of the stressor, (b) characteristics of the target subjects (e.g., a child or adolescent, a parent and the family environment), (c) characteristics of the environment (e.g., family member's reactions and level of support from family members and members of the community), and (d) the children's and adolescents' cognitive processing of the fire experience. Additionally, they identified several important mediators (e.g., social support and coping) and moderators (e.g., parent's reactions) of the outcomes. Their initial analyses suggest that many children report distress following this event. Additionally, a small percentage of children and adolescents and their parents meet diagnostic criteria for psychiatric disorders, including PTSD and major depression. An important mediator of these outcomes in children and adolescents appears to be coping ability, another protective factor. Parent reactions seem to moderate the relationship between loss and health outcome (Jones & Ollendick, 2002). Their preliminary analyses make a strong case for early psychological assessment and intervention following residential fire.

A major goal in all this work has been to develop interventions to assist injured children, adolescents, and parents in coping with the consequences of fire-related trauma. As a result, a number of behavioral interventions have been developed for children to use in fire emergencies, like fire and emergency detection, fire evacuation, anxiety control, and dialing 9-1-1.

Primary Prevention

Jones and colleagues (Jones, 1980) have conducted extensive research to identify and validate behavioral steps to assist children's ability to cope effectively with emergency situations. In one program, they taught a group of youngsters in a Head Start program how to perform emergency phone dialing in case of fire. Children first learned their own addresses and phone numbers. Then they were taught how to actually contact the fire department in case of fire. This procedure was later refined and expanded to teach 3rd graders how to recognize a variety of emergency situations (Jones, Kazdin, & Haney, 1981a), and take appropriate preventive action. Firefighters from the United States and Canada socially validated the behavioral sequences learned. Fire safety skills have also been taught to children who are retarded (Jones & Thornton, 1987), blind children and adolescents (Jones, Van Hasselt, & Sisson, 1984), and elderly people (Haney & Jones, 1982).

Secondary and Tertiary Prevention

In another set of studies, Jones and Randall (1994) and Jones and McDonald (1986) developed and tested an intervention strategy labeled "Rehearsal Plus" (R+), targeting a variety of skills including fire evacuation, refusal skills, and fear reduction (Corbin, Jones, & Schulman, 1993; Hillman, Jones, & Farmer, 1986; Jones, McDonald, Fiore, Arrington, & Randall, 1990; Jones, Ollendick, McLaughlin, & Williams, 1989; Williams & Jones, 1989). Using behavioral and cognitive strategies, specific skills were enhanced using positive reinforcement, modeling and rehearsal, and knowledge was increased through changes in beliefs and elaborative rehearsal to enhance learning, retention, and appreciation of such skills.

Using this model, researchers helped two children develop competencies across the domains of behavioral, cognitive, and affective functioning. The R+ strategy was also used with an 11-year-old boy and his 7-year-old sister, who were forced to relocate after a recent house fire. Treatment consisted of eight weekly 50-minute sessions, in which valid and adaptive ways of reprocessing the event were provided to the older child. Additionally, inaccurate perceptions and beliefs were challenged and changed. Systematic desensitization and deep muscle relaxation procedures were also administered to reduce levels of fear and anxiety associated with the fire. Both children learned fire evacuation skills that enhanced their sense of self-efficacy (in the event of another fire) and reduced feelings of panic and guilt that were associated with not knowing what to do in the previous fire emergency. At posttest, both children showed decreases in levels of depression and significant drops across each symptom cluster of PTSD (Jones & McDonald, 1986).

A Model of Preventive Intervention for Children and Fire

We now provide brief examples of how components of a prevention model could be integrated into portions of a treatment strategy.

Step 1: Documenting the Need for Intervention

The therapist carries out objective assessment of the children's functioning during and following the fire. This step is important because we know from prior research with 212 children and adolescents after Hurricane Andrew that perceptions of the disaster and reactions to the emergency were the most salient predictor of distress afterwards (Jones, Cunningham, Weddle, Frary, & Kaiser, 2001).

A thorough clinical assessment of the psychological consequences of the fire will determine if intervention is necessary. Primary assessment instruments could include a Fire Questionnaire (Jones & Ribbe, 1990), the Children's Depression Inventory (Kovacs, 1985), Horowitz's scale (Horowitz, Wilner, & Alvarez, 1979), and the Diagnostic Interview (Reich & Welner, 1990). The Fire Emergency Behavioral Situations Scale (Jones, 1988) has also been used to assess emergency functioning.

Step 2: Determining and Validating the Skills to Teach

This step involves determining and then shaping fire safety skills children will need to cope with future fire emergency situations. One common fear among children and adolescents who survived fires is the fear of another fire in which they are likely to be seriously injured or killed. Therefore, behaviors necessary to evacuate a burning house are targeted for change. Earlier studies found that children who said they could "change the situation" were more likely to engage in adaptive, problem-focused coping, whereas those who felt they could not were more likely to engage emotion-focused coping (Jones & Randall, 1994). Consistent with Bandura's (1997) assertion that coping beliefs, such as appraisal and coping efficacy, play a major role in determining coping efforts in disaster situations, children were taught evacuation skills in an attempt to enhance their sense of self-efficacy.

Step 3: Deciding How to Teach Skills

In this step, a variety of effective skill-enhancement strategies are used, including verbal instructions, demonstration and modeling, role-playing, simulation, feedback, and positive reinforcement. These active educational methods are far more preferable than passive didactic approaches.

Step 4: Determining When to Teach Skills

Skills needed to successfully evacuate in a fire emergency requires that children acquire these skills before they encounter the emergency. Teaching, practice, and feedback are helpful to prepare children for a possible emergency before it happens.

Step 5: Selecting Interventionists and Training Settings

Training can take place in a clinic, school, or the home. Trained clinical psychologists or trained assistants usually administer the intervention. The children's parents are also encouraged to provide assistance and social support by reinforcing acquisition and practicing skills in the home. This component increases the likelihood that skills will generalize to settings other than where the training was conducted.

Step 6: Obtaining Community-Wide Involvement

Communities can be helpful in providing resources, assisting the identification of at-risk children, and advocating for programs that improve children's mental health and recovery. Schools, fire departments, police departments, and health departments can all assist. Organizations including the National Fire Protection Association, the Federal Emergency Management Agency, as well as a variety of insurance companies can also help by incorporating behavioral components of the program (e.g., "stop, drop, and roll") into their own programs.

In summary, although only a few behavioral scientists have been involved in fire emergency behavioral management, important progress has been made in identifying psychological consequences and implementing behavioral interventions with children. Research has shown the value of prevention, early assessment and treatment in reducing the psychological effects of serious burn injuries. Most important, modified intervention strategies are now being developed and systematically explored in hopes of managing individual and family dynamics that might help children and communities recover from fire emergencies more quickly.

RECOVERING FROM COLLECTIVE VIOLENCE IN WAR-TORN COUNTRIES

Collective violence in its various forms receives a high degree of public attention. Conflicts between nations and groups, terrorism, genocide, rape as a weapon of war, and torture occur daily in many parts of the world. The World Health Organization (WHO) estimates that 310,000 people died from war-related injuries in 2000 alone, ranging from 1 per 100,000 population in high-income countries to 6.2 in low-income and middle-income countries. Worldwide, the highest rates of war-related deaths were found in the WHO African Region (32.0 per 100,000; Zwi, Garfield, & Loretti, 2002). The psychological effects of these events, and efforts of victims to recover from them, have important public health and mental health implications (Volkan, 2000). The WHO World Report on Violence and Health documented the health and mental health impact in the aftermath of collective violence in war-torn countries, and pointed toward individual and national rehabilitation as one of the major social and public health challenges in the aftermath of armed conflict (Zwi, Garfield, & Loretti, 2002).

Collective violence is defined as "the instrumental use of violence by people who identify themselves as members of a group . . . against another group or set of individuals, in order to achieve political, economic or social objectives" (Zwi et al., 2002, p. 215). Half the countries of the world are currently postconflict societies in transition from repressive pasts to democracy (Rosenberg, 1999). Even a cursory glance across cultures reveals the powerful influence of past collective violence such as ethnic conflicts, wars, international and civil strife, or state-sanctioned repression on the lives of the individuals who suffered, as well as within the societies themselves (Staub, 1999). Psychologists can play an important role in recognizing these global problems, and assisting individuals and countries in coming to terms with war-related atrocities.

Those governments that are the successors to those responsible for collective violence face twin tensions that require balancing. One is the need to maintain current political stability, the second, to provide justice for those who suffered and an accounting from those who perpetrated the crimes of prior regimes. How countries choose to confront their past has significant impact on the future course of their society. Whether or not they pursue prosecution of the perpetrators or ensure a context for people and communities to tell their stories of suffering and survival has important implications for recovery.

Amnesty

Granting amnesty to those who perpetrated violence is one response that has created intense debate in international circles (Orentlicher, 1991; Scharff, 1996; Zalaquett, 1993). As one author asserts, "It is morally defensible to say that amnesty is a reasonable price to pay for peace" (Boraine, as cited by Hamber & Kibble, 1999, pp. 28–29). Some in the human rights community, however, contend that providing amnesty to prior regimes contributes to a culture of impunity that exacerbates the injustices suffered by the victims of those regimes. The relationship of amnesty to the psychological processing of trauma is unclear and a question that warrants close examination by psychologists.

There is some suggestion by researchers who have analyzed the South African Truth and Reconciliation Commission and its after-effects that "(p)ast perpetrators can, and often do, get involved in other types of violence (largely criminal acts) albeit not directly 're-offending' of political violence" (Hamber, 1997; see also Hamber & Kibble, 1999; Simpson, 1998). These authors question whether the continuing instances of police torture and deaths in police custody can be linked to the failure to prosecute those responsible for apartheid-related violence. Similarly, they link the often-significant rise in crime in postconflict societies to the provision of amnesty.

Truth Commissions

Truth commissions have been used in about two-dozen countries (Hayner, 2001) as the mechanism for collecting the narratives of torture, murder, abduction, assassination, and execution perpetrated against a group or individuals. These could be people who stood in opposition to the prevailing political ideology, whether they be students, union leaders, journalists, those who worked to empower the poor, who challenged the government, or are simply considered political opposition forces. They were often considered political enemies of the state and beaten or tortured. Although there is no single model for a truth commission, their aim is to write an historical record of the abuses of the past through the testimony of survivor-victims.

Truth commissions' investigations collect testimony from those who have experienced state sponsored violence. From these accounts they characterize the *pattern* of abuses, rather than the substantiation of any one person's experiences. Depending on their mandate, the investigation is often coupled with recommendations for structural changes within the country that would prevent the recurrence of the abuses of the past. A further intent is to contribute to the creation of a "culture of human rights" that would serve as protection against the recurrence of such abuses. In South Africa, for example, in addition to hearings from individuals about their experience of torture, investigations were conducted into industries such as banking, mining, and the media. War crimes trials, in contrast, seek to punish the authors of policies and perpetrators of practices that resulted in human rights violations of earlier periods.

Psychological Impact

Psychological consequences of collective violence and trauma for survivors include fear and passivity for both direct survivors and the broader general population. In addition to a profound sense of fear of others and social isolation, many survivors report being overwhelmed by memories and flashbacks typical of posttraumatic stress disorder symptoms. One person described the pervasive fear this way: "After they took him away, I spent ten days awake taking care of my two babies, because I was certain they were also going to take them away from me. The greatest harm that we have endured is never feeling secure" (Statement to the Chilean National Commission on Truth and Reconciliation; Berryman, 1993).

Other fears include being abducted and tortured, implicating a friend or loved one, being betrayed by a neighbor or colleague for real or imagined advantage. Fear also becomes an isolating force. Once socially isolated and divided, not knowing whom to trust, people ultimately become passive to further acts of collective violence. Other effects of collective violence include an alteration of stimulus regulation that has underlying biological correlates (van der Kolk & Greenberg, 1987). Data suggest that substance abuse rates, aggressive behavior, gang related activity among adolescents, and suicide are high in those societies that have survived ethnic conflict, war, or other repression. Each of these activities may have linkages to what has been termed "addiction to trauma," resulting in high levels of other risk taking behaviors (van der Kolk & Greenberg, 1987).

Complicated mourning is another common consequence of collective violence. Without a body to bury (much less, information about what happened to their loved ones), survivors are unable to use the rituals that are necessary for dealing with death. As a result, survivors often remain rooted in endless grief. The present cannot be fully experienced and is colored by the grief of the past, which colors current relationships. Reconstructing the past through truth-telling (as in truth commissions) can help the individual and the community recover from collective violence and live more actively in the present.

There is a powerful social and psychological function in a truth commission's work. By testifying before a truth commission, people affected psychologically by collective violence can tell their story of fear and isolation and for the first time put their experience into words. Truth commissions provide the context for individual storytelling and for sharing community grief. This public acknowledgement and recognition of what happened to individuals and families inhibits the potential for collective denial of the events of the past. The community's processing the trauma in the context of truth commissions can be an important part of the rehabilitation process for individuals and restorative for communities.

Unfortunately little is known regarding the effectiveness of truth commissions, amnesty, and war tribunals in ameliorating the effects of trauma in war-torn countries. This is an important opportunity for psychologists to contribute solutions and assist future research related to the recovery from collective violence in war-torn countries.

CONCLUSION

Injuries remain a critical community health problem. This chapter has introduced psychologists to issues and opportunities in research and practice related to community injury prevention and control. We have illustrated how community health promotion, youth violence, responses to fire emergencies, and recovery from collective violence all benefit from taking a psychological or behavioral science approach.

Although specific unintentional injuries and violence may take place in settings like the school, home, or playground, all injuries occur within the context of a community. The contributions of psychology to this area will be more fully realized as psychologists and public health researchers and practitioners work side-by-side. Both the American Psychological Association (APA) and federal agencies within the U.S. government are important resources for psychologists who want to increase their involvement in research and community action for injury control. For example, the National Center for Injury Prevention and Control (CDC, 2002a), the National Institute for Mental Health (National Institutes of Health, 2000), and the American Psychological Association (APA, 1996) have all published research agendas that provide many opportunities for psychologists to become more involved.

"Psychology Builds a Healthy World," the theme of APA's 2001 initiative, focuses on the opportunity to improve health through the contributions of psychology. The initiative presents new opportunities and new challenges to the field of psychology to apply the psychologists' tools, skills, and concepts to the public health problem of injury. Psychologists complement the work of epidemiologists and other public health practitioners working on injury problems in schools, families, and communities. Psychologists bring a clinical, developmental, and community focus to our efforts to reduce the burden of injuries.

Injury prevention needs psychology. More than 10 years ago, Spielberger and Frank (1992) outlined injury control as a promising field for psychologists. Yet even today, models, theories, and behavior-change strategies are underrepresented in injury prevention research, and behavioral and social science approaches to injury prevention are still underutilized and underfunded. The CDC–APA joint conference on behavioral and social science approaches to public health and the subsequent book that followed (Schneiderman, Speers, Silva, Tomes, & Gentry, 2001), went a long way toward stimulating change. Behavioral science has been applied successfully to a number of public health problems, and there is a developing empirical literature that supports its efficacy for injury prevention and control (Sleet, Hopkins, & Singer, 2003)

This is an exciting time to examine injuries from a behavioral perspective, because it is clear that both psychologists and injury professionals recognize the value of behavioral approaches (DiLillo, Peterson, & Farmer, 2002; Gielen & Girasek, 2001; Gielen & Sleet, 2003; Liller & Sleet, in press; Lutzker & Whitaker, in press; Thompson, Sleet, & Sacks, 2002; Solomon & Kington, 2002). APA and its Past President Norine Johnson have now taken further steps to provide a platform for these two groups to work together.

This chapter, the results of a symposium on "Injury and Violence Prevention in the Community," is a demonstration of APA's commitment to the role of psychology in community health generally, and to injury and violence prevention specifically. The symposium highlighted areas where psychologists and public health workers are aligned. Because of the empirical rigor that psychology offers, the application of behavioral and social science theories in injury prevention will help us understand more specifically how behavior and injuries are interlinked. Such information will be valuable in designing injury intervention, prevention, and rehabilitation programs. We salute the APA for including injury prevention as an important component in community health. The time has come to work together.

REFERENCES

American Psychological Association, Human Capital Initiative Coordinating Committee. (1996). *Reducing violence: A research agenda.* Washington, DC: Author.

Bablouzian, L., Freedman, E. S., Wolski, K. E., & Fried, L. E. (1997). Evaluation of a community based childhood injury prevention program. *Injury Prevention, 3*(1), 14–16.

Bandura, A. (1997). *Self-efficacy: The exercise of control.* New York: W. H. Freeman.

Berryman, P. E. (Trans.). (1993). *Report of the Chilean National Commission on Truth and Reconciliation.* Notre Dame, IN: Notre Dame Law School.

Centers for Disease Control and Prevention. (2002a). *CDC injury research agenda.* Atlanta, GA: National Center for Injury Prevention and Control.

Centers for Disease Control and Prevention. (2002b). Youth risk behavior surveillance—United States, 2001. *Morbidity and Mortality Weekly Report, 51* (SS-04), 1–64.

Centers for Disease Control and Prevention. (2003). *Web-based Injury Statistics Query and Reporting System (WISQARS)* [database online]. Retrieved February 25, 2003, from National Center for Injury Prevention and Control: http://www.cdc.gov/ncipc/wisqars

Clamp, M., & Kendrick, D. (1998). A randomized controlled trial of general practitioner safety advice for families with children under 5 years. *British Medical Journal, 316,* 1576–1579.

Corbin, S., Jones, R. T., & Schulman, R. S. (1993). Drug refusal behavior: The relative efficacy of skills-based and information-based treatment. *Journal of Pediatric Psychology, 18,* 769–784.

Davis, R. M., & Pless, I. B. (2001). BMJ bans "accidents." *British Medical Journal, 322,* 1320–1321.

DeTurch, M. A., Chih, I.H., & Hsu, Y. P. (1999). Three studies testing the effects of role models on product users' safety behavior. *Human Factors, 41*(3), 397–412.

DiLillo, D., Peterson, L., & Farmer, J. (2002). Injury and poisoning. In T. J. Boll (Series Ed.), S. B. Johnson, N. W. Perry, & R. H. Rozensky (Vol. Eds.), *Handbook of clinical health psychology: Vol. 1. Medical disorders and behavioral applications* (pp. 555–582). Washington, DC: American Psychological Association.

Dowswell, T., Towner, E., Simpson, G., & Jarvis, S. N. (1996). Preventing childhood unintentional injuries: What works? A literature review. *Injury Prevention, 2,* 140–149.

Dunn, C., DeRoo, L., & Rivara, F. (2001). The use of brief interventions adapted from motivational interviewing across behavioral domains: A systematic review. *Addiction, 96,* 1725–1742.

Farrell, A. D., Meyer, A. L., & Dahlberg, L. L. (1996). Richmond Youth Against Violence: A school-based program for urban adolescents. *American Journal of Preventive Medicine, 12*(Suppl. 5), 13–21.

Fields, S. A., & McNamara, J. R. (2003). The prevention of child and adolescent violence: A review. *Aggression and Violent Behavior, 8,* 61–91.

Geller, E. S. (1998). *The psychology of safety.* Boca Raton, FL: CRC Press.

Geller, E. S., Berry, T. D., Ludwig, T. D., Evans, R. E., Gilmore, M. R., & Clarke, S. W. (1990). A conceptual framework for developing and evaluating behavior change interventions for injury control. *Health Education Research, 5*(2), 125–138.

Geller, E. S., Elder, J., Hovell, M., & Sleet, D. A. (1991). Behavioral approaches to drinking-driving interventions. In W. Ward & F. M. Lewis (Eds.), *Advances in health education and promotion* (Vol. 3, pp. 45–68). London: Jessica Kingsley.

Gielen, A. (Ed.). (2002, March). Injury and domestic violence prevention [Special issue]. *Patient Education and Counseling, 46*(3).

Gielen, A., & Girasek, D. (2001). Integrating perspectives on the prevention of unintentional injuries. In N. Schneiderman, M. Speers, J. Silva, H. Tomes, & J. Gentry (Eds.), *Integrating behavioral and social sciences with public health* (pp. 203–230). Washington, DC: American Psychological Association.

Gielen, A., & Sleet, D. A. (2003). Applications of behavior-change theories and methods to injury prevention. *Epidemiologic Reviews, 25*(1).

Green, L. W., & Kreuter, M. K. (1999). *Health promotion planning: An educational and ecological approach* (3rd ed.). Mountain View, CA: Mayfield Publishing.

Greenberg, H. S., & Keane, A. (1997). A social work perspective of childhood trauma after a residential fire. *Social Work in Education, 19,* 11–22.

Hamber, B. (1997). Living with the legacy of impunity: Lessons for South Africa about truth, justice, and crime in Brazil. *Latin American Report, 13*(2), 4–16.

Hamber, B., & Kibble, S. (1999). *From truth to transformation: South Africa's Truth and Reconciliation Commission.* Johannesburg, South Africa: Centre for the Study of Violence and Reconciliation.

Hammond, W. R., & Prothrow-Stith, D. (2001). The epidemic of homicide and violence. In R. L. Braithwaite & S. E. Taylor (Eds.), *Health issues in the Black community* (2nd ed., pp. 151–166). San Francisco: Jossey-Bass.

Haney, J. I., & Jones, R. T. (1982). Programming maintenance as a major component of a community-centered preventive effort: Escape from fire. *Behavior Therapy, 13,* 47–62.

Hawkins, J. D., Herrenkohl, T. I., Farrington, D. P., Brewer, D., Catalano, R. F., Harachi, T. W., et al. (1998). A review of predictors of youth violence. In R. Loeber & D. P. Farrington (Eds.), *Serious and violent juvenile offenders: Risk factors and successful interventions* (pp. 106–146). Thousand Oaks, CA: Sage.

Hayner, P. B. (2001). *Unspeakable truths: Confronting state terror and atrocity.* New York: Routledge.

Hillman, H., Jones, R. T., & Farmer, L. (1986). The acquisition and maintenance of fire emergency skills: Effects of rationale and behavioral practice. *Journal of Pediatric Psychology, 11,* 247–258.

Holtgrave, D. R., Doll, L. S., & Harrison, J. (1997). Influence of behavioral and social science on public health policy making. *American Psychologist, 52,* 154–166.

Horowitz, M. J., Wilner, N., & Alvarez, W. (1979). Impact of events scale: A measure of subjective stress. *Psychosomatic Medicine, 41,* 209–218.

Huesmann, L., Guerra, N., Miller, L., & Zelli, A. (1992). The role of social norms in the development of aggression. In H. Zumkley & A. Fraczek (Eds.), *Socialization and aggression.* New York: Springer.

Hungerford, D. W., & Pollock, D. A. (Eds.). (2002). *Alcohol problems among emergency department patients: Proceedings of a research conference on identification and intervention.* Atlanta, GA: National Center for Injury Prevention and Control, Centers for Disease Control and Prevention.

Institute of Medicine. (1999). *Reducing the burden of injury: Advancing prevention and treatment.* Washington, DC: National Academy Press.

Johnston, B. D., Rivara, F. P., Droesch, R. M., Dunn, C., & Copass, M. (2002). Behavior change counseling in the emergency department to reduce risk: A randomized control trial. *Pediatrics, 110*(2), 267–274.

Jones, R. T. (1980). Teaching children to make emergency telephone calls. *Journal of Black Psychology, 6,* 81–93.

Jones, R. T. (1988). The Fire Emergency Behavioral Situations Scale. In M. Hersen & A. S. Bellack (Eds.), *Dictionary of behavioral assessment techniques* (pp. 224–226). New York: Pergamon Press.

Jones, R. T., Cunningham, P., Weddle, J. D., Frary, R., & Kaiser, L. (2001). The psychological effects of Hurricane Andrew on ethnic minority and Caucasian children and adolescents: A case study. *Cultural Diversity and Ethnic Minority Psychology, 7,* 103–108.

Jones, R. T., Kazdin, A. E., & Haney, J. I. (1981a). A follow-up to training emergency skills. *Behavior Therapy, 12,* 716–722.

Jones, R. T., Kazdin, A. E., & Haney, J. I. (1981b). Social validation and training of emergency fire safety skills for potential injury prevention and life saving. *Journal of Applied Behavior Analysis, 14*, 249–260.

Jones, R. T., & McDonald, D., III (1986). Childhood injury: A prevention model for intervention. *Education and Treatment of Children, 9*, 307–319.

Jones, R. T., McDonald, D. W., Fiore, M. F., Arrington, T., & Randall, J. (1990). A primary preventive approach to children's drug refusal behavior: The impact of rehearsal-plus. *Journal of Pediatric Psychology, 15*, 211–223.

Jones, R. T., & Ollendick, T. H. (2002). The impact of residential fire on children and their families. In A. La Greca, W. Silverman, E. Vernberg, & M. Roberts (Eds.), *Helping children cope with disasters: Integrating research and practice* (pp. 175–199). Washington, DC: American Psychological Association.

Jones, R. T., Ollendick, T. H., McLaughlin, K. J., & Williams, C. E. (1989). Elaborative and behavioral rehearsal in the acquisition of fire emergency skills and the reduction of fear of fire. *Behavior Therapy, 20*, 93–101.

Jones, R. T., & Randall, J. (1994). Rehearsal-plus: Coping with fire emergencies and reducing fire-related fears. *Fire Technology, 30*, 432–444.

Jones, R. T., & Ribbe, D. P. (1990). *The child fire questionnaire*. Unpublished manuscript. Virginia Polytechnic Institute and State University, Blacksburg, VA.

Jones, R. T., & Ribbe, D. P. (1991). Child and adolescent victims of fire: Psychological consequences. In J. Freedy (Chair), *Short- and long-term effects of trauma in children and adolescents*. Symposium conducted at the annual meeting of the American Psychological Association, San Francisco, CA.

Jones, R. T., & Thornton, J. L. (1987). The acquisition and maintenance of emergency evacuation skills with mildly to moderately retarded adults in a community living arrangement. *Journal of Community Psychology, 15*, 205–215.

Jones, R. T., Van Hasselt, V. B., & Sisson, L. A. (1984). Emergency fire safety skills: A study with blind adolescents. *Behavior Modification, 8*, 59–78.

Kaniasty, K. Z., Norris, F. H., & Murrell, S. A. (1990). Received and perceived social support following natural disaster. *Journal of Applied Social Psychology, 20*, 85–114.

Keane, A., Jepson, C., Pickett, M., Robinson, L., McCorkle, R., & Lowery, B. (1994). Psychological distress in survivors of residential fires. *Social Science and Medicine, 38*, 1055–1060.

Kellam, S. G., Rebok, G. W., Ialongo, N., & Mayer, L. S. (1994). The course and malleability of aggressive behavior from early to middle school: Results of a developmental epidemiologically based preventative trial. *Journal of Child Psychology, Psychiatry, and Allied Disciplines, 35*, 259–281.

Kovacs, M. (1985). CDI (The Children's Depression Inventory). *Psychopharmacology Bulletin, 21*, 995–998.

Krause, T. (1997). *The behavior based safety process*. New York: Van Nostrand Reinhold.

Krim, A. (1983). *Families after urban fire: Disaster intervention* (MH29197). Washington, DC: National Institute of Mental Health.

Krug, E. G., Dahlberg, L. L., Mercy, J. A., Zwi, A. B., & Lozano, R. (Eds.). (2002). *World report on violence and health*. Geneva, Switzerland: World Health Organization.

Leslie, J. (2001). Behavioural safety: Extending the principles of applied behavioral analysis to safety in fires in public buildings. In *Proceedings of the 2nd International Symposium on Human Behavior in Fire* (pp. 1–10). London: Interscience Communications.

Liller, K, & Sleet, D. A. (Eds.). (in press). Health behavior and injury control [Special issue]. *American Journal of Health Behavior*.

Lipsey, M. W., & Derzon, J. H. (1998). Predictors of violent or serious delinquency in adolescence and early adulthood: A synthesis of longitudinal research. In R. Loeber & D. P. Farrington (Eds.), *Serious and violent juvenile offenders: Risk factors and successful interventions* (pp. 86–105). Thousand Oaks, CA: Sage.

Lonsway, K. A. (1996). Preventing acquaintance rape through education: What do we know? *Psychology of Women Quarterly, 20,* 229–266.

Lutzker, J. R., & Whitaker, D. J. (in press). The expanding role of behavior analysis and support: Current status and future directions. *Behavior Modification*.

Mercy, J. A., & Hammond, W. R. (2001). Learning to do violence prevention well. *American Journal of Preventive Medicine, 20,* 1–2.

Meyer, A. L., & Farrell, A. D. (1998, November). Social skills training to promote resilience in urban sixth-grade students: One product of an action research strategy to prevent youth violence in high-risk environments. *Education and Treatment of Children, 21*(4), 461–488.

Miller, T. R., Covington, K., & Jensen, A. (1997). *Costs of injury by major cause, United States, 1995: Cobbling together estimates.* Calverton, MD: Children's Safety Network: Economics and Insurance Resource Center, Pacific Institute for Research and Evaluation.

National Center for Injury Prevention and Control. (2001). *Injury fact book 2001–2002.* Atlanta, GA: Centers for Disease Control and Prevention.

National Committee for Injury Prevention and Control. (1989). Injury prevention: Meeting the challenge. *American Journal of Preventive Medicine* (Suppl.).

National Fire Protection Association. (1999). *Fire loss in the U.S. during 1999.* Retrieved from the National Fire Protection Association Web site: http://www.nfpa.org

National Institutes of Health. (2000). *Pathways to health: Charting the science of brain, mind, and behavior—A research strategic plan for the NIMH FY2000–2001.* Bethesda, MD: National Institute for Mental Health.

National Research Council, Committee on Trauma Research. (1985). *Injury in America: A continuing public health problem.* Washington, DC: National Academy Press.

O'Conner, P. J. (1982). Poisoning prevention: Results of a public media campaign. *Australian Paediatrics Journal, 18*, 250–252.

Orentlicher, D. F. (1991). Settling accounts: The duty to prosecute human rights violations of a prior regime. *The Yale Law Journal, 100*, 2537–2615.

Orpinas, P., Kelder, S., Frankowski, R., Murray, N., Zhang, Q., & Mcalister, A. (2000). Outcome evaluation of a multi-component violence-prevention program for middle schools: the Students for Peace Project. *Health Education Research, 15*, 45–58.

Pless, I. B. (1978). Accident prevention and health education: Back to the drawing board? *Pediatrics, 62*, 431–435.

Reich, W., & Welner, Z. (1990). *Diagnostic interview for children and adolescents— Revised.* St. Louis: Washington University.

Roberts, M., Fanurik, D., & Layfield, D. A. (1987). Behavioral approaches to preventing childhood injuries. *Journal of Social Issues, 43*(2), 105–118.

Rosenberg, T. (1999). Afterword: Confronting the painful past. In M. Meredith (Ed.), *Coming to terms: South Africa's search for truth* (pp. 327–370). New York: Public Affairs.

Scharff, M. P. (1996). Swapping amnesty for Peace: Was there a duty to prosecute international crimes in Haiti? *Texas International Law Journal, 31*(1), 1–41.

Scheckner, S., Rollin, S. A., Kaiser-Ulrey, C., & Wagner, R. (2002). School violence in children and adolescents: A meta-analysis of the effectiveness of current interventions. *Journal of School Violence, 1*(2), 5–33.

Schneiderman, N., Speers, M. A., Silva, J. M., Tomes, H., & Gentry, J. H. (Eds.). (2001). *Integrating behavioral and social sciences with public health.* Washington, DC: American Psychological Association.

Shechtman, Z. (1999). Bibliotherapy: An indirect approach to treatment of childhood aggression. *Child Psychiatry and Human Development, 30*(1), 39–53.

Sheridan, R. L., Hinson, M. I., Liang, M. H., Nackel, A. F., Schoenfeld, D. A., Ryan, C. M., et al. (2000). Long-term outcome of children surviving massive burns. *Journal of the American Medical Association, 283*, 69–73.

Simpson, G. (1998). *A brief evaluation of South Africa's Truth and Reconciliation Commission: Some lessons for societies in transition.* Johannesburg, South Africa: Centre for the Study of Violence and Reconciliation.

Sleet, D. A., & Gielen, A. (1998). Injury prevention. In S. S. Gorin & J. Arnold (Eds.), *Health promotion handbook* (pp. 247–275). St. Louis, MO: Mosby, Inc.

Sleet, D. A., Hollenbach, K., & Hovell, M. (1986). Applying behavioral principles to motor vehicle occupant protection. *Education and Treatment of Children, 9*(4), 320–333.

Sleet, D. A., Hopkins, K., & Singer, H. H. (2003). *Bibliography of behavioral science research in unintentional injuries.* Atlanta, GA: Centers for Disease Control and Prevention.

Sleet, D. A., & Lonero, L. (2002). Behavioral strategies for reducing traffic crashes. In L. Breslow (Ed.), *Encyclopedia of public health* (pp. 105–107). New York: McMillan.

Sleet, D. A., & Mercy, J. M. (2003). Promotion of safety, security, and well-being. In M. H. Bornstein, L. Davidson, C. L. M. Keyes, K. A. Moore, & The Center for Child Well-being (Eds.), *Well-being: Positive development across the life course* (pp. 81–97). Mahwah, NJ: Erlbaum.

Sleet, D. A., & Rosenberg, M. L. (1997). Injury control. In D. F. Scutchfield & C. W. Keck (Eds.), *Principles of public health practice* (pp. 337–349). New York: Delmar Publishers.

Snider, D. E., & Satcher, D. (1997). Behavioral and social sciences at the Centers for Disease Control and Prevention. *American Psychologist, 52*(2), 140–142.

Solomon, S. Kington, R. (2002). National efforts to promote behavior-change research: Views from the Office of Behavioral and Social Science Research. *Health Education Research, 17,* 495–499.

Spielberger, C. D., & Frank, R. G. (1992). Injury Control: A promising field for psychologists. *American Psychologist, 47,* 1029–1030.

Staub, E. (1999). The origins and prevention of genocide, mass killing, and other collective violence. *Peace and Conflict: Journal of Peace Psychology, 5*(4), 303–335.

Streff, F. M., & Geller, E. S. (1986). Strategies for motivating safety belt use: The application of applied behavior analysis. *Health Education Research, 1,* 47–59.

Tarnowski, K. J. (Ed.). (1994). *Behavioral aspects of pediatric burns.* New York: Plenum Press.

Taylor, R. B., Ureda, J. R., & Denham, J. W. (1982). *Health promotion: Principles and clinical applications.* Stamford, CT: Appleton and Lange.

Thompson, N. J., Sleet, D. A., & Sacks, J. J. (2002). Increasing the use of bicycle helmets: Lessons from behavioral science. *Patient Education and Counseling, 46*(3), 191–197.

Thornton, T. N., Craft, C. A., Dahlberg, L. L., Lynch, B. S., & Baer, K. (2000). *Best practices of youth violence prevention: A sourcebook for community action.* Atlanta, GA: Centers for Disease Control and Prevention, National Center for Injury Prevention and Control.

Thornton, T. N., Craft, C. A., Dahlberg, L. L., Lynch, B. S., & Baer, K. (2002). *Best practices of youth violence prevention: A sourcebook for community action* (rev. ed.). Atlanta, GA: Centers for Disease Control and Prevention.

Towner, E. (1995). The role of health education in childhood injury prevention. *Injury Prevention, 1,* 53–58.

Towner, E., & Dowswell, T. (2002). Community-based childhood injury prevention interventions: What works? *Health Promotion International, 17*(3), 273–284.

U.S. Department of Health and Human Services. (2001). *Youth violence: A report of the Surgeon General.* Rockville, MD: U.S. Department of Health and Human Services, Centers for Disease Control and Prevention, National Center for

Injury Prevention and Control; Substance Abuse and Mental Health Services Administration, Center for Mental Health Services; and National Institutes of Health, National Institute of Mental Health.

U.S. Preventive Services Task Force. (1996). *Guide to clinical preventive services* (2nd ed.). Baltimore: Williams & Wilkins.

U.S. Public Health Service. (1979). *Healthy people: The Surgeon General's report on health promotion and disease prevention*. Washington, DC: Department of Health, Education, and Welfare.

van der Kolk, B. A., & Greenberg, M. S. (1987). The psychobiology of the trauma response: Hyperarousal, constriction, and addiction to traumatic reexposure. In B. A. van der Kolk (Ed.), *Psychological trauma*. Washington, DC: American Psychiatric Press.

Volkan, V. D. (2000). Traumatized societies and psychological care: Expanding the concept of preventive medicine. *Mind and Human Interaction, 11*(3), 177–194.

Wasserman, G. A., Miller, L. S., & Cothern, L. (2000). Prevention of serious and violent juvenile offending. *Juvenile Justice Bulletin.*

Williams, A. F., Wells, J. K., & Farmer, C. M. (2002). Effectiveness of Ford's belt reminder system in increasing seat belt use. *Injury Prevention, 8*(4), 293–296.

Williams, C. E., & Jones, R. T. (1989). Impact of self-instructions on response maintenance and children's fear of fire. *Journal of Clinical Child Psychology, 18*, 84–89.

Wilson, F., Dwyer, F., & Bennett, P. (2003). Prevention of dog bites: Evaluation of a brief educational intervention program for preschool children. *Journal of Community Psychology, 31*(1), 75–86.

World Health Organization Global Consultation on Violence and Health. (1996). *Violence: A public health priority* (Document No. WHO/EHA/SPI.POA.2). Geneva, Switzerland: Author.

Yung, B., & Hammond, W. R. (1995). *PACT: Positive Adolescent Choices Training— A model for violence prevention groups with African-American youth*. Champaign, IL: Research Press.

Zalaquett, J. (1993). Introduction to the English edition. In P. E. Berryman (Trans.), *Report of the Chilean National Commission on truth and reconciliation* (pp. xxiii– xxxiii). Notre Dame, IN: Notre Dame Law School.

Zaza, S., & Thompson, R. S. (Eds.). (2001). The guide to Community Preventive Services: Reducing injuries to motor vehicle occupants: Systematic reviews of evidence, recommendations from the Task Force on Community Preventive Services, and expert commentary. *American Journal of Preventive Medicine, 21*(4S), 1–90.

Zwi, A. B., Garfield, R., & Loretti, A. (2002). Collective violence. In E. G. Krug, L. L. Dahlberg, J. A. Mercy, A. B. Zwi, & R. Lozano (Eds.), *World report on violence and health* (pp. 213–239). Geneva, Switzerland: World Health Organization.

III

BUILDING HEALTHY WORKPLACES

8

WORKING TOGETHER: BALANCING HEAD AND HEART

JAMES CAMPBELL QUICK, JOANNE H. GAVIN, CARY L. COOPER, AND JONATHAN D. QUICK

Part III of this volume is about building healthy workplaces, an increasing concern as the boundaries between the work and home environments soften, the spillover effects from one environment to the other become better understood, and the workplace becomes increasingly the venue through which health is addressed for many people in the world. This part is composed of three chapters. The first is this chapter, which explores the two dimensions of working together, one an intrapersonal dimension and the other an interpersonal dimension. The following chapter presents four dimensions of healthy work, and the third chapter examines health issues at work.

This chapter is an extension of James Campbell Quick's Presidentially Invited Address on healthy workplaces at the 109th Annual Convention of the American Psychological Association. Partial support for the address came during a Faculty Development Leave from the University of Texas at Arlington. The authors would like to thank John A. (Jack) Walters, Vice President, Human Resources, Alcon Laboratories, Inc., for the inspiration for the main chapter title. The authors would like to thank John (Jack) Dovidio, David J. Gavin, Harry Levinson, and Sheri Schember Quick for contributions, suggestions, and comments on earlier drafts of this chapter.

This chapter sets forth a personal message of intrapersonal integrity and integration as well as a collective message of cooperation and collaboration in the workplace. The chapter has as its psychological foundation a dual drive theory of human nature in which both the need to achieve and the need to feel secure are accepted as compelling and legitimate. By developing a deeper understanding and appreciation of our own feelings and emotions, we can learn to work from our hearts as well as our heads. At a collective level, this requires balancing the processes of competition with cooperation and collaboration. This chapter offers illustrations and organizational examples throughout.

Next, chapter 9 has four independent yet interrelated contributions by Quick, Piotrkowski, Jenkins, and Brooks. Each author brings a unique perspective and professional expertise to address a specific dimension of healthy work. On the basis of Paul Rosch's (2001) identification of job stress as a health epidemic, Quick calls for psychologists to take leadership roles in organizations for prevention and to develop the practice of organizational therapy for treatment. Piotrkowski brings our attention to the relationship between work and family life and calls for the promotion of the health of vulnerable families through a new generation of research. Jenkins addresses the low frequency, high impact health risk of workplace violence using the public health notions of prevention, including workplace surveillance systems, and calls for the preventive management of this organizational problem. Brooks addresses the unique occupational case of the professional athlete, focusing on lifestyle issues and potential challenges to healthy work and lifestyles within this select group.

Chapter 10 addresses health at work, with contributions from Cantor, Boyce, and Repetti. Boyce studies and intervenes on issues of workplace safety, relating to behaviors, rather than to equipment safety. Repetti studies the impact of occupational health on the health of families. Repetti devotes particular attention to how parental experiences at work affect children's health, and promotes the interrelatedness of these two domains of life. Finally, Cantor is concerned with workers' preparation for postwork lives, beyond their health and wealth, so that they spend their time in purposeful and fulfilling ways.

THERE IS A PUBLIC NEED

The United States is at the center of a global economic village in the midst of what is the second great period of globalization in modern world history. If one looks across the economic, political, social, and military institutions of our society, the United States is a strong and mighty nation. In fact, the United States is the dominant world leader today, across the board. It is a rich and prosperous land, a land of great wealth and abundant resources. In 2000, John Reed was the number one paid CEO in America, making $293,000,000 during the year (Lavelle with Jespersen, 2001). Stunning!

Yet, not all is well. In the midst of this rich and prosperous land of milk and honey there is also a sense of anxiety, stress, and suffering. This has been called the age of anxiety (Twenge, 2000). The corporate warfare of the 1980s and 1990s goes on across a competitive industrial landscape. People continue to be anxious about job loss and a secure place of employment. Although working carries with it social and psychological benefits, there are also risks, such as job insecurity and job loss. Lee Iacocca, the then CEO of the new Chrysler Corporation in the early 1980s, noted these risks and the costs of unemployment when he asked the United States government to guarantee loans to enable Chrysler to work its way to financial health. Or, as he pointed out, the United States government could either guarantee the loans, or start paying unemployment benefits to tens of thousands of unemployed autoworkers.

The picture is not significantly different in the United Kingdom (UK) and parts of Europe. Beginning during the years of Margaret Thatcher and beyond, the UK economy has become increasingly Americanized. This has been economically and financially positive, yet with some social and personal costs as well. For example, the divorce rate in the pre-Thatcher UK was the lowest in the European Union (EU). By the year 2000, the divorce rate in the UK was the highest in the EU. Thus, along some dimensions, it may not be advantageous to model American strength. Excessive attention to economic activity and financial gain may come at social and human costs that are not worth bearing.

Our premise is that it is in our collective, public, and national best interest to have people both healthy and productive, in America, in the UK, and around the world. Healthy and productive work is what we should be collectively and individually striving to achieve (Murphy & Cooper, 2000). In many ways, America is the Promised Land and she must reclaim her inheritance of good-spirited people who can achieve great things through collective and collaborative work effort while caring for each other with support and concern. Psychology has important roles to play in fostering productive effort and supportive compassion in the workplace. This is the center of our concern in this chapter.

HOW CAN PSYCHOLOGY HELP?

Psychology has already done much to help in the healthy and productive work arena. For example, Steve Sauter, Joe Hurrell, Larry Murphy,

Naomi Swanson, and other National Institute for Occupational Safety and Health (NIOSH) team members as well as Gwen Keita and Gary VandenBos at the American Psychological Association (APA) forged the productive APA-NIOSH Cooperative Agreement to advance the healthy workplace agenda. For the unemployed, Rick Price at the Michigan Prevention Research Center offers the JOBS (Job-Search Workshop) Program, in America and around the world. We are not going to review this established body of work and practice here; you may read about that elsewhere. In this chapter we want to discuss working together and relationships in the workplace. The double meaning in the title, although not originally intended, is one we want to elaborate along both the intrapersonal and interpersonal dimensions.

A Personal Message

There is a personal message here. The message is that work is personally healthier if we balance our heads with our hearts. The message is that we are healthier at work if we balance our thinking with our feeling, our thoughts with our emotions. There are deep within us two instinctual drives that lead us, on the one hand, to explore the world and, on the other hand, to connect with each other (Hallowell, 1999). Achievement and connection are both important to individual long-term mental and physical health. Levinson, Price, Munden, Mandl, and Solley (1962) recognize the need for organizations to meet employees' dependency needs through his concept of the psychological contract. This implicit contract is a series of mutual expectations that, if reciprocally satisfying, contribute to mental health.

The dual instinctual drives are manifest in the workplace in the concepts of pressure and support. Spielberger has repeatedly found these two factors as the underlying constructs in his Job Stress Survey (Vagg & Spielberger, 1998). These two stress factors are job pressure and lack of organizational support. If we balance pressure and challenge with support and concern, we create one of the conditions for healthy work relationships. We found this in our field study at Alcon Laboratories headquarters, where high demands for achievement are coupled with human resource support systems that show concern for health and well-being (Quick, Cooper, Gavin, & Quick, 2002).

Psychologist James Pennebaker (1990, 1997) shows us the pathways to achieving the balance between head and heart. Pennebaker's research and practice in confession, confiding in others, and expressive writing elaborates the gateways for overcoming inhibition and opening a deeper dialogue between our heads and our hearts, enabling us to achieve a richer and better understanding of our emotions and emotional lives. His research is particularly relevant to stressful and traumatic events, such as job loss, yet has wider applicability as well (Spera, Buhrfeind, & Pennebaker, 1994). The tools and insights he offers can help each of us gain a better understanding of who we are and how we feel. Let us suggest that when our heads and our hearts are disconnected is when we are at greatest risk of doing harm at work, either to ourselves or to others. Alternatively, when our heads and our hearts connect, when we achieve balance in thought and feeling, and feeling and action, we can act in helpful and healthy ways.

Emotional Intelligence

The process of connecting head and heart has come, in recent times, to be thought of as *emotional intelligence*. Goleman (1998) defined emotional intelligence as the capacity for recognizing our own feelings and those of others, for motivating ourselves, and for managing emotions well in ourselves and in our relationships (p. 319). It is the ability to identify and regulate feelings and use this information to motivate, plan, and achieve in life (Salovey, Mayer, Goldman, Turvey, & Palfai, 1997). People who are high in emotional intelligence can connect the head and heart and use this connection to make the best, most healthy decisions. Decisions are made from neither a purely emotional perspective nor a purely logical one. Rather, decisions are made with the most effective combination of logical decision-making processes informed and guided by our feelings.

Figure 8.1 suggests the two-way, intrapersonal dialogue implied through this process. The intrapersonal dialogue involves the brain and the heart, the logical and the emotional. The brain actually has three levels of functioning, the lowest level being in the brainstem. The brainstem, or reptilian brain, handles all of our automatic functions, such as breathing and activation under stressful conditions. The next higher level in the brain is the limbic level, which is the seat of feeling and emotion. The limbic brain handles feeling, emotion, and processes related to interpersonal connectedness. It is linked to the heart and cardiovascular system, as the figure suggests. If feeling and emotion are aroused, then the heart and cardiovascular system are activated. The top level of the brain, the cerebral cortex, is where we think and carry on abstract and rational functions. The cerebral brain handles logic, abstract reasoning, organizing processes, and intellectual activities. A failure in the internal dialogue between thinking and feeling, thought and emotion, head and heart can lead to unhealthy and adverse consequences. Figure 8.1 embodies the communication at the center of emotional intelligence.

Executive Health and Trust

This intrapersonal message has particular applicability for executives, many of whom experience inner conflicts and tensions with which they are not well acquainted (Levinson, 1985). For this reason and because of the

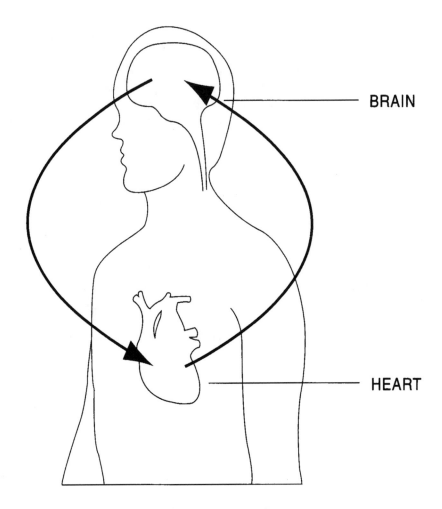

BRAIN

HEART

Figure 8.1. An intrapersonal dialogue between head and heart.

increasing pressures of the current competitive industrial landscape, executive health has become an increasingly important issue for individuals and organizations (Quick, Gavin, Cooper, & Quick, 2000). Hirschhorn (1990) offered a healthy model for executives and leaders on this new competitive landscape. He called for executives to help followers understand tasks and challenges on this new industrial landscape through a process of being both vulnerable and supportive. Their vulnerability leaves them open to new, important information and inputs for high-quality decision making, whereas their supportive posture lends reassurance and felt security to those with whom they work, building trusting bonds at work. This is a new and challenging way for many executives to function because being vulnerable and strong at the same time does require a balance of one's head and heart. Doing so can enable an executive to make difficult decisions and take firm action in compassionate ways.

Joel Brockner's research in the heartland of organizational restructuring and downsizing concluded that trust in executives and organizational authorities matters in difficult situations such as organizational downsizing (Brockner, Siegel, Daley, Tyler, & Martin, 1997). The establishment of trust seems to be a potent force in overcoming the otherwise adverse reactions that employees may display in reaction to decisions leading to unfavorable outcomes, such as job loss. Trust can come from the heart, or from the head. We interpret Brockner's work as a call for executives to be trustworthy and compassionate, which should not be confused with soft or indecisive. Trust can come from emotional connection, and it can come from personal dependability. A theme in Brockner's work seems to be that the effects of what we do depend on how we do it. There are very different consequences, both individually and collectively, for actions that are heartfelt and those that are heartless. One of Dr. Joseph Grant's proudest achievements during the most difficult period in his life, which was the loss of the bank he chaired and all of his personal resources, was establishment of the trusting and cooperative relationships among his management team in the bank (Grant, 1996).

The Collective Message

There is a collective message here as well and it concerns diversity in the workplace and competition and cooperation. The American free enterprise system is built on Adam Smith's (1776/1909) notions of free enterprise along with the extraordinary efforts of diverse groups of immigrants in America during the first great period of globalization in the late 1800s (Friedman, 2000). We are again seeing diversity as a leading edge issue in the current period of globalization (Cox & Blake, 1991). The ability of organizations to again find strength in the cooperative efforts of strong, diverse people from widely varied cultural backgrounds has implications for organizational competitiveness in the global village. Assessment and diagnosis to enhance organizational health has individual and collective benefits (Levinson, 2002).

Competition and cooperation are intractable interpersonal processes that are often in dynamic tension at work. As competition increases, we experience the stress and challenge that enhance motivation and effort, but only up to a point (Loehr, 1997). When competition and competitive behavior goes to the extreme, it is dysfunctional and destructive. Over-the-top competition and stress tear down individuals and organizations. The challenge is to manage our personal and collective competitive drives. At the limbic level, the stress response assumes there is an enemy to be fought, if not killed. Hence, at times like these it may be critical that our head talks to our heart so that we do not act wrongly based solely on emotion. To be healthy, competition must be managed and balanced with cooperation.

Organizations can put this knowledge of balancing competition and cooperation to work in helping create healthier work environments. This is not new knowledge, but rather knowledge that we have had collectively in America over the past 100 years. Why have we failed to fully put this knowledge to work? The calls for cooperation, not divisive competition, are embedded in Fredrick Winslow Taylor's testimony before the Special Committee of the House of Representatives under authority of House Resolution 90 (Taylor, 1939) and in Walter B. Cannon's writings about stress and the fighting emotions following World War I (Cannon, 1929).

Frederick Taylor is probably best known for his uniquely American approach to the standardization of work in a way that helped people from diverse cultural backgrounds and with different languages to perform common work tasks. However, the limitation with this approach to standardizing work is that you cannot standardize human behavior (Buckingham & Coffman, 1999). Although executives may want to eliminate variance at work, and this may have benefits when standardizing parts or processes, it becomes counterproductive to attempt to standardize people's behavior. Rather than changing people at work, Buckingham encourages executives to help people become more of who they already are. This is the approach of positive psychology: build on ability and strength, enhancing each, rather than fighting to overcome weakness.

What is little known and less cited in Taylor's work are some key elements in his testimony before the U.S. Congress. During his second day of testimony (Friday, January 26, 1912), he wanted to call the Committee's attention

> to the bitterness that was stirred up in this fight before the men finally gave in, to the meanness of it, and the contemptible conditions that exist under the old piecework system, and to show you what it leads to. (Taylor, 1939, p. 83)

This part of his testimony focused on the competition and conflicts of the 2–3-year period he experienced as a gang boss at Midvale Steel Company. Portraying the destructiveness of this period, some of his own behavior and the personal toll on his own health, Taylor goes on in his testimony to call for a cooperative working relationship between labor and management. In essence, recognizing from personal experience that competition can be destructive in the workplace, Taylor calls for reconciliation between labor and management, for a cooperative spirit in the working relationship. Scientific management in his view was not a whip to use on labor but a paradigm for work analysis. Although Taylor made important contributions to work and task analysis and he espoused the desirability of cooperative work behavior, his system of scientific management, when put into practice, often squeezed the creativity and humanity out of people (Mintzberg, 1994).

Cannon (1929) came to a very similar conclusion about cooperative behavior from a far different set of research and experience. On the basis of his laboratory research establishing the framework for understanding stress and his field experience as a member of the Harvard Medical team in Europe during World War I, he concluded that the fighting emotions and instincts can be very destructive. He too calls for cooperation in contrast to competition, suggesting that

> the great war of mankind is that against pain, disease, poverty and sin; ... War of man against man, in this view, becomes dissension in the ranks. (Cannon, 1929, p. 384)

Although born of experience early in the century, Cannon's core concepts are echoed in Cascio's psychological and financial research at the end of the century (1998; Cascio, Young, & Morris, 1997; Morris, Cascio, & Young, 1999). We do not build healthier companies, either interpersonally or financially, through employment downsizing alone and by "killing" people off. As I listened to a Fortune 100 executive talk about the waves of layoffs he led during the 1990s, he said it was just like when he was a Marine Corps first lieutenant in Vietnam, putting people in body bags to come back home to America. Although employment downsizing in fact may be necessary, it must be coupled with other restructuring activities in the organization to be effective. Brockner's research clearly suggests that if downsizing is done with fairness, justice, and a heart, it can lead to significantly more positive outcomes for both those who leave and those who stay. Treating people that leave, as well as those that stay, right and fairly does pay dividends over time.

How can organizations put more of this knowledge to work? Maybe we can take a chapter from the military, as Walter Cannon did early in the century. Also, we might take a chapter from education, where addressing diversity in the classroom has been a key concern since the beginning of the Civil Rights Movement.

The U.S. Military

Whereas segregation characterized most of the first 200 years of U.S. military history, that changed after World War II. The American military services became integrated and remain so. The result has been remarkable and positive, leaving the U.S. Army as one American institution that contradicts the prevailing race paradigm of Black failure (Moskos & Butler, 1997):

It is an organization unmatched in its level of racial integration. It is an institution unmatched in its broad record of black achievement. It is a world in which the Afro-American heritage is part and parcel of the institutional culture. It is the only place in American life where whites are routinely bossed around by blacks. (Moskos & Butler, 1997, p. 2)

This achievement demonstrates the collective success found in individuals rising above themselves, overcoming their personal competitive drives, and becoming part of something much bigger than any one of them alone. This sort of collective success is born of cooperative behavior, behavior that is taught and learned.

Another example of the collective success of cooperative United States military behavior occurred in the downsizing and closure of the largest aircraft maintenance depot in the U.S. Air Force as a result of President Bill Clinton signing the BRAC (Base Realignment and Closure) order in July 1995. The closure of the San Antonio Air Logistics Center at Kelly Air Force Base, Texas is the largest federal closure event in the history of the Department of Defense, affecting the livelihoods of more than 13,000 military and federal employees. Major General Lewis G. Curtis set the priorities clearly from the outset: fulfill the mission of supporting Air Force combat readiness first and, a very close second, take care of all the people. In the early stages of this industrial restructuring event, Major General James Childress hired full-time clinical psychologist, Dr. Charles Klunder, to engage in (a) surveillance of the mental health of the workforce and (b) prevention programming to enhance health and coping skills for supervisors and employees. Klunder designed the Transition Life Advisor Program as the centerpiece of his intervention activities. In contrast to Eastern Airlines, where more than 50 suicides preceded its final demise, Kelly experienced only one suicide, the only fatality during the process. No incidents of workplace violence occurred and more than $33 million in complaint cost avoidance were realized. However, no one person can nor did attempt to claim the credit for this cooperative and collective success. In addition to Major General Curtis' senior leaders and his organizational clinical psychologist, the general's civilian personnel officer, the chaplains, the medical staff, and trained supervisors were all part of TEAM Kelly. During much of the 6-year process, this maintenance depot continued to carry about 40% of the U.S. Air Force workload to keep the combat fleet in the air (Quick, Tetrick, Adkins, & Klunder, 2003).

Cooperation and Competition in the Classroom

In an educational context, Aronson, Blaney, Stephan, Sikes, and Snapp (1978) framed a paradigm for cooperative learning that they labeled the

Jigsaw classroom. The ultimate goal of Jigsaw learning is to teach the skill of cooperation so as to enable its use, not to make people totally out of place in a competitive society in which competitive behaviors abound. Although there is competition in society and in the classroom, and competition is about winning, they believed it possible to achieve cooperative learning, too. Their premise was that emotional development and traditional knowledge, skill, and ability acquisition are not necessarily incompatible. By requiring interdependence among students, Aronson and his colleagues were able to have students of different races work together in a helpful way without sacrificing excellence.

Central to the Jigsaw cooperative learning concept are listening skills, especially reflective listening skills, which help build cooperation. In addition, processing feelings and emotions becomes a central element in the communication process and cooperative interactions enhance prosocial behavior through empathy. This does not mean that there is no place for competition or competitive behaviors. Johnson and Johnson (1987) addressed competitive learning, as well as cooperative learning. They also distinguished between intergroup competition and interpersonal competition, noting that competitive learning can stimulate teamwork. They went on to elaborate important skills for competitive learning, much as Aronson and colleagues (1978) outlined skills for cooperative learning. These competitive learning skills include the ability to play fair, be a good winner and a good loser, enjoy competition, the ability to monitor where one stands in the competition, and to recognize the limitations of the results of a competition so as to not overgeneralize or exaggerate the results.

CONCLUSION

What we can learn from the classroom is that cooperation and competition each have a place in learning and in the achievement of excellence. Excellence can be achieved through collaborative effort and through positive interdependence. Excellence can be achieved through inclusion; it does not require exclusion. Table 8.1 summarizes the paradigms, benefits, rules, skills, and limitations of each of these two strategies for interpersonal relationships in the workplace. Healthy competition requires a sense of fair play, an open environment of clear rules, and the capacity to be both a good winner and a good loser, because competition is founded on a win-lose paradigm. Team competitions blend the use of cooperative and competitive skills.

Working together takes all of us. One person holding out can disrupt an entire collaborative system. One person whose heart is in the wrong place can cause damage to us all in the workplace. One competitor who has not disclosed the name of his or her game to everyone else can disrupt

TABLE 8.1
Cooperation and Competition

	Cooperation	Competition
Paradigm	Win–Win	Win–Lose
Benefits	Positive interdependence Mutual support Felt security	Personal challenge Individual competence Experienced mastery
Emphasis	Interpersonal support	Individual achievement
Required skills	Open communication Trust and trustworthiness Interpersonal relations	Monitor one's position Fair play Individualistic skills
Deemphasizes	Individual competence	Interpersonal comfort

a cooperative system, turning it into a competitive system in which everyone may end up losing.

Whereas winning is the desired outcome of the competitive game, it is all too often the case at work that a win-lose paradigm results in lose-lose, also a viable option in this framework. By striving for balance between head and heart, by striving for fair play and a balance between cooperation and competition in the workplace, we may ultimately come closer to achieving win-win dynamics, which are at the center of our vision for healthy and productive workplaces.

REFERENCES

Aronson, E., Blaney, N., Stephan, C., Sikes, J., & Snapp, M. (1978). *The jigsaw classroom.* Beverly Hills and London: Sage.

Brockner, J., Siegel, P. A., Daley, J. P., Tyler, T., & Martin, C. (1997). When trust matters: The moderating effect of outcome favorability. *Administrative Science Quarterly, 42,* 558–583.

Buckingham, M., & Coffman, C. (1999). *First, break all the rules.* New York: Simon & Schuster.

Cannon, W. B. (1929). Alternative satisfactions for the fighting emotions. In B. Cannon (Ed.), *Bodily changes in pain, hunger, fear, and rage* (2nd ed., pp. 377–392). New York and London: D. Appleton-Century Company.

Cascio, W. F. (1998). Learning from outcomes: Financial experiences of 300 firms that have downsized. In M. Gowing, J. Kraft, & J. C. Quick (Eds.), *The new organizational reality* (pp. 55–70). Washington, DC: American Psychological Association.

Cascio, W. F., Young, C. E., & Morris, J. R. (1997). Financial consequences of employment-change decisions in major U.S. corporations. *Academy of Management Journal, 40*(5), 1175–1180.

Cox, T. H., Jr., & Blake, S. (1991). Managing cultural diversity: Implications for organizational competitiveness. *Academy of Management Executive, 5*(3), 45–56.

Friedman, T. L. (2000). *The Lexus and the olive tree.* New York: Vintage Anchor Publishing.

Goleman, D. (1998). *Working with emotional intelligence.* New York: Bantam Books.

Grant, J. M. (1996). *The great Texas banking crash: An insider's account.* Austin, TX: University of Texas Press.

Hallowell, E. M. (1999). *Connect: 12 vital ties that open your heart, lengthen your life, and deepen your soul.* New York: Pantheon Books.

Hirschhorn, L. (1990). Leaders and followers in a postindustrial age: A psychodynamic view. *Journal of Applied Behavioral Science, 26,* 529–542.

Johnson, D. W., & Johnson, R. T. (1987). *Learning together and alone: Cooperative, competitive, and individualistic learning* (2nd ed.). Englewood Cliffs, NJ: Prentice-Hall.

Lavelle, L., with Jespersen, F. F. (2001, April 16). Executive pay. *Business Week,* p. 76.

Levinson, H. (1985). *Executive stress.* New York: New American Library.

Levinson, H. (2002). *Organizational assessment: A manual.* Washington, DC: American Psychological Association.

Levinson, H., Price, C. R., Munden, K. J., Mandl, H. J., & Solley, C. M. (1962). *Men, management, and mental health.* Cambridge, MA: Harvard University Press.

Loehr, J. E. (1997). *Stress for success.* New York: Times Business.

Mintzberg, H. (1994). *The rise and fall of strategic planning.* New York: The Free Press.

Morris, J. R., Cascio, W. F., & Young, C. E. (1999, Winter). Downsizing after all these years. *Organizational Dynamics,* 78–87.

Moskos, C. C., & Butler, J. S. (1997). *All that we can be: Black leadership and racial integration the army way.* New York: Basic Books.

Murphy, L. R., & Cooper, C. L. (2000). *Healthy and productive work: An international perspective.* London: Taylor & Francis.

Pennebaker, J. W. (1990). *Opening up: The healing power of expressing emotions.* New York: Guilford Press.

Pennebaker, J. W. (Ed.). (1997). *Emotion, disclosure, and health.* Washington, DC: American Psychological Association.

Quick, J. C., Cooper, C. L., Gavin, J. H., & Quick, J. D. (2002). Executive health: Self-reliance for challenging times. In C. L. Cooper & I. T. Robertson (Eds.), *International review of industrial and organizational psychology* (Vol. 17, pp. 187–216). New York: Wiley.

Quick, J. C., Gavin, J. H., Cooper, C. L., & Quick, J. D. (2000). Executive health [Special issue]. *Academy of Management Executive, 14,* 1–134.

Quick, J. C., Tetrick, L. E., Adkins, J. A., & Klunder, C. (2003). Occupational health psychology. In A. M. Nezu, C. M. Nezu, & P. A. Geller (Eds.), *Handbook of psychology: Health psychology* (Vol. 9, pp. 569–589). Hoboken, NJ: John Wiley & Sons.

Rosch, P. J. (2001). The quandary of job stress compensation. *Health and Stress, 3,* 1–4.

Salovey, P., Mayer, J. D., Goldman, S. L., Turvey, C., & Palfai, T. P. (1997). Emotional attention, clarity, and repair: Exploring emotional intelligence using the trait meta-mood scale. In J. W. Pennebaker (Ed.), *Emotion, disclosure, and health* (pp. 125–154). Washington, DC: American Psychological Association.

Smith, A. (1909). *An inquiry into the nature and causes of the wealth of nations.* In C. J. Bullock (Ed.), *The Harvard classics* (Vol. 10). New York: Collier. (Original work published 1776)

Spera, S. P., Buhrfeind, E. D., & Pennebaker, J. W. (1994). Expressive writing and coping with job loss. *Academy of Management Journal, 37,* 722–733.

Taylor, F. W. (1939). Taylor's testimony before the special house committee. In F. W. Taylor (Ed.), *Scientific management* (pp. 5–287). New York and London: Harper & Brothers Publishers.

Twenge, J. M. (2000). The age of anxiety? Birth cohort change in anxiety and neuroticism, 1952–1993. *Journal of Personality and Social Psychology, 79*(6), 1007–1021.

Vagg, P. R., & Spielberger, C. D. (1998). Occupational stress: Measuring job pressure and organizational support in the workplace. *Journal of Occupational Health Psychology, 3*(4), 294–305.

9

FOUR DIMENSIONS OF HEALTHY WORK: STRESS, WORK–FAMILY RELATIONS, VIOLENCE PREVENTION, AND RELATIONSHIPS AT WORK

JAMES CAMPBELL QUICK, CHAYA PIOTRKOWSKI, LYNN JENKINS, AND YOLANDA BRUCE BROOKS

This chapter is a composite of four independent yet interrelated contributions related to the central issue of healthy work and a healthy world. Each of the authors brings a unique perspective and professional expertise to address a specific dimension of health at work. Although there is some overlap and some interdependence among the four sections of the chapter, each section stands largely as the contribution of the section author to the larger issue of how to build a healthy world at work and beyond. The resulting chapter is a composite of independent and interdependent perspectives that fit under the larger umbrella of healthy workplaces.

The first section provides an overview of stress and health in organizations. Paul Rosch (2001) of the American Institute of Stress calls job stress a health epidemic needing medical and psychological treatment. Since the early research on organizational stress, the public health notions have been applied to the stress process, with attendant concerns for workplace surveillance and preventive interventions. This section considers related issues, such as unemployment, which have spillover effects on health at work. Occupational health psychology is a specialty in psychology aimed at enhancing healthy work. The section then recommends that psychology build healthier workplaces through chief psychological officers in organizations and by elaborating a framework for organizational therapy.

The second section brings our attention to the relationship between work and family life and discusses the limitations of current research in this field. It notes that families in the United States receive little government or institutional support to fulfill their important social responsibilities, so they struggle on their own to meet work and family obligations. It is further suggested that single parents in low-wage jobs have particular difficulty balancing work and family, but they have been largely invisible to work and family researchers. The section then calls attention to promoting the health of these vulnerable families through a new generation of research.

The third section addresses the low-frequency, high-impact health risk of violence in the workplace. It uses the public health notions of prevention, including workplace surveillance systems, to outline strategies for the prevention of workplace violence.

The fourth section addresses the unique occupational case of the professional athlete from the perspective of a professional sports consultant. The section focuses on the lifestyle issues and potential challenges to healthy work- and lifestyles with this select group. Areas for potential clinical investigation and intervention are also identified.

STRESS AND HEALTH AT WORK

Robert Kahn and his associates' seminal studies in role conflict and ambiguity placed psychology in the midst of understanding organizational and work stress (Kahn, Wolfe, Quinn, Snoek, & Rosenthal, 1964). Prior to the early 1960s, stress was primarily a medical concept based on classic research by physicians Walter B. Cannon (1935) and Hans Selye (1976). By the early 1980s, stress and psychological disorders in the workplace had become one of the top ten occupational health hazards in America (Millar, 1984; Sauter, Murphy, & Hurrell, 1990). By the end of the century, Rosch (2001) suggested that job stress had reached epidemic proportions, based on data from the National Institutes of Health on working hours, increases in working hours, job losses, absenteeism, and turnover data. What has and what can psychology do to address the job stress epidemic?

Stress at Work

Job and work stress with their associated health risks had their foundations in the early days of the Industrial Revolution, which sprang from the factories and mills of Manchester, England, in the mid-1800s. Over the next 100 years these factories and mills gave way to large, modern corporations in the industrialized world, which were the subject of concern for Kahn and colleagues (1964). Psychiatry had an early concern with industrial mental hygiene with the "preventive management" of Elkind (1931), who applied a national mental hygiene agenda to workplace issues of industrial relations, human nature in organizations, management, and leadership. The American Psychological Association (APA) formed a cooperative agreement with the National Institute for Occupational Safety and Health (NIOSH) to address job stress and psychological disorders in the workplace (Murphy, Hurrell, Sauter, & Keita, 1995; Sauter & Hurrell, 1999). This three-pronged initiative aimed to design strategies for healthy workplace design, health promotion at work, and surveillance of health risks (Landy, Quick, & Kasl, 1994).

Healthy Workplace Design

Although Abraham Maslow (1965/1998) called for healthy work environments as early as the 1960s, Murphy and Cooper (2000) presented the most recent definition and evidence concerning healthy and productive work. Much happened in the intervening 40 years. An international tradition aimed at defining and encouraging the healthy workplace design through the identification of physical and psychosocial health risk factors coupled with redesign interventions to enhance mental health and psychological well-being grew up in the intervening years (Hurrell & Murphy, 1992; Quick, Murphy, & Hurrell, 1992; Sauter, Murphy, & Hurrell, 1990). The healthy workplace design tradition places priority on the characteristics of the work environment.

Individual Health

Individuals come to work with their own characteristics, not all of which are healthy. Von Dusch (1868) was the first to call attention to excessive involvement in work as a health risk factor for cardiovascular problems. His observations suggest that the work environment does not cause all stress. This view is broadly consistent with Lazarus' (1995) psychological theory of work stress and with Levinson's (1985) psychoanalytic theory of executive stress. These theories of stress look to the individual and the individual's responses to explain stress at work. Whereas these theories serve as bases for psychotherapeutic interventions for job stress, health promotion activities and other more behavioral interventions are alternatives to enhance individual health at work (Ilgen, 1990).

Person–Environment Fit

Edwards (1996) examined the competing versions of person–environment fit theory, which aim to explain stress at work by considering both factors in the environment and in the individual. This view holds that stress cannot be fully explained by either environmental factors or individual factors.

Surveillance of Health Risks at Work

Assessment and surveillance activities are important for the measurement of workplace stress and to the enhancement of organizational health (Adkins, 1999). Many measures of stress are available for the workplace, including one developed by NIOSH. In her pioneering work, Adkins used the Occupational Stress Inventory to measure organizational demands and stressors, individual strains, and personal coping resources in a variety of organizations (Osipow & Spokane, 1992). Her results show marked organizational variance among these various measures, yet broadly show a clear link between stress and strain. The Job Stress Survey is a second and emerging assessment measure that consistently identifies two factors across work contexts (Vagg & Spielberger, 1998). These are job pressure and lack of organizational support.

Stress Factors Beyond the Workplace

Stress factors beyond the workplace are important to a more complete understanding of stress and health at work. Specifically, the interface between work and family, with the potential spillover effects that may occur, is a subject of increasing significance. In addition, unemployment, or the lack of work, is a major source of distress for an important minority in many industrialized nations.

The Work–Family Interface

One of the more important arenas in a person's non-work life is the family, and the work–family interface has been found important in understanding a person's health at work as well as at home (Piotrkowski, 1979). Although some individuals may be able to partition the various elements of their lives into different roles, such as work roles and family roles, spillover effects do occur.

Unemployment

Work may be stressful, but we have known for decades that the distressful effects of unemployment may even be more devastating from a psychological point of view (Levi et al., 1984). The Michigan Prevention Research Center's JOBS (Job-Search Workshop) program aims to help reemploy and enhance the mental health of those who fall into this sector of the potential work population (Vinokur, Schul, Vuori, & Price, 2000).

Preventive Stress Management

Prevention is always the best public health strategy for any disease epidemic. Quick, Quick, Nelson, and Hurrell (1997) have translated and applied the public health notions of prevention to organizational stress, framing the theory of preventive stress management. This theory is one of ten major theories of organizational stress (Cooper, 1998). If job stress has become an epidemic in America and other industrialized nations, then prevention holds the best hope for addressing this epidemic (Elkin & Rosch, 1990). Using the public health and preventive medicine model, Quick and colleagues (1997) classified prevention strategies into primary, secondary, and tertiary. Primary prevention aims to modify and manage the demands of the work environment. Secondary prevention aims to modify and manage the individual's response to these demands. Tertiary prevention aims to help and provide aid to those in frank distress.

Occupational Health Psychology

Occupational health psychology (OHP) is consistent with these public health notions and has a primary focus on the prevention of injuries and illnesses, and the enhancement of health (in contrast to the treatment of injuries and illnesses) by creating safe and healthy working environments (Sauter & Hurrell, 1999). OHP continues to use the three-stage strategy of primary, secondary, and tertiary prevention for the management of stress and the enhancement of psychological health at work (Quick & Tetrick, 2003).

Psychology Builds a Healthier World at Work

In addition to managing organizational stress, preventing psychological disorders in the workplace, and enhancing mental health at work through OHP, how can psychology help build a healthier world at work in our new organizational reality (Gowing, Kraft, & Quick, 1998)? First, psychologists can become chief psychological officers in organizations. Second, psychologists can develop the professional practice of organizational therapy.

Psychologists as CPOs

Organizations often have many chiefs: chief executive officer (CEO), chief operational officer (COO), chief financial officer (CFO), chief information officer (CIO), and so on. These "chief" officers are responsible for the critical resources and processes that influence the health of the organization. People may be the most important resource in any organization, especially in the information age. Yet responsibility for their support and development is often dispersed to functions such as personnel and human resources, the medical department, employee assistance programs for counseling and psychotherapy, and possibly an industrial chaplainry for their spiritual needs. Psychologists can become CPOs (chief psychological officers, or alternatively chief people officers). A key role for a CPO in an organization is to integrate the specialties on the human side of the enterprise. These specialties include human resource professionals, physicians and medical personnel, clinical psychologists and counselors, safety professionals, security forces, industrial–organizational psychologists, and chaplains and spiritual advisors. These professionals offer employees and executives a range of expertise. They are most effective when organized into functional role interrelatedness so as to complement and supplement each other as they serve individuals' health and safety needs at work. Psychology has a strategic opportunity to build on the pioneering work of U.S. Air Force Lieutenant Colonels Joyce Adkins and Charles Klunder, who were the CPOs for their respective commanding generals during the largest industrial restructuring activity in the history of the Department of Defense from 1994 through 2001 (Quick, Tetrick, Adkins, & Klunder, 2003).

Organizational Therapy

Frost and Robinson (1999) are concerned with the toxins and emotional pain that are all too often endemic to organizational life. Although their focus is on the health risks for those organizational heroes who absorb much of this emotionally toxic material at work, what also comes through their work is the fact that these organizational heroes do not have formal organizational roles for engaging in their therapeutic and curative activities. Edgar Schein (Quick & Gavin, 2000), in wrestling with essentially the same problem, suggested that what is needed is an evolving practice of organizational therapy to help heal organizations. Although healthy organizational systems may have natural homeopathic agents and immune systems that metabolize these psychological toxins and emotional pain, psychology can take the lead in crafting mechanisms, systems, and roles that help to metabolize the unhealthy energies that inevitably yet unintentionally emerge in many work organizations.

CURRENT RESEARCH NEEDS AND LIMITATIONS IN THE FIELD OF WORK AND FAMILY RELATIONS

Work and family are two critical spheres of human activity. Theory on the relationship between these two domains has been shaped by important social and economic changes. With industrialization, work and family came to be viewed as separate domains and workers were treated as if they had no families. In the 20th century, theories in sociology and psychology provided theoretical justifications for the male breadwinner family and the separation of work and family. In sociology, structural-functionalism held that the total separation of work and family realms was functionally necessary to avoid occupational competition between husbands and wives that would threaten marital stability. In psychology, attachment theory warned of dire consequences to children's development if the mother–infant bond were disrupted by separation. Therefore, when researchers did examine links between work and family, they focused on problems caused by male unemployment and by female employment: Depression-era research examined the effects of unemployment on family roles and relationships, whereas the influx of mothers into the labor force during the 1960s and 1970s spurred research on the supposed negative effects of women's employment on children and on marriage, as well as studies of the new dual-earner family (for reviews of these early research literatures, see Kanter, 1977; Piotrkowski & Gornick, 1987; Piotrkowski & Hughes, 1993; Piotrkowski, Rapoport, & Rapoport, 1987).

Over the past 20 years, there has been yet another significant shift in the way we think about the relationship between work and family life. As the employment of mothers and wives has become normative and economically necessary, we have come to recognize that all employees face complex challenges in negotiating paid work and family roles, to an understanding that work and family systems may affect each other, and to public discourse on how best to help employees balance obligations to their jobs and to their families.

With these changing views of work and family has come a literal explosion of work–family research within the social and behavioral sciences, as well as schools of nursing, social work, and management (Westman & Piotrkowski, 1999). In psychology alone, work–family research is conducted by clinical, social, developmental, family, organizational, and occupational health psychologists. Most research has focused on (a) the effects of work on family life rather than the effects of family life on work outcomes, and (b) on negative outcomes rather than positive ones. Despite numerous criticisms of this imbalance, this research emphasis is consistent with the relative powerlessness of families vis-à-vis the workplace, the lack of public work and family policy, and an emphasis on promoting health and well-being in families.

In the United States, families receive little support from government and other institutions to assist their enormously important functions: the socialization of the young, the care and nurturing of all family members—including older people—and the economic support of the household through paid work. In the delicate and challenging endeavor of meeting obligations to families and employers, workers and their families are at a distinct disadvantage. Economically dependent on their jobs, most employees have little say in the policies and organization of work that affect them and their families, and the use of individual coping strategies are relatively ineffective in managing workplace stressors (Pearlin & Schooler, 1978). Family members have even less input in how work is organized. Therefore, it is not surprising that studies consistently find that employees report greater interference from work to family than vice versa (e.g., Burke & Greenglass, 1999; Frone, Russell, & Cooper, 1992b; Gutek, Searle, & Klepa, 1991; Netemeyer, Boles, & McMurrian, 1996). The Family and Medical Leave Act of 1993 (FMLA) partly redressed this imbalance of power by protecting some workers' jobs while they care for new or ill family members, but not all workers are covered by this legislation. Corporate work–family life initiatives and the emergence of a work–family consulting industry represent the acknowledgment by corporations that employees' families must be taken into account. However, these initiatives generally have been aimed at minimizing the family's intrusion into the workplace, maintaining productivity, and retaining skilled employees (Parasuraman & Greenhaus, 1997). Research evidence indicates these programs and policies are only marginally effective in reducing work–family conflict (Gottlieb, Kelloway, & Barham, 1998; Kossek & Ozeki, 1999b).

Given the lack of public and institutional support for families, employees and their families are left on their own to find child care, juggle demanding work schedules, protect themselves from stressful workplace conditions, and so forth. Although we can acknowledge that relations between work and family are bidirectional and that certain working conditions and policies may have beneficial effects on families, our first priority must be to identify those workplace conditions and organizational policies that interfere with family well-being so they can be addressed. As yet, however, work–family research has limited usefulness for policymakers, employers, practitioners, and families. This section describes these limitations and provides suggestions for how to address them.

Limited Theory

Because work–family research spans many disciplines and specialization areas within disciplines, theory-building has been limited. Terminology is inconsistent and there are no agreed-upon central questions, no overarching generally recognized theories, and no systematic knowledge-building across disciplines (Allen, Herst, Bruck, & Sutton, 2000; Barnett, 1998; Lambert, 1990; Westman & Piotrkowski, 1999). For example, constructs such as "spillover," "carryover," and "crossover" are used interchangeably and inconsistently. Thus, knowledge remains fragmented and rudimentary.

In the past two decades, work–family research in psychology has focused on employees' experience of conflict between work and family roles (Greenhaus & Beutell, 1985) as the central mediator between work life and family life (Frone, Russell, & Cooper, 1992a). Work-to-family conflict and family-to-work conflict have been distinguished theoretically and empirically, and both their antecedents and consequences have been widely studied. For example, we have learned that work-to-family conflict is related to job dissatisfaction and burnout and to mental and physical strain (see reviews by Allen et al., 2000, and Kossek & Ozeki, 1999a). We also have learned that the antecedents of work-to-family conflict include classic job stressors such as excessive work demands and lack of autonomy (e.g., Frone et al., 1992a).

Yet this conceptual framework is too narrow. The almost singular focus on work–family conflict as a favored research variable means that other important direct and indirect processes linking work and family life have been neglected (Lambert, 1990; Piotrkowski, 1998). For example, few studies have examined if and how children learn about managing work–family dilemmas or the impact of adverse parental working conditions on their views, development, and behavior (e.g., Barling, 1986; Galinsky, 1999). Similarly, most Americans do not work the standard 9-to-5 work week (Presser, 1995), but we know very little about how these schedules affect family relationships and other family members. Other neglected topics include the effects of work-related injury and illness on families and the costs and benefits of the various coping strategies families use to manage difficult work situations and work–family conflict. An interesting example is provided by Presser and Cain (1983) who found that young, dual-earner families manage child care through "split-shift" arrangements, with mothers and fathers working different shifts. Although young couples are able to manage their child care this way, one wonders if this arrangement also may have some adverse consequences for marital satisfaction, problem solving, and intimacy. Absent systematic empirical research on such multiple processes and their outcomes, we are left with limited theory and inadequate knowledge to guide practitioners working with families.

Weak Methodology

Typical research designs still involve the collection of cross-sectional data, limiting causal conclusions. Moreover, data usually are collected only from the employee, which may artificially inflate associations between predictors and outcomes because of common method variance. A further problem is that "the family" has all but disappeared from current work–family research. With some exceptions, the individual employee remains the unit of analysis (Barnett, 1998; Westman & Piotrkowski, 1999), even when organizational outcomes (e.g., turnover) or family outcomes (e.g., family satisfaction or distress) are studied. The collection of data from and about other family members remains the exception.

Measures of work–family conflict suffer from the additional problem of requiring respondents to make causal attributions, an approach long-abandoned in research on occupational stress. As an example, a typical item from a work–family conflict scale states, "Because my work is so demanding, I am often irritable at home" (Stephens & Sommer, 1996; also see Netemeyer et al., 1996). In their longitudinal study of work–family conflict, Kelloway, Gottlieb, and Barham (1999) concluded that reports of work-to-family conflict may result from an attribution process "whereby employees who experience stress 'scapegoat' their work." They found that work-to-family conflict did not predict psychological strain measured 6 months later; instead, strain 6 months earlier predicted work-to-family conflict 6 months later.

Limited Populations

A final significant limitation of current work–family research is the strong middle-class bias that has rendered the low-wage, low-skilled worker and his or her family all but invisible. Work–family research continues to focus on married, White, middle-class professionals and managers, a problem sometimes noted but rarely redressed. These latter populations are easy to study because they provide adequate response rates to mailed surveys, they speak English, and they are relatively easy to access. When low-wage workers are included in rare representative community samples, education and income are treated as nuisance variables to be controlled.

Yet, low-wage workers represent an important segment of our population; they are disproportionately represented among women, people of color, immigrants, and single parents. In 1995, 7.5 million workers were living in poverty (Hale, 1997), and millions of others were living in near poverty. One particularly vulnerable group of such workers is mother-only families. In 2000, over 75% of unmarried mothers were in the labor force (Current Population Survey, 2001). Even when they worked full-time, year round, in 1993 11% of mother-only families did not earn enough to lift their families out of poverty (Rodgers, 1996). Often financially strapped and with little household support, these women are subject to working conditions—such as limited autonomy—that are known to increase work–family conflict.

They also are more likely to work nonstandard shifts and weekends, making it especially difficult to locate child care (Presser & Cox, 1997). Family supports such as the FMLA have limited usefulness to these women (Hyde, Essex, Clark, Klein, & Byrd, 1996), particularly if they lack paid sick leave and vacations. They also lack a second income that would assist them in taking unpaid leave, and the FMLA provision requiring an employee to have worked at least 1,250 hours for a year with his or her current employer falls heavily on poor women who are especially likely to be new hires, to move in and out of the labor force, and to work part-time for small employers, who are exempt from the FMLA (Piotrkowski & Kessler-Sklar, 1996). Yet we know very little of the unique challenges these women face in combining work and parental roles, how well they manage, or how best to assist them (Oliker, 1995). The problems they face are not unique to poor women, but also plague other low-wage workers and their families.

There are several reasons why we cannot assume that findings from White professionals and managers generalize to low-skill and low-wage workers. Some working conditions are especially problematic for this latter population. They are more likely to face unique workplace stressors that include physical hazards and discomfort, nonstandard shifts, and limited or no sick leave. Non-White workers also must confront racial harassment and nonmarried women are more likely to face sexual harassment (Swanson, Piotrkowski, Keita, & Becker, 1997), with unknown consequences for family well-being and family role functioning. It also is likely that processes linking work to family life, as well as outcomes, differ by race and ethnicity. Economic resources also shape the strategies families have available to manage work–family conflicts and problems. Thus, an affluent family may hire a live-in nanny to care for their children, while low-income families rely on a patchwork of help from neighbors and relatives and low-quality day care.

This middle-class bias also seriously limits the application of our findings, because work–family research is not addressing the problems and needs of our most vulnerable workers and their families. As a result, work–family research has little relevance to the important policy debates about how to support vulnerable families, a problem noted by Kelly (1988) that still persists. Private sector work–family initiatives also favor professional and management employees and have been limited to large, corporate employers who can afford them. But most people are not managers or professionals, and half of all workers in the private sector work in establishments with fewer than 100 employees (Wiatrowski, 1994). As Googins (1997) has noted, "the working poor do not generally work in family-friendly corporations and are not well represented in work-and-family initiatives" (p. 228).

The Next Generation of Work–Family Research

It is time for a new generation of work–family research that aims to build theory and systematic knowledge that can be used to guide clinicians working with couples and families, to inform supportive work–family public policy, and to help unions and employers—large and small—develop cost-effective workplace strategies to ameliorate conflicts between work and home and negative effects of work on families.

This agenda points to new research directions. Work–family research needs to be truly interdisciplinary, so that integrated theory is developed that incorporates complex conceptualizations of the family, the workplace, and individual development (Piotrkowksi, 1998). Within psychology, cross-specialization research teams could integrate theoretical perspectives from organizational, family, developmental, occupational health, and clinical psychology. One benefit of this approach is that it would move work–family research beyond the individual as the sole unit of analysis to include family-level outcomes, such as the parent–child relationship, marital stability, and family "cohesion" (Piotrkowski & Staines, 1991) and to the inclusion of data from and about other family members. It is possible, for example, that the same working conditions affect family members differently. This approach would allow for a better and broader understanding of the costs and benefits of different working arrangements for all family members. Gathering data from more than one family member also can minimize the problems associated with relying solely on the self-report of the employee. Examples of this broader approach already exist within the work–family field (e.g., MacEwen, Barling, & Kelloway, 1992; Piotrkowski & Katz, 1982; Repetti, 1989; Repetti & Wood, 1997; Westman & Etzion, 1995).

In addition to incorporating family outcomes in work–family research, a cross-disciplinary approach would be useful in identifying a wider array of working conditions for study and a wider array of processes linking work life to family life, beyond work–family conflict. Such processes include socialization processes, the moderating effects of spousal undermining or support, family coping strategies, and so forth. Measures of work–family conflict that do not require respondents to make causal attributions also would represent a methodological improvement, as would longitudinal designs that allow stronger causal inferences to be made.

To meet our obligations to the well-being of our most vulnerable workers and their families, it also is essential that work–family researchers focus attention on ethnic minorities, low-wage workers, and single parents. The Personal Responsibility and Work Opportunity Reconciliation Act of 1996 (welfare reform) gives new urgency to this problem, as the safety net of public assistance has disappeared for most poor women with dependent children. These women will enter low-quality, low-wage jobs lacking even the most basic family supportive benefits. Kelly (1988) also has encouraged the examination of work–family relations among the urban "underclass," who work in the informal underground economy. This shift toward the study of low-wage families will require a commitment to more cumbersome data collection strategies that go beyond the mailed survey, and to the development of culturally appropriate measures in other languages (e.g., Marin & Marin, 1991). It also may require less conventional methods of sampling, because of the difficulties inherent in studying work in the informal, underground economy. Such research will need to pay particular attention to cultural differences in how families manage work and family obligations, and to the processes linking work to home.

Finally, we need to anticipate how changing demographics and changes in the workplace affect relations between people's work and families' lives. For example, we need to learn more about work–family relations among contingent workers and the "sandwich generation" of workers—typically women—who are caring for dependent children and elderly parents (e.g., Lee, 1997), about the impact of the new job insecurity on families (Lewis & Cooper, 1999) and about "telework," which blurs the boundaries between work and home (e.g., Standen, Daniels, & Lamond, 1999). In all these ways, work–family research can inform public policy and organizational and clinical practice to support the development of healthy families.

WORKPLACE VIOLENCE: RESEARCH, RISK FACTORS, AND PREVENTION STRATEGIES

In recent years, violence in the workplace has received considerable attention in the popular press and among safety and health professionals. From 1994–1998, there were an average of 921 workplace homicides each year. These homicides included an average of 147 supervisors or proprietors in retail sales, 84 cashiers, 65 taxicab drivers, 51 managers in restaurants or hotels, 65 police officers or detectives, and 52 security guards annually (Bureau of Labor Statistics [BLS], 2000). An additional 2 million workers were assaulted each year (Bureau of Justice Statistics [BJS], 1998). Death or injury should not be an inevitable result of one's chosen occupation, nor should these staggering figures be accepted as a cost of doing business in our society.

Purpose and Scope

The purpose of this section is to review what is known about fatal and nonfatal violence in the workplace to determine the focus needed for prevention and research efforts. This document also summarizes issues to be addressed when dealing with workplace violence in various settings such as offices, factories, warehouses, hospitals, convenience stores, and taxicabs.

Although no definitive strategy will ever be appropriate for all workplaces, we must begin to change the way work is done in certain settings to minimize or remove the risk of workplace violence. We must also change the way we think about workplace violence by shifting the emphasis from reactionary approaches to prevention, and by embracing workplace violence as an occupational safety and health issue.

Defining workplace violence has generated considerable discussion. Some would include in the definition any language or actions that make one person uncomfortable in the workplace; others would include threats and harassment; and all would include any bodily injury inflicted by one person on another. Thus the spectrum of workplace violence ranges from offensive language to homicide, and a reasonable working definition of workplace violence is as follows: violent acts, including physical assaults and threats of assault, directed toward people at work or on duty. Most studies to date have focused primarily on physical injuries, because they are clearly defined and easily measured. But this section examines data from multiple sources and acknowledges differences in definitions and coverage to learn as much as possible from these varied efforts.

The circumstances of workplace violence also vary and may include robbery-associated violence; violence by disgruntled clients, customers, patients, inmates, and so forth; violence by coworkers, employees, or employers; and domestic violence that finds its way into the workplace. These circumstances all appear to be related to the level of violence in communities and in society in general. Thus the question arises: Why study workplace violence separately from the larger universe of all violence? Several reasons exist for focusing specifically on workplace violence:

- *Violence is a substantial contributor to death and injury on the job.* NIOSH data indicate that homicide has become the second leading cause of occupational injury death, exceeded only by motor-vehicle-related deaths (Jenkins, 1996). Estimates of nonfatal workplace assaults vary dramatically, but a reasonable estimate from the National Crime Victimization Survey is that approximately 2 million people are assaulted while at work or on duty each year (BJS, 1998).
- *The circumstances of workplace violence differ significantly from those of all homicides.* For example, 75% of all workplace homicides in 1993 were robbery-related; but in the general population, only 9% of homicides were robbery-related, and only 19% were committed in conjunction with any kind of felony (robbery, rape, arson, etc.; Federal Bureau of Investigation [FBI],

1994). Furthermore, 47% of all murder victims in 1993 were related to or acquainted with their assailants (FBI, 1994), whereas the majority of workplace homicides (because they are robbery-related) are believed to occur among people not known to one another. Only 17% of female victims of workplace homicides were killed by a spouse or former spouse (Windau & Toscano, 1994), whereas 29% of the female homicide victims in the general population were killed by a husband, ex-husband, boyfriend, or ex-boyfriend (FBI, 1994).

- *Workplace violence is not distributed randomly across all workplaces but is clustered in particular occupational settings.* More than half (56%) of workplace homicides occurred in retail trade and service industries. Homicide is the leading cause of death in these industries as well as in finance, insurance, and real estate. Eighty-five percent of nonfatal assaults in the workplace occur in service and retail trade industries (BLS, 1994). As the United States economy continues to shift toward the service sectors, fatal and nonfatal workplace violence will be an increasingly important occupational safety and health issue.

- *The risk of workplace violence is associated with specific workplace factors such as dealing with the public, the exchange of money, and the delivery of services or goods.* Consequently, great potential exists for workplace-specific prevention efforts such as bullet-resistant barriers and enclosures in taxicabs, convenience stores, gas stations, emergency departments, and other areas where workers come in direct contact with the public; locked drop safes and other cash-handling procedures in retail establishments; and threat assessment policies in all types of workplaces.

Homicide in the Workplace

NIOSH Data

Data from the National Traumatic Occupational Fatalities (NTOF) Surveillance System indicate that 12,863 workplace homicides occurred during the 16-year period from 1980 through 1995, with an average workplace homicide rate of 0.70 per 100,000 workers (NIOSH, 2001). NTOF is an ongoing, death-certificate-based census of traumatic occupational fatalities in the United States, with data from all 50 states and the District of Columbia. NTOF includes information for all workers ages 16 or older who died from an injury or poisoning and for whom the certifier noted a positive response to the "injury at work" item on the death certificate. For additional discussion of the NTOF system and the limitations of death certificates for the study of workplace homicide, see Castillo and Jenkins (1994).

Sex

The majority (80%) of workplace homicides between 1980 and 1995 occurred among male workers. The leading cause of occupational injury death varied by sex, with homicides accounting for 12% of all occupational injury deaths among male workers and 42% among female workers (NIOSH, 2001). Although homicide is the leading cause of occupational injury death among female workers, male workers have more than three times the risk of work-related homicide (1.0 per 100,000 workers for males versus .3 per 100,000 workers for females).

Age

The largest number of workplace homicides occurred among workers ages 25–34 years, whereas the rate (per 100,000 workers) of workplace homicide increased with increasing age. The highest rates of workplace homicide occurred among workers ages 65 years and older; the rates for these workers were more than twice those for workers ages 55–64 years. This pattern held true for both male and female workers (NIOSH, 2001).

Race

Although the majority of workplace homicide victims were White (71%), Black workers (1.4/100,000) and workers of other races (2.0/100,000) had the highest rates of work-related homicide.

Industry and Occupation

During the 16-year period 1980–1995, the greatest number of deaths occurred in the retail trade (4,917) and service (2,329) industries, whereas the highest rates per 100,000 workers occurred in retail trades (1.7); public administration (1.4); and transportation, communication, and public utilities (1.0). At the more detailed levels of industry, the largest number of deaths occurred in grocery stores, eating and drinking places, taxicab services, and justice and public order establishments. Taxicab services had the highest rate of work-related homicide.

Bureau of Labor Statistics Data

Information from the Bureau of Labor Statistics (BLS) Census of Fatal Occupational Injuries (CFOI) Program identifies the same high-risk demographic and occupational groups as NIOSH NTOF data and allows description of the circumstances of workplace homicides beginning in 1992. According to the BLS data for 1999, 77% of the homicides occurred during a robbery or other crime and 10% were attributed specifically to coworkers or former employees (BLS, 2000). The CFOI system uses multiple sources, including administrative documents from federal and state agencies (e.g., death certificates, medical examiner records, workers' compensation reports, and regulatory agency reports) as well as news reports and follow-up questionnaires to business establishments (Windau & Toscano, 1994).

Discussion

Despite differences in data collection and the resulting total number of homicides reported by the NTOF and CFOI fatality surveillance systems, the ranking of high-risk industries and occupations is consistent, with taxicab drivers and chauffeurs, law enforcement and security personnel, and retail trade workers experiencing the greatest risks and the largest numbers of workplace homicides. Findings about the distributions by demographic characteristics are also remarkably similar (Castillo & Jenkins, 1994; NIOSH, 1996; Toscano & Weber, 1995; Windau & Toscano, 1994).

Differences in leading causes of occupational injury death by sex can be attributed at least in part to variations in employment patterns (Jenkins, 1994). For example, homicide is the leading cause of occupational injury death for female workers because they are exposed less frequently than male workers to hazards such as heavy machinery and work at elevations. The same is also true for differences among industries in leading causes of death. Workers in retail trade, services, finance, insurance, and real estate are not exposed to the same kinds of hazards as workers in construction, agriculture, forestry, fishing, mining, or transportation, communication, and public utilities. These factors are extremely important to the future direction of occupational safety and health as employment patterns shift from traditional heavy industry to retail trade and service sectors. Workplace homicide must be addressed to continue the trends of decreasing numbers and rates of occupational injury deaths (Jenkins et al., 1993; Stout, Jenkins, & Pizatella, 1996).

Elevated rates of workplace homicide among workers ages 65 and older may be attributable to a number of factors, including a decreased ability to survive injury or the perception that such workers are softer targets (Jenkins, Layne, & Kisner, 1992).

Nonfatal Assaults in the Workplace

Victimization Studies

Limited information is available in the criminal justice and public health literature regarding the nature and magnitude of nonfatal workplace violence. The criminology literature contains a few victimization studies that include designation of victimizations that occurred at work. Using the 1982 Victim Risk Supplement to the National Crime Victimization Survey, Lynch (1987) used log linear modeling to examine workplace victimizations with regard to demographic variables as well as features of the workplace. Features of the workplace included exposure to and public access to the workplace, local travel, overnight trips, perceived dangerousness of the neighborhood and the workplace, and the frequency with which money was handled on the job. These analyses indicated that the risk of workplace victimization was related more to the task performed than to the demographic characteristics of the person performing the job. Factors related to an increased risk for workplace victimization included routine face-to-face contact with large numbers of people, the handling of money, and jobs that required routine travel or that did not have a single worksite. Using a 1983 crime survey in the metropolitan Washington, DC, area, Collins and Cox (1987) found results similar to those of Lynch: The delivery of passengers or goods and dealing with the public were the factors associated with an increased risk for workplace assault. State-specific studies of workplace assaults using workers' compensation data have also been conducted, as have industry- and occupation-specific studies; a summary of these appears in Castillo (1995).

Estimated Magnitude of the Problem

There are varying estimates of the magnitude of nonfatal assaults in U.S. workplaces. The first comes from the BLS Annual Survey of Occupational Injuries and Illnesses (ASOII). The ASOII is an annual survey of approximately 174,000 private establishments. This survey excludes the self-employed, small farmers, and government workers. These data indicate that 16,600 workplace assaults occurred in 1999; these represented 1% of all cases involving days away from work (BLS, 2001).

Another estimate of assaults in the workplace comes from the National Crime Victimization Survey (NCVS), an annual, national, household-based survey of more than 100,000 individuals ages 12 or older. NCVS data for 1992–1996 indicate that each year, nearly 2 million people were assaulted while at work or on duty (BJS, 1998). Twelve percent of workplace victimizations resulted in injuries.

When workplace victimizations were analyzed by type of work setting, these data indicate that 56% occurred in private companies, 37% occurred among government employees, and 7% of the victims were self-employed (BJS, 1998). BJS points out in its report that government workers make up only 16% of the workforce and thus appear to be suffering a disproportionate share of the attacks; it should also be noted that risk factors such as dealing with the public and delivery of services are common among government employees. In addition, all local, state, and federal law enforcement are included in this category.

When individuals in the NCVS were asked whether the workplace victimization was reported to the police, 56% indicated that it was not. For 30% of respondents, the reason cited for not reporting to the police was that the incident was reported to another official such as a company security guard; another 21% believed the incident to be a private or personal matter (BJS, 1998).

Discussion

Nonfatal assaults in the workplace clearly affect many workers and employers. Although groups at high risk for workplace homicide and nonfatal workplace assaults share similar characteristics such as interaction with the public and the handling of money, there are also clear differences. For example, groups such as health care workers are not at elevated risk of workplace homicide, but they are at greatly increased risk of nonfatal assaults. Castillo (1995) suggested that some of the distinctions between fatal and nonfatal workplace assaults can be attributed to differences between robbery-related violence and violence resulting from the anger or frustration of customers, clients, or coworkers, with robbery-related violence being more likely to result in a fatal outcome. The premeditated use of firearms to facilitate robberies is also likely to influence the lethality of assaults in the workplace.

Risk Factors and Prevention Strategies

Risk Factors

A number of factors may increase a worker's risk for workplace assault, and they have been described in previous research (Castillo & Jenkins, 1994; Collins & Cox, 1987; Davis, 1987; Davis, Honchar, & Suarez, 1987; Kraus, 1987; Lynch, 1987; NIOSH, 1993; NIOSH 1996). These factors include

- contact with the public;
- exchange of money;
- delivery of passengers, goods, or services;
- having a mobile workplace such as a taxicab or police cruiser;
- working with unstable or volatile people in health care, social service, or criminal justice settings;
- working alone or in small numbers;
- working late at night or during early morning hours;
- working in high-crime areas;
- guarding valuable property or possessions; and
- working in community-based settings.

Prevention Strategies

Environmental designs. Commonly implemented cash-handling policies in retail settings include procedures such as using locked drop safes, carrying small amounts of cash, and posting signs and printing notices that limited cash is available. It may also be useful to explore the feasibility of cashless transactions in taxicabs and retail settings through the use of machines that accommodate automatic teller account cards or debit cards. These approaches could be used in any setting where cash is currently exchanged between workers and customers.

Physical separation of workers from customers, clients, and the general public through the use of bullet-resistant barriers or enclosures has been proposed for retail settings such as gas stations and convenience stores, hospital emergency departments, and social service agency claims areas. The height and depth of counters (with or without bullet-resistant barriers) are also important considerations in protecting workers because they introduce physical distance between workers and potential attackers. Consideration must nonetheless be given to the continued ease of conducting business; a safety device that increases frustration for workers or for customers, clients, or patients may be self-defeating.

Visibility and lighting are also important environmental design considerations. Making high-risk areas visible to more people and installing good external lighting should decrease the risk of workplace assaults (NIOSH, 1993).

Access to and egress from the workplace are also important areas to assess. The number of entrances and exits, the ease with which nonemployees can gain access to work areas because doors are unlocked, and the number of areas where potential attackers can hide are issues that should be addressed. This issue has implications for the design of buildings and parking areas, landscaping, and the placement of garbage areas, outdoor refrigeration areas, and other storage facilities that workers must use during a work shift.

Numerous security devices may reduce the risk for assaults against workers and facilitate the identification and apprehension of perpetrators. These include closed-circuit cameras, alarms, two-way mirrors, card-key access systems, panic-bar doors locked from the outside only, and trouble lights or geographic locating devices in taxicabs and other mobile workplaces. Personal protective equipment such as body armor has been used effectively by public safety personnel to mitigate the effects of workplace violence.

Administrative controls. Staffing plans and work practices (such as escorting patients and prohibiting unsupervised movement within and between clinic areas) are included in the California Occupational Safety and Health Administration Guidelines for the Security and Safety of Health Care and Community Service Workers (State of California, 1993). Increasing the number of staff on duty may also be appropriate in any number of service and retail settings. The use of security guards or receptionists to screen people entering the workplace and controlling access to actual work areas has also been suggested by security experts.

Work practices and staffing patterns during the opening and closing of establishments and during money drops and pickups should be carefully reviewed for the increased risk of assault they pose to workers. These practices include having workers take out garbage, dispose of grease, store food or other items in external storage areas, and transport or store money.

Policies and procedures for assessing and reporting threats allow employers to track and assess threats and violent incidents in the workplace. Such policies clearly indicate a zero tolerance of workplace violence and provide mechanisms by which incidents can be reported and handled. In addition, such information allows employers to assess whether prevention strategies are appropriate and effective. These policies should also include guidance on recognizing the potential for violence, methods for defusing or de-escalating potentially violent situations, and instruction about the use of security devices and protective equipment. Procedures for obtaining medical care and psychological support following violent incidents should also be addressed. Training and education efforts are clearly needed to accompany such policies.

Behavioral strategies. Training employees in nonviolent response and conflict resolution has been suggested to reduce the risk that volatile situations will escalate to physical violence. Also critical is training that addresses hazards associated with specific tasks or worksites and relevant prevention strategies. Training should not be regarded as the sole prevention strategy but as a component in a comprehensive approach to reducing workplace violence. To increase vigilance and compliance with stated violence prevention policies, training should emphasize the appropriate use and maintenance of protective equipment, adherence to administrative controls, and increased knowledge and awareness of the risk of workplace violence.

Developing and Implementing a Workplace Violence Prevention Program and Policy

The first priority in developing a workplace violence prevention policy is to establish a system for documenting violent incidents in the workplace. Such data are essential for assessing the nature and magnitude of workplace violence in a given workplace and quantifying risk. These data can be used to assess the need for action to reduce or mitigate the risks for workplace violence and implement a reasonable intervention strategy. An existing intervention strategy may be identified within an industry or in similar industries, or new and unique strategies may be needed to address the risks in a given workplace or setting. Implementation of the reporting system, a workplace violence prevention policy, and specific prevention strategies should be publicized company-wide, and appropriate training sessions should be scheduled. The demonstrated commitment of management is crucial to the success of the program. The success and appropriateness of intervention strategies can be monitored and adjusted with continued data collection.

A written workplace violence policy should clearly indicate a zero tolerance of violence at work, whether the violence originates inside or outside the workplace. Just as workplaces have developed mechanisms for reporting and dealing with sexual harassment, they must also develop threat assessment teams to which threats and violent incidents can be reported. These teams should include representatives from human resources, security, employee assistance, unions, workers, management, and perhaps legal and public relations departments. The charge to this team is to assess threats of violence (e.g., to determine how specific a threat is, whether the person threatening the worker has the means for carrying out the threat, and so forth) and to determine what steps are necessary to prevent the threat from being carried out. This team should also be charged with periodic reviews of violent incidents to identify ways in which similar incidents can be prevented in the future. Note that when violence or the threat of violence occurs among coworkers, firing the perpetrator may or may not be the most appropriate way to reduce the risk for additional or future violence. The employer may want to retain some control over the perpetrator and require or provide counseling or other care, if appropriate. The violence prevention policy should explicitly state the consequences of making threats or committing acts of violence in the workplace.

A comprehensive workplace violence prevention policy and program should also include procedures and responsibilities to be taken in the event of a violent incident in the workplace. This policy should explicitly state how the response team is to be assembled and who is responsible for immediate care of the victims, reestablishing work areas and processes, and organizing and carrying out stress debriefing sessions with victims, their coworkers, and perhaps the families of victims and coworkers. Employee assistance programs, human resource professionals, and local mental health and emergency service personnel can offer assistance in developing these strategies.

Responding to an Immediate Threat of Workplace Violence

For a situation that poses an immediate threat of workplace violence, all legal, human resource, employee assistance, community mental health, and law enforcement resources should be used to develop a response. The risk of injury to all workers should be minimized. If a threat has been made that refers to particular times and places, or if the potential offender is knowledgeable about workplace procedures and time frames, patterns may need to be shifted. For example, a person who has leveled a threat against a worker may indicate, "I know where you park and what time you get off work!" In such a case, it may be advisable to change or even stagger departure times and implement a buddy system or an escort by security guard for leaving the building and getting to parking areas. The threat should not be ignored in the hope that it will resolve itself or out of fear of triggering an outburst from the person who has lodged the threat. If someone poses a danger to himself or others, the employer should notify appropriate authorities and take action.

Dealing With the Consequences of Workplace Violence

Much discussion has also centered around the role of stress in workplace violence. The most important thing to remember is that stress can be both a cause and an effect of workplace violence. That is, high levels of stress may lead to violence in the workplace, but a violent incident in the workplace will most certainly lead to stress, perhaps even to posttraumatic stress disorder. The data from the National Crime Victimization Survey (BJS, 1998) show compelling evidence for the need to be aware of the impact of workplace violence. Employers should therefore be sensitive to the effects of workplace violence and provide an environment that promotes open communication; they should also have in place an established procedure for reporting and responding to violence. Appropriate referrals to employee assistance programs or other local mental health services may be appropriate for stress debriefing sessions after critical incidents.

Current Efforts and Future Directions: Research and Prevention

Although researchers have begun collecting descriptive information about workplace violence, a number of research questions remain:

- What are the specific tasks and environments that place workers at greatest risk?
- What factors influence the lethality of violent incidents?
- What are the relationships of workplace assault victims to offenders?
- Are there identifiable precipitating events?
- Were there any safety measures in place?
- What were the actions of the victim and did they influence the outcome of the attack?
- What are the most effective prevention strategies?

These questions should also be addressed in developing violence prevention strategies for specific workplaces.

A number of these questions were raised in 1990 at a workshop convened by NIOSH. They continue to require attention through the collaborative research and prevention efforts of public health, human resource, and criminal justice professionals. A number of other recommendations were made by a panel of experts in interpersonal violence on directions for NIOSH in this area (NIOSH, 1992). These recommendations have been implemented or initiated and include efforts to

- improve the quality of death certificate data,
- compare findings from NTOF, the National Center for Health Statistics, and the Federal Bureau of Investigation,
- conduct evaluation research to determine the effectiveness of various prevention strategies,
- disseminate information on workplace homicide risk,
- examine possibilities for collection and analysis of data on nonfatal workplace violence, and
- increase collaboration between public health and criminal justice agencies.

In the fall of 1993, NIOSH released an alert on preventing homicide in the workplace (NIOSH, 1993) and encouraged employers, workers, unions, and others with a vested interest to look at their workplaces and take immediate action to reduce the risk for workplace homicide. In related efforts, NIOSH responded to numerous requests from the media, resulting in print, radio, and television coverage of the data and the NIOSH prevention message: Although no single intervention strategy is appropriate for all workplaces and no definitive strategies can be recommended at this time, immediate action should be taken to reduce the toll of workplace homicide on our nation's workforce. This message still holds true and applies not only to workplace homicide but to all workplace violence. Clearly, violence is pervasive in U.S. workplaces, accounting for 1,071 homicides in 1994 and approximately 2 million nonfatal assaults each year (BJS, 1998). NIOSH continues to pursue research and prevention efforts to reduce the risk of workplace violence for the nation's workers. The murder of an average of 20 workers each week is unacceptable and should not be considered the cost of doing business in our society.

BUILDING A HEALTHY WORK–LIFESTYLE BALANCE FOR PROFESSIONAL ATHLETES AND THEIR FAMILIES

Lifestyle Issues in Professional Sports

Imagine being called into the office for your performance evaluation. Upon entering the office, you discover not only your boss, but hundreds of others are present to contribute to the analysis. Every detail of your performance has been recorded on videotape, each action has been statistically analyzed, and a MANOVA (multivariate analysis of variance) computed to compare this week's performance with that of previous weeks. In addition, individuals who are totally unrelated to your workplace, many of whom you have never met, are continually evaluating your performance and broadcasting their assessments via print media, radio, television, and the Internet. This process occurs week after week, month after month, over the entire course of your career. How many of us would subject ourselves to this degree of scrutiny?

Many in our society perceive professional athletes as "having it all"—money, big houses, expensive cars, and fame and adulation—all based on their endeavors on the field of play. But the challenges associated with performing one's daily work in a high visibility workplace (i.e., the football field or the hockey arena) often go unrecognized. There are inherent drawbacks to sports fame. Fans are notoriously fickle. Athletes find that they may be worshipped one moment as the hero, while in the next be condemned as villain (a situation referred to as "going from the penthouse to the outhouse").

The public is often oblivious to the high (many say unrealistic) expectations for these modern-day gladiators. Many professional athletes decry their unwanted role model status, the intense public scrutiny, and lack of privacy. However, these cries fall on deaf ears. Fans often behave as if they are entitled to know everything about their heroes and heroines, leading many elite athletes to feel that they are "living their life in a fishbowl."

The sacrifices made in pursuit of athletic glory are also overlooked or ignored by the public. Athletic success often requires a single-minded devotion to one's sport, leaving little time or energy for elements of life that most people take for granted. To achieve and maintain dominance on the court or the playing field, athletes often neglect family, friends, and hobbies. For high-level athletes, their sport often becomes a "job" long before they cash a paycheck. Studies have estimated that collegiate student athletes devote 30 to 60 hours per week to their sport (Miller, 1999). In many environments, any interest or activity that is not directly related to one's sport is viewed as a distraction.

Many individuals who reach the professional ranks have been singled out at an early age due to their athletic prowess. They have been groomed for a sports career and toward this end they have led lives that have been highly structured for them (summer camps, workouts, practices, and so forth). At the same time, they have been sheltered from other responsibilities and experiences, and in many ways protected from everyday problems and concerns. In addition, because of the fame and adoration that is frequently heaped on athletes in our society, many grow up being constantly catered to and deferred to, leading to a sense of privilege and entitlement.

This combination of an all-consuming "work" environment and sheltered upbringing can result in an individual who is markedly underdeveloped in other areas of his or her life. This development pattern has been termed *identity foreclosure*: that is, the individual "forecloses" on a convenient or comfortable role and fails to explore alternative identities (Marcia, 1966). In the sports environment, such foreclosure can contribute to an "exclusive athletic identity" (Brewer, Van Raalte, & Linder, 1993). This condition is characterized by an inability to identify and describe self-worth outside of athletic descriptions. This type of identity may also pose an impediment to important personal growth and development that is "unmasked" when the player's athletic career comes to an end (Murphy, Petitpas, & Brewer, 1996; Werthner & Orlick, 1990).

The odds against any individual becoming a professional athlete are astronomical. According to data compiled by the National Collegiate Athletic Association, in any given year there are more than 1,450,000 high school athletes playing football and basketball in the United States. However, there are fewer than 400 new professional positions available in these sports each year: less than one professional rookie position for every 3,600 aspirants (Hagwell, 1998). On the basis of these numbers it should be clear that once he or she overcomes all of the hurdles faced by the aspiring professional athlete, the rookie has then joined a very small, select, and basically closed society. The rookie also finds that initiation into this group comes at a considerable cost.

With lightning speed, the newly turned professional athlete is consumed by a myriad of activities, issues, obligations, and expectations—before ever stepping foot on the professional field or court. The game they have played, to this point for enjoyment and competition, is now not only their livelihood, but has become *the* foundation of self-identity and social support. No longer can they simply "play" the game; they must integrate new business and social factors as well. In addition, many rookie professionals must now learn for the first time to deal with life outside of a highly sheltered and supportive environment.

Family members of exceptional athletes (particularly parents, partners and significant others) also face challenges with the transition to the professional realm. They often feel that friends and members of their extended family do not understand the issues faced by their famous offspring or spouse, or how this newfound fame affects them as a family. Indeed, wives and mothers of players in the National Football League and the National Basketball Association have formed their own organizations to provide support and information to one another (Broussard, 1998).

Challenges to a Healthy Work Life in Professional Sports

Professional athletes are confronted with the same types of psychological issues that are experienced by those in the general society. Elements of the professional athletic lifestyle can comprise barriers to establishing and maintaining an effective therapeutic relationship with clinicians. If not appreciated by the provider, these aspects can give an impression of disinterest and a lack of commitment or disengagement on the part of the athlete.

The sports environment in the United States creates a climate that discourages athletes from seeking or accepting care for physical and psychological ailments. A "sport ethic" has been described (Hughes & Coakley, 1991) that dictates that one must "play with pain." Seeking treatment is implicitly (or explicitly) viewed as a sign of weakness (Linder, Brewer, Van Raalte, & DeLange, 1991). In this intensely competitive environment, perception can determine the degree of success in sustaining the professional athlete status. If a player is perceived to have problems that could impede his or her athletic performance, the exposure of such problems can be the "kiss of death" to a professional sports career.

An additional potential impediment to careseeking by athletes relates to the "star power" that is bequeathed upon celebrities in our society. As a result of this perceived power, elite athletes frequently find themselves besieged with requests and demands from every quarter. It often seems as if even casual acquaintances expect something from them (money, time, the enhanced status that accompanies being associated with them). The response to such constant demands may be a deep-seated suspicion and distrust of anyone outside of "their world." The athlete shares him or herself only with other players, family, and possibly a small circle of friends (Begel & Baum, 2000). This can eventually result in significant social isolation. Although many individuals in our society are reluctant to seek psychological help, the self-protective isolation adopted by many professional athletes can exacerbate this avoidance.

If these barriers to seeking care are overcome, a variety of non-clinical factors and influences can impinge on the provision of care to this group. Dr. Joseph Pursch is a substance abuse specialist whose practice includes a number of professional athletes. He describes the impact of celebrity on the clinical encounter:

> When I have a sports star in my office for the first time, I can expect all of the buttons on my telephone to be lit up. . . . His agent is on one line to tell me he has a beer commercial lined up for his client that can't be shot if it is known he is an alcoholic. . . . The coach wants to know how soon he can play; the hospital administrator wants to make a public announcement; and the star's lawyer wants it quiet. A TV network demands

a full report. Agents for the Players Association and the team have their interests, and his wife and ex-wife (and maybe a girlfriend) want to be assured his income will continue, and all of this is before I have even taken his blood pressure. (Cowart, 1986, p. 2646)

Role of the Therapist in Attaining and Maintaining a Healthy Work and Life Balance

Although there are unique or magnified elements of mental health care for professional athletes, in the majority of cases their assessment and treatment is identical to treatment of others seeking care for psychological issues. Basic principles of problem identification, differential diagnosis, investigation of stressors and contributing factors, and assessment of coping skills and support network must be applied. This diagnostic and therapeutic approach must be applied within the context of the professional sports arena.

The primary psychological problems seen in athletes in therapy are stress related, specifically: anxiety and stress, depression, eating disorders, and substance abuse (Brewer & Petrie, 1995; Petrie & Diehl, 1995; Petrie, Diehl, & Watkins, 1995). The life of the professional athlete is, more than most, one of constant instability and transition. These transitions may be related directly to the athlete (i.e., being traded or released from the team, injury, retirement) or to the work environment (coaches fired, entire teams moved from one city to another, etc.). Transitions, uncertainty, and the constant pressure to perform at a high level result in a significant degree of stress. A variety of psychological interventions have been proposed to assist athletes in stress management, recovering from injury and in some cases, preventing injuries. These include relaxation, goal setting, positive self-talk, and imagery (Ieleva & Orlick, 1991; Wiese-Bjornstal & Smith, 1993; Yukelson & Murphy, 1993).

In counseling professional athletes, as with all counseling, trust building and empathetic understanding are essential. Trying to understand the athlete's point of view, and communicating that understanding to the individual can establish the foundation for a trusting therapeutic relationship. Explicit acknowledgement of the unique aspects of the professional athlete's work life and lifestyle may also aid in nurturing this relationship and establishing a foundation of trust.

Therapeutic techniques and approaches that may prove useful in treating professional athletes include

- acknowledging the variety of emotions that the athlete is experiencing, normalizing their emotions and concerns, predicting their responses, and reframing their issues;
- assessing coping skills and assisting the athlete in developing and using healthy coping mechanisms; and

- providing assistance in expanding identity beyond athletics. Encourage non-sports related activities, active planning for life beyond sports. Help them recognize transferable skills (Murphy, 1995; Petitpas, Champagne, Chartrand, Danish, & Murphy, 1997). Assessment tools like Myers-Briggs or stress inventories (i.e., Moos) may be helpful.

As with most individuals, the social support system of athletes is frequently a key contributor to their psychological health and well-being (Brewer, Jeffers, Petitpas, & Van Raalte, 1994). Assessing these support networks and advising the athlete on ways to effectively use them can be of tremendous benefit. As in other settings, the support system of professional athletes usually consists of family and a few close friends. Coworkers (in this instance, coaches and teammates) may also be important components of the support network for professional athletes (Wiese, Weise, & Yukelson, 1991). A therapeutic approach based on family systems theory can often be useful in treating athletes (Zimmerman, 1999). With the athlete's permission, discussion with family, friends, and coaches can provide an opportunity to reinforce the important role that these individuals play in the treatment process. Reinforcing appropriate interventions on their part and educating them regarding useful therapeutic techniques can also be of benefit.

Clinicians in a sports environment must recognize that, in addition to providing support to the athlete, this network may often be the cause of or a significant contributor to the psychological issues that bring the athlete into therapy. In many cases, as a result of the financial windfall that often accompanies a professional contract, the athlete may find that their role in the family system has, almost overnight, gone from one of child or sibling to head of household. At times players will create businesses or opportunities to put family members and friends on their "payroll," resulting in additional role confusion (player as "boss" to Mom or Dad). The attendant responsibilities and obligations may prove overwhelming for a young adult who is still struggling to develop a sense of independence and a mature self-identity.

In other instances, the family support system may have been only minimally effective prior to the athlete entering the professional realm. The increased stress and intense public scrutiny may erode this tenuous foundation of support. The athlete then redefines his support network, often leading to further conflict.

Unique Clinical Aspects of Professional Athletes

As previously acknowledged, most of the problems leading to mental health care in professional athletes are common to many workplace environments (stress and anxiety, depression, marital or relationship issues, lack of balance between personal and professional life). However, there are some conditions that are unique to, or experienced differently by athletes.

Substance Abuse

The athlete with drug addiction is a case in point. As exemplified by Dr. Pursch's description in the previous section, the assessment and treatment process are infringed on from many directions. In addition to these multiple distracters, the lifestyle of the athlete and the culture of professional sports make it extremely difficult for sustained treatment and follow-up (Cowart, 1986). If a player is suspended from competition due to substance abuse, he or she is not allowed to participate in team practices, meetings, or other activities. Because most athletes do not live in the same cities as their families of origin, suspension essentially removes and isolates the player from his only major source of support (the team). He or she is not able to work and may then become vulnerable to increased abuse of the substances. At the same time the athlete is without access to those relationships that may stabilize and minimize his or her abusive tendencies. Additionally, the athlete's struggles with sobriety are often played out on a highly public stage.

Retirement

Another example of a unique athletic psychological experience relates to retirement and end of career. According to statistics compiled by the National Football League Office of Player Development, the average player spends 3.5 years in the NFL. This "professional lifespan" is similar for other professional sports. Consequently, the career of most pro athletes "peaks" at a very early age (typically in their mid- to late 20s). As already discussed, many of these individuals have devoted the majority of their waking hours to athletic accomplishments. This transition to former athlete is often traumatic:

> The pampered treatment he has long received may have left him without basic skills for coping with life. Now he suddenly confronts a mystifying world that is normal to most. The countless people who have long stroked his ego may have left him with an unrealistic appraisal of himself and his value to the world, and now he suddenly confronts a society that is indifferent to his physical skills and is asking if he has any others . . . . He has long felt himself invincible . . . but now he must confront his own wretched mortality. (Myslenski, 1986, p. 20)

With retirement comes a host of losses: the loss of income; loss of identity and status; the loss of the routines, rituals, and the adrenaline rush of competition; and loss of the camaraderie of team. There may be feelings of helplessness and shame. These losses often trigger a grief reaction in retired players. The period following retirement is an extremely vulnerable phase. According to National Football League surveys, during the first 4 years after retirement players are at increased risk of marital separation and divorce, and are more susceptible to developing or worsening problems with substance abuse (G. Troupe, NFL Senior Director of Player and Employee Development, personal communication, April 2001).

Schedules and Continuity

Scheduling and appointment issues frequently arise when treating professional athletes. Professional athletes work year round. The off-season is devoted to strength and conditioning—a vital part of their success once the season begins. They have very full schedules and may have very little time off during traditional business hours. It is expected that practitioners working with professional athletes will maintain a high level of flexibility. Players expect clinicians to work around *their* schedules.

Many pro athletes find it challenging to keep scheduled appointments because they are not accustomed to making such appointments, and they have been conditioned to expect that others will work with them at whatever point they decide to make themselves available. At the high school and collegiate levels, the athlete is typically not responsible for designing his or her schedule. Such details are usually handled by coaches or by advisors within the department of athletics. Most of the athlete's time evolves around their sport's schedule. There is little if any time for the athlete to be involved in other extracurricular activities. Once the athlete reaches the professional level, his or her time is even more consumed by sports-related activities. Free time is diminished, with the possible exception of the off-season. So much is "handled" for elite athletes (by team and coaches, agents, or personal assistants) that the need or the opportunity to develop personal time management skills is often eliminated. In addition, responsibilities to team and to sport are expected to override all other obligations. For example, a player may schedule (or have scheduled for them) an appointment "outside" of the sports system. This could be to explore a business opportunity or a clinical encounter. The team makes a last minute change in the schedule— a common occurrence—resulting in a conflict with keeping the appointment. The athlete then exacerbates the problem by failing to call to cancel or change the appointment. Such behaviors are reinforced by the general acceptance of this lack of courtesy and consideration by many who are accustomed to working with elite athletes.

In anticipation of such events, a discussion of expectations around time and scheduling issues early in the treatment process is warranted. Clarifying what will and will not be viewed as acceptable behavior, and consequences of deviation from this agreed-upon norm may prevent problems down the line.

Additional complications can arise as a result of the "revolving door" nature of professional sports (trades, injury, salary cap, etc.). Players have limited job stability and are literally "here today, gone tomorrow." A player may be traded without notice and report to work in another city within 24 hours. This can pose significant challenges to continuity in the treatment process.

Confidentiality Issues

The issues related to confidentiality in the professional sports arena are as critical as they are controversial. The practitioner may at times have difficulty identifying exactly *who* is the client, and be challenged by how information is disseminated and used within this setting. If clinicians are hired by a team or a sports league, there are usually expectations on the part of the hiring party that sensitive information about individuals will be shared. This can place the mental health practitioner in an unfamiliar and uncomfortable position.

Information such as the psychological history and family dynamics would typically be considered private and confidential by a clinician. However, intimate details are commonly included in the scouting reports used by coaches and teams in their "hiring" process for players. The dilemma the practitioner may encounter is determining to whom the information will be provided and how it will be used.

Professional sports organizations are typically unaccustomed to the appropriate management of highly confidential clinical information. Most athletes do not appreciate the sensitive nature of information revealed through the psychological and psychiatric evaluations that are often performed at the behest of interested teams. Therefore, sensitive and revealing information about that athlete's state of psychological functioning could be revealed indiscriminately to those within and outside of the sports organization.

Dual relationships abound within the professional sports arena. This has historically been a controversial area in the practice of psychology. It is imperative that the clinician understands the culture of professional sports, and clearly defines his or her role and establishes appropriate boundaries. One key is to always keep in mind exactly who the "client" is (league, team, or athlete) and how the needs of that client can be most effectively and confidentially addressed.

It is also incumbent upon the clinician to educate key individuals within the organization regarding the importance of client privacy and the need to severely limit access to sensitive information. Educating the player about such issues serves to empower the player, and may aid in building a bond of trust with the psychologist.

Final Thoughts

A recent front-page article in *USA Today* discusses the increasing interest in young athletes turning professional. The article discusses lucrative professional contracts offered to today's young stars. The athletes featured in this article were 12 years old (Brady & Rosewater, 2001).

The difficulties experienced by professional athletes as a result of under-developed life skills have been well documented. Many of these problems have been described in players who have entered the professional sports arena from college. What will be the long-term effects on those athletes who bypass college altogether?

Increasingly, the need for psychological consultation and intervention is being recognized in the world of professional sports. The need for more research providing empirical evidence, insight, and understanding into the coping and adjustment aspects of the professional athlete is clear. Other areas requiring exploration include effective methods of developing life skills, and studies of family issues in professional sports.

The issues have been presented before us. Psychologists, like elite athletes, must train and prepare for the challenge.

REFERENCES

Adkins, J. A. (1999). Promoting organizational health: The evolving practice of occupational health psychology. *Professional Psychology: Research and Practice, 30,* 129–137.

Allen, T. D., Herst, D. E. L., Bruck, C. S., & Sutton, M. (2000). Consequences associated with work-to-family conflict: A review and agenda for future research. *Journal of Occupational Health Psychology, 5,* 278–308.

Barling, J. (1986). Fathers' work experience: The father–child relationship and children's behavior. *Journal of Occupational Behavior, 7,* 61–66.

Barnett, R. C. (1998). Toward a review and reconceptualization of the work/family literature. *Genetic, Social, and General Psychology Monographs, 124*(2), 125–182.

Begel, D., & Baum, A. L. (2000). The athlete's role. In D. Begel & R. W. Burton (Eds.), *Sport psychiatry* (pp. 55–56). New York: W.W. Norton & Company.

Brady, E., & Rosewater, A. (2001, August 24). The need to star at 12. *USA Today,* pp. 1A, 5A.

Brewer, B. W., Jeffers, K. E., Petitpas, A., & Van Raalte, J. L. (1994). Perceptions of psychological interventions in the context of sport injury and rehabilitation. *The Sport Psychologist, 8*(2), 176–188.

Brewer, B. W., & Petrie, T. A. (1995). A comparison of injured and non-injured football players on selected psychosocial variables. *Academic Athletic Journal,* 11–18.

Brewer, B. W., Van Raalte, J. L., & Linder, D. (1993). Athletic identity: Hercules' muscle or Achilles' heel? *International Journal of Sport Psychology, 24*, 237–254.

Broussard, C. (1998, August 24). Pro basketball: Trying to lift up each other's arms; Pro players' mothers help themselves cope. *The New York Times*, p. C1.

Bureau of Justice Statistics. (1998). *Workplace violence, 1992–96. BJS Special Report: National Crime Victimization Survey* (NCJ-168634). Washington, DC: U.S. Government Printing Office.

Bureau of Labor Statistics. (1994). *Work injuries and illnesses by selected characteristics, 1992*. Washington, DC: U.S. Department of Labor, Bureau of Labor Statistics.

Bureau of Labor Statistics. (2000). *National census of fatal occupational injuries, 1999* (BLS News USDL-00-236). Washington, DC: U.S. Department of Labor, Bureau of Labor Statistics.

Bureau of Labor Statistics. (2001). *Lost-worktime injuries and illnesses: Characteristics and resulting time away from work, 1999* (BLS News, USDL-01-71). Washington, DC: U.S. Department of Labor, Bureau of Labor Statistics.

Burke, R., & Greenglass, E. R. (1999). Work–family conflict, spouse support, and nursing staff well-being during organizational restructuring. *Journal of Occupational Health Psychology, 4*, 327–336.

Cannon, W. B. (1935). Stresses and strains of homeostasis. *American Journal of the Medical Sciences, 189*, 1–14.

Castillo, D. N. (1995). Nonfatal violence in the workplace: Directions for future research. In C. Block & R. Block (Eds.), *Trends, risks, and interventions in lethal violence: Proceedings of the Third Annual Spring Symposium of the Homicide Research Working Group* (pp. 225–235). Washington, DC: National Institute of Justice.

Castillo, D. N., & Jenkins, E. L. (1994). Industries and occupations at high risk for work-related homicide. *Journal of Occupational Medicine, 36*, 125–132.

Collins, J. J., & Cox, B. G. (1987). Job activities and personal crime victimization: Implications for theory. *Social Science Research, 16*, 345–360.

Cooper, C. L. (1998). *Theories of organizational stress*. Oxford, England: Oxford University Press.

Cowart, V. (1986). Road back from substance abuse especially long, hard for athletes. *Journal of the American Medical Association, 256*(19), 2645–2649.

Current Population Survey. (2001). *Employment characteristics of families summary*. Retrieved June 20, 2003, from the U.S. Department of Labor, Bureau of Labor Statistics: http://www.bls.gov/bls/newsrels.htm

Davis, H. (1987). Workplace homicides of Texas males. *American Journal of Public Health, 77*, 1290–1293.

Davis, J., Honchar, P. A., & Suarez, L. (1987). Fatal occupational injuries of women, Texas 1975–1984. *American Journal of Public Health, 77*, 1524–1527.

Edwards, J. R. (1996). An examination of competing versions of the person–environment fit approach to stress. *Academy of Management Journal, 39*, 292–339.

Elkin, A. J., & Rosch, P. J. (1990). Promoting mental health at the workplace: The prevention side of stress management. *Occupational Medicine: State of the Art Review*, 5, 739–754.

Elkind, H. B. (Ed.). (1931). *Preventive management: Mental hygiene in industry*. New York: B. C. Forbes.

Federal Bureau of Investigation. (1994). *Uniform crime reports for the United States, 1993*. Washington, DC: U.S. Department of Justice.

Frone, M. R., Russell, M., & Cooper, M. L. (1992a). Antecedents and outcomes of work–family conflict: Testing a model of the work–family interface. *Journal of Applied Psychology*, 77, 65–78.

Frone, M. R., Russell, M., & Cooper, M. L. (1992b). Prevalence of work–family conflict: Are work and family boundaries asymmetrically permeable? *Journal of Organizational Behavior*, 13, 723–729.

Frost, P., & Robinson, S. (1999). The toxic handler: Organizational hero—and casualty. *Harvard Business Review*, 77, 97–106.

Galinsky, E. (1999). *Ask the children. What America's children really think about working parents*. New York: William Morrow.

Googins, B. K. (1997). Sharing responsibility for managing work and family relationships: A community perspective. In S. J. Parasuraman & J. H. Greenhaus (Eds.), *Integrating work and family* (pp. 220–231). Westport, CT: Quorum Books.

Gottlieb, B. H., Kelloway, E. K., & Barham, E. (1998). *Flexible work arrangements: Managing the work–family boundary*. Chichester, England: John Wiley & Sons.

Gowing, M. K., Kraft, J. D., & Quick, J. C. (1998). *The new organizational reality*. Washington, DC: American Psychological Association.

Greenhaus, J. H., & Beutell, N. J. (1985). Sources of conflict between work and family roles. *Academy of Management Review*, 10, 75–88.

Gutek, B. A., Searle, S., & Klepa, L. (1991). Rational versus gender role explanations for work–family conflict. *Journal of Applied Psychology*, 76, 560–568.

Hagwell, S. R. (Ed.). (1998). *A career in professional athletics: A guide for making the transition*. Overland Park, KS: The National Collegiate Athletic Association.

Hale, T. W. (1997, September). The working poor. *Monthly Labor Review*, 47–48.

Hughes, R. H., & Coakley, J. (1991). Positive deviance among athletes: The implications of overconformity to the sport ethic. *Sociology of Sport Journal*, 8, 307–325.

Hurrell, J. J., Jr., & Murphy, L. R. (1992). Psychological job stress. In W. N. Rom (Ed.), *Environmental and occupational medicine* (pp. 675–684). New York: Little, Brown.

Hyde, J. S., Essex, M. J., Clark, R., Klein, M. H., & Byrd, J. (1996). Parental leave: Policy and research. *Journal of Social Issues*, 52(3), 91–109.

Ieleva, L., & Orlick, T. (1991). Mental links to enhanced healing: An exploratory study. *The Sport Psychologist*, 5, 25–40.

Ilgen, D. R. (1990). Health issues at work: Opportunities for industrial/organizational psychology. *American Psychologist, 45,* 273–283.

Jenkins, E. L. (1994). Occupational injury deaths among females: The U.S. experience for the decade 1980 to 1989. *The Annals of Epidemiology, 4*(2), 146–151.

Jenkins, E. L. (1996). Workplace homicide: Industries and occupations at high risk. *Occupational Medicine State of Art Reviews, 11*(2), 219–225.

Jenkins, E. L., Kisner, S. M., Fosbroke, D. E., Layne, L. A., Stout, N. A., & Castillo, D. N. (1993). *Fatal injuries to workers in the United States, 1980–1989: A decade of surveillance; national profile* (DHHS [NIOSH] Publication No. 93-108). Washington, DC: U.S. Government Printing Office.

Jenkins, E. L., Layne, L. A., & Kisner, S. M. (1992). Homicide in the workplace: The U.S. experience, 1980–1988. *American Association of Occupational Health Nurses Journal, 40,* 215–218.

Kahn, R. L., Wolfe, R. P., Quinn, R. P., Snoek, J. D., & Rosenthal, R. A. (1964). *Organizational stress: Studies in role conflict and ambiguity.* New York: John Wiley & Sons.

Kanter, R. M. (1977). *Work and family in the United States: A critical review and agenda for research and policy.* New York: Russell Sage.

Kelloway, E. K., Gottlieb, B. H., & Barham, L. (1999). The source, nature, and direction of work and family conflict: A longitudinal investigation. *Journal of Occupational Health Psychology, 4,* 337–346.

Kelly, R. F. (1988). The urban underclass and the future of work–family relations research. *Journal of Social Behavior and Personality, 3*(4), 45–54.

Kossek, E. E., & Ozeki, C. (1999a). Bridging the work–family policy and productivity gap: A literature review. *Community, Work, and Family, 2*(1), 7–32.

Kossek, E. E., & Ozeki, C. (1999b). Work–family conflict, policies, and the job-life satisfaction relationship: A review and directions for organizational behavior-human resources research. *Journal of Applied Psychology, 83,* 139–149.

Kraus, J. F. (1987). Homicide while at work: Persons, industries, and occupations at high risk. *American Journal of Public Health, 77,* 1285–1289.

Lambert, S. J. (1990). Processes linking work and family: A critical review and research agenda. *Human Relations, 43,* 239–257.

Landy, F., Quick, J. C., & Kasl, S. (1994). Work, stress and well-being. *International Journal of Stress Management, 1*(1), 33–73.

Lazarus, R. S. (1995). Psychological stress in the workplace. In R. Crandall & P. L. Perrewe (Eds.), *Occupational stress: A handbook* (pp. 3–14). Washington, DC: Taylor & Francis.

Lee, J. A. (1997). Balancing elder care responsibilities and work: Two empirical studies. *Journal of Occupational Health Psychology, 2,* 220–228.

Levi, L., Brennar, S. O., Hall, E. M., Hjelm, R., Saolvaara, H., Arnetz, B., et al. (1984). The psychological, social, and biochemical impacts of unemployment in Sweden. *International Journal of Mental Health, 13,* 1–2, 18–34.

Levinson, H. (1985). *Executive stress*. New York: New American Library.

Lewis, S., & Cooper, C. L. (1999). The work–family research agenda in changing contexts. *Journal of Occupational Health Psychology, 4*, 382–393.

Linder, D. E., Brewer, B. W., Van Raalte, J. L., & DeLange, N. (1991). A negative halo for athletes who consult sport psychologists: Replication and extension. *Journal of Sport and Exercise Psychology, 13*, 133–148.

Lynch, J. P. (1987). Routine activity and victimization at work. *Journal of Quantitative Criminology, 3*, 283–300.

MacEwen, K. E., Barling, J., & Kelloway, E. K. (1992). Effects of short-term role overload on marital interactions. *Work and Stress, 6*, 117–126.

Marcia, J. E. (1966). Development and validation of ego-identity status. *Journal of Personality and Social Psychology, 3*, 551–558.

Marin, G., & Marin, V. O. B. (1991). *Research with Hispanic populations*. Newbury Park, CA: Sage.

Maslow, A. H. (1998). *Eupsychian management*. Homewood, IL: R. D. Irwin. (Original work published 1965)

Millar, J. D. (1984). The NIOSH-suggested list of the ten leading work-related diseases and injuries. *Journal of Occupational Medicine, 26*, 340–341.

Miller, P. (1999). *Life skills development in high-level sport*. Paper presented at the 7th International Post-Graduate Seminar on Olympic Studies. Olympia, Greece.

Murphy, L. R., & Cooper, C. L. (2000). *Health and productive work: An international perspective*. Philadelphia: Taylor & Francis.

Murphy, L. R., Hurrell, J. J., Jr., Sauter, S. L., & Keita, G. P. (Eds.). (1995). *Job stress interventions*. Washington, DC: American Psychological Association.

Murphy, S. M. (Ed.). (1995). *Sports psychology interventions*. Champaign, IL: Human Kinetics.

Murphy, S. M., Petitpas, A., & Brewer, B. W. (1996). Identity foreclosure, athletic identity and career maturity in intercollegiate athletes. *The Sports Psychologist, 10*, 239–246.

Myslenski, S. (1986). Rookies at reality. *Chicago Tribune Magazine, 32*, 20.

National Institute for Occupational Safety and Health. (1992). *Homicide in U.S. workplaces: A strategy for prevention and research* (DHHS [NIOSH] Publication No. 92-103). Morgantown, WV: U.S. Department of Health and Human Services, Public Health Service, Centers for Disease Control.

National Institute for Occupational Safety and Health. (1993). *NIOSH alert: Request for assistance in preventing homicide in the workplace* (DHHS [NIOSH] Publication No. 93-109). Cincinnati, OH: U.S. Department of Health and Human Services, Public Health Service, Centers for Disease Control and Prevention.

National Institute for Occupational Safety and Health. (1996). *Current Intelligence Bulletin 57– Workplace violence: Risk factors and prevention strategies* (DHHS [NIOSH] Publication No. 96-100). Cincinnati, OH: U.S. Department of Health and Human Services, Public Health Service, Centers for Disease Control and Prevention.

National Institute for Occupational Safety and Health. (2001). *Fatal injuries to civilian workers in the US 1980–1995 (National Profile)* (DHHS [NIOSH] Publication No. 2001–129). Cincinnati, OH: U.S. Department of Health and Human Services, Public Health Service, Centers for Disease Control and Prevention.

Netemeyer, R. G., Boles, J. S., & McMurrian, R. (1996). Development and validation of work–family conflict and family–work conflict scales. *Journal of Applied Psychology, 81,* 400–410.

Oliker, S. J. (1995). Work commitment and constraints among mothers on welfare. *Journal of Contemporary Ethnography, 24,* 165–194.

Osipow, S. H., & Spokane, A. R. (1992). *Occupational Stress Inventory: Manual, research version.* Odessa, FL: Psychological Assessment Resources.

Parasuraman, S. J., & Greenhaus, J. H. (Eds.). (1997). *Integrating work and family.* Westport, CT: Quorum Books.

Pearlin, L. I., & Schooler, C. (1978). The structure of coping. *Journal of Health and Social Behavior, 19,* 2–21.

Petitpas, A., Champagne, D., Chartrand, J., Danish, S., & Murphy, S. (1997). *Athletes guide to career planning.* Chicago: Human Kinetics.

Petrie, T. A., & Diehl, N. S. (1995). Sport psychology in the profession of psychology. *Professional Psychology: Research and Practice, 26,* 288–291.

Petrie, T. A., Diehl, N. S., & Watkins, C. E., Jr. (1995). Sports psychology: An emerging domain in the counseling psychology profession? *The Counseling Psychologist, 23,* 535–545.

Piotrkowski, C. S. (1979). *Work and the family system.* New York: Free Press.

Piotrkowski, C. S. (1998, May). *An overview of research on work and family life.* Paper presented at the international conference Public Health in the 21st Century: Behavioral and Social Science Contributions, sponsored by the National Institute for Occupational Safety and Health and the American Psychological Association, Washington, DC.

Piotrkowski, C. S., & Gornick, L. K. (1987). Effects of work-related separations on children and families. In J. Bloom-Feshbach & S. Bloom-Feshbach (Eds.), *The psychology of separation and loss* (pp. 267–299). San Francisco: Jossey-Bass.

Piotrkowski, C. S., & Hughes, D. (1993). Dual-earner families in context. In F. Walsh (Ed.), *Normal family processes* (2nd ed., pp. 185–207). New York: Guilford Press.

Piotrkowski, C. S., & Katz, M. (1982). Indirect socialization of children: The effects of mothers' jobs on academic behavior of children. *Child Development, 53,* 1520–1529.

Piotrkowski, C. S., & Kessler-Sklar, S. (1996). Welfare reform and access to family-supportive benefits in the workplace. *American Journal of Orthopsychiatry, 66,* 538–547.

Piotrkowski, C. S., Rapoport, R. N., & Rapoport, R. (1987). Families and work. In M. B. Sussman & S. K. Steinmetz (Eds.), *Handbook of marriage and the family* (pp. 251–283). New York: Plenum.

Piotrkowski, C. S., & Staines, G. L. (1991). Job stress and the family. *Business Insights, 7*(1), 22–27.

Presser, H. B. (1995). Job, family and gender determinants of nonstandard work schedules among employed Americans in 1991. *Demography, 32,* 577–598.

Presser, H. B., & Cain, V. S. (1983). Shift work among dual-earner couples with children. *Science, 10,* 18–25.

Presser, H. B., & Cox, A. G. (1997, April). The work schedules of low-educated American women and welfare reform. *Monthly Labor Review,* 25–34.

Quick, J. C., & Gavin, J. H. (2000). The next frontier: Edgar Schein on organizational therapy. *Academy of Management Executive, 14,* 30–44.

Quick, J. C., Murphy, L. R., & Hurrell, J. J., Jr. (1992). *Stress and well-being at work: Assessments and interventions for occupational mental health.* Washington, DC: American Psychological Association.

Quick, J. C., Quick, J. D., Nelson, D. L., & Hurrell, J. J., Jr. (1997). *Preventive stress management in organizations.* Washington, DC: American Psychological Association.

Quick, J. C., & Tetrick, L. E. (2003). *Handbook of occupational health psychology.* Washington, DC: American Psychological Association.

Quick, J. C., Tetrick, L. E., Adkins, J. A., & Klunder, C. (2003). Occupational health psychology. In A. M. Nezu, C. M. Nezu, & P. A. Geller (Eds.), *Handbook of psychology: Health psychology* (Vol. 9, pp. 569–589). Hoboken, NJ: John Wiley & Sons.

Repetti, R. L. (1989). Effects of daily workload on subsequent behavior during marital interaction: The roles of social withdrawal and spouse support. *Journal of Personality and Social Psychology, 57,* 651–659.

Repetti, R. L., & Wood, J. (1997). Effects of daily stress at work on mothers' interactions with preschoolers. *Journal of Family Psychology, 11,* 90–108.

Rodgers, H. R. (1996). *Poor women, poor children* (3rd ed.). Armonk, NY: M. E. Sharpe.

Rosch, P. J. (2001). The quandary of job stress compensation. *Health and Stress, 3,* 1–4.

Sauter, S. L., & Hurrell, J. J., Jr. (1999). Occupational health psychology: Origins, content, and direction. *Professional Psychology: Research and Practice, 30,* 117–122.

Sauter, S. L., Murphy, L. R., & Hurrell, J. J. (1990). Prevention of work-related psychological distress: A national strategy proposed by the National Institute of Occupational Safety and Health. *American Psychologist, 45,* 1146–1158.

Selye, H. (1976). *Stress in health and disease.* Boston: Butterworths.

Standen, P., Daniels, K., & Lamond, D. (1999). The home as a workplace: Work–family interaction and psychological well-being in telework. *Journal of Occupational Health Psychology, 4,* 368–381.

State of California. (1993). *Guidelines for security and safety of health care and community service workers.* Sacramento, CA: Division of Occupational Safety and Health, Department of Industrial Relations.

Stephens, G. K., & Sommer, S. M. (1996). The measurement of work to family conflict. *Educational and Psychological Measurement, 56,* 475–486.

Stout, N. A., Jenkins, E. L., & Pizatella, T. J. (1996). Occupational injury mortality rates in the United States: Changes from 1980 to 1989. *American Journal of Public Health, 86,* 73–77.

Swanson, N. G., Piotrkowski, C. S., Keita, G. P., & Becker, A. B. (1997). Occupational stress and women's health. In S. Gallant, G. P. Keita, & R. Royak-Schaler (Eds.), *Health care for women: Psychological, social, and behavioral influences* (pp. 147–159). Washington, DC: American Psychological Association.

Toscano, G., & Weber, W. (1995). *Violence in the workplace: Compensation and working conditions.* Washington, DC: U.S. Department of Labor, Bureau of Labor Statistics.

Vagg, P. R., & Spielberger, C. D. (1998). Occupational stress: Measuring job pressure and organizational support in the workplace. *Journal of Occupational Health Psychology, 3*(4), 294–305.

Vinokur, A. D., Schul, Y., Vuori, J., & Price, R. (2000). Two years after a job loss: Long-term impact of the JOBS program on reemployment and mental health. *Journal of Occupational Health Psychology, 5*(1), 32–47.

Von Dusch, T. (1868). *Lehrbuch der herzkrankheiten* [Textbook of heart disease]. Leipzig: Verlag von Wilhelm Engelman.

Werthner, P., & Orlick, T. (1990). Retirement experiences of successful Olympic athletes. *International Journal of Sport Psychology, 17,* 337–363.

Westman, M., & Etzion, D. (1995). Crossover of stress, stain and resources from one spouse to another. *Journal of Organizational Behavior, 16,* 169–181.

Westman, M., & Piotrkowski, C. S. (1999). Work–family research in occupational health psychology. *Journal of Occupational Health Psychology, 4,* 301–306.

Wiatrowski, W. J. (1994). Small businesses and their employees. *Monthly Labor Review, 117*(10), 29–35.

Wiese, D. M., Weise, M. R., & Yukelson, D. (1991). Sport psychology in the training room: A survey of athletic trainers. *The Sports Psychologist, 5,* 15–24.

Wiese-Bjornstal, D. M., & Smith, A. M. (1993). Counseling strategies for enhanced recovery of injured athletes within a team approach. In D. Pargman (Ed.), *Psychological bases of sports injury* (pp. 149–182). Morgantown, WV: Fitness Information Technology.

Windau, J., & Toscano, G. (1994). *Workplace homicides in 1992: Compensation and working conditions, February 1994.* Washington, DC: U.S. Department of Labor, Bureau of Labor Statistics.

Yukelson, D., & Murphy, S. (1993). Psychological considerations in injury prevention. In P. A. F. H. Renstrom (Ed.), *Sport injuries: Basic principles of prevention and care* (pp. 321–333). Cambridge, MA: Blackwell Scientific.

Zimmerman, T. S. (1999). Using family systems theory to counsel the injured athlete. In R. Ray & D. M. Wiese-Bjornstal (Eds.), *Counseling in sports medicine* (pp. 111–126). Champaign, IL: Human Kinetics.

10

ENSURING HEALTHY WORKING LIVES

DOROTHY W. CANTOR, THOMAS E. BOYCE, AND RENA L. REPETTI

Psychologists can and should be bringing their knowledge and expertise to the understanding of workplace health. Sometimes we first have to make the case to those in the workplace that our work will be of benefit to them. There is often a perception that psychological matters are too "soft" and therefore inappropriate for the factory or executive offices. If we are working in the area of workplace safety, the case is fairly easily made that our efforts will be beneficial. If we are interested in preparing employees for effective retirement, we may have to convince the human resources departments that this planning is as essential as the financial planning and healthy lifestyle efforts that they offer to their employees. For those interested in child health outcomes, the task is more complicated because the results are less directly observable in the workplace.

It is up to us to establish our credibility and with that, a level of trust, that will allow us in. How do we best do that? All of us have been able to get in the front door and do research and interventions. We note that it

Dr. Boyce would like to thank the students in his behavioral safety lab for their continued support and desire to improve quality of life. A special thanks is extended to Horacio Roman who assisted in the creation of some of the figures appearing in this chapter. Dr. Repetti's preparation of this chapter was supported by National Institute of Mental Health Grant R29-48593.

is important to understand the company hierarchy to know whom to approach. You have to know the system to know how to access it. Then, you have to convince people either that what you are planning to do will be of significant advantage to them and their employees or that what you will be doing will demonstrate their interest in their employees' welfare. There clearly needs to be a balance between the demands of the research or intervention and the perceived relevance of the issue to the employer and employees.

To make ourselves welcome in the corporate world, we also need to speak in a language that lay people can understand and market our interventions as solutions that complement current initiates. We need to demonstrate the effectiveness of our treatments with data in a form that is easy to interpret. And we need to reduce the response effort needed to adopt our behavior change innovations.

It is somewhat different for clinicians who work with individuals around workplace issues. Their task is to create a niche market by distinguishing themselves from the many therapists to whom people in their communities can turn for help. They need to educate themselves about the problems that people face at work and learn appropriate ways to intervene, which may be different from the skills and techniques they have used with patients with diagnosable conditions.

Each of the authors of this chapter has had a role in workplace research and intervention. Dr. Boyce studies and intervenes on issues of workplace safety relating to behaviors, rather than to equipment safety. Dr. Repetti studies the impact of occupational health on the health of families, promoting the interrelatedness of the two. And Dr. Cantor is concerned with how workers prepare themselves for their postwork lives, beyond their health and wealth, to how they will spend their time and continue to feel purposeful and fulfilled. This chapter is based on the integration of those topics and those experiences.

MOTIVATING HEALTH AND SAFETY AT WORK: SIMPLE SOLUTIONS FOR SIGNIFICANT PROBLEMS

Building a work culture that supports healthy choices among employees requires attention to three dynamic factors: the person (individual differences: biology, cognitions, and experiences); the environment (resources: including tools, equipment, and structure of the work setting); and behavior (safe vs. at-risk performance). These factors are dynamic and reciprocal in that influencing one factor necessarily influences the others (Bandura, 1997). For example, changes in the *environment* generally have an effect on people's *behaviors*, which can impact their attitudes, a *person* factor. Attitudes can

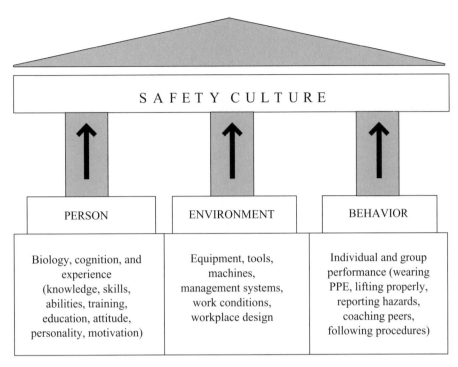

SAFETY CULTURE

PERSON	ENVIRONMENT	BEHAVIOR
Biology, cognition, and experience (knowledge, skills, abilities, training, education, attitude, personality, motivation)	Equipment, tools, machines, management systems, work conditions, workplace design	Individual and group performance (wearing PPE, lifting properly, reporting hazards, coaching peers, following procedures)

Figure 10.1. The Safety Triad, described by Geller (2001), provides the basis for effective behavior-based safety intervention. PPE = personal protective equipment.

be reliably measured through self-report and a body of research suggests a correspondence between what people say and what they do (e.g., Bandura, 1997; Boyce & Geller, 1999; Rogers-Warren & Baer, 1976).

Building an effective health and safety culture requires employees to accept responsibility for the health and safety of themselves *and* others. That is, employees need to be motivated to *behave* in ways that set the healthy example and make the work *environment* more safe, while paying attention to individual *person* factors. In this way, employees are continually involved in the safety process. The relationship among these three dynamic factors is depicted in the Safety Triad (Geller, 1996) presented in Figure 10.1.

For motivating health and safety, however, behavior is the key factor. Specifically, it is best to first motivate safety-related behaviors because attitudes will follow (cf. Festinger, 1957). That is, targeting behaviors directly for intervention (e.g., written prompts, behavioral feedback, incentive or rewards, and self-management) leads to changes in behavior that prevent injury and ultimately can result in attitude change. And, more behavior change leads to more attitude change, and so on. Regardless, in most cases of work-related injuries and illness, people's attitudes are not harming them, their behaviors are. Therefore, a good wellness program will first target behaviors directly for change, involve intervention agents to support changes in behavior, and provide the resources necessary to keep the effort involved in making healthy choices at a minimum (Winett, 1995). In fact, Winett and others have argued that if salad bar establishments were as available as fast-food hamburger establishments, more people would be eating salads.

A Flow of Behavior Change Model for Large-Scale Intervention

To maximize the effectiveness of a health and safety program, we must understand the source of at-risk behavior. From the perspective of behavior analysis, people behave for two reasons: (a) to receive pleasant consequences and (b) to escape or avoid unpleasant consequences. However, not all consequences are created equal. Specifically, research has shown that, all else remaining the same, consequences that occur soon after a response, are certain to occur when the response occurs, and are sufficient enough in size to be wanted or avoided will be more effective than consequences that are improbable, delayed, and insufficient. Given this, it is easy to understand why unhealthy responses or bad habits are acquired.

Consider the natural consequences of smoking. When someone lights a cigarette, they often do so "during a break from work." The cigarette is often correlated with escape from a potentially aversive work situation. In addition, with each puff of the cigarette, the smoker ingests nicotine, which directly affects the pleasure centers of the brain (immediate, sizable, and certain reinforcement), and often smokers congregate together such that pleasant social consequences may also maintain smoking behavior. On the other hand, the natural negative consequences of smoking, although sizeable (e.g., illness or death), are not certain (many smokers never do get sick), and are delayed (the effects of smoking are cumulative over years of smoking).

Our experiences with the consequences of behavior tell us what outcome to expect if engaging in different behaviors (Bandura, 1997; Skinner, 1953). As Malott (2001) suggested, if a smoker were told "you will certainly die 10 years from the time of your first puff of cigarette smoke," few people would ever start smoking. However, this is not the case. The negative health consequences of many health and safety behaviors are too delayed and not probable enough to have an impact on current behavior, relative to the more immediate and desirable positive consequences of the at-risk behavior. In short, an effective wellness program needs to compete with the natural consequences of the at-risk behavior.

Characteristics of Behavior and Behavioral Intervention

Certain interventions work better or worse depending on the relationship between the complex factors of the Safety Triad and whether the target behavior is other-directed, self-directed, or automatic (Watson & Tharp, 1997). Most operant or "voluntary" safety behavior starts as a result of following instructions or modeling the example set by someone else. Behavior with this characteristic has been called "other-directed" (Geller, 2001) presumably because it is motivated by powerful social consequences rather than directly by the consequences the behavior itself produces.

After initial learning, some people may internalize the instructions and make adjustments in their behavior as a result of the knowledge they have acquired. Indeed, if behavior cannot be attributed to response–consequence contingencies that are soon, certain, and sizable enough to shape behavior, rules can be said to control the behavior. Such behavior is considered rule-governed (Malott, 1992) and has been called "self-directed" (Geller, 2001). It presumably results from mediation by the individual performer him or herself (Boyce & Geller, 2001; Stokes & Baer, 1977), as when in organizational settings, safety behaviors may be prompted by warning signs and maintained by a written commitment to perform them (cf. Geller & Lehman, 1991).

Finally, if the behavior has been performed consistently and frequently for a period of time it can appear automatic. In this case, responding is said to be fluent. Fluent behavior is likely maintained by the reinforcing consequences produced directly by the response. At this point we often say that a habit has been formed. This habit may be desirable or harmful depending on the consequences it provides. Regardless, fluent responding is easily retained, can be performed over long periods of time, and can be applied in a variety of settings and in the face of distraction (Binder, 1996). These are certainly desirable characteristics in the context of healthy behaviors, but also contribute to the difficulty of changing an at-risk habit as described previously. For this reason it is important to understand the history of consequences an individual has with respect to a health-related behavior that is targeted for intervention.

The Basics of Behavior Change

In the behavior-based safety literature, relationships among environmental antecedents, behaviors, and the consequences produced by the behaviors have been studied to understand why certain at-risk behaviors occur. As depicted in Figure 10.2, the three-term contingency (i.e., antecedent–behavior–consequence [A-B-C] model) is the cornerstone of analyzing behavior and designing effective behavior-improvement interventions (Geller, 1996; Skinner, 1953). Put simply, antecedents, such as safety signs, education, policies, and incentives are thought to direct behavior. That is, they provide instructional information or tell us what to do. Antecedents are useful when it has been determined that health and safety problems are a

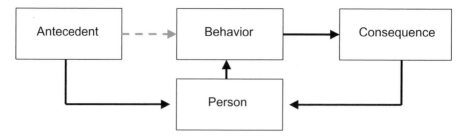

Figure 10.2. The antecedent–behavior–consequence model of behavior analysis demonstrating sensitivity of current contingencies to individual differences.

result of workers not "knowing" what to do. If workers know what to do and understand the rationale for behaving in a healthy manner (e.g., avoiding injury), more education and training will not increase the frequency of desired behaviors. In fact, a significant amount of money has been wasted by organizations who all too often "re-train" employees as a means of correcting undesired performance (Binder, 1998). If employees know what to do, they do not need more information. They need motivation. Indeed, Boyce and Geller (1999) demonstrated that an industry-based program to motivate safety-belt use among workers at a manufacturing facility was only effective when the intervention provided a consequence more probable and sizable than the threat of a fine resulting from a statewide belt-use law.

Consequences, such as feedback, praise, rewards, or penalties, are said to motivate behavior. With our knowledge that people generally behave to get pleasant consequences or to avoid unpleasant consequences, we can understand that consequence-focused interventions are best when people know what to do, but don't do it regularly (Geller, 2001). Specifically, we are more likely to engage in behaviors that produce desirable out-comes or help us escape or avoid undesirable outcomes. Effective response–consequence contingencies can be arranged by others in the work environment. However, for health-related behaviors, self-management interventions may be required. Self-management is presumed to gain its effectiveness from a self-directed perspective (Geller, 2001), and it is in this sense the contingencies are thought to be mediated by the individual (Boyce & Geller, 2001).

Although people will reliably respond to remove themselves from or prevent aversive situations, punishment is often ineffective because it is not administered consistently or soon after a behavior that is not wanted. Therefore, punishment as a behavior change strategy is not recommended because most people respond to punishment only if the person who can enforce a policy (e.g., a police officer) is present. On the other hand, positive consequences tend to be "relived" (Geller, 2001) and produce longer-term, more durable behavior change presumably because they invoke easier to follow rules (Malott, 2001). Using positive consequences also prevents the occurrence of unwanted side effects such as acting out, which is often produced by punishment. This phenomenon was described by Skinner (1971) as *countercontrol*. Countercontrol can undermine the benefits of an intervention to increase safety and health, because it often results in the appearance of other at-risk behaviors (O'Neill, Lund, & Ashton, 1985).

To summarize, a motivational intervention cannot benefit people unaware of certain risks or the appropriate safe behavior. And, instructional or awareness signs will not influence the behaviors of those already aware of the risks, but who choose to take the risk anyway. People at the self-directed and automatic stages will not benefit from a motivational intervention, but may be amenable to a self-management intervention. It is presumed that in organizations with poor safety records, motivation for safety is lacking because the consequences for competing responses, such as production and free time, are more powerful than the consequences for working safely.

Characteristics of Behavior-Based Health and Safety Processes

The behavior-based approach to achieving an effective safety culture is a process of involving workers in defining the ways they are most likely to be injured, seeking their involvement and obtaining their buy-in, and asking them to observe coworkers to determine progress in the reduction of at-risk behaviors (Geller, 1996). This may be accomplished by a core group of "in-house" facilitators who champion the process or by each worker with minimal efforts and time requirements. As summarized from Geller (1996, 2001), following is a list of six principles identified and described by behavioral scientists to be definitive of behavior-based safety. These characteristics are best achieved with a simple observation and feedback process. Making observations a regular part of the workday can serve as an antecedent and direct appropriate safety-related behaviors. Using the information obtained from observations to provide workers feedback on safety improvement (or areas in need of attention) is a consequence that can motivate desired changes in safety-related behaviors.

The six defining characteristics of behavioral safety include the following:

1. Focus interventions on observable behaviors.
2. Look for external (system) factors to both understand and improve behaviors.
3. Direct behaviors with activators; motivate behaviors with consequences.
4. Focus on positive consequences.

Critical Behavior Checklist for Personal Protective Equipment

Observation period (dates): _____

Observer: _____

	TOTAL NUMBER OF EMPLOYEES OBSERVED	NUMBER OF EMPLOYEES OBSERVED USING ALL REQUIRED PPE

PPE (For Observed Area)	SAFE OBSERVATION (Proper Use of PPE)	AT-RISK OBSERVATION (Improper or No Use of PPE)
Gloves		
Safety Glasses/Shield		
Hearing Protection		
Safety Shoes		
Hard Hat		
Lifting Belt		
TOTAL		

Figure 10.3. A typical critical behavior checklist for making behavioral observations and quantifying the significance of health and safety behavior problems and intervention effectiveness. PPE = personal protective equipment.

5. Apply the scientific method to develop, improve, and evaluate interventions.
6. Use theory to integrate information, but not limit possibilities.

Behavioral observations are the key to a successful behavior-based safety process and necessary for building an effective safety culture. Observations are made using a "critical behavior checklist" such as one depicted in Figure 10.3.

If done properly, organizations will see increased employee ownership of workplace health and safety, improved worker morale, increased management–worker communication, and improved productivity and quality. These will also lead to a reduction in worker injuries and worker compensation costs. The literature has demonstrated straightforward and unmistakable benefits of a BBS approach for reducing work-related injuries (cf. Guastello, 1993).

EFFECTS OF BEHAVIOR-BASED SAFETY
AT A LARGE MANUFACTURING FACILITY

The study reported next highlights the implementation and benefits of a behavior-based safety (BBS) intervention in a work environment. The description of research and data were adapted from Geller, Boyce, DePasquale, Pettinger, and Williams (1998).

Participants and Setting

Participants were 476 hourly and salary employees at an engine bearing manufacturing plant in southwest Virginia. The population of employees ranged in age from 19 to 63 years (M = 42), and employee tenure at the facility ranged from 6 months to more than 25 years (M = 16). The proportion of hourly to salary workers was approximately five to one, and the workforce and hours worked were stable throughout the course of the study.

Procedure

The BBS process began by training volunteer safety facilitators from representative work areas on first shift ($n = 8$) and second shift ($n = 6$) in the basic principles and procedures of this approach. Following two intensive 8-hour education and training sessions for the safety facilitators, the remaining employees across three shifts received a 4-hour version of BBS education and training.

Both shifts implemented the same customized BBS process. Specifically, for 9 weeks the safety facilitators of the Shift 1 workers ($n = 230$) and Shift 2 workers ($n = 210$) made behavioral observations. Observations were made on behavioral checklists designed by the Shift 1 facilitators and distributed to Shift 2 facilitators. On each shift, one facilitator was responsible for collecting completed observation cards. These data were collected two times a month at facilitator meetings scheduled and led by a research assistant.

Data were graphed and posted on a safety bulletin board located at the highly traveled entrance to the production areas. Facilitator involvement was assessed by the number of observations taken on each shift.

Results

Figure 10.4 depicts a cumulative record of this organization's lost work-days for 18 months prior to and 18 months following the BBS process. The figure shows a marked decrease in lost days due to injuries following the introduction of BBS education and training, observation and feedback, and

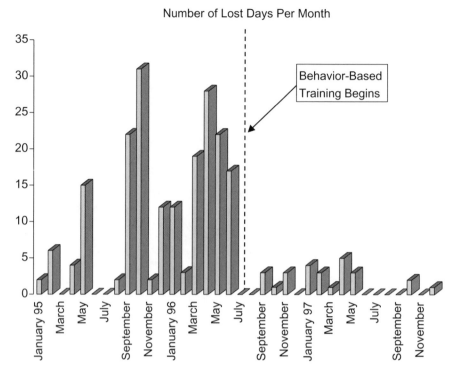

Figure 10.4. Lost workdays incurred by the organization studied in Pettinger, Boyce, and Geller (in press) prior to and after the introduction of a comprehensive behavior-based safety intervention.

several additional intervention processes. Specifically, a mean of 10.9 lost days ($n = 197$) per month occurred prior to BBS; whereas after the intervention, a mean of 1.4 days ($n = 26$) were lost per month due to injury.

In addition, on the basis of the average cost per injury at this facility for the 2 years prior to the introduction of BBS, this prominent reduction in lost workdays was reported by the organization to have saved approximately $200,000 in worker's compensation. The cost of the entire BBS process was approximately $55,000. This is a net savings of $145,000 over the course of 18 months.

Conclusion

Behavior-based approaches to injury control have several advantages over other approaches: (a) they can be administered by individuals with minimal professional training, (b) they can reach people in the setting in which the problems occur (e.g., assembly line or administrative office), and (c) the leaders in these settings can be taught the behavior-change tech-

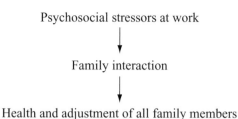

Psychosocial stressors at work

↓

Family interaction

↓

Health and adjustment of all family members

Figure 10.5. The social-ecological approach to occupational health suggests that family outcomes are associated with parental job stressors that are reported by work–family researchers.

niques most likely to work under specific circumstances. Research has also shown this approach to be cost-effective, primarily because behavior-change techniques are straightforward and relatively easy to administer, and because intervention progress can be readily assessed by on-site personnel monitoring target behaviors.

Behavior-based approaches to safety focus on systematically studying the effects of various interventions on target behaviors by first defining the target behavior in a directly observable and recordable way. The behavior is then observed and recorded in its natural setting. Finally, interventions based on the A-B-C model assist in directing and motivating healthy choices in settings in which the natural consequences of behaving typically promote risk.

PARENTS' EXPERIENCES AT WORK AND THEIR CHILDREN'S HEALTH

A social-ecological perspective on human development and health calls our attention not only to the immediate settings in which individuals live, such as their work and family environments, but also to the relations among those settings and the larger social contexts in which the settings are embedded (Bronfenbrenner, 1989). This approach encourages us to consider the consequences of psychosocial factors at work not merely for the worker him- or herself, but also for the quality of life in his or her family and, ultimately, the health and development of all family members. This perspective is illustrated here by a discussion of research on psychosocial stressors at work and health outcomes in children. As shown in Figure 10.5, the general model underlying this research suggests that stress at work has an impact on the employed individual's behavior at home. According to the model, if stress at work is chronic, it can influence stable patterns of family interaction. Over time, social relationships in the family influence the health and adjustment of all members.

Work–Family Research

The work–family research literature suggests that occupational factors can play a role in shaping the quality of family life, particularly parent–child interaction. (See Perry-Jenkins, Repetti, & Crouter, 2000, for an overview.) Several work–family processes have been studied. For example, some investigators have examined socialization that can take place at work, examining occupational conditions like the complexity of tasks performed and autonomy at work as predictors of parenting style. Greenberger, O'Neil, and Nagel (1994) found that parents whose jobs were more complex offered verbal explanations to their children that were of higher quality than was the case for parents with less complex work. Another line of work considers the transfer of job stress into the family. This research literature suggests that chronic occupational stress can lead to greater parent–child conflict and less parental nurturing, particularly when job stress is associated with feelings of overload or role conflict (conflict between the roles of worker and parent; Perry-Jenkins et al., 2000).

Some work–family researchers have attempted to study how stress at work affects behavior at home by observing the short-term association between a stressful day at work and family interaction later that evening. The evidence suggests that there are at least two short-term behavioral responses to daily job stress. One, *negative emotion spillover,* occurs when feelings of frustration, anger, or disappointment at work lead to greater irritability, impatience, or more power assertion at home (Repetti, 1994). The other, *social withdrawal,* occurs when parents withdraw both behaviorally and emotionally from family interaction following high stress days at work (Repetti, 1994; Repetti & Wood, 1997). Social withdrawal may be an adaptive response, at least in the short-run. Withdrawal may help adults to cope in the short term with certain types of stressors (Repetti, 1992), and it may also buffer the transmission of negative emotions from parents to their children (Larson & Gillman, 1999).

However, under conditions of chronic occupational stress, the cumulative effects of daily stressors appear to have little or no beneficial effects. A negative long-term impact can be observed both in the employed individual's emotional and psychological functioning, and in interactions with children that become less sensitive and responsive, and more negative and conflictual (Perry-Jenkins et al., 2000). Research in this area suggests that occupational stressors, such as work pressure, poor supervision, and a negative social climate at work, are often linked to parent–child outcomes through individual psychological mediators, such as feelings of role overload, work–family conflicts, and psychological distress (e.g., Crouter, Bumpus, Maguire, & McHale, 1999; Galambos, Sears, Almeida, & Kolaric, 1995; Greenberger et al., 1994; MacDermid & Williams, 1997; Repetti, 1994).

These consistent findings in the research literature do not necessarily reflect uniform effects of job stress. Individual, family, and social context differences exert important influences on the transfer of stress from work to family. Responses to occupational stressors are shaped by individual differences in personality, health, coping style, and social support resources. Other characteristics of the job, such as the nature of the work being performed and the number and flexibility of work hours, as well as family characteristics, such as marital satisfaction and the number and ages of children in the home, are critical in shaping stress transfer processes (Perry-Jenkins et al., 2000). Thus, although research suggests that chronic job stress can have a long-term negative impact on the parent–child relationship, those associations are moderated by individual differences and other social context factors.

The Link to Children's Health

How might parents' experiences with stress at work influence the health and well-being of their offspring? My colleagues Shelley Taylor and Teresa Seeman and I (Rena Repetti) have argued that because much social, emotional, and biological development takes place through interactions with family members, the family social environment is a critical starting point for understanding health trajectories throughout life. Our review of research literatures in several different fields suggested that certain family characteristics create a cascade of risk, one that begins early in life by creating vulnerabilities (and exacerbating preexisting biological vulnerabilities) that lay the groundwork for long-term physical and mental health problems (Repetti, Taylor, & Seeman, 2002). The risky family characteristics fall into two broad categories: overt family conflict, as manifested in recurrent episodes of anger and aggression, and deficient nurturing, especially family relationships that are cold, unsupportive, and neglectful. Our model describes a succession of developmental processes whose course can be influenced by risky family environments. According to the model, early disruptions in the processes continue to have an impact on development in future stages. For example, disturbances in physiologic and neuroendocrine system regulation, especially dysregulated biological responses to stress, can have cumulative long-term adverse effects on health. Deficits in the processing of emotions and in social competence are the two other key developmental pathways through which family environments may influence long-term physical and mental health.

The risky families model can contribute to the social-ecological approach to occupational health described here. The family outcomes associated with parental job stressors that are reported by work–family researchers—less sensitive and responsive, and more negative and conflictual, parent–child interactions (Perry-Jenkins et al., 2000)—are risky family characteristics. Thus, the risky families analysis supports the second half of the model depicted in Figure 10.5 by suggesting a set of processes that link family interaction with child health. To the extent that parental job stressors result in family social interactions that are less sensitive and supportive, or more negative and conflictual, there will be an impact on the development of children's biological responses to stress, emotion regulation, and social competence. According to the risky families model, these developmental processes have cascading effects over time, with clinical and subclinical manifestations of problems in mental and physical health most frequently manifested later in life (Repetti et al., 2002).

In the work–family research literature, findings of a direct association between an individual's experiences of stress at work and the well-being of other family members are often referred to as *cross-over effects*. These effects are often elusive, sometimes observed, sometimes not (Perry-Jenkins et al., 2000). There are at least three reasons why cross-over effects have been difficult to detect, particularly in small heterogeneous samples. As explained next, cross-over effects are weak, they are variable, and researchers may be looking in the wrong places for them. First, and most obviously, cross-over effects are relatively weak. There are multiple biological, environmental, and behavioral factors that are direct sources of influence on physical and emotional well-being. As has been argued here, parents' occupations have an *indirect* influence; the effects of stress at work are mediated through their impact on parents and the parent–child relationship. Second, cross-over effects are variable. As suggested above, work–family linkages are moderated by individual differences and other social context factors. As a result, there are significant differences among families in their vulnerability to the effects of parental job stressors; some individuals and families may be immune to the negative effects of job stress (Perry-Jenkins et al., 2000)

Third, and perhaps most important, researchers may be searching for cross-over effects in the wrong places. To successfully integrate a social-ecological approach into research on occupational and family health, it is important to correctly identify the "health outcome" of interest. According to the risky families model, the impact of family relationships on adjustment and health are usually not observed until adolescence or adulthood (Repetti et al., 2002). Instead, during childhood, work–family cross-over effects would be most likely found in the intermediate pathways. These dysregulated developmental processes then act as precursors to physical and mental health outcomes observed in adolescence and adulthood. Therefore, work–family researchers interested in assessing the effects of parental job stressors on children should consider assessing their regulation of biological, emotional, and social responses, especially in stressful situations.

Conclusion

A social-ecological perspective on health and development suggests that parents' experiences at work have an impact on the family social environment and the health and development of all family members. This section has focused on the potential negative consequences of stressors at work for families and child development, highlighting current knowledge in this area and promising directions for future research.

WHEN WORK LIFE ENDS: PLANNING AHEAD FOR HEALTHY RETIREMENT

Millions of Americans are over 40, thinking about retirement, and planning for it by saving a lot of money in their 401Ks, eating well, and exercising. They are going to live longer than any generation before them, and many of them are retiring earlier than their parents did. They will have 25 years and more good quality life when their work life ends. Unless they begin to consider how they will spend their time postretirement, we will have a major segment of our population that is healthy, wealthy, and bored. Psychologists have the opportunity to direct people's attention to planning how they will spend their time when their work life ends. And further, we can help people to explore themselves in a way that will help them to find the best answers for them and their individual needs and interests. We can help them answer the question: "What do you want to do when you grow up?"

Growing Up Is a Lifelong Process

Growth does not end at age 20. It is a lifelong process of recreating yourself as circumstances change. In a well-lived life, growth only stops when we die. Each life is a work in progress. That means that change is always possible.

Growth is an essential life component. It is as vital as meeting our existential needs (that is, the material and physical things we need to survive) and our reference needs (our need to be with others).

The common wisdom is that people die when they retire. In truth, although some die, most do not. Rather, clinical experience tells us that many become depressed. Even people who "retire" from childrearing and homemaking may suffer: Studies of empty-nest women who had not been gradually increasing their interests and activities over the years found the women to feel lost, aimless, and depressed (Cooper & Gutmann, 1987). They, too, had lost their jobs. One man sold his successful retail business at 55, moved to Florida, and was thrilled at the prospect of playing golf every day. Six months later he was depressed and told his son, "I'm no Arnold Palmer." He decided to follow his lifetime passion for the stock market. He studied, took the necessary exams, and spent the rest of his life as a stockbroker. He never worked excessively. He did not need the money. But he was never depressed, either, and he continued to play golf on weekends, as he had all his life.

Carol Ryff (1995) has described six dimensions of adult well-being. They are

1. Self-acceptance,
2. Positive relations with others,
3. Autonomy,
4. Environmental mastery,
5. Purpose in life, and
6. Personal growth.

Ryff noted that the first four stay fairly stable throughout an adult life. But older adults come up short on the last two. They lack goals, directedness, and aims, and they stop developing and expanding. The result is a diminished sense of well-being. But it is a preventable phenomenon if psychologists help people plan their lives as they age. We can provide "retirement inoculation."

Understanding the Role of Work in Life

The first step in the process is coming to a realization of the role that work plays in our lives. Ask people to list 15 things that they get from their work besides money. This exercise is designed to get them to think beyond the usual "I have enough money to retire" and the notion that money is the only reward of work. Responses run the gamut from status and power, to a place to go every day, to social interaction, and weekends. In other words, people come to recognize that in addition to the financial aspect of work meaning, there are social (interactive) and psychological (self-image) aspects (Mor-Barak, 1995). Clearly, whatever people do beyond their work lives will have to offer many of the important rewards that they got from work.

Another telling exercise is to complete the sentence, "I am a _____." Most people fill in the blank with their occupation or job title. If they have no other interests, they have lost their identity when they stopped working. In his book, *The Virtues of Aging* (Carter, 1998), former President Jimmy Carter "names" himself thusly,

> At different times in my life I have introduced myself as a submariner, farmer, warehouseman, state senator, governor, or even president, if that was necessary. I might have added where I lived, but that was about it. Now, even though not holding a steady job, I could reply that

I am a professor, author, fly fisherman, or woodworker. I could add American, southerner, Christian, married or grandfather. (pp. 89–90)

Keeping a variety of identities and options going, he writes, "is a good indication of the vitality of our existence."

If what you do is a good fit with who you are, at any age, you will be more content and satisfied. If you are so engrossed that you wonder where the time went, you feel happier. "Fit" increases the likelihood of being involved in that way. Our task as psychologists is to help people find that "fit" for themselves, by helping them embark on a process of self-evaluation.

Reviewing Life at Various Stages

Those of us who work psychodynamically consider that the clue to who we are now lies in what happened to us earlier in our lives. Thus, the best source of that "fit" is a historic view of one's development, with particular focus on the questions that relate to occupational and avocational choices. We can lead people through a review of their childhood and adolescence, their main working years, and the great plateau of midlife.

For example, we can ask people what they dreamed of being as children. Few became what they dreamed of being. But in that dream lies a first clue as to what intrigued them as children, and might be rekindled. Why do we give up those early dreams? We see them as impractical, like the man who did not think he could support himself as a director or producer, but in retirement is on the Board of Directors of a prominent theater company in a major city, and also directs plays at his grandchildren's school. We are influenced by our parents, like the woman who did not become a nurse because her mother said she would just be emptying bedpans. Today, she volunteers at a hospice, where among the other things she does, she empties bedpans. We follow the crowd and do what our peers are doing. Women in my generation became secretaries, nurses, or teachers, and did not see any other possibilities for themselves. We "fall into" some career path because our first job was in a particular industry and there we stay for life. The dream may not be one that can be fulfilled now, but it holds a clue to who we were and what excited and motivated us in our early years. The kid who wanted to be an astronaut has grown into the adult who would like adventure and challenging frontiers.

Another telling question is who our heroes and heroines have been. Thinking about the characteristics of those whom we admire is often a clue to what we would like to be ourselves. Sometimes, as in the case of former Texas governor Ann Richards, the only available heroine has been fictitious because no strong women have been available to emulate (Cantor & Bernay, 1992).

We can look at how we made our choices in the central core of life. Did we choose a college ourselves? Did we select a major because it really intrigued us or because it was what was expected? We need to consider some questions about our first job. Did we choose it intentionally or take what was available? Did we give ourselves freedom to experiment? Did we go for the safe and sure, or the brash and brave? Did we follow a path dictated by family expectations, or one in revengeful rejection of those family expectations? Were our earliest job experiences exciting and exhilarating or disappointing and discouraging?

It is important to honestly appraise what we love and hate about work, as well as what we are good and not good at doing. Listen to Jack, a school guidance counselor:

> I'm pretty good at interacting with the students and with some of the other counselors and teachers. I like helping the kids with some of their personal problems. On the downside, I hate the paperwork, especially totally pointless reports. Can't stand gabby workshops that I have to attend. (Cantor, 2000, p. 132)

He knows what he *doesn't* want to do when he retires!

Knowing What Motivates Us

In planning for the future, it is important to appraise what has motivated us in life. Some motivators to consider are the degree to which we need intellectual activity, physical activity, spiritual attention, friendships, family attachments, and applause and recognition. We need to consider our general activity comfort level. That is, are we at the couch potato or whirling dervish end of the activity scale? We also need to assess our risk comfort level. Some of us are more comfortable with the familiar, tried, and true. Others enjoy the excitement of the unknown. Knowing where we are comfortable will help direct our choice of postwork activity.

Knowing What Activates Us

Further refinement of the planning process comes from knowing our strong suits and roadblocks. People need to understand that their roadblocks, or resistances, are not bad qualities, but rather characteristics of themselves that need to be taken into account so that they will not get in the way. The goal is to name them and work with or around them. Here are a few examples.

When it comes to initiating action, the strong suit is being a self-starter. The person with a roadblock recognizes the need for a push, and having recognized it, takes some actions. These might be finding a "pusher," or pushing oneself by creating a structure and designing self-assignments.

Another consideration is setting reasonable goals. The strong suit is setting goals that are within reach or a slight stretch. The roadblock is setting goals so high that they discourage any attempt to meet them or so low that achievement is not gratifying. For older people, well-being occurs when they revise their goals to reflect possibilities as well as the limitations for achievement and maintenance.

Other activators to be considered are how well we make choices, proceed independently, overcome obstacles, change course, strike a balance, follow through, experience a sense of achievement, and find pleasure.

It helps to recapture a childlike way of learning, thinking, and being. Too often, as people get older, they get stuck in familiar ways of doing things and are loath to try new things for risk of failing, or looking foolish. We need to encourage people to be curious, gather information, find people to play with, find people who will help, take chances, make mistakes, and proceed with trial and error. If we can behave that way again, we can experiment with new passions, try something new and reject it if it is not what we imagined, and move on until we find the good "fit" we were looking for.

Conclusion

It can be said that we are not old as long as we have goals and purpose in life. Those goals can shift and change as we age, but they must be ever present. This is a process to be revisited every several years, as a means of reevaluating and planning. When we have helped people to adopt this way of thinking about their postwork years, we will have provided them with the tools they need to make the rest of their lives gratifying. They will remain mentally healthy into old, old age.

SOME FINAL THOUGHTS

Psychologists have been present in the workplace for many years, in the defined role of industrial-organizational psychologists. They have provided myriad services that have been valued and appreciated by the corporate sector.

What we have suggested here is an expanded view of psychology's potential contribution to the workplace, particularly in the sphere of health. We have talked about health in terms of occupational safety, children's well-being, and postwork life. These are but a sample of the ways in which psychologists can be of service. Over the next decades, we will be seeing new applications of psychological research and interventions in the workplace. It makes consummate sense. Adults spend about one-third of their time at work. If that is where they are, then that is where the best of psychological science and practice must reach them.

REFERENCES

Bandura, A. (1997). *Self-efficacy: The exercise of control*. New York: W. H. Freeman.

Binder, C. (1996). Behavioral fluency: Evolution of a new paradigm. *The Behavior Analyst, 19*, 163–197.

Binder, C. (1998). The six boxes™: A descendent of Gilbert's behavior engineering model. *Performance Improvement, 37*(6), 48–52.

Boyce, T. E., & Geller, E. S. (1999). Attempts to increase vehicle safety-belt use among industry workers: What can we learn from our failures? *Journal of Organizational Behavior Management, 19*, 27–44.

Boyce, T. E., & Geller, E. S. (2001). Applied behavior analysis and occupational safety: The challenge of response maintenance. *Journal of Organizational Behavior Management, 21*(1), 31–60.

Bronfenbrenner, U. (1989). Ecological systems theory. In R. Vasta (Ed.), *Annals of child development: A research annual. Vol. 6: Six theories of child development: Revised formulations and current issues* (pp. 187–249). Greenwich, CT: JAI Press.

Cantor, D. W. (2000). *What do you want to do when you grow up?* New York: Little, Brown & Co.

Cantor, D. W., & Bernay, T. (1992). *Women in power: The secrets of leadership*. Boston: Houghton-Mifflin.

Carter, J. (1998). *The virtues of aging*. New York: Ballantine Books.

Cooper, K. I., & Gutmann, D. L. (1987). Gender identity and ego mastery style in middle-aged, pre-and post-empty nest women. *Gerontologist, 27*, 347–352.

Crouter, A. C., Bumpus, M. F., Maguire, M. C., & McHale, S. M. (1999). Linking parents' work pressure and adolescents' well-being: Insights into dynamics in dual-earner families. *Developmental Psychology, 35*, 1453–1461.

Festinger, L. (1957). *A theory of cognitive dissonance*. Stanford, CA: Stanford University Press.

Galambos, N. L., Sears, H. A., Almeida, D. M., & Kolaric, G. C. (1995). Parents' work overload and problem behavior in young adolescents. *Journal of Research on Adolescence, 5*(2), 201–223.

Geller, E. S. (1996). *The psychology of safety*. Boca Raton, FL: CRC Press.

Geller, E. S. (2001). *Psychology of safety handbook*. Boca Raton, FL: CRC Press.

Geller, E. S., Boyce, T. E., DePasquale, J. P., Pettinger, C. B., & Williams, J. W. (1998). *Critical success factors for behavior-based safety*. Final report submitted to the National Institute for Occupational Safety and Health (Grant #1 RO1 OH03374-01/02).

Geller, E. S., & Lehman, G. R. (1991). The buckle-up promise card: A versatile intervention for large-scale behavior change. *Journal of Applied Behavior Analysis, 24,* 91–94.

Greenberger, E., O'Neil, R., & Nagel, S. K. (1994). Linking workplace and homeplace: Relations between the nature of adults' work and their parenting behaviors. *Developmental Psychology, 30,* 990–1002.

Guastello, S. J. (1993). Do we really know how well our occupational accident prevention programs work? *Safety Science, 21,* 445–463.

Larson, R. W., & Gillman, S. (1999). Transmission of emotions in the daily interactions of single-mother families. *Journal of Marriage and the Family, 61,* 21–37.

MacDermid, S. M., & Williams, M. L. (1997). A within-industry comparison of employed mothers' experiences in small and large workplaces. *Journal of Family Issues, 18,* 545–566.

Malott, R. W. (1992). A theory of rule-governed behavior and organizational behavior management. *Journal of Organizational Behavior Management, 12,* 45–65.

Malott, R. W. (2001). Occupational safety and response maintenance: An alternate view. *Journal of Organizational Behavior Management, 21,* 85–102.

Mor-Barak, M. E. (1995). The meaning of work for older adults seeking employment: The generativity factor. *International Journal of Aging and Human Development, 41,* 325–344.

O'Neill, B., Lund, A. K., & Ashton, S. (1985). Mandatory belt use and driver risk taking: An empirical evaluation of the risk compensation hypothesis. In L. Evans & R. Schwing (Eds.), *Human behavior and traffic safety* (pp. 93–107). New York: Plenum Press.

Perry-Jenkins, M., Repetti, R. L., & Crouter, A. C. (2000). Work and family in the 1990's. *Journal of Marriage and the Family, 62,* 981–998.

Pettinger, C. B., Boyce, T. E., & Geller, E. S. (in press). Behavior-based safety and employee involvement: Differential effects during training versus implementation. *Journal of Safety Research.*

Repetti, R. L. (1992). Social withdrawal as a short-term coping response to daily stressors. In H. S. Friedman (Ed.), *Hostility, coping, and health* (pp. 151–165). Washington, DC: American Psychological Association.

Repetti, R. L. (1994). Short-term and long-term processes linking job stressors to father–child interaction. *Social Development, 3,* 1–15.

Repetti, R. L., Taylor, S. E., & Seeman, T. E. (2002). Risky families: Family social environments and the mental and physical health of offspring. *Psychological Bulletin, 128,* 330–366.

Repetti, R., & Wood, J. (1997). The effects of daily stress at work on mothers' interactions with preschoolers. *Journal of Family Psychology, 11,* 90–108.

Rogers-Warren, A., & Baer, D. M. (1976). Correspondence between saying and doing: Teaching children to share and praise. *Journal of Applied Behavior Analysis, 9,* 335–354.

Ryff, C. D. (1995). Psychological well-being in adult life. *Current Directions in Psychological Science, 4,* 99–103.

Skinner, B. F. (1953). *Science and human behavior.* New York: Macmillan.

Skinner, B. F. (1971). *Beyond freedom and dignity.* New York: Knopf.

Stokes, T. F., & Baer, D. M. (1977). An implicit technology of generalization. *Journal of Applied Behavior Analysis, 10,* 349–367.

Watson, D. L., & Tharp, R. G. (1997). *Self-directed behavior: Self-modification for personal adjustment* (3rd ed.). Monterey, CA: Brooks/Cole.

Winett, R. A. (1995). A framework for health promotion and disease prevention programs. *American Psychologist, 50,* 341–350.

IV

AFTERWORD

FUTURE DIRECTIONS FOR PSYCHOLOGY AND HEALTH

NORINE G. JOHNSON

There comes a moment in time that lets the future in.
—Robert Kennedy

Psychology is at that moment in time of which Robert Kennedy spoke. We are at the threshold of a major leap forward in expanding the role of our science and practice in the design and implementation of health services and policy within our nation. The research is clear; any division between mind and body is arbitrary, capricious, and detrimental to the health of individuals, families, communities, and our nation. With the bylaw approval of change in the American Psychological Association's (APA) mission statement, organized psychology has declared to itself and to others that it is a health discipline and that we, as psychologists, have as a primary mission the promotion of health.

First let us look at what we are doing to recognize the major role of health within our discipline by briefly reviewing recent actions within APA's central office. Then I will suggest a five-part vision for psychology in the future in which psychology collaborates with others, using state of the art research and interventions, to build a healthy world.

AMERICAN PSYCHOLOGICAL ASSOCIATION
HEALTH-RELATED ACTIVITIES

In 2001–2002 Russ Newman, PhD, JD, Executive Director of the APA Practice Directorate, chaired an APA work group which reviewed health-related activities within the association. These activities provide a telescopic lens for looking into psychology's future directions in health as they span a breadth of psychology research, education, practice, public information, and policy initiatives.

Psychology scientists are looking at the role of behavior in health promotion and disease prevention. Psychology educators are preparing health-related unit lesson plans for high school teachers and curriculums are changing across the educational spectrum from undergraduate to doctoral studies to reflect the increased knowledge regarding the role of psychology in health. Psychology public advocates are working on policies to reduce health disparities and to increase funding for psychology research and training in health related activities. The work continues on HIV/AIDS prevention, women's health, and issues in the workplace that promote health and enhance well-being.

Psychology practice activities include new procedure codes for the diagnosis and treatment by psychologists of patients with physical health diagnoses. In addition, the APA is working with the World Health Organization to develop an International Classification of Functioning, Disability, and Health that would provide an alternative system of diagnosis to the *Diagnostic and Statistical Manual of Mental Disorders* (4th ed.). The Practice Directorate facilitated psychology practice and research collaboration to study the effect of psychological interventions on cardiovascular disease and cancer. And, as noted earlier, the results are supportive of psychologically based interventions that both decrease the likelihood of future similar disease events and potentially lower medical cost.

A VISION FOR PSYCHOLOGY AND HEALTH

There are five parts to the vision of psychology that emerged from the "Psychology Builds a Healthy World" initiative. The following discussion includes a vision in which there would be (a) endorsement of a biopsychosocial model of health research and health care; (b) increased collaborative involvement of psychology and psychologists in health research and health care; (c) expansion of biopsychosocial health education and training; (d) enactment of health policies that increase access, reduce health disparities, and promote improved quality of life as well as prolonging life; and (e) a public better informed of the psychosocial aspects of health.

Enact a Biopsychosocial Model of Health Research and Health Care

The first vision is that our nation, including federal, state, and local governments, would enact a biopsychosocial model of health research and health care. Structural and funding changes consistent with the model would be incorporated and programs inconsistent with the model would be replaced. The first to go should be policy that allows the capricious carve-out of mental health services within some managed care systems. The public health system would become more collaborative as behavioral interventions joined medical interventions to address the contributing cultural causes of death and injury. There would be a prioritizing of research to correct the imbalance noted in the 10/90 report so that increased dollars would go for large-scale longitudinal research to investigate health interventions from a biopsychosocial perspective (Global Forum for Health Research, 2002). Report after report from national policy institutes pile on data to support a biopsychosocial model of health research and health care. A biopsychosocial model enables and encourages designing wellness and prevention research and interventions. The major killing illnesses of humans all have large psychosocial components. Psychological influences—behavior, cognition, and emotion, together with cultural influences such as race, ethnicity, socioeconomic status, and gender—account for, at a minimum, 50% of the death and illnesses in the United States. And yet, the structure and funding of our health care system is based on arcane divisions between the mind and the body. Isn't it time to remove the line between health and mental health and to develop a collaborative system of health care in our nation that provides access and quality for all? Endorsing a biopsychosocial model is a major step in equalizing and enhancing health care.

Increase Collaborative Involvement of Psychology and Psychologists in Health

Organized psychology must aggressively take the next steps in supporting psychologists' increased involvement in all areas of health. This means a concerted effort to obtain psychologists' expanded recognition as providers in health care delivery services, as primary investigators in health research efforts, and in interdisciplinary health education and training. Increased involvement of psychologists in multiyear collaborative health research would allow more of our scientists to devise complex research designs with multimodal interventions that investigate the impact of psychological, behavioral, and biological mechanisms on health outcomes.

The interest in nanoscience has increased funding and hence discoveries exponentially without a parallel investment in the psychological effects of such knowledge or the potential of such knowledge. It is not just psychologists or social scientists who are asking for another look at how our research dollars are allocated. In the April 2002 issue of *Science*, Jonathan Rees' essay decisively bemoaned the reduction in patient-oriented research for the heralded genocentric view of discovery. He concludes by stating that science is better served by a breadth of methods, including clinical science, which looks to "solving disease based on the experience of seeing, thinking about, and treating individual patients" (p. 701). This approach also recognizes the importance of psychological variables and individual practitioners.

Innumerable psychology researchers work in untold hundreds of areas of health: psychopharmacology, psychobiology, social neuroscience, and so forth. But there are still so many questions to be investigated. The vision of Psychology Builds a Healthy World embraces the conclusions of the Institute of Medicine report (2002) "Informing the Future": (a) societal-level phenomena are critical determinants of health; (b) population groups have a characteristic pattern of disease and injury over time; (c) the environmental approaches can be successful; and (d) behavioral interventions have succeeded in improving health behaviors.

Psychology researchers are doing critical investigations in all these areas but the amount of support is not comparable with the scope of the health problems being studied. A more even distribution of resources between biomedical and biopsychosocial research would be the first step in realigning our country's health resources with the health problems faced by our population.

Increased involvement of psychologists in using the next generation of psychological interventions would expand the benefits for patients of interventions based in psychological practice. Susan Pick (chap. 5, this volume) called for psychologists to develop and deliver practical applications of the research to intervene in the health lives of people throughout the world:

> We, as psychologists, have a unique opportunity to act as mediators for the application of the theories that serve as the basis for our academic and professional lives. By using the practical tools of program development, evaluation systems, and instrument development, we are able to apply our theories about human nature and behavior in ways that address the very practical needs of the populations we serve. . . . Now, more than ever before, there is a recognition of the importance of strengthening human capital as a means of strengthening economic and social development.

Changes in classification, new diagnostic and treatment codes, techniques appropriate for health and mental health issues strengthen the case for removing the arbitrary division between physical health practitioners and mental health practitioners. The new International Classification system with its emphasis on functioning, disability, and health, and six new health and behavior CPT codes (American Medical Association, 2001) provide increased opportunities for psychological knowledge and professional skills to be used directly within the health system.

There have been major shifts in the role of psychology practitioners within the nation's health system. A significant majority of psychologists identify themselves as health service providers, health psychologists, neuropsychologists, primary care psychologists, rehabilitation psychologists, and occupational health psychologists. And a growing number work directly in medicine's house in behavioral medicine, genetics, and epidemiology. In the health care service arena we must remove the barriers between the delivery of health and mental health services. This book has chapter by chapter documented the behavioral, emotional, and social conditions that affect physical health and how physical health affects mental health. Yet psychologists are still not reimbursed at parity with their medical colleagues for their involvement with patients with primary health problems.

Opportunities are expanding, but for the sake of patients' total well-being our service delivery systems need to embrace an interdisciplinary approach to health care in which psychology is an equal partner. Any list of expanding opportunities would become quickly limited because the rate of expansion has achieved exponential proportions. Let me at least name a few of those areas that currently have very limited psychological involvement but appear on the cusp of expanding development: the field of injury; culturally appropriate and sensitive health care; prescription privileges; genetic screening; occupational health psychology; and private practitioners and groups with niche market expertise in an ever broadening range of health and illness issues.

In the spring of 2002, New Mexico's passage of prescription privileges for psychologists opened up a practice opportunity for psychologists that has been an increasing priority for the APA for almost 25 years. Dr. Patrick DeLeon, whose insight and leadership began the long march to legislative enactment, believes that the RxP agenda represents the best of psychology seeking to effectively serve the public good and is a sign of a maturing profession.

Human genomics, as Susan McDaniel and colleagues wrote in their chapter (chap. 2, this volume), have moved beyond prenatal testing of single gene disorders to more complex configurations that give probabilities or estimated chances for the development of certain diseases without being able to conclusively predict one way or another. Psychologists need to be part of the team that engages from the beginning with the individuals considering genetic testing and with the family in cases of familial illness because the impact of the decision on their lives is so long-lasting and stressful. Also part of psychology practitioners' role is to alert the public and policymakers to the long-range effects of decisions about genetic testing and the need for individuals and families to have the ongoing services of a psychologist as part of the health package.

I asked practitioners about the role of health issues in their practices. Three issues were consistently reported. There was an increase in clients with concurrent health problems and the health problems spanned a broad range and were not just centered on cancer and heart disease. And the psychologists found their general background was transferable but they wanted more formal training in health psychology to be available.

Expand Biopsychosocial Health Education and Training

The history of psychology's interest in health education is traced by some as far back as William James and G. Stanley Hall. The APA began formal discussions of the role of psychology in medical education around 1911. But it was not until after World War II that psychology and health began to show significant growth and development in medical schools.

For the past several decades, psychologists' roles as teachers and trainers within medical and tertiary settings have expanded and become better integrated with other health professions. More doctoral programs are preparing psychologists to work in health care settings. For many psychologists today their first work experience is in a medical setting. This was true for me. In 1968 after finishing my internship in the Psychiatry Department at University Hospitals in Cleveland, Ohio, I was asked to stay on and accept a position as the first psychologist to work in the departments of Pediatrics, Neurology, and Endocrinology. It was one of the most exciting years of my professional life as we all sat on the cutting edge, wondering what psychology had to offer these medical departments. I went with the medical students, interns, and residents to clinics where we sometimes saw as many as 200 patients a day. There was no predicting what type of issue we would confront. After several months, the medical departments were apparently satisfied enough with the role of psychology that they funded, for the first time, a psychology health position.

Today's health psychology is significantly more specialized and sophisticated from those early days when a few of us were beginning to consult regularly with medical personnel about health issues and the interface with mental health. Specialized training has included areas such as clinical health psychology, neuropsychology, and rehabilitation psychology. A trend in medical education is providing expanding opportunities for psychologists to participate and have key roles in the education and training of family and community primary care physicians and other health care professions. As envisioned by Victor De La Cancela in this book, behavioral scientists are key to the development and delivery of a curriculum that promotes essential skills in providing family–oriented, comprehensive care to medical residents.

However, in addition to the doctoral training of psychologists who choose a health-oriented psychology specialty, psychology must formally incorporate into its core curriculum state-of-the-art psychology and health knowledge and interventions. We must provide our new graduates with foundational knowledge of the biopsychosocial health research and interventions. We must attract diversity in our students that parallels the richness and strengths of the diversity in our culture. And we must infuse our curriculums and training with knowledge of the cultures in our nation and the influence of ethnicity, race, socioeconomic status, and gender on health and well-being.

We must have faculty that is actively engaged in health research and health interventions. Our accredited internships and postdoctoral training programs must include psychology and health in medical settings, community settings and in traditional mental health settings. The Veterans Administration training programs are outstanding examples of psychology's longstanding commitment to quality internship and postdoctoral training in psychology and health. APA's advocacy efforts recently were successful in establishing the first federal program targeted to graduate education in psychology. Starting in 2002, the Graduate Psychology Education program in the Bureau of Health Professions' appropriation for $2 million will be available to train health service psychologists in accredited psychology programs. This competitive program is consistent with the biopsychosocial approach to health and provides awards for work with underserved populations, including children, older people, victims of abuse, the chronically ill or disabled and in areas of emerging needs, which will foster an integrated approach to health care services, address access for underserved populations, and build on the interrelatedness of behavior and health.

Psychology must address the question of how to educate and train established professionals for a changing marketplace in health services with a challenge to increase the rigor of self-assessment. The range of expanded education and training opportunities spans from high school psychology courses, through the undergraduate curriculum, to graduate school and professional psychology training, to internship and postdoctoral training, and of course lifelong learning and retooling.

Most established professionals who want to expand their practices in health psychology or new niches, such as working with heart disease patients, do not choose to return to school or to enter an organized postdoctoral training program. These professionals need continuing education that ethically equips them to retool for an expansion of their practices. The Internet is increasingly being used to bring state of the art psychology into distant communities and homes. However, as a vehicle for education it sounds easier than it is to actually implement in a coherent way. The Practice Directorate's new portal is one new tool that can potentially meet the needs for information about emerging areas of practice.

Psychology needs to develop continuing education programs in emerging and newly recognized specialty areas. These continuing education programs should be collaboratively developed by researchers, educators, and practitioners and use new technologies to make them accessible and affordable. The format for psychology continuing education requires even greater expansion from the old face-to-face classroom exposures. Psychology needs to have well-designed evaluations appropriate for the changes in continuing education. In addition to the current evaluations of process and content at the time of the encounter, psychology needs evaluations of expanding competencies over time.

Belar and colleagues (2001) proposed a template for self-assessment instruments specially designed for psychology practitioners who want to ethically expand their professional practices. The template contains targeted questions that are recommended to be used to self-assess readiness to provide psychological services to patients with physical health problems. It remains an empirical question whether or not a psychologist can use self-assessment techniques such as this template to competently and ethically evaluate a move into the diversity of health care practice settings that are becoming available.

Enact Health Policies That Increase Access, Reduce Health Disparities, and Promote Improved Quality of Life as Equally Important as the Prolonging of Life

We must be ready to accept the challenge of the Institute for the Future (2000) to meet the needs of increasing proportions of African American, Asian American, Latino and Latina, and Native American patients. We must be ready to provide services that are culturally appropriate. We must be ready to have services that include awareness of complex issues related to the underdiagnosis of certain conditions and diseases among minority groups, the effects of lifestyle and cultural differences on health status, the implications of the diverse genetic endowment of the population, and the impact of patterns of assimilation on health status.

"Psychologists have known for years what many policymakers are only now discovering: mental health is health, and psychologists provide health care services for more than mental health problems" (Johnson, 2001, p. 5). Rather than pitting men against women, ethnic group against ethnic group, socioeconomic group against socioeconomic group, what this book and this chapter advocates is that health policy, funding, research, and interventions, are respectful of these psychosocial influences.

There is growing evidence of the adverse effect of negative health behaviors such as excessive eating and smoking and that positive health behaviors, including exercise and nutritional improvements, can enhance immune responses. Can we as biopsychosocial scientists and practitioners influence public policy to take the next steps necessary to demonstrate what are the effective intervention components? The effort does not lack for person power—we have the scientists, we have the practitioners. The next step into the future requires a significant expansion of resources for public and private health to address the sociobehavioral causes of illness as called for in the Institute for the Future (2000), U.S. Department of Health and Human Services (2000), and Institute of Medicine (2002) reports.

Increased access means making a commitment to low socioeconomic groups, the unemployed, children, youth, and older people—all groups not covered under our dominant national system with its heavy reliance on business to protect the support for health. For too long our country's health policies have resulted in undercare and fragmented care for many of its citizens because of the stigma of mental health. The integration of health and mental health means equity of funding that recognizes the major ingredients to good health are psychosocial factors, healthy behaviors, and reducing risk factors. Public policies need to recognize that one's health affects one's mental health and vice versa. And in reality, it is impossible to separate the two, and therefore, there must be adequate funding commensurate with the effect of psychosocial factors on one's health.

It is not just enough to add new policies; we need to advocate for the removal of policies that provide obstacles to integrated health care, such as the carve-outs for mental health services and policies that do not support collaborative care across disciplines. Public policy must equably fund professions—psychologists, primary care physicians, social workers, and similar disciplines' involvement in the type of integrated health care discussed throughout this book.

Funding for health care is like a hermit crab. If its home is not big enough, it will simply leave and find another home. That is what is happening in health care. Because the resources are not adequate for the needs the problems move to new homes, like the justice system. For example, in 2000 I was one of three APA delegates, along with Drs. Ronald Levant and APA Past President Robert Resnick, to the U.S. Surgeon General's conference on Mental Health in Children. We learned that dollars removed from adolescent mental health in Chicago were showing up, dollar for dollar, in the juvenile justice system. Teens with mental health problems unable to find appropriate services within the mental health systems were committing crimes that resulted in their incarceration. Are we really saying as a nation, we would rather put our teens in jail than provide appropriate integrated mental health and health services at the community level?

Good primary care is where it all comes together. Psychologists also need to continue to advocate for the movement of health services to primary care with an integration of professionals with specialization in behavioral and social-cultural health as part of the primary health team. Primary care promotes prevention if the health personnel are given the time to take appropriate inventory of the patient's health and develop knowing relationships over time. Primary care promotes the family approaches so vital for the prevention and intervention in certain diseases also covered earlier in this chapter.

Community, family, and workplace interventions also are the model for integrated care that focuses on improved quality of life as well as life extension. My vision of public policy will promote wellness and prevention as well as appropriate care for the psychosocial aspects of illness in communities, in families, and at work, as well as within individuals. Community primary care should be funded at an appropriate level throughout various systems in our country. The populations who would be significantly better served by this health approach are our most vulnerable—the poor, ethnic minorities, children and youth, and older people.

Increase Public Knowledge of Psychology and Health

My vision is that on a daily basis the public will have ready access to current state of the art psychological health research and effective psychosocial interventions. To do that, psychology must increase the availability to the public of its research and interventions. APA's Public Information Directorate, under Executive Director Rhea Farberman, and the APA Practice Directorate, under Russ Newman, have made giant leaps forward in the amount and type of psychology information getting to the public. Although significant progress has been made recently, we need to allocate even more of our resources—financial, administrative, and energy—in developing and implementing a strategic plan that prioritizes informing the public. I would include in the plan a psychology journal with the power to reach the public as is seen in *Science* or the *New England Journal of Medicine*, to name two examples. As our premier journal gets known as "the place" to find the newest psychology research and interventions and as the writing becomes more "public friendly," there will be increased coverage of psychology. With regularity and, hence, predictability, the media will know there is a reliable authentic source for psychological information that is news.

Psychology also needs to increase its presence in the visual media and on radio. During my 2001 APA Presidential year I did several television appearances on CNN and public television. The CNN shows and a PBS show were designed to give the public psychological information to cope with the anxiety that followed the 9-11 terrorist attacks. APA's partnership in the PBS film 5 *Girls* was a unique opportunity for the association. Another valuable partnership occurred when the APA Practice Directorate partnered with MTV on a video "Warning Signs" to alert the public to the signs in teens of depression and potential violence. The show was broadcasted several times on national TV as part of a larger campaign. The media is eager for information about health and psychology. We have the knowledge and we are learning how to communicate it—for this step we are not dependent on others changing either models or funding. It is time; the opportunity is right.

CONCLUSION

Simply said, health needs to be envisioned as a right, equally available to all. We need a commitment as a nation to a form of universal health care that promotes access, eliminates disparities, integrates physical health and mental health, recognizes the importance of psychosociocultural factors in health. We need funding that lets the dollars flow commensurate with the research findings on the significant extent of behavior, cognition, emotion, and social cultural influences on health. As psychologists we need to take the lead in fighting for the right of all people to the best care possible, whatever the health need.

REFERENCES

American Medical Association. (2001). The new International Classification system with its emphasis on functioning, disability and health and six new health and behavior CPT codes. *American Medical Association, New Codes*, p. 39.

Belar, C. D., Brown, R. A., Hersch, L. E., Hornyak, L. M., Rozensky, R. H., Sheridan, E. P., et al. (2001). Self-assessment in clinical health psychology: A model for ethical expansion of practice. *Professional Psychology: Research and Practice, 32*, 135–141.

Global Forum for Health Research. (2002). *The 10/90 report on health research 2001–2003*. Geneva, Switzerland: World Health Organization.

Institute for the Future. (2000). *Health and health care 2010: The forecast, the challenge*. San Francisco: Jossey-Bass.

Institute of Medicine. (2002). *Informing the future: Critical issues in health*. Washington, DC: Author.

Johnson, N. G. (2001). Psychology's mission includes health: An opportunity. *Monitor on Psychology, 32*(5), 5.

Rees, J. (2002). Complex disease and the new clinical sciences. *Science, 296*, 698–701.

U.S. Department of Health and Human Services. (2000). *Healthy people 2010: Understanding and improving health.* Washington, DC: Government Printing Office.

AUTHOR INDEX

Numbers in italics refer to listings in the reference sections.

Rosenthal, R. A., 234, *268*
Rosewater, A., 265, *265*
Ross, C. E., 107, 121, *132*
Rossouw, J. E., 124, *132*
Roter, D. L., 112, 114, 119, *129, 132*
Roth, B. J., 110, *132*
Roth, S., 20, *31*
Rothman, A. J., 7, *29*
Roussus, S., 177, 178, *183*
Royak-Schaler, R., 105, 119, *128, 133*
Rozanski, A., 65, *74*
Rozensky, R. H., *126, 309, xix, xxii*
Rubel, A. J., 172, *182*
Rubenstein, A., 6, *31*
Rubenstein, L. V., *126*
Ruddock, A., 158, *184*
Ruiz, M. G., 148, *153*
Rule, W. R., 110, *133*
Runyon, D. K., 159, *181*
Russell, D. E. H., 158, *183*
Russell, M., 240, 241, *267*
Ryan, C., 60, *74, 214*
Ryff, C. D., 11, *29*, 290, *296*

Sacks, J. J., 208, *215*
Sadava, S. W., 109, *130*
Saftlas, A. F., 91, *103*
Saia-Lewis, T. L., 66, *74*
Sala, J., *28*
Saldana, L., 83, *102*
Saldívar, A., 145, *152*
Salley, A., *129*
Salovey, P., 7, *29*, 223, *232*
Sanders, D. E., 163, *182*
Sanders, M., *29*
Sanderson, M., *100*
Sandman, D., 107, 115, *133*
Sanz, G., *28*
Saolvaara, H., *268*
Satcher, D., 190, *215*
Saundars, B. E., *182*
Sauter, S. L., 234, 235, 237, *269, 271*
Savage, I., 115, *133*
Scharff, M. P., 205, *214*
Scheckner, S., 192, *214*
Schneider, T. R., 23, *29*
Schneiderman, N., 23, *30, 208, 214, xx, xxii*
Schoenfeld, D. A., *214*
Schooler, C., 240, *270*

Schreiner, B., 64, *75*
Schuerman, J. R., 159, *181*
Schul, Y., 237, *272*
Schulman, R. S., 202, *209*
Scott, K., 88, *104*
Seaburn, D., 50, *73*
Seal, D. W., 125, *128*
Searle, S., 240, *267*
Sears, H. A., 286, *294*
Sears, S. F., 66, 67, 69, 71, *74*
Sechrist, K. R., 107, *135*
Sedlak, A. J., 84, *103*
Seeman, T. E., 287, *295*
Seifert, M. H., 113, *131*
Seligman, M. E. P., 6, *30*
Selye, H., 234, *271*
Severson, H. H., 117, *130*
Shechtman, Z., 191, *214*
Sheehan, D. V., *74*
Shelton, D., 110, *133*
Sheperd, J. B., 125, *129*
Sheridan, E. P., *126, 309*
Sheridan, J., 120, *130*
Sheridan, R. L., 200, *214*
Sherman, S. J., 18, *29*
Shike, M., 111, *135*
Shock, S., 81, *104*
Shumaker, S. A., 119, *130, 133*
Shurman, R. A., 50, *74*
Siegel, P. A., 9, *27*, 225, *230*
Siegler, I. C., *126*
Sikes. J., 228, *230*
Silva, J. M., 23, *30, 208, 214*
Silverstein, J. H., *73*
Simantov, E., 107, *133*
Simpson, G., 190, 205, *210, 214*
Singer, B., 11, *29*
Singer, H. H., 208, *214*
Sirles, E. A., 159, *184*
Sirois, B., *74*
Sisson, L. A., 192, 202, *212*
Skidmore, J. R., 109, *128*
Skinner, B. F., 278, 279, 281, *296*
Skinner, C., *126*
Skrabski, A., 107, *130*
Sleet, D. A., 187, 190, 191, 192, 195, 208, *210, 213, 214, 215*
Slemmons, M., *72*
Smith, A., 225, *232*, 260, *272*
Smith, B. L., 106, *129*
Smith, T. R., 119, *133*

Wiese-Bjornstal, D. M., 260, *272*
Wild, T. C., 18, *30*
Wilkerson, J. C., 114, *128*
Williams, A. F., 192, *216*
Williams, C. E., 202, 212, *216*
Williams, D. G., 107, *135*
Williams, E., 171, *183*
Williams, J. B., *74*
Williams, J. E., 108, *135*
Williams, J. W., 283, *294*
Williams, M. L., 286, *295*
Williams, R., 169, 170, *182, 184*
Williams, R. B., *126*
Williamson, D. F., *101*
Wilner, N., 203, *211*
Wilson, F., 191, *216*
Wilson, M. H., 81, 82, *104*
Wilson, R. W., 107, *135*
Winawer, S. J., 111, *135*
Windau, J., 247, 249, *272*
Winder, C., 159, *183*
Windle, J. R., 66, 69, *71, 74*
Winett, R. A., 278, *296*
Winter, R. O., 167, 173, *180*
Wolf, M. E., 91, *101*
Wolfe, D. A., 87, 88, 89, *104*
Wolfe, R. P., 234, *268*
Wolff, T., 175, 177, *184*
Wolski, K. E., 191, *209*
Wood, J., 244, *271*, 286, *295*
Wood, M., 165, *183*
Worden, J. K., 23, *29*

Worell, J., 6, *28, 30*
World Health Organization, 5, *30*, 193, 204, *216*
Worldwide UNDP Human Development Report, 26, *30*
Woznick, L. A., 15, *30*
Wyatt, G. E., 158, 159, *184*
Wynne, L. C., 52, *75*

Yee, P. Y., 120, *135*
Yocum, D., *135*
Young, C. E., 227, *231*
Young, T. L., 83, *104*
Yukelson, D., 260, 261, *272, 273*
Yung, B., 196, *216*

Zager, K., 6, *31*
Zalaquett, J., 205, *216*
Zautra, A. J., 20, *31*, 121, *135*
Zaza, S., 192, *216*
Zelli, A., 192, *211*
Zhang, Q., *214*
Zibecchi, L., *128*
Ziegelstein, R. C., *27*
Zimmerman, R., 83, *104*
Zimmerman, T. S., 261, *273*
Zull, J., *29*
Zwi, A. B., 193, 204, 205, *213, 216*
Zyzanski, S., 169, *184*

SUBJECT INDEX

Chronic disease
    gender comparisons, 107
    role of psychology in management
        of, 13–18
Community health psychology, 8
    advocacy efforts, 155, 179
    characteristics of healthy communi-
        ties, 175
    child sexual abuse prevention, 156–
        162
    common features of community ini-
        tiatives, 175–176
    conceptual basis, 155
    culturally-sensitive clinical practice,
        166, 171–174
    curriculum for family medicine prac-
        tice, 162–174
    historical development, 174–175
    injury prevention, 185–193, 207–
        208
    model programs, 177–179
    needs assessment, 146
    prescription for health, 12
    qualities of successful programs,
        176–178
    role of psychologist in, 155–156,
        164, 171, 178–179, 185
    socioeconomic factors in, 23
    stress conceptualization, 19–20
    violence prevention, 185, 207–208
Community Oriented Primary Care, 165
Competitive behavior, 225–226, 229–230
Confidentiality, 264
Contraception, 140, 141, 148
Cooperative behavior, 225–229
Cooperative learning, 228–229
Coping skills
    domestic violence prevention, 94–95
    gender differences, 107–108
    protective function, 7
Curtis, Lewis G., 228

Defibrillator, implantable cardioverter,
    14, 65–70
DeLeon, Patrick, 303
Depression
    cardiovascular disease management
        and, 13, 50
    gender differences in diagnostic prac-
        tice, 26

physical health and, 122
    in retirement, 289–290
Diabetes
    developmental considerations in
        management of, 59–64
    epidemiology, 16, 59
    family challenges, 64–65
    medical care, 59
    role of psychology in management
        of, 16
Diagnostic and Statistical Manual of Mental
    Disorders, 300
Domestic violence. See Intimate partner
    violence

Ecobehavioral approach, child maltreat-
    ment assessment in, 85
Education and training of practitioners,
    304–306
    community health curriculum, 162–
        174
Emotional functioning
    effects of workplace stress in family,
        286
    gender differences, 107, 122
    gender inequalities in human sexual-
        ity, 141
    intrapersonal dialogue, 223
    physical health and, 122
Emotional intelligence, 223
Ethical practice in genetic counseling,
    51, 52

Family and Medical Leave Act, 240, 243
Family functioning
    adolescent connectedness, 40–46
    biopsychosocial model of health, 8
    child maltreatment, 84–87
    childhood diabetes management,
        64–65
    connectedness, 38
    effects of domestic violence, 95–99
    family member with implantable
        cardioverter defibrillators, 67–68,
        69–70
    genetic risk of illness, 52
    health of children of working par-
        ents, 287–289
    injury prevention, 79–80, 83–84

parent–child interaction skills training, 85–87

perception of home as sanctuary, 77–78

school violence incidents and, 38

sociocultural conceptualizations, 35–36

stresses for professional athletes, 258, 261

violence prevention intervention, 8, 35–36, 38–39, 41–42, 43–46, 79–80

workplace relations and, 9, 220, 234, 236, 239–245, 285–287

Federal Child Abuse Prevention and Treatment Act, 84

Feminist thought, 6

Fire emergencies, 199–204

Gender issues
assessment and diagnostic practice, 26

caregiver role, 120

concepts of health behavior, 108–111, 113

experience of pain, 113

within gender differences, 106

health differences, 24–26, 106

health research, 105

inequalities in human sexuality, 140–146

stress experience, 120, 121–122, 123

substance use patterns, 111

youth violence, 39–40

See also Men's health; Sexuality and sexual behavior; Women's health

Genetic illness
cost of screening, 52

ethical issues, 51, 52

future of health care, 51–52

risk assessment, 52–53

role of psychologist in assessment and treatment, 52–53, 55–58, 303–304

single gene disorders, 53–57

Governmental intervention
environmental safety regulation, 82

perception of home as sanctuary and, 77–78

support for families, 240

Health and health care, generally
conceptualization of, 3–4, 5–6, 10–11, 49–50, 301

gender differences, 24–26, 106

gender issues, 105–106

Healthy World Initiative goals, 4–5

medical research, 119–120

poverty and, 22–23

preventive medicine, 11, 12

psychological stress and, 19–20, 121–122

racial and ethnic factors in, 20–22, 119

role of psychology in, 5, 299–309

strengths orientation, 7

See also Health behavior; Men's health; Women's health

Health behavior
at-risk behaviors, 278

behavioral change in the workplace, 276–279, 281–285

behavioral change models, 279–281

community needs assessment, 146

cultural concepts of gender in, 108–111, 113

educational interventions, 308–309

experience of pain and, 113

gender differences, 25, 105–106, 107–108, 119

health maintenance plans, 116–117

of professional athletes, 259

public policy interventions, 307–308

racial and ethnic differences, 110, 119

screening participation, 12–13

strengths orientation, 117–118

work stress and, 285, 287–289

Healthy People 2010, 79

Healthy World Initiative, 4
systemic approach, 7–8

HIV. See Human immunodeficiency virus/AIDS

Home Accident Prevention Inventory, 86

Hormonal system, 123

Human immunodeficiency virus/AIDS
community health programs, 164

epidemiology, 16–18

gender differences in risk, 26, 125

preventive intervention, 125, 148, 149–150

role of psychology in management of, 16–17

Identity foreclosure, 258
Immune function, stress and, 20
Injury, accidental
    at-risk behavior, 278
    automobile-related, 187
    child maltreatment and, 84–85
    conceptualization of intentionality
        in, 81
    definition, 77, 79, 80–81, 187
    epidemiology, 187
    fire-related, 199–200
    gender differences, 26, 108
    intentional violence and, 79
    sequelae, 187–190
    social costs, 80, 186
    sources, 187
    See also Injury prevention
Injury prevention
    behavioral targets, 82–83, 191, 192,
        276–285
    caregiver interventions, 83–84
    characteristics of behavioral safety,
        281–282
    child maltreatment as target of,
        85–87
    children's preparation for fire emer-
        gencies, 199, 201–204
    combined strategies, 192–193
    community health initiatives, 185–
        193, 207–208
    conceptual development, 190
    educational interventions, 191–192
    environmental targets, 82
    in the home, 77–78
    public health approach, 79, 190
    role of psychology in, 23–24, 78–80,
        81, 84, 99–100, 208–209
    strategies, 81–84, 190–191
    in the workplace, 276–279, 281–285
Insurance, 12
    access to care and, 22
Interdisciplinary approach
    biopsychosocial model of health
        care, 50, 52–53, 70–71, 301
    child sexual abuse interventions, 180
    in future of health care, 301–304
    violence and injury prevention, 79
    work–family research, 244
Intimate partner violence
    effects on families, 95
    epidemiology, 91–93

interventions, 94–99
    legal intervention, 95, 98–99
    risk factors, 93
    sequelae, 93
    women's health issues, 120–121

Job Stress Survey, 236

Legal system, domestic violence interven-
    tions, 95, 98–99
Lower Outer Cape Community Coali-
    tion, 177–178

Mammography, 12, 22–23
Men's health
    denial and concealment in, 115
    emotional functioning, 107
    experience of pain, 113
    health attitudes and behaviors, 105–
        106, 107–111
    health maintenance plan, 116–117
    help-seeking behavior, 112, 113–114
    mortality, 106–107
    occupational injury and violence,
        248, 249
    physician–patient relationship, 112
    risk perception, 115–116
    sexual dysfunction, 113
    social support networks, 116
    strategies for improving, 111–118,
        146–151
    stress response and, 107–108
    violence, concepts of maleness and,
        8, 39
    See also Gender issues
Mental health, generally
    APA mission statement, 5
    genetic risk, 52
    physical health and, 3–4, 7, 10–11,
        50
    in primary care, 4, 8, 50
    role of psychology in chronic disease
        management, 13–18
    strengths orientation, 6–7
    See also Biopsychosocial model
Mexican Institute for the Study of Family
    and Population, 140, 142–151
Military services, 227–228

Mortality
     automobile-related, 108
     cancer, 15
     cardiac disease, 65
     child maltreatment, 84
     demographic patterns, 107
     fire-related, 199–200
     gender comparison, 106–107
     injury-related, 186, 187
     psychosocial factors in, 18–26
     racial and ethnic differences, 22,
          106, 107
     sociocultural factors in, 18
     socioeconomic status and, 22–23
     tobacco use-associated, 18
     war-related, 204
Myotonic dystrophy, 52–58

National Center for Cultural Compe-
          tence, 166
National Institute on Drug Abuse, 19
National Violence Against Women
          Survey, 92
Newman, Russ, 300, 308

Obesity, 119
Occupational health psychology, 234,
          237
Occupational Stress Inventory, 236
Organ transplantation, 14

Pain experience, 113
Personal Responsibility and Work Oppor-
          tunity Reconciliation Act, 244–
          245
Planned Activities Training, 87
Positive psychology, 6–7, 117–118
Posttraumatic stress disorder
     after fire exposure, 201
     in family violence, 98
Poverty
     health and, 22–23
     women's health and, 118–119
     working poor, 243, 244–245
Prescribing authority, 303
Preventive interventions
     biopsychosocial approach, rationale
          for, 11–12

child maltreatment, 160
children's preparation for fire emer-
          gencies, 201–204
community health curriculum for
          family medicine practitioners,
          162–174
genetic counseling, 51–52
improving men's health, 111–118
improving women's health, 124–125
invasion of home privacy and, 78
medical research patterns, 22
in physical health care, 11, 12
psychosocial causes of illness and
          death, 18–26
retirement planning, 10
role of psychology in chronic disease
          management, 13–18
strengths orientation, 6
substance abuse among youth, 8–9
in workplace, 9
workplace stress, 237
     See also Injury prevention; Screen-
          ing; Violence prevention
Primary care
     community health curriculum for res-
          idents and interns, 162–174
     genetic counseling in, 51–52
     mental health care and, 4, 8, 50
     role of psychologist in, 164, 308
Project 12-Ways, 85
Project SafeCare, 85–86
Protective factors
     coping skills, 7
     strengths orientation in psychology,
          6
Psycho-neuro immunology, 20
Public education, 308–309
Public health policy
     environmental safety regulation, 82
     future challenges and opportunities,
          139–140, 306–308, 309
     global issues, 17
     theory to action model, 140, 151
     violence and injury prevention, 79,
          190, 193–194, 197–198

Race and ethnicity
     culturally-sensitive clinical practice,
          163, 166, 171–174, 196, 306
     ethnic conflict, 205

for professional athletes, 260, 261–264
unemployment, 237
workplace, 221, 233–238, 285–287
Substance abuse
among professional athletes, 262
child abuse and, 26
diabetes and, 63
patterns among youth, 8
prevention among youth, 8–9
role of psychology in preventing/treating, 19
social attitudes and beliefs, 19
social costs, 19
See also Alcohol use; Tobacco use
Suicide, 187
Survivor therapy, 57, 96–97
after collective violence, 206–207

Taylor, Frederick W., 226–227
Theory of Reasoned Action, 144
Therapeutic relationship
men's health attitudes and behavior, 112–118
work with professional athletes, 260–261
in workplace psychology, 276
Tobacco use
gender socialization and, 111
mortality and morbidity related to, 18
patterns among women, 119
Transplantation technology, 14
Transtheoretical Model of Behavior Change, 144
Truth commissions, 206–207

Unemployment, 237, 239
United Nations, 17
Universal health care, 309

Violence
accidental injury and, 79
adolescent exposure, 88
in association with crime, 246–247
cultural concepts of maleness and, 8, 39, 110–111, 141
definition, 77, 193, 246

in intimate relationships, 91–93
occupational risk, 247, 248–249, 251
prevalence, 194
protective factors, 195
risk factors, 195
in schools, 36–39, 44
social costs, 194
toward women, 24, 26, 120–121
in war, 204–207
in workplace, 220, 234, 245–251
youth behavioral trends, 39–40, 194
See also Child maltreatment; Sexual abuse; Violence prevention
Violence prevention
in adolescent relationships, 87–91
child maltreatment, 85–87
community health initiatives, 207–208
domestic violence, 94–99
family connectedness in, 41–42, 43–46
family systems approach, 8, 35–36, 38–39
in the home, 77–78
immediate threat, 254–255
intervention effectiveness evaluation, 196
interventions with youth, 195–199
public health approach, 79, 193–194, 197–198
role of psychology in, 23–24, 78–80, 99–100, 208–209
in workplace, 251–256

War, 204–207
Women's health
biological factors, 122–124
curriculum for family medicine practice, 163–164
determinants of, 106
employment issues, 239, 242–243
environmental context, 118–120
gender inequalities in human sexuality, 140
health attitudes and behaviors, 107–108, 119
individual differences, 122
interpersonal context, 120–122
intimate partner violence, 91–93
medical research and, 119–120

Women's health, *continued*
mortality, 106–107
obesity, 119
occupational injury and violence, 248, 249
racial and ethnic differences, 119
sexually-transmitted disease risk, 26
strategies for improving, 124–125, 146–151
stress experience and, 120, 121–122
tobacco use patterns, 119
violence toward women, 24, 26
See also Gender issues
Women's Health Initiative, 124
Workplace
competitive behavior in, 225–226, 229–230
cooperative behavior in, 225–230
cross-disciplinary research, 244
designs for health, 235, 251–252
diversity in, 225
downsizing effects, 9, 225, 227
dual drives model of needs fulfillment in, 220, 222
executive health, 223–225
family functioning and, 9, 220, 234, 236, 239–245, 285–287
gender differences in stress experience, 120
health goals, 221, 222–223
health of children of working parents, 287–289
historical developments, 235
intervention rationale, 9
issues of concern, 9
motivating safety-related behaviors in, 276–279, 281–285
needs fulfillment in, 220, 222, 290–291
organizational therapy, 238
person–environment fit, 236
preventive interventions, 237
research methodology, 241–243
research needs, 240–241, 244–245, 255–256
research trends, 235, 239–240
role of psychology in, 220, 221–227, 234, 237–238, 275–276, 293–294
sports professionals, 256–265
standardization in, 226
stress in, 221, 233–238
surveillance of health risks, 236
trust relationships in, 225
unemployment stress, 237, 239
U.S. economic performance, 220–221
violence in, 220, 234, 245–256
See also Retirement
World Health Organization, 300

Youth
adolescent relationship violence, 87–91
diabetes management in, 59–63
diabetes trends, 8
family relations in adolescence, 40–46
health of children of working parents, 287–289
injury prevention strategies, 82–84
parent–child interaction skills training, 85–87
peer relations, 45, 195
preparation for fire emergencies, 199–204
professional athletes, 257–258, 265
role models, 42–44
substance use patterns, 8
violence prevention, 195–199
violent behavior trends, 39–40, 194
See also Child maltreatment
Youth Relationships Program, 88–89

ABOUT THE EDITORS

Ronald H. Rozensky, PhD, ABPP, is professor and chair of the Department of Clinical and Health Psychology at the University of Florida. He is board certified in both clinical and clinical health psychology. Dr. Rozensky is the founding and current editor of the *Journal of Clinical Psychology in Medical Settings* and has published 5 textbooks and more than 30 journal articles on the science and practice of psychology in health care settings. He has served as chair of two American Psychological Association (APA) boards, the Board of Professional Affairs and the Board of Educational Affairs, and currently serves on the APA Council of Representatives. He is a past president of the Illinois Psychological Association. He was elected to the National Academy of Practice as a Distinguished Practitioner in Psychology, is the recipient of the Illinois Psychological Association's Distinguished Psychologist Award and the APA's Karl F. Heiser Presidential Award for Advocacy, and was named the Association of Medical School Psychologists' Distinguished Educator. He cochaired the APA Presidential Initiative "Psychology Builds A Healthy World" and chaired the APA Presidential Initiative "Health Psychology Through the Life Span." Dr. Rozensky was awarded a $1 million grant from the Substance Abuse and Mental Health Administration to help found the National Rural Behavioral Health Center located at the University of Florida.

Norine G. Johnson, PhD, is past president of the American Psychological Association (APA). Her 2001 Presidential Initiative, "Psychology Builds a Healthy World," served as a foundation for this book. Her other edited books include *Beyond Appearance: A New Look at Adolescent Girls* (with M. C. Roberts and J. Worell; APA, 1999) and *Shaping the Future of Feminist Psychology: Education, Research, and Practice* (with J. Worell; APA, 1997).

Dr. Johnson was the director of psychology and psychology training at Franciscan Hospital for Children in Boston and introduced innovative psychological programs in health and rehabilitation for the patients and their families. She is a clinical assistant professor in the Neurology Department at Boston University and was one of three psychology representatives to the Surgeon General's conference on Children and Mental Health. Dr. Johnson received an Honorary Doctorate of Science from DePauw University, 2002, and an Honorary Doctorate of Letters from the Massachusetts School of Psychology, 2001.

Carol D. Goodheart, EdD, is in independent practice in Princeton, New Jersey, and is an author and editor of numerous books, chapters, and articles on psychology and health. She currently serves as a member of the Board of Directors of the American Psychological Association (APA). Dr. Goodheart cochaired the APA Presidential Initiative "Psychology Builds a Healthy World" and the APA Congressional Initiative on Serious Illness, a series of briefings on cancer, heart disease, and chronic diseases, for the U.S. Congress. She is a past president of APA's Division 42 (Psychologists in Independent Practice). Dr. Goodheart is a fellow of the APA, a Distinguished Practitioner in the National Academy of Psychology, and a recipient of the Distinguished Psychologist of the Year Award from both Psychologists in Independent Practice and the New Jersey Psychological Association.

W. Rodney Hammond, PhD, is director of the Division of Violence Prevention within the National Center for Injury Prevention and Control at the Centers for Disease Control and Prevention (CDC) in Atlanta, Georgia. The division oversees prevention research and programs in youth violence, intimate partner violence, child maltreatment, sexual assault, and suicide prevention. He is a fellow of the American Psychological Association (APA) and APA's Division 38 (Health Psychology). His research and programmatic publications have focused on violence as a public health concern, especially youth violence. He developed Project PACT (Positive Adolescents Choices Training), distinguished by its impressive violence prevention outcomes for at-risk youth. He is author and executive producer of the series *Dealing With Anger: A Violence Prevention Program for African American Youth*, which has been nationally recognized for its unique contribution as a culturally sensitive violence prevention program. His efforts also extend to international affairs. He works closely with the World Health Organization (WHO) headquarters in Geneva, Switzerland, and with the Regional WHO Centers in Japan and the Americas. He was the CDC representative to the Health Working Group of the Gore-Mbecki Bilateral Commission to the Republic of South Africa. He has received the U.S. Department of Health and Human Service Secretary's Award for Distinguished Service for his efforts in public health and mental health collaboration.

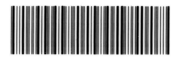